Poetry On & Off the Page

avant-garde & **modernism studies**

General Editors

Marjorie Perloff

Rainer Rumold

Consulting Editors

Peter Fenves

Stephen Foster

Christine Froula

Françoise Lionnet

Robert von Hallberg

Poetry On & Off the Page

Essays for

Emergent Occasions

MARJORIE PERLOFF

Northwestern

University Press

Evanston

Illinois

Northwestern University Press
Evanston, Illinois 60208-4210

Copyright © 1998 by Marjorie Perloff.
Published 1998 by Northwestern University Press.
All rights reserved.
Printed in the United States of America

Second paperback printing 2000

ISBN 0-8101-1561-1

Library of Congress Cataloging-in-Publication Data

Perloff, Marjorie.
Poetry on & off the page : essays for emergent occasions /
Marjorie Perloff.
p. cm. — (Avant-garde & modernism studies)
Includes bibliographical references (p.   )
ISBN 0-8101-1561-1 (pbk. : alk. paper)
1. American poetry—20th century—History and criticism—
Theory, etc. 2. American poetry—20th century—
History and criticism. 3. Experimental poetry, American—
History and criticism. 4. Modernism (Literature)—United
States. 5. Poetics. I. Title. II. Series: Avant-garde and mod-
ernism studies.
PS323.5.P48 1998
811'.509—dc21   97-50432
                                                        CIP

Contents

Acknowledgments

The following essays appeared, most in somewhat different form, in the following publications and are reprinted here by permission:

"Postmodernism/Fin de Siècle: Defining 'Difference' in Late Twentieth-Century Poetics," as "Postmodernism/Fin de siècle: The Prospects for Openness in a Decade of Closure," *Criticism* 35 (March 1993): 161–92.

"Tolerance and Taboo: Modernist Primitivisms and Postmodernist Pieties," in *Prehistories of the Future: The Primitivist Project and the Culture of Modernism,* ed. Elazar Barkan and Ronald Bush (Stanford: Stanford University Press, 1995), 339–54.

" 'Barbed-Wire Entanglements': The 'New American Poetry,' 1930–32," as "Barbed-Wire Entanglements: The New American Poetry 1930–32," *Modernism/Modernity* 2 (January 1995): 145–75.

"Lucent and Inescapable Rhythms: Metrical 'Choice' and Historical Formation," as " 'Lucid and Inescapable Rhythms': Metrical 'Choice' and Historical Formation," in *What Is a Poet?,* ed. Hank Lazer (Tuscaloosa: University of Alabama Press, 1987), 84–114; reprinted in *The Line in Poetry,* ed. Robert Frank and Henry Sayre (Urbana: University of Illinois Press, 1988), 13–40.

"After Free Verse: The New Nonlinear Poetries," in *Close Listening: Poetry and the Performed Word,* ed. Charles Bernstein (New York: Oxford University Press, 1998).

"What We Don't Talk about When We Talk about Poetry: Some Aporias of Literary Journalism," *PN Review* 115 (May–June 1997): 17–25. Printed in different form in *Grub Street and the Ivory Tower: Literary Journalism and Literary Scholarship from Fielding to the Internet,* ed. Jeremy Treglown and Bridget Bennett (Oxford: Oxford University Press, 1998).

"English as a 'Second' Language: Mina Loy's 'Anglo-Mongrels and the Rose,' " in *Mina Loy: Essays on the Poetry,* ed. Keith Tuma and Maeera Schreiber (Orono, ME: National Poetry Foundation, 1998).

"Poetry in Time of War: The Duncan-Levertov Controversy," *PN Review* 112 (November–December 1996): 33–38.

"How Russian Is It: Lyn Hejinian's *Oxota,*" *Parnassus: Long Poem Issue* 17 (spring 1993): 186–209.

"What Really Happened: Roland Barthes's Winter Garden / Christian Boltanski's Archives of the Dead," *Artes* 2 (1995): 110–25.

" 'Inner Tension/In Attention': Steve McCaffery's Book Art," *Visible Language* 25, no. 2/3 (1992): 173–91; special issue on "The Artist's Book: The Text and Its Rivals," ed. Renée Hubert.

"The Music of Verbal Space: John Cage's 'What You Say . . . ,' " in *Sound States: Acoustical Technologies and Modern and Postmodern Writing,* ed. Adalaide Morris (Chapel Hill: University of North Carolina Press, 1997).

"The Morphology of the Amorphous: Bill Viola's Videoscapes," as "The Morphology of the Amorphous: The Videoscapes of Bill Viola," *Salt* 10 (1997): 131–42.

Introduction

The fourteen essays in this collection all date from the past decade; indeed, with one exception (essay 5, "Lucent and Inescapable Rhythms"), from the past five years. These are, as my subtitle suggests, occasional essays, written for specific conferences, symposia, or edited volumes. The period of writing intersects with work on *Wittgenstein's Ladder* (1996), and no doubt the concerns of that book—with the process whereby "ordinary" language becomes "poetic"—also figure in these essays, although many of the latter deal not with poetry as such but with such cognate art constructs as the memoirs of Michel Leiris, the photographs of Eugene Atget, Berenice Abbott, and Robert Frank, the simulated documentaries of Christian Boltanski, the bookworks of Johanna Drucker and Steve McCaffery, the mesostic texts of John Cage, the video art of Bill Viola, and the criticism of Roland Barthes. The essays were composed for very different venues (a symposium on postmodernism at the University of Washington, a conference on the relationship of literary journalism to literary scholarship at the University of Warwick, a John Cage festival sponsored by the Museum of Contemporary Art in Warsaw), and have been published in an unlikely assortment of places, ranging from volumes on specific topics like primitivism (*Prehistories of the Future*) and acoustical technologies (*Sound States*), to scholarly journals like *Modernism/Modernity* and *American Literary History,* to such "little magazines" as the British *PN Review* and the Australian *Salt.*

Poetry On & Off the Page makes no attempt to advance a linear argument, much less to "cover" a unified field. Yet the essays do share a common project—one initiated in *The Poetics of Indeterminacy* (1981)—of mapping the historical changes and ruptures that characterize twentieth-century poetics. Whether writing about the "mongrel" language of Mina Loy's poetry in the 1920s or reconsidering the literary friendship of Robert Duncan and Denise Levertov in the 1960s or tracking the dissolution of "free verse" in the 1990s, I have sought to describe the formations and transformations of literary and artistic discourses, as these discourses have evolved in their dialogue with history, culture, and society.

Consider the way we talk about periods and *isms*—especially the two Big Ones of our century, modernism and postmodernism. The past decade has witnessed important reconsiderations of the modernist canon: Cary Nelson's valuable *Repression and Recovery* (1989), for example, brings to light the work of proletarian, African-American, and women poets whose work had been wholly "repressed" by what Nelson calls the "narrow" and "patriarchal" modernist canon constructed by "academic literary history." Yet Nelson's aim is less to enlarge the existing canon than to replace the old canon by a new, more satisfactory one. *Repression and Recovery* thus sets the stage for the many studies that continue to search for *the* definitive modernism or postmodernism, *the* thirties and *the* fifties. Such studies usually contain assertions on the order of "Modernism has been held to be X, but I shall argue that it is Y." In his recent *Our America* (1995), for example, Walter Benn Michaels equates American "modernism" with "nativism," the equivalence depending, however, on the omission of all those (T. S. Eliot, Ezra Pound, Gertrude Stein, Djuna Barnes, Wallace Stevens) whose poetry doesn't fit into the nativist paradigm.

I find myself wary of such holistic paradigms: my own concern, as "Postmodernism / Fin de Siècle" (essay 1) testifies, is with the gradual transformations of a given *ism* as well as with the *differences* that arise within it. Modernist primitivism, for example, must be understood, so I argue in "Tolerance and Taboo" (essay 2), in its own historical context: the preoccupation of Michel Leiris with violence toward women, for example, is complicated by the writer's own adolescent experience during World War I. Again, in studying the small-press publication of the American thirties (essay 3, " 'Barbed-Wire Entanglements': The 'New American Poetry,' 1930–32"), I discovered that the "protest literature" label applied to the decade is largely inaccurate, that, especially in the early years of the decade, a literature, no longer "modernist," in the sense that James Joyce and Ezra Pound were modernists, but by no means "socialist realist" either, comes into being, a literature (and there are parallels in the visual arts) characterized by abstraction, irony, pastiche, and elaborate stylization. Along similar lines, " 'A Step Away from Them': Poetry 1956" (essay 4) makes the case that the poetics of the "tranquillized fifties" (Robert Lowell's term) were much more conflicted and poignant than we tend to assume. Indeed, the work of such "apolitical" poets as Frank O'Hara and John Ashbery emerges as at least as responsive to the public discourse of the day as is the more overtly "radical" poetry of Allen Ginsberg.

The map of twentieth-century poetry thus becomes an increasingly differentiated and complex space. "English as a Second Language" (essay 8) argues that Mina Loy's poetic language, usually linked to that of her American contemporaries Marianne Moore and William Carlos Williams, must be understood as a complex confluence of rival strains: British versus East European–Jewish, European versus American, and male avant-garde versus the new feminist sensibility of the teens and twenties. "Poetry in Time of War" (essay 9) considers how those close "Black Mountain" poet-friends, Robert Duncan and Denise Levertov turn out to have almost diametrically opposite views of the poet's function in society. And "How Russian Is It" (essay 10) studies the intersection of a "language" poetics with the tradition of the epic novel in verse, as represented by Pushkin's *Eugene Onegin.*

A second area of historical change that I find enormously interesting is that of metrical formation, free verse, and the verse/prose relation-ship—areas that I discuss in "Lucent and Inescapable Rhythms" (essay 5) and "After Free Verse" (essay 6). It is usually assumed that poets have a "choice," that they can write in whatever form—sonnet, villanelle, ode, prose poem, free verse paragraph—that strikes their fancy. True, most contemporary poets tend to write "free verse," whatever that is, but why they use it and how it relates to their culture is rarely discussed. Yet, as I suggest in tracing a line from Goethe's "musical" lyric to Rimbaud's prose poetry, to William Carlos Williams's free verse, Samuel Beckett's "associative rhythm," and, beyond these, to the "measure" of the page itself—a page that has, I believe, replaced the line as the poet's basic unit—prosodic choice is never arbitrary. It is an important index not only to the ethos of the individual poet but to the larger culture and historical moment. Visual or postconcrete poetry, which was dismissed, not so long ago, as a mere sideline and declared by most critics and reviewers not to be poetry at all (see "What We Don't Talk about When We Talk about Poetry," essay 7) has now come into its own. In the technological and digital culture of the late century, "Wr-eye-tings," as such poetry is called by an Internet group of that name, is moving to center stage: witness a thick 1996 compendium called *Experimental-Visual-Concrete: Avant-Garde Poetry Since the 1960s,* edited by K. David Jackson, Eric Vos, and Johanna Drucker for Rodopi. Drucker's own artist's book *Narratology* is discussed in "Postmodernism / Fin de Siècle" (essay 1) and Steve McCaffery's visual poetics in "Inner Tension / In Attention" (essay 12).

A third area of historical change, closely linked to these transformations in the materiality of the text, concerns the relationship of poetry and poetics to other media. These relationships—for example, poetry/video art, poetry/photography, or poetry/performance—have again received little attention in scholarly and critical discourse, which continues to assume, as I note in essay 7, that poems are poems—lineated texts, usually divided into stanzas, surrounded by white space and designed to be read silently to oneself. There is, of course, a large literature today on the breakdown of the "great divide" between high and popular culture and of what looks to be a sinister and large-scale media takeover. But what is less understood is that, however vapid or pernicious commercial television may be, there are remarkable artists like Bill Viola (see essay 14, "The Morphology of the Amorphous") who use the video medium precisely to make art constructs (part visual, part sonic) that consciously position themselves in the line of an earlier poetic practice. Or who, like Roland Barthes in *Camera Lucida* (see essay 11, "What Really Happened: Roland Barthes's Winter Garden/Christian Boltanski's Archives of the Dead"), have produced a text that is part autobiographical memoir, part semiotic critique, part photo-essay, part lyric meditation, even as Christian Boltanski has reimagined what "documentary" photography might look like and what it "tells" us. Media crossovers are not, of course, anything new, but what *is* new is that artists who might, in an earlier time, have become painters or poets, now choose to be video artists or performance poets or makers of bookworks, or, like John Cage (see essay 13, "The Music of Verbal Space"), workers in what Joyce called the "verbivocovisual."

But if art conventions and norms undergo such large-scale historical changes, what, if any, are the constants in poetic discourse? How can one read Ezra Pound against John Donne or, for that matter, Charles Bernstein against Ezra Pound? Here the issue of value, for so long held to be merely irrelevant, if not embarrassing, comes in. It is true that if poetry is defined simply as that which people of all types and talents who produce it, call by that name, then the resulting anarchy can be controlled only by imposing external grids—nationality, race, gender, ethnicity—that serve as exclusionary markers.

Such increasingly restrictive identitarian categories raise more problems than they can solve, foregrounding, as they do, work that is often ephemeral in every respect *but* its sociocultural position and that is hence quickly displaced by other work. Paradoxically, it is only in examining the specificities within designated groupings that one becomes aware of the larger constants characterizing the literary and artistic texts that continue to make a difference. However significant, for example, the transformations in sound structure that I trace in "Lucent and Inescapable Rhythms" (essay 5), I am struck, every time I read the texts in question, by how brilliantly each one responds to its particular poetic donnée.

"You might think," said Wittgenstein, "aesthetics is a science telling us what's beautiful—almost too ridiculous for words. I suppose it ought to include also what sort of coffee tastes good." Writing, as I do, under the sign of Wittgenstein, I would not dream of advancing a definition of poetry, much less of art in general, but common sense makes it hard to take issue with the Poundian precept that "Poetry is news that stays news." It withstands, in other words, any number of successive readings, generating new meanings, new forms, new values for successive generations. Whether a particular poem X or picture Y does in fact accomplish this feat is always open to debate—there can be no absolutes or fixed values in art. But what actually finds itself *not* being debated is the vast preponderance of writing (or painting or photography) in our century (most of it, incidentally, by white men) that has disappeared without a trace. True, there are hitherto culturally, ethnically, or politically marginalized artists whose work urgently demands reconsideration, and there are important "repressed" texts that must be resurrected. But if one reads, say, the *New York Times Book Review* for a given decade of the century, as I do in "What We Don't Talk about When We Talk about Poetry" (essay 7), one quickly learns that most of what has been published since the founding of the review at the turn of the century has simply melted into thin air. The most obscure former bestseller may, of course, have significance for those whose primary focus is on cultural and ideological paradigms. But when it comes to *rereading* rather than *reading for,* to the "news" that will stay" "news" for a subsequent generation, to a poetics of engagement rather than a hermeneutics of suspicion, such texts—and there are thousands in our crowded century—have become largely irrelevant.

Indeed, my own experience in the classroom consistently reminds me that the power of the *poetic* is irresistible, that, once exposed to the more radical experiments of the second half of our century, students can't get enough. This past spring, for example, my graduate seminar in Postmodern Poetics had a heated debate on the meaning of the word "crystal" in Robert Smithson's art writings. Crystals, for that matter, were turning up in any number of poetry texts we were reading: Clark Coolidge's *The Crystal Text*, Christian Bök's *Crystallography*, and Susan Howe's *Chanting at the Crystal Sea*. And what about that surreal rock sequence in Bill Viola's video piece *Hatsu Yume?*

Are these versions of the "Great Crystal" as Ezra Pound conceives it in the *Cantos?* Or, to the contrary, *di*versions produced by an ethos largely antithetical to Pound's modernism? These are the kinds of questions that interest me. How Russian is Lyn Hejinian's long "Russian" poem *Oxota?* How close to "concrete poetry" are the concrete-derived visual poetics of Steve McCaffery or Joan Retallack? And why is it that the poetry of Mina Loy has suddenly become so relevant to our own poetries? The end of the century is a good moment to confront such poetic turnings.

* * *

I have generally not brought the essays, recent as they are, up to date, but some have been altered quite a bit since their original presentation or publication, largely because I have wanted to incorporate the very useful feedback from the audiences who heard these pieces as talks.

The lectures are divided into two sections, "Histories and Issues" (essays 1–7) and "Cases" (essays 8–14). The second set of seven essays focuses on individual writers or artists, but they are not, in kind, different from the first set, so I have simply numbered them consecutively.

The production of writing for particular occasions depends largely on the generosity, receptiveness, and goodwill of individual conference conveners, lecture committee organizers, and editors. In the course of the past decade, I have been more than fortunate in these associations, as well as in having so many friends, colleagues, and students with whom I can thrash out issues of mutual interest. There are more persons to be thanked than I can possibly cite here, but the following must be mentioned: Charles Altieri, David Antin, Luigi Ballerini, Martha Banta, Elazar Barkan, Charles Bernstein, Robert Bertholf, Ronald Bush, Robert Creeley, Michael Davidson, Dubravka Duric, Craig Dworkin, Ulla Dydo, Robbert Flick, Albert Gelpi, Alan Golding, Kenneth Goldsmith, Michael Golston, Thomas Hines, Renée Riese Hubert, Burton Hatlen, Susan Howe, Gordon Hutner, Jerzy Kutnik, Edward Larissy, Herbert Leibowitz, Herbert Lindenberger,

Kathryne Lindberg, Ming-Qian Ma, Steve McCaffery, Karen MacCormack, Jerome McGann, Adalaide Morris, Peter Quartermain, Jean-Michel Rabaté, Susan Rankaitis, Rima Dell Reck, Brian Reed, Joan Retallack, Michael Schmidt, Maeera Schreiber, Jeremy Treglown, Keith Tuma, Susan Vandenborg, and Robert von Hallberg.

Hank Lazer, who organized the now famous "What Is a Poet?" conference held at the University of Alabama in 1984, where I delivered the talk that was to become the earliest essay (essay 5) in this collection, deserves a special debt of gratitude for his excellent advice as to the selection and organization that went into this book. I am very grateful to Rainer Rumold of Northwestern, who first suggested to me that it would be useful to put together my essays of the last decade, and to Susan Harris of Northwestern University Press for being, as always, such a clear-eyed, perceptive, and exemplary editor.

Histories and Issues

1. Postmodernism / Fin de Siècle

Defining "Difference" in Late
Twentieth-Century Poetics

It is now more than twenty years ago that a SUNY-Binghamton professor named William Spanos—a Heideggerian student of poetics bent on opposing everything the New Criticism, in which he had been trained, stood for—founded a journal called *boundary 2,* subtitled *An International Journal of Postmodern Literature.* The title is emblematic of the period: the lower-case *boundary 2* points to the desire and need for new parameters, new margins—a "second" way to define literature. "International" means, in sixties- or seventies-speak, European as well as American; the first issue of *boundary 2* features an essay on Foucault by Edward Said and another on the *Nouveau Roman* by Bruce Morrisette, side by side with Warren Tallman's piece on William Carlos Williams's short stories, Joseph Riddel's deconstructionist essay on Wallace Stevens, and James Curtis's essay on Marshall McLuhan and French structuralism. The poetry published in the issue may also be considered "international" since there is a thirty-five-page portfolio of work by the Greek poet Yannis Ritsos.

But it is the word *literature* in the title that I find especially interesting. For, although poststructuralist theory is already much in evidence (witness Edward Said on Foucault, Riddel on Stevens via Paul de Man, and Spanos himself on the postmodern imagination via Heidegger), the journal's focus is very much on literature, it still being a given, in 1972, that "literary" journals, published as they were by English or comparative literature departments, would concentrate, from however radical a point of view, on literary texts.

Consider, for example, David Antin's seminal essay "Modernism and Postmodernism: Approaching the Present in American Poetry," published in the first issue. Antin writes from the perspective of the practicing poet who was also beginning to make a name for himself as a performance artist and art critic, having recently been appointed chair of the newly formed Visual Arts department of the University of California—San Diego. His *boundary 2* essay brilliantly dismantles what he calls the "closed verse tradition" of late modernist poetry from Delmore Schwartz to W. D. Snodgrass. "What we have called the 'modern' for so long," Antin declares, "is thoroughly over"; accordingly, the recycling of the symbolist lyric (Antin dismisses W. D. Snodgrass's *After Experience* as "an updated version of *A Shropshire Lad*"), as well as the recycling of collage (e.g., Robert Lowell's "attenuated history collage" in "Concord" or "For the Union Dead"), can only be retrograde.[1] Over against Snodgrass and Lowell, Antin sets Charles Olson, the then hero of the poetic counterculture; Olson's "disregard for metrical organization and for a poetical frame that wraps things up" (DA 117) is considered exemplary. Indeed, following the scenario first made prominent by Donald Allen in *The New American Poetry* (1960), Antin describes the "great explosion of American poetry" in the sixties as the final rejection of the "closed-verse" tradition of neomodernist, late New Critical poetry, in favor of a more direct and spontaneous poetry based on natural utterance, on the breath. The "opening of the field" by the Black Mountain and Beat poets, by the New York school and the San Francisco Renaissance, so the argument goes, was animated by "the underlying conviction that poetry was made by a man [*sic*] on his feet talking" (DA 131). As such, the poetic text was to be understood less as an object than as a "score" or "notation" to be actualized in performance, the implication of such "scoring" being that "phenomenological reality is 'discovered' and 'constructed' by poets" (DA 132–33). And further: postmodernist poetics meant the turn from Pound and Eliot to the neglected work of Gertrude Stein and John Cage, the poetry of Dada and Surrealism, and "the poetry of nonliterate and partially literate cultures" (DA 133): in the case of the latter, Antin is of course thinking of the ethnopoetics movement spearheaded by his friend and fellow poet Jerome Rothenberg. Indeed, one of the early issues (spring 1975) of *boundary 2* was a special issue on "The Oral Impulse in Contemporary American Poetry," featuring the work of Rothenberg and again Antin.

To reread Antin's 1972 essay in the mid-nineties is to become aware of how much our assumptions about postmodernism have changed. The essay's frame of reference is, to begin with, resolutely *literary*, the issue being who has inherited and who should inherit the poetic mantle of the great modernists: such neomodernists as Robert Lowell, who carry on, in attenuated form, the symbolist collage tradition of *The Waste Land* and the *Cantos*, or such "phenomenological" poets as Olson and Creeley? Closed verse versus open form, the metrical line versus the "breath," poetry as product versus poetry as process, symbolism versus immanence (as Charles Altieri put it in another important essay published in *boundary 2* in 1973),[2] and so on. But although the poem as autonomous artifact is rejected, Poetry itself remains an autonomous realm, contaminated neither by culture nor by theory nor by any of the discourses that surround it. It is also the case that just about all of Antin's poets, whether Good Guys or Bad Guys, are white men. Indeed, the "field" that is supposedly "opening" is, at the practical level, the setting of a polite athletic contest (hockey? soccer?), where the Harvard team captained by Robert Lowell plays the Harvard team captained by Charles Olson. To put it another way: Antin, who is obviously a member of the Olson team, is theorizing his own practice, telling us what kind of poetry he wants to produce (the utterance of "a man on his feet talking") and why.

But there is another assumption Antin makes—an assumption shared by Altieri's "From Symbolism to Immanence," by James Breslin's *From Modern to Contemporary* (even though Breslin is careful not to use the P-word), and for that matter, by my own *Poetics of Indeterminacy*—namely the assumption that *poetry matters*.[3] Poetic discourse, in early formulations of postmodernism, is not just a site to be contested and intersected by other discourses, for—and this is the corollary assumption—there is such a thing as *poetic value*. Not only is Olson "better" than a member of the other team like Snodgrass; Ginsberg is judged to be better than Ferlinghetti, Denise Levertov (one of the few women poets regularly cited in the seventies) is better than May Swenson, Frank O'Hara better than Ted Berrigan.

These twin assumptions—the value of poetry and the ability to discriminate specific poetic value—are just as central to discussions of the other arts. In 1972 art with a capital A still mattered, and it mattered that Jasper Johns was "better" than a second-generation abstract expressionist like Norman Bluhm. Merce Cunningham was judged to be more "interesting" than Murray Feldman. And so on. Indeed, theorizing postmodernism, during the first decades of its usage, was animated by the belief— and here *boundary 2* was quite typical—that postmodernism represents everything that is radical, innovative, forward-looking—*beyond,* if not contra, mere modernism, and is thus distinguished from the mass of writing or painting or architecture, which, far from challenging modernism, merely carries on its traditions.

It is interesting to reread Ihab Hassan in this regard. Hassan's first book, after all, was called *The Literature of Silence* (1967), and made the case for a "new literature" written in the wake of Dachau and Hiroshima, a literature whose "total rejection of Western history and civilization" leads either to the apocalyptic violence and obscenity of a Henry Miller or a Norman Mailer or the silence, randomness, and indeterminacy of Samuel Beckett or John Cage. By 1971, Hassan referred to this "change in Modernism" as postmodernism and drew up the first of his famous lists or tables, a table made up of binary oppositions:[4]

Modernism	Postmodernism
1. Urbanism	1. The Global Village (McLuhan), Spaceship Earth (Fuller), the City as Cosmos—Science Fiction. Anarchy and fragmentation.
2. Technologism	2. Runaway technology. New media, art forms. Boundless dispersal by media. The computer as substitute consciousness or extension of consciousness.
3. Elitism	3. Antielitism, antiauthoritarianism. Diffusion of the ego. Participation. Community. Anarchy.
4. Irony	4. Radical play. Entropy of meaning. Comedy of the absurd. Black Humor. Camp.
5. Abstraction	5. New Concreteness. Found Object. Conceptual Art.
6. Primitivism	6. Beat and Hip. Rock Culture. Dionysian Ego.
7. Eroticism	7. The New Sexuality. Homosexuality, Feminism, Lesbianism. Comic pornography. Repeal of Censorship.

| 8. Antinomianism. Beyond Law. Non Serviam. | 8. Counterculture. Beyond alienation. Counter Western "ways." Zen, Buddhism, Hinduism. The occult, apocalypticism. |
| 9. Experimentalism. Formal innovation. New language. | 9. Open form, discontinuity, improvisation. Antiformalism. Indeterminacy. Aleatory structure. Minimalism. Intermedia. |

Hassan's frame of reference is, on the face of it, much broader than Antin's: he draws on fiction as well as poetry, on philosophy, the visual arts, and certain well-known critical texts like Lionel Trilling's *Beyond Culture*. Urbanism, for example, is exemplified by Baudelaire, Proust, Rilke, Eliot, and Dos Passos; Technologism, by Cubism, Futurism, and Dada, with a reference to Wylie Sypher's *Literature and Technology*, and the entry on Modernist Antinomianism alludes to Nathan A. Scott's *The Broken Center*. The postmodern column is similarly eclectic, transurbanism (the Global Village) being represented by Buckminster Fuller, Marshall McLuhan, science fiction, and so on.

But like Antin, and like almost everyone who wrote on the subject in the seventies, postmodernism was where it was happening, where the excitement was. Not because the individual writers of modernism (Pound, Eliot, Rilke, Mann) were not perhaps greater than those of postmodernism, but because PoMo was presented as being open, antielitist, antiauthoritarian, participatory, anarchic, playful, improvisational, rebellious, discontinuous—and even, in Hassan's words, ecologically active, otherwise known as Green. To write from a postmodernist perspective, in these years, thus involved a romantic faith in the open-endedness of literary and artistic discourse, in the ability of these discourses to transform themselves, to go beyond existing models and improve on them. As such, this utopian phase of postmodernism was very much an inside view, a witnessing on the part of the poets themselves (and Hassan used all manner of typographical devices and fragmentary forms so as to ally himself with the poets) that there was still a cutting edge.

Within a decade, a curious reversal had set in. By 1978, Hassan, always something of a barometer, published an essay called "Culture, Indeterminacy, and Value," that contained more references to Foucault and de Man than to McLuhan or Cage or Burroughs. The essay is written under the sign of Nietzsche and makes much of the "disappearance" of man as a "concrete figuration of history" (IHPT 52–53). And the 1982 "Towards a Concept of Postmodernism" begins with a catalog of names that "may serve to adumbrate postmodernism," a catalog that opens with the following: Jacques Derrida, Jean-François Lyotard, Michel Foucault, Hayden White, Jacques Lacan, Gilles Deleuze, R. D. Laing, Norman O. Brown, Herbert Marcuse, Jean Baudrillard, Jürgen Habermas, Thomas Kuhn, Paul Feyerabend, Roland Barthes, Julia Kristeva, Wolfgang Iser, the Yale critics. The list then turns to dancers, composers, artists, architects, and "various authors" from Beckett and Borges to John Ashbery and Robert Wilson (IHPT 85). But theory, specifically French theory, is clearly at the center of the enterprise. The open form or process model celebrated by David Antin now gives way to the "semantic instability" of Derrida, and since the construction of the text as trace structure, as a tissue of differences, can be applied to writings of any period, the examples begin to come from established writers, primarily of the nineteenth century—Rousseau and Shelley, Marx and Mallarmé, Nerval and Nietzsche. Not reading the New but rereading the familiar in the light of the New Theory—this becomes the order of the day.

The widespread acceptance of Jean-François Lyotard's paradigm presented in *La Condition postmoderne* (1979; English translation 1984) marks this shift from what we might call Antin's pragmatics of postmodernism (the inside view of the practicing poet) to the broader cultural definition of the term as it is used today. When Lyotard defines the *postmodern* as "incredulity toward metanarratives," when he describes the "two major versions of such narratives of legitimation" as that of the liberation of humanity (justice) and the speculative unity of all knowledge (truth), the term *modernism* points, not as in Antin or Hassan's case, to the particular literary and art movements of the early twentieth century, but to the larger *modernity* of Enlightenment discourse, specifically to the various progress models of the nineteenth century, which are central to Lyotard's discussion.[5] But when Lyotard declares that in postindustrial society the "grand narrative has lost its credibility" (PC 37), that "modernist" statements of legitimation, whether regarding truth (e.g., "The earth revolves around the sun") or regarding justice (e.g., "The minimum wage must be set at *x* dollars") no longer hold, one wonders if Lyotard's own metanarrative of delegitimation can really account for the specific changes that have occurred in Western societies over the last few decades.

Why, to begin with, *the* not *a* "postmodern condition," and why the singular form of the noun? Perhaps because *The Postmodern Condition* is itself a metanarrative—the story of how, in the face of post–World War II scientific knowledge, technology, and information theory, the de-legitimation of the "grand" metanarratives has set in. Interestingly, the Lyotard paradigm continues to make the case for *difference,* for openness (the "essay," he says, is postmodern; the fragment, still modern), and, in a famous formulation, for the *unpresentable,* perceptible in "presentation itself; that which denies itself the solace of good forms" (PC 81). But in practice, respect for difference has now hardened into a set of norms and prescriptions that leave very little room for the free play, the anarchy, the indeterminacy and disjunctive form that used to be considered character-istic of postmodernism.

Consider the position of Fredric Jameson, whose *Postmodernism; or, The Cultural Logic of Late Capitalism* is surely the best-known and most widely respected discussion of the subject. It is worth remembering that Jameson wrote the foreword to the English translation of Lyotard's *La Condition postmoderne* and that, although he subjects Lyotard's argument to a more orthodox Marxist spin, he too believes that we have come to an end of the "great master narratives." The title chapter of *The Cultural Logic of Late Capitalism,* first published in 1984 in the *New Left Review,* designates "one fundamental feature of all the postmodernisms," "the effacement in them of the older (essentially high-modernist) frontier between high culture and so-called mass or commercial culture. . . . The postmodernisms have, in fact, been fascinated precisely by this whole 'degraded' landscape of schlock and kitsch, of TV series and Reader's Digest culture, of advertis-ing and motels, of the late show and the grade-B Hollywood film."[6] And since postmodern culture (also known as media culture, consumer society, or information society) is thus "degraded" by its capitalist economic base, its products no longer shock or offend, as did the oppositional art of the modernist avant-garde. The "constitutive features" (note the assurance of that term) of the postmodern are now described as follows:

a new depthlessness, which finds its prolongation both in contempo-rary "theory" and in a whole new culture of the image or the simu-lacrum; a consequent weakening of historicity, both in our relationship to public History and in the new forms of our private temporality, whose "schizophrenic" structure (following Lacan) will determine new types of syntax or syntagmatic relationships in the more temporal arts;

a whole new type of emotional ground tone . . . [and] the deep constitutive relationships of all this to a whole new technology, which is itself a figure for a whole new economic world system. (FJ 6)

The "new type of emotional ground tone," also called the "waning of affect in postmodern culture" (FJ 10), refers, of course, to the dissolution of the subject, with the consequent dissolution of "unique style" and the replacement of parody by pastiche ("blank parody").

I don't think I need spell out here the influence this analysis of postmodernism was to have on the theorizing of the eighties. From Andreas Huyssen's *After the Great Divide* (1986), which similarly defines postmodernism, although less pessimistically than Jameson, as the breakdown of the modernist "frontier" between high art and mass culture, to Rosalind Krauss's scornful rejection of what she calls the "sublimation model" ("According to this model, the function of art is to sublimate or transform experience, raising it from ordinary to extraordinary, from commonplace to unique, from low to high; with the special genius of the artist being that he or she has the gifts to perform this function"),[7] the discourse of postmodernism has referred, as if to a set of incontrovertible facts, to postmodern "depthlessness," the simulacrum, the death of the subject, the nondifferentiation of "art" and popular culture, and so on.

Whether or not we adhere to these particular paradigms of the postmodern, it is interesting to note how the terminology of the early seventies, when discussions of postmodernism still had a quasi-utopian cast, has subtly shifted. What David Antin and Ihab Hassan characterized as the openness associated with the postmodern ("Open, discontinuous, improvisational, indeterminate, or aleatory structures") imperceptibly turns into "depthlessness," with all its negative associations of mere surface, shallowness, superficiality. The erasure of boundaries between the traditional genres and media becomes the "contamination" of all art works by the "'degraded' landscape of schlock and kitsch," playfulness hardens into simulacrum, "decreation" into the death of the subject ("there is no longer," says Jameson, "a self present to do the feeling" [FJ 51]), and Derridean *différance* as deferral is gradually replaced by the very specific difference of identity politics, difference as marker or label. Indeed, despite all the talk of rupture, transgression, antiformalism, the breaking of the vessels—in Lyotardian terms, the delegitimation of the great metanarratives—there seem to be more rules and prescriptions around than ever. Such familiar modernist/postmodernist pairs as "hierarchy"/"anarchy" and

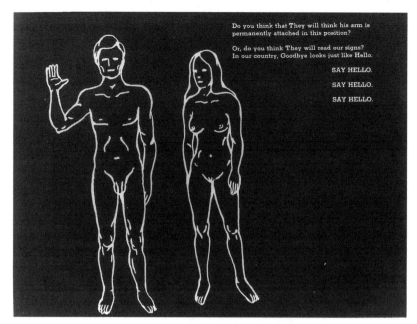

Within the image:

Do you think that They will think his arm is
permanently attached in this position?

Or, do you think They will read our signs?
In our country, Goodbye looks just like Hello.

SAY HELLO.

SAY HELLO.

SAY HELLO.

Figure 1. Laurie Anderson, "Say Hello," *United States.*

"Master Code"/"idiolect" (see IHPT 91) are now being called into question, ironically enough, by the establishment of new hierarchies and master codes—the return, we might say, of the Law of the Father.

An important essay by Craig Owens, called "The Discourse of Others: Feminists and Postmodernism," which appeared in the Hal Foster collection *The Anti-Aesthetic* (1983), may serve to dramatize this subtle shift. In a section subtitled "A Remarkable Oversight," Owens apologizes for the "gross critical negligence" of an earlier reading he had performed on Laurie Anderson's well-known image, in her multimedia performance piece *United States,* of a nude man and woman (a cartoon version of Adam and Eve), in which the man's right arm is raised at a ninety-degree angle while the woman, shorter than the man and hands at her sides, faces toward him. In the performance, Anderson's voice-over (amplified to sound like a male voice) tells us, "In our country, we send pictures of our sign language into Outer Space. We are speaking our sign language in these pictures. Do you think that They will think his arm is permanently attached in this position? Or do you think They will read our signs? In our country, Goodbye looks just like Hello" (figures 1 and 2).[8]

Here is Owens's original commentary on this captioned image:

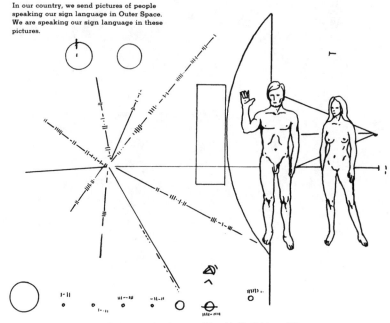

Figure 2. Laurie Anderson, "Say Hello," *United States.*

Two alternatives: either the extraterrestrial recipient of the message will assume that it is simply a picture, that is, an analogical likeness of the human figure, in which case *he* might logically conclude that male inhabitants of Earth walk around with their right arms permanently raised. Or *he* will somehow divine that this gesture is addressed to *him* and attempt to read it, in which case *he* will be stymied, since a single gesture signifies both greeting and farewell, and any reading of it must oscillate between these two extremes. The same gesture could also mean "Halt!" or represent the taking of an oath, but if Anderson's text does not consider these two alternatives that is because it is not concerned with ambiguity, with multiple meanings engendered by a single sign; rather two *clearly defined but mutually incompatible* readings are engaged in blind confrontation in such way that it is impossible to choose between them. (AA 60, my emphasis on "he")

This passage represents Owens as quintessential Derridean: his source seems to be *Of Grammatology* or possibly *Writing and Difference,* and

French feminist constructions, based on Lacan, still seem far away: witness the use of the masculine pronoun throughout. As he himself now confesses:

> In my eagerness to rewrite Anderson's text in terms of the debate over determinate versus indeterminate meaning, I had overlooked something. . . . For this is, of course, an image of sexual difference, or rather, of sexual differentiation according to the distribution of the phallus—as it is marked and then re-marked by the man's right arm, which appears less to have been raised than erected in greeting. . . . Like all representations of sexual difference that our culture produces, this is an image not simply of anatomical difference, but of the values assigned to it. Here the phallus is . . . the signifier of privilege, of the power and prestige that accrue to the male in our society. . . . For in this (Lacanian) image, chosen to represent the inhabitants of Earth for the extraterrestial Other, it is the man who speaks, who represents mankind. The woman is only represented; she is (as always) already spoken for. (AA 61)

Here is Owens speaking in his role as New Feminist. The sexual differentiation he now notes is certainly central to Anderson's cartoon (one wonders how Owens could have missed it the first go-round), but I am not sure its identification cancels out his earlier reading, with its focus on the American equation of "Goodbye" with "Hello," an equation that parodies more than the obvious inequity of gender roles in our culture. "Anderson's blunt question ['Do you think that They will think his arm is permanently attached in this position?']," writes Herman Rapaport in a discussion of *United States,* "is expressionless, exposing the fatuousness of 'big science,' the silly presupposition that aliens are going to be able to read our 'signs.' She suggests that in a postmodern culture scientists are so overspecialized that when it comes to basic questions they are enormously obtuse. No one has noticed that saying 'hello' is exactly the same as saying 'good-bye,' that even if aliens could read our signs, they would be confused."[9] It is difficult to see how this aspect of Anderson's witty parody can be ignored, but Owens does ignore it in his zeal to demonstrate that his second reading "corrects" the first: difference as signifying gap ("two clearly defined but mutually incompatible readings") thus gives way to clear-cut gender difference: it is the man who speaks, the woman who is always already spoken for.

Is this then the New Enlightenment of third-stage (the first is exemplified by Antin's poetics, the second by Derridean deconstruction) postmodernism? And if so, what has happened to postmodernism's fabled openness and decenteredness? For not only is Owens telling us how to read Anderson's image, telling us *what it means,* as unequivocally as Brooks and Warren once told us what the word "design" means in Robert Frost's poem by that name, but this assertive statement ("it is the man who speaks") is embedded in a larger discourse that is not without its own coercions. Owens's essay begins as follows:

> Decentered, allegorical, schizophrenic . . . —however we choose to diagnose its symptoms, postmodernism is usually treated, by its protagonists and antagonists alike, as a crisis of cultural authority, specifically of the authority vested in Western European culture and its institutions. That the hegemony of European civilization is drawing to a close is hardly a new perception; since the mid-1950s, at least, we have recognized the necessity of encountering different cultures by means other than the shock of domination and conquest. (AA 57)

But even as he makes this declaration, Owens cites the following: Lévi-Strauss, Derrida, Ricoeur, Baudrillard, Foucault, Kristeva, and Barthes. Seven French theorists named within the space of two pages. And on the third page (AA 59), the combined authority of Lacan and Foucault advances the following hypothesis:

> The *modernist* avant-garde . . . sought to transcend representation in favor of presence and immediacy; it proclaimed the autonomy of the signifier, its liberation from the "tyranny of the signified"; "postmodernists instead expose the tyranny of the *signifier,* the violence of its law. . . . It is precisely at the legislative frontier between what can be represented and what cannot that the postmodern operation is being staged—not in order to transcend representation, but in order to expose that system of power that authorizes certain representations while blocking, prohibiting, or invalidating others.

Here is the move we have already observed from what is, so to speak, a seventies Derridean paradigm to an eighties Foucauldian-Lacanian one. Aside from Anderson, Owens's exempla of "prohibited" representations include Martha Rosler's *The Bowery in Two Inadequate Descriptive Systems,* Dara Birnbaum's *Technology/Transformation: Wonder Woman,* and assorted photos and film stills by Sherrie Levine, Cindy Sherman, and Barbara Kruger. But however interesting such exempla of "gender-specific" artworks may be, it is important to note that the works of Anderson and Rosler, Birnbaum and Levine, Sherman and Kruger remain just that: *exempla,* demonstrating how valid Lacan's discussion of the Law of the Father, Lyotard's notion of the postmodern "unrepresentable," and Foucault's analysis of the power system are. Ironically, then, the women artists in question continue to be victimized—if not by the patriarchy of modernist critique and the art market, then by the French theoretical model, which their work so nicely illustrates.[10] The real power, in other words, belongs not to the postmodern artist (Anderson, Sherman) but to the poststructuralist theorist whose principles validate the work.

No wonder, then, that recent handbooks on postmodernism—and they are now legion—reduce what was once the excitement of the Cutting Edge to a list of rules and prescriptions that make one almost long for the days of *Understanding Poetry.* Take Brenda K. Marshall's *Teaching the Postmodern,* published by Routledge in 1992.[11] The introduction opens with a page of what are evidently intended to be *parole in libertà,* as Marinetti dubbed them (see figure 3). Notice that the very first word in this "visual poem" is our old friend *différance,* but there is precious little difference in this list of the Big Names, whether of theorists (Kristeva, Barthes, Derrida, Foucault, Althusser, and such American variants as Hutcheon [Linda] and de Lauretis [Teresa]), or fiction writers (Morrison, Carter, Rushdie, Wolf, Coetzee), or Big Theory Terms (genealogy, historiography, deconstruction, structuralism, ideology, intertextuality, subject position, Marxism, etc.). What is, so to speak, the poem's refrain is the word *language,* which appears four times! Language, it seems, is centrally important. But how?

Marshall begins with the Piety of the Day: "Crucial to an understanding of the postmodern moment is the recognition that there is no 'outside' from which to 'objectively' name the present." Of course not: no *hors texte,* no transcendental signified, no metanarrative, no essentialist norms by which to judge production: "The postmodern moment is an awareness of being within, first, a language, and second, a particular historical, social, cultural framework. . . . There can be no such thing as objectivity. . . . That does not mean that we are paralyzed or helpless; rather, it means that we give up the luxury of absolute Truths, choosing instead to put to work local and provisional truths" (BM 3). Having made this obligatory gesture to some kind of Uncertainty Principle, Marshall now proceeds briskly to tell us what postmodernism is all about:

Postmodernism is about language. About how it controls, how it determines meaning, and how we try to exert control through language.

Introduction

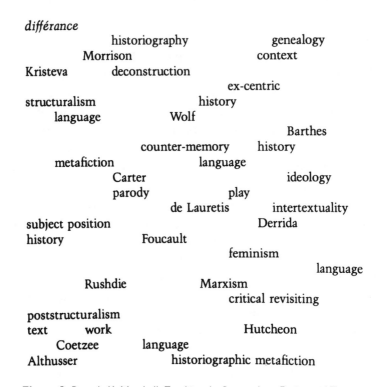

différance

        historiography   genealogy

     Morrison   context

Kristeva   deconstruction

                     ex-centric

structuralism   history

   language   Wolf

                        Barthes

        counter-memory   history

   metafiction   language

      Carter   ideology

      parody   play

         de Lauretis   intertextuality

subject position   Derrida

history   Foucault

             feminism

                  language

   Rushdie   Marxism

            critical revisiting

poststructuralism

text   work   Hutcheon

  Coetzee   language

Althusser   historiographic metafiction

Figure 3. Brenda K. Marshall, *Teaching the Postmodern: Fiction and Theory.*

About how language restricts, closes down, insists that it stands for some *thing*. Postmodernism is about how "we" are defined within that language, and within specific historical, social, cultural matrices. It's about race, class, gender, erotic identity and practice, nationality, age, ethnicity. It's about difference. It's about power and powerlessness, about empowerment, and about all the stages in between and beyond and unthought of. . . . It's about those threads that we trace, and trace, and trace. But not to a conclusion. To increased knowledge, yes. But never to innocent knowledge. To better understanding, yes. But never to pure insight. Postmodernism is about history. But not the kind of

"History" that lets us think we can know the past. . . . It's about chance. It's about power. It's about information. And more information. And more. And. And that's just a little bit of what postmodernism [is]. (BM 4)

Thus it is that postmodernism enters the classroom. "The word postmodernism," adds the author, "does not refer to a period or a 'movement'. It isn't really an 'ism'; it isn't really a thing. It's a moment but more a moment in logic than in time. Temporally, it's a space" (BM 5). If this sounds more like *The Cat in the Hat* ("It isn't really an 'ism'; it isn't really a thing") than like a serious attempt to understand what is happening in late twentieth-century culture, it is unfortunately not atypical. Nor are the exercises that follow this introduction—for example, "Critique of Representation and J. M. Coetzee's *Foe*"; "Critique of Subjectivity and Michel Tournier's *Friday*"—which dutifully go through the motions of reading selected contemporary novels through the prisms provided, once again, by Derrida and Foucault.

How did we ever get ourselves into this mode of critical thinking? And should we therefore, as many critics now suggest,[12] abandon the P-word as useless, a word subject to the closure that everywhere threatens the demand for difference? If we do give up the term, moreover, can we designate our period—excuse me, moment—vis-à-vis earlier moments in any meaningful way? In what follows, I make some tentative suggestions, coming back to the question of a "postmodern" as opposed to a "modernist" poetics.

Differences/Diversities

The gradual but wholesale reversal of PoMo terminology between the late sixties and the early nineties suggests that the fin de siècle may well be as different from the sixties and early seventies as those decades were from the twenties and thirties. Yet the standard opposition between modernism and postmodernism does not take this continuing evolution into account. Theorists either push modernism further and further back into the past, as do Lyotard and Habermas; this gives us three centuries of modernist (Enlightenment) discourse against which to measure what is happening in the delegitimating present. Or we do the opposite: we push modernism further and further toward the present, so as to include postwar figures like Beckett and Pinter, Georges Perec and *film noir*, Jackson Pollock and

Figure 4. Vincent van Gogh, *A Pair of Boots.*

Philip Johnson, thus setting aside postmodernism as referring to German neo-Expressionism or cyberpunk or the performance art of the eighties.

We cannot, in short, come to terms with postmodernism until we decide what modernism was. "From the modernism that you want," David Antin has quipped, "you get the postmodernism you deserve." If, for example, modernism is equated with Enlightenment discourse from the *Encyclopedia* to World War II, then Lyotard may well be right to insist that postmodernism means incredulity to the *grands récits* of progress and scientific advancement. If, on the other hand, modernism is taken to refer to the first three decades or so of the twentieth-century, then it is hard not to infer that any number of great modernists—Kafka, Brecht, Musil, Kraus, Leiris, Celine, Bataille, Pound, Stevens, Williams—had already lost faith in those metanarratives of knowledge and social justice. Again, if modernism is equated with Anglo-American modernism, then the attribution of order and hierarchy, organic form and autonomy, centering and aesthetic distance may well be applicable; if, on the other hand, we focus on continental Europe, on, say, Italian Futurism and Dada, on Apollinaire and Cendrars, or on Klee and Tatlin, the picture is quite different.

It is, I think, the drive toward totalization and hence toward closure that bedevils current discussions of postmodernism. Consider what we might call the synecdochic fallacy. In *Postmodernism; or, The Cultural Logic of Late Capitalism,* Jameson makes an extended comparison between Van Gogh's well-known painting of peasant shoes (figure 4), which he calls "one of the canonical works of high modernism," and Andy Warhol's *Diamond Dust Shoes* (figure 5). Whether we interpret the Van Gogh as an "act of compensation," a "willed and violent transformation of a drab peasant object world into the most glorious materialization of pure color in oil paint," or, in Heideggerian terms, as a re-creation of "the whole missing object world which was once [the shoes'] lived context," the "disclosure of what the equipment, the pair of peasant shoes *is* in truth" and hence "the unconcealment of [their] being," reading the painting, Jameson posits, is "*hermeneutical,* in the sense in which the work in its inert, objectal form is taken as a clue or a symptom for some vaster reality which replaces it as its ultimate truth" (FJ 8).

Warhol's *Diamond Dust Shoes,* by contrast, doesn't speak to anything beyond itself; rather, this "random collection of dead objects hanging together on the canvas like so many turnips" functions as a set of commodity fetishes. In an "inversion of Van Gogh's Utopian gesture," Jameson argues, "the external and colored surface of things—debased and contaminated in advance by their assimilation to glossy advertising images—has been stripped away to reveal the deathly black-and-white substratum of the photographic negative which subtends them" (FJ 9). As such, Warhol's work exemplifies the "new depthlessness" and the "waning of affect" which Jameson, as I noted above, takes to be the distinguishing features of the postmodernist "culture of the simulacrum" (FJ 6, 10).

What interests me here is less the specific characterization of the respective paintings than the claim that the part ipso facto stands for the whole. Van Gogh's is "one of the canonical works of high modernism"; Warhol is "the central figure in contemporary visual art" (FJ 8). And so a late nineteenth-century painter who was one of the least appreciated and most cruelly marginalized artists of his own day is compared to an American artist who has become the icon of self-promotion, publicity, and commercial success. Is Warhol really Van Gogh's postmodernist counterpart, or should we more accurately compare the former to a salon painter like Bouguereau, who similarly knew how to manipulate the public and become a star? Or, to take the other side of the parallel, suppose we compare Van Gogh not to Warhol but to Jasper Johns. The "modernist" "disclosure of what the equipment, the pair of peasant shoes, *is* in truth," the emergence of the painted "entity . . . into the unconcealment of its being,

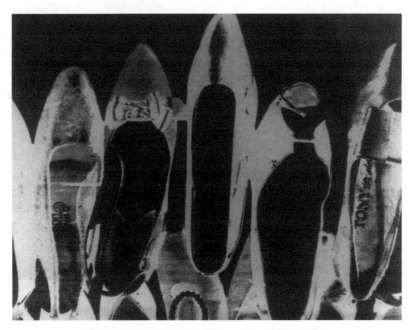

Figure 5. Andy Warhol, *Diamond Dust Shoes* (1980).

by way of the mediation of the work of art," has a perfect counterpart in Johns's paintings of coat hangers and light bulbs, beer cans and paint brushes, the various *Alphabets* and number series.

A Warhol silkscreen cannot, in any case, "represent" *the* postmodern any more than John Portman's Bonaventure Hotel (another Exhibit A in Jameson's lexicon of postmodernism; see FJ 38–44) can represent the "new depthlessness" of architecture over against the International Style of Le Corbusier and Gropius. Common sense suggests that whatever the "hyperspace" of the Bonaventure is or isn't, its modernist counterpart is not a Bauhaus monument but, say, New York's art deco Waldorf Astoria, the grand commercial hotel of the thirties and forties, even as the Bonaventure, with its revolving skytop cocktail lounge and "reflective glass skin [that] repels the city outside" (FJ 42), is a popular building of our own day.

Van Gogh/Warhol; Le Corbusier/Portman: these would-be synecdoches, representing the modern and postmodern respectively, also display a curious way of relating the European to the American. If modernism is regularly considered a European phenomenon, postmodernism is almost by definition "born in the U.S.A." This means that although Van Gogh's most logical postmodernist successor might well be the Belgian

Marcel Broodthaers, now recognized as a seminal figure in the development of postconceptual art, pride of place must nevertheless be given to the quintessential American product of late capitalism, Andy Warhol. Note that neither in his discussion of pastiche nor in his differentiation of postmodern from modern architecture does Jameson feel obliged to justify the U.S.-centrism of his position. Indeed, despite the lip service currently paid to multiculturalism, one often has the sense that the only thing that matters in U.S. culture . . . is U.S. culture. True, that culture is divided up into dozens of marginalized, disempowered, and minority subsets: African American, Chicana/o, Native American, Asian American, gay and lesbian, and so on. But the requisite for all these groups turns out to be U.S. citizenship: the Other, it seems, does not include the literatures of other nations or in other languages.

"What postmodernism taught us," writes David Harvey, "was that difference and heterogeneity matter, and that the language in which we represent the world, the manner of discourse, ought to be the subject of careful reflection. But it did not teach us how to negotiate differences in fruitful ways, nor did it tell us how to go about the business of communicating with each other after we had carefully deconstructed each others' language."[13] We could take this a step further and argue that the concept of difference, as liberating as it seemed in the seventies, has now been replaced by a bland diversity that, as the poet Charles Bernstein observes in *A Poetics,* harks back "to New Critical and liberal-democratic concepts of a common readership that often . . . have the effect of transforming unresolved ideological divisions and antagonisms into packaged tours of the local color of gender, race, sexuality, ethnicity, region, nation, class, even historical period: where each group or community or period is expected to come up with—or have appointed for them—representative figures we all can know about."[14]

Unlike difference, Bernstein argues, *diversity* "presupposes a common standard of aesthetic judgment or implicitly aims to erect a new common standard. In this context, diversity can be a way of restoring a highly idealized concept of a unified American culture that effectively quiets dissent" (CB 4–5). And he adds:

> Too often the works selected to represent cultural diversity are those that accept the model of representation assumed by the dominant culture in the first place. "I see grandpa on the hill / next to the memories I can never recapture" is the base line against which other versions play:

"I see my yiddishe mama on hester street / next to the pushcarts I can no longer peddle" or "I see my grandmother on the hill / next to all the mothers whose lives can never be recaptured" or "I can't touch my Iron Father / who never canoed with me / on the prairies of my masculine epiphany." Works that challenge these models of representation run the risk of becoming more inaudible than ever within mainstream culture. (CB 6)

A similar point is made by Henry Louis Gates Jr. in a 1991 essay for *American Literary History.* "If black authors are primarily entrusted with producing the proverbial 'text of blackness'," he writes, "they become vulnerable to the charge of betrayal if they shirk their duty. . . . Representational democracy [here Gates is citing the black British filmmaker Isaac Julian and the media theorist Kobena Mercer], like the classic realist text, is premised on an implicitly mimetic theory of representation as correspondence with the 'real.'"[15]

Which is to say that essentialism has by no means been put to rest and that metanarrative, far from having been abandoned, has reappeared in the new guise of an elaborate plot of ethnic amelioration. Consider the following poem by a young Chicano writer, published, like Gates's essay, in 1991:

The Willow
Las Cruces, New Mexico
Spring 1964

I loved a tree in my boyhood, a tree
In my grandfather's garden, a weeping
willow whose ancient limbs longed
upwards, then arched downwards, perfect
bows which reached so low, so low
the leaves brushed the grass as if to
sweep it clean. I played alone among
the arches of leaves, pulling the green

limbs around myself as if they were the
great arms of God. They held me tight.
I was so loved in that embrace of leaves.

And then sickness came

to the garden one spring, the old willow
wrapped in a shroud of bugs. I could only

watch, could not touch it. I shouted
at the tree, and told it to live, and

though it fought to breathe without
leaves, neither my voice nor the rain
could heal it. So the tree was chopped,
stripped limb by limb until there was

only a stump. And the stump, too
was pulled from the ground — pulled
so harshly that even the roots came up

shaking the whole garden.[16]

Ironically, nothing in the poem except its designated locale, Las Cruces, New Mexico, identifies the poet's ethnicity or class. Its author, Benjamin Alire Sáenz, has taken on the most familiar of romantic models: the nature poem in which a particular speaker remembers a particular incident that taught him a lesson — in this case, the lesson that suffering and death are inevitable. The beloved tree, significantly a weeping willow, predictably stands in "my grandfather's garden"; the boy predictably plays under its "arches of leaves," and feels loved and protected by God. But since there is always a serpent in paradise, one spring "sickness came"; a blight struck the tree and it had to be chopped down. Its dismemberment, moreover, became the occasion for excessive human force: "so harshly" was the tree stump "pulled from the ground" that "even the roots came up / shaking the whole garden." The boy who has witnessed this surgery will never be the same.

Even the quatrain form of "The Willow" places it in the romantic tradition, as it comes down to us from Wordsworth to Houseman, and as it no doubt came down to Benjamin Sáenz in the creative writing workshop. Yet, in what we might take as a kind of postmodern giveaway, the poem seems ill at ease with the formal constraint of the quatrain, the syntax being that of straightforward prose: "I shouted at the tree, and told it to live, and though it fought to breathe without leaves, neither my voice nor the rain could heal it." And further: the omission of rhyme and inclusion of one-line units — "And then sickness came," and "shaking the whole garden" — identify "The Willow" as a contemporary poem, a poem that cannot quite reproduce the paradigm it has so earnestly chosen to follow.

To encourage this kind of writing in the name of ethnic diversity is to assume that the "marginalized" have the right (perhaps even the duty) to use what would otherwise be considered well-worn clichés because these groups have hitherto been denied all access to poetic speech, because their voices have been suppressed by the dominant culture. But such validation is based on the further assumption that a poem like "The Willow" is an "authentic" representation of Chicano subjectivity, an assumption that is again an instance of what I have called the synecdochic fallacy. Indeed, the irony is that the refusal to submit the poems of the marginalized to any kind of serious critique accomplishes nothing so much as the marginalization of poetry itself. For even as publishers are dutifully bringing out anthologies of Native American or Chicana/o or Asian-American poetry, we all know that the action has passed elsewhere. For every poetry review in the major papers and journals, there are fifty reviews of biographies, of political books, of media studies and self-help manuals. As for intellectuals, poetry as discourse cannot begin to matter in the ways that theory or cultural study matters. And theory has, as my example from Craig Owens suggests, remained almost exclusively Eurocentric, primarily French and (increasingly) German. A seminar on Bourdieu or Deleuze, on Habermas's concept of the public sphere or Judith Butler's Hegelianism will draw a lot more students than any seminar on contemporary poetry, however oppressed the constituency in question.

And yet, to tap for a moment into a more genuine and robust romanticism than the attenuated version we find in poems like "The Willow," "Without Contraries is no progression." And again: "Improvement makes strait roads; but the crooked roads without Improvement are roads of Genius." The opposition to the bland call for diversity on the one hand, and to the gloomy emphasis on the "new depthlessness" on the other, is coming, once again, not from the professional critics but from poets. The difference is that the new poets are themselves working theorists like Susan Howe, whose *My Emily Dickinson* and *The Birthmark* weave together poetic, historical, and critical discourse, or like Steve McCaffery, whose *North of Intention* and *Rational Geomancy: The Collected Research Reports of the Toronto Research Group 1973–82* (the latter with the late Canadian poet bpNichol) take the theorems of Derrida and Lacan, Kristeva and Althusser for a playful spin that produces fanciful and fictive verbal/visual configurations as "creative" as they are "critical." In a 1992 issue of *Raddle Moon* (#11), a section called "Women / Writing / Theory" features work by Johanna Drucker, Norma Cole, Laura Moriarty, and others that cannot be categorized as "theory" or "poetry," the texts in question always already being "both/and."

Consider a recent poem by Alfred Arteaga:

"The Small Sea of Europe"

—At the end of the eighteenth century, Hindu law, insofar as it can be described as a unitary system, operated in terms of four texts that "staged" a four-part episteme defined by the subject's use of memory: *sruti* (the heard), *smitri* (the remembered), *sastra* (the learned-from-another), and *vyavahara* (the performed-in-exchange).

—Gayatri Chakravorty Spivak

In Europe's small sea,
a system of exchange:
forms of life
and motion in sign.

The Case in Point—

Verkehr:
"the motion of women, of slaves,
in sleep
congested automobiles, trunks
with drugs"

Verkehr,
from the Sanscrit, (small sea),
vyavahara:
performance traffic,
former act of transformation,
an 'exchange.'
Ecos escritos: *Sruti, Smitri, Sastra*
three sisters in myth, very
sources of Europe, Western Man
the very sounds slipping: 3Ss, sans (é)crit
3 Ss:
3Ss: ecos escritos (S grito)

Again, then,
Verkehr:
S_1 in the automobile besides S_2, S_3
At the wheel, 'Sister . . . ' furtive, slave-like
movements (escape? from/to/what/where?)

But who can drive? Of course, S_2 remembers,
tells, S_1 hears, inserts the key,
demonstrates, S_3 learns, starts the motor: of
course, escape, With-Drugs o wild & steering slaves
through furtive traffic, changing lanes, exchanging
places of courses, escape:
Sruti hears, Smriti recalls, Sastra learns from an other:
S *verkehr:* vyavahara
a performance, vyavahara,
the S sound of abandon.

(Or) Again:
Sastra (née 'furtive slave') learned
furtive from
Sruti (née 'furtive slave') heard
furtive from
Smitri (née 'furtive slave') remembers
furtive from
the small sea of history, the big C of capital,
first squirt of legend, transcendental quill
and myth-inks, rib stain here first
no ear, no hearing, across which sheets first
defined smear.

I remember Smitri, in the dictionary
Verkehr:
"fast women in cars escape with drugs"
like Texas, but this is Berlin
to Paris, night rides hard riding off course
3 woman Ss written off across this old sad continent
fast esses, stained-fast essences, the Ss senses (S sense)
of woman defi(l/n/)ed.

Some big *Dichtung*
this place, ace.

London, 1988.[17]

Cantos, in which this poem appears, is a book written in tongues (Spanish/English). "The Small Sea of Europe" adds Sanskrit and German to the linguistic mix, and its epigraph from Gayatri Spivak's well-known essay "Can the Subaltern Speak?," together with its locale (London), place the poem in what is a discourse evidently quite alien to that of Benjamin Sáenz's "The Willow"—the discourse of the international theory community where Spivak is read and studied. Alfred Arteaga probably came across her work at Santa Cruz, where he received a doctorate in Renaissance literature before taking a job at Berkeley.

But he is also a Chicano poet, and it is the intersection of the different (and often conflicting) forms of agency at play that generate his own poetic language. What, the poem seems to ask, is the relationship of subaltern languages (Hindi, Chicano) to the dominant discourse of "The Small Sea of Europe," the irony being that Hindi derives from Sanskrit, which stands at the origin of the Indo-European languages, including the Spanish of the colonized "slaves," whose images merge with those of the "fast women in cars [who] escape with drugs," who now make the headlines. Europe is a "small sea" in relation to the globe, hence the conquistadors' felt necessity of crossing the "small sea" to the New World. Then, too, the journey from Berlin to Paris to London, where the poem was written, has the shape of a "small C" on the map, and the small sea is also the English Channel, which divides England from the Continent.

The "system of exchange," in this context, refers not only to traffic as transportation (*Verkehr*), to the drug traffic that is part of our daily life and the slave traffic which is part of our collective memory (*sruti, smitri, sastra*), but to the exchange of phonemes and letters as well:

> Sanscrit (small Sea) . . .
> sans (é)crit . . .
> ecos escritos (S grito) . . .
> fast esses . . . [on the model of "negresses" or "goddesses"]
> Ss senses (S sense) . . .
> woman defi(l/n)ed . . .

and so on. The three women involved in what may be a sting operation are identified only as S_1 S_2 S_3; they remain nameless and faceless, despite the poet's desire to endow them with the mythic weight of memory: with *sruti* (the heard), *smitri* (the remembered), and *sastra* (the learned-from-another). The "S sound" is thus the "sound of abandon," the invocation of the three graces or muses or goddesses ("fast esses, stained-fast essences") that can do nothing to recover the past. Not memory, but only performance-in-exchange (*vyavahara*), the "three sisters" regarded as so many "furtive slaves." The "small sea of history" is, after all, controlled by the "big C of capital."

Pun, paragram, double entendre: Arteaga's poem emerges as a *Dichtung* without *Wahrheit,* a journey into time and space to recapture the past (which doesn't exist). What, after all, is "this place" which contains "ace" within its word boundaries, "ace" which is again "a *ce*" — the small c of "sans(c)rit"? The "unitary system," whether of Hindu law as Spivak describes it or of Spanish colonial history, has become so many missing links — "myth-inks" smeared on blank sheets.

Arteaga has written a complex meditative poem that interrogates and extends the current theorizing on the "subaltern" question, a question that evidently preoccupies him even as it has preoccupied a critic of a different culture and gender like Gayatri Spivak. To classify such a poem as Chicano is to elide the important differences between it and the neoromantic model we find in Benjamin Sáenz's "The Willow," a model whose tacit assumption that the lyric is a univocal and authentic form of self-expression seems oddly out of key with the discourses of the 1990s in which it is implicated.

If Arteaga's poetics have little in common with Sáenz's, how do they relate to the "postmodern" poetics of the 1960s with which I began? In one sense, "The Small Sea of Europe" is not all that different from, say, Charles Olson's "The Kingfishers," which provided David Antin with his Exhibit A in the *boundary 2* essay. Both are poems including history; both splice together a series of seemingly unrelated cultural and mythological references; both pun on letters and numbers. The difference is that for Arteaga, poetic discourse is no longer held together by the authority of what Antin called "a man on his feet talking" (Olson's "I hunt among stones"). Indeed, "The Small Sea of Europe" refuses to privilege speech over writing, refuses what the poem itself refers to as the *sans(é)crit.* The once central Olsonian subject now occupies the interstices of the narrative, lines like "I remember Smitri" serving as sudden reminders that the events described have actually been witnessed by someone.

This calling into question of authorial control, mimetic speech, and "normal" syntax has been carried even further by other poets of the nineties. I conclude with two variations on this theme. The first is a short prose text called "Staged Dialogue with Failed Transit Actiant Opposition" by the British-born Canadian poet Steve McCaffery.[18] Here the emphasis is less on the problems of history and memory that concern Arteaga than on the look and sound of everyday life in the videated, Larry-King-Live 1990s:

Hello and also. Why do you live? I live because there is a house upon a street somewhere, a house I was born in. It's made of bricks. Is correct. Yes, many things are made of bricks. Bridges and walls and special cups are made of bricks. Excellent. So why do you like sport? Yes, sport is often my favourite, especially the sport of chess. That's played on boards and sometimes ice. Is ice also your favourite? My favourite is books if there's lots of them. My name is Sidney Lanier. I was once a writer. I have many books with names and sometimes thicker ones on the front porch of a house. Sometimes my house is sunny that way and once a week it will always be tuesday. Do you also like the name of Sidney Lanier? Not as a book but as a day yes. Wonderful. Now what hobbies have you got? I have the noun cooking which is my favourite. Especially some lamb and stew of lamb and chickens too that cannot fly. How do you like jetplanes? If they are eggs I like to fry them in a pan as fat as possible. Fat or flat? Yes. Either will do. The kitchen also is a place to sing. Moths sing with mouths and also beards. Precisely. I too like music especially when sometimes the songs are old. Oaktrees are old. Me too. Many days pass in which I wish to write a complete history of forests. When I say that I smile. Alders are best. Terrific. Me too. Are skies not the best? The ones that seem to be yesterday's clouds. No. We say these sounds are like a twittering pond. Ponds describe fish because today I am hungry. I know this because angles cut across my entire interior appetite. The word stomach is worse. I know a word to lead to stars and the decription of a moon as thick but wide. Excellent. Me too. What else can be known? That soup can be cooked but mud thrown is ground lost. Does each work invoke a simile? On mountains yes. Is there a fire? Perhaps. Not especially. That too is the case. Terrific. What is your name? My name is Herbert Kinsella but Abigail is best. Such difference is value. Why do they rise? Because horses are discontented by the hair. Me too. I reach a room and recognize that anything is placed to soften forms. Which forms do you like? Perhaps motion or charm or eyes soaked in wine. Yes. Tall glasses are best. The ones that have knees. Would you still like a chair? Speech yes, and a quiet bath before the ark. When true is I do not.

Here everything depends on linguistic deformation, the "making strange" of everyday dialogue and discourse. My second example comes from the domain of the artist's book, although that name no longer quite fits the digital productions now designed to make language "visible." In

1994, the poet–visual artist Johanna Drucker published, in an edition of seventy copies, a book called *Narratology*. According to the colophon, Drucker first wrote the text in a child's notebook, reworked it a number of times, and then put it on the computer together with a series of images "culled, copied, transformed, redrawn, and then computer manipulated before being Quarked [Quark Express is a software program] into the dummies, output on Linotronic, and then turned into polymer plates."[19] This process allows for a variety of impositions, juxtapositions, and cut-ups. After each page of text was digitally transferred to the polymer plate, Drucker then printed the book on Rives lightweight paper and handpainted the images. It was then "handbound in die-stamped covers, Franklin Gothic and Memphis have been used throughout, but much distorted through various Quark features."

Narratology: "the stories according to which I thought my life would be lived, which shaped my expectations," as Drucker explains in a text appended to her book. "Living one's life" is now "in/through writing/representation, not outside it, inside it, or in opposition." Thus Drucker's pseudo–romance tale, with its innocent little girl born into the perfect fifties nuclear family, growing up, daydreaming, meeting all the wrong young men, suffering absurd mishaps, and finally encountering Dream Man, thus "pull[ing] back," as the narrator puts it, "from a commitment to real time and place." Onto this romance plot Drucker has grafted a number of conflicting discourses—economic, science fiction, Victorian romance, television soap opera—discourses, moreover, that are intermittent rather than continuous and that are further complicated by their visual appearance: the text makes use of varied fonts, type sizes, and format (plain, bold, italic), and the "illustrations," deliciously ironic versions of stills from the teenage and women's magazines of the period, use faces copied from old photographs (especially snapshots of Johanna Drucker herself) and submit these figures to "colorful" hand-painting so that the "slick" photo images, so reminiscent of the advertising page, with its display of clothes and bodies and its catchy titles and captions, becomes something other.

No two pages of *Narratology* are quite alike. Consider the following page (figure 6) about halfway through the book. The young girl in the upper left-hand corner (the face seems to be the artist's own) is a cross between Cinderella (wearing an apron and holding her dust rag) and the typical blonde young girl at the breakfast table. Above the table, another

DOMESTIC

His tongue protruded through the mucous membrane of her emotional **defenses**, taking the plunge which **ripped** her heart **loose** from its bearings. Pressing home his advantage he maneuvered **the** lip service to contractual **arrangements** as carefully into place as **his** keys in his jeans were wedged to advertise the **other** advantages he had recently grown into. But the story on the late breaking **news** did not include the reversal of fortune she **had** suffered by being **forced** to remain after school these long afternoons without adequate transportation. Deep bitterness accumulated **behind** the dam of blocked movement as she stayed trapped between **the** seasons of vacation and the **seasons** of unrest. Splinters from a pier she'd known in the intimate proximity of **childhood** now rose to the surface of the skin, **begging to be** let free from the wounds into which they had **found** their way.

APPARATUS

TROPHY WIFE TO A CANNIBAL
Rise to the occasion little dove of my heart, and let us rejoice in the efficiency of the loaded cartridge which replays the old relief effort before our eyes. Projected on the screen it hid the house that hid our crumbling hopes and threw the global scale of the disaster back into a domestic frame while it shook the foundations of our intimate relations to their molten core.

Figure 6. Johanna Drucker, from *Narratology*.

young girl (or is she the same one?) in a fifties ballerina-length green pinafore supports a huge console TV that is larger than herself, as if to remind us that this was the Age of Television, the first stage of seduction by the Big Box.

On the right side of the page is a slinky female figure, stretching her arms as if after sleep, in a transparent, clingy nightgown (or evening dress) that gives her the appearance of a mermaid: we can see her breasts and what looks like a chastity belt. Since this dress too is green, the woman, labeled "Trophy Wife to a Cannibal," may well be the young girl on the left grown up into jaded housewife. "Trophy," moreover, fits the mermaid image: this woman has been fished out of somewhere. "Rise to the occasion little dove of my heart," we read in the fine print beneath the title, "and let us rejoice in the efficiency of the loaded cartridge which replays the old relief effort before our eyes."

Indeed, the girl in the green nightgown (and pointy black pumps) is, like the girl images on the left, seen as so much "DOMESTIC APPARATUS: **HIS** tongue protrudes through the mucous membrane," not of her lips or any other body part but, in perfect contemporary psychobabble "of her emotional **defenses**." The lover "maneuvered **the** lip service to contractual arrangements," and the girl's reversal of fortune comes from "being **forced** to remain after school these long afternoons without adequate transportation"—a real fate-worse-than-death in the age of Meals on Wheels. The heroine is "trapped between **the** seasons of vacation and the **seasons** of unrest." Here there are no memories rising to the surface of the consciousness but "Splinters from a pier she'd known in the intimate proximity of **childhood** [that] now rose to the surface of the skin." And so on. The sexual and the contractual, the erotic and the economic are never far apart. Cliché follows cliché, only to move toward the inevitability of the **APPARATUS,** presented in 1½-inch boldface block letters. Meanwhile, there is a writing-through the text, produced by the boldface words read in sequence. "His defenses ripped loose the arrangements his other news had forced behind the seasons, childhood begging to be found." And this too fits into Drucker's scheme of things, childhood indeed regularly "begging to be found" in the midst of those defenses and arrangements. To be "found," the female protagonist would have to be "let free," and that seems, at the moment, to be an unlikely prospect.

Are Drucker's *Narratology* and McCaffery's "Staged Dialogue" to be characterized as postmodern art works? Yes and no. Certainly, these texts have come a long distance from the more utopian postmodernism envisioned by David Antin and his fellow poet-critics in the early seventies. *boundary 2* itself, as I remarked earlier, has long since opted for cultural critique rather than literary criticism, its "editorial collective" (the epithet is indicative) and contributors engaging primarily in theoretical polemics, especially with regard to postcolonialism, race, and gender. In this sense, the 90s have literally inverted the 60s ethos.

Yet if we look again at the right-hand column of Ihab Hassan's table, it is curious to note that the postmodern attributes here listed—for example, under 3 ("Diffusion of the ego") or 9 ("Open form, discontinuity . . . Intermedia")—are certainly applicable to the poetries of the nineties: witness Arteaga, Drucker, and McCaffery. In this sense, it seems quite premature to talk about the "death of postmodernism." Perhaps, then, the time has come to avoid *pronunciamentos,* whether pro or con, about *"the* postmodern condition" and to try to keep an open mind on the postpost days we are now witnessing, days for which we don't yet have a name and whose postpeople we can't quite conceptualize. In the words of Laurie Anderson, "do you think They will read our signs?"

—Combien de kilomètres a-t-il fallu que nous fassions pour nous sentir
enfin au seuil de l'exotisme!"

—Michel Leiris, *L'Afrique fantôme* 1

2. Tolerance and Taboo

Modernist Primitivisms and
Postmodernist Pieties

Exoticism, as Michel Leiris knew, can take many forms, not the least of
which is the contemporary urge to eliminate it once and for all, to demonstrate that we are all equal and that, so far as history goes, an enlightened
"we" who live at the end of the twentieth century can see the hidden and
not-so-hidden colonialism, racism, and sexism of the early twentieth century as in itself it really was. In her highly praised study *Gone Primitive:
Savage Intellects, Modern Lives* (1990), for example, Marianna Torgovnick
is scornful of modernist definitions and ideas about the primitive, which
"all take the West as norm and define the rest as inferior, different, de-
viant, subordinate, and subordinatable." 2 "We simply do not have," she
mourns, "a neutral, politically acceptable vocabulary," the "best we can
do" thus being "to uncover, from a political and cultural perspective, the
kinds of work key terms like *primitive* have performed within modern and
postmodern culture and the kinds of work they have evaded and short-
changed" (GP 21).

But of course words like "evaded" and "short-changed" are themselves
loaded, suggesting that there is a correct (as in politically correct) way
to regard "the primitive" and the "work" it *should* perform in our culture. Oddly—and I shall come back to this issue—*Gone Primitive* seems
to have learned little from a book that appeared just two years earlier and
on which it is heavily dependent for its information, subject matter, and

even its specific examples, namely James Clifford's *Predicament of Culture* (1988), which argued eloquently that "the words of ethnographic writing . . . cannot be construed as monological, as the authoritative statement about, or interpretation of, an abstracted, textualized reality." [3] When Torgovnick does cite Clifford, it is to remark (accurately enough) about his omission of the role gender plays in the construction of "the primitive," an omission that places Clifford in the long line of those first-world male (and sometimes, like Margaret Mead, even female) ethnographers who have victimized the Other.[4] Thus, in an ironic reversal, the ethnographer takes the place of the "primitive" in the "them" versus "us" game.

Fieldwork, in this scheme of things, is devalued as old-fashionedly empiricist, as is any sort of firsthand experience of ethnographic acts and their objects of investigation—the knowledge, for starters, of the languages both of the investigators and the investigated. The preferred method is to know what one wants to prove—in this case, that modernism was riddled with racism, sexism, and colonialism—and then to proceed to collect one's supporting exempla, the game being to ignore all "evidence" that might point in a contrary direction. Ironically, then, we are now witnessing an increasing body of scholarship on oppressed groups that, in its zeal to track down the oppressors, reinscribes the very oppression and subordination it seeks to descry. And further: such would-be oppositional discourse curiously reverts to the very binary model poststructuralist critics have assiduously claimed to be undermining. In what follows, I take Torgovnick's interrogation of modernist primitivism as my example.

Chapter 5 of *Gone Primitive*, "The Many Obsessions of Michel Leiris," begins with the following thumbnail sketch:

> Michel Leiris is a French novelist, poet, and man of letters, but also and by profession, an ethnographer who has written a massive and important book on African art. Intellectually, he has traveled with his culture, moving from Surrealism in the twenties and thirties, to Existentialism after World War II, to, more recently, a poststructuralist concern with language. He has been the intellectual bridesmaid of figures better known in this country, like Georges Bataille and Jean-Paul Sartre. (GP 105)

Whatever audience Torgovnick is writing for here, surely it cannot be an audience in any way familiar with French literature or culture, much less with Michel Leiris or problems of African ethnography. "A graduate seminar at Duke in Spring 1988," explains this professor of English in her preface, "was indefatigable in providing me with information and with evidence that primitivism was everywhere present in contemporary culture" (GP x). Hers, one surmises, is a projected readership not likely to be offended by such inaccuracies as that Leiris was a "bridesmaid" (an odd vulgarism) of Sartre, or that Leiris's interest in language *followed* his surrealist phase (which was, incidentally, never fully surrealist), when in fact it coincided with it. And further: only a fairly narrowly drawn American audience would not question Torgovnick's assertion that the "best-known work in English on Leiris," a special issue of *SubStance* edited by Jean-Jacques Thomas, conceives of the writer as "ethnographic hero" and ignores (in the case of Mary Ann Caws's essay) his terrible mysogyny. What Torgovnick doesn't say is that this issue appeared as long ago as 1975 when gender theory was in its infancy and that, from the sixties to the present, a rich secondary literature on Leiris has come into being, critics from Maurice Blanchot, Philip Lejeune, and Susan Sontag to Rosalind Krauss, James Clifford, and Denis Hollier writing major commentary on this complex and brilliant writer.[5]

Then, too, the cultural production Torgovnick investigates seems oddly unrelated to questions of the actual production and reception of Leiris's autobiography. The critic bases her entire reading of Leiris's *Manhood* (*L'Age d'homme*, 1939) on its "inspiring icon" in the form of Lucas Cranach's diptych *Lucrece and Judith* (1536), reproduced on the book's cover (see GP 109). But although Cranach's diptych is indeed central to Leiris's autobiography, the original 1939 edition published in Paris by Gallimard does not reproduce the painting at all (it first appeared in the 1946 edition, where *L'Age d'homme* is preceded by the introductory essay, "De la littérature considérée comme une tauromachie"). The 1966 Livre de Poche edition has on its cover a blown-up detail of Judith's torso, the gender of the headless figure, holding what seems to be its own head in its left hand, being ambiguous; and the 1973 Folio paperback edition depicts Judith as a semi-abstract playing-card figure, a kind of Queen of Hearts.[6] Indeed, the first time Cranach's Lucrece and Judith become, so to speak, Leiris cover girls is in the 1984 North Point Press translation by Richard Howard (a translation originally published by Grossman in 1968). And when the University of Chicago Press recently reissued this edition, North Point having gone out of business, the cover design and format were retained.

Leiris's "mysogynist" cover (which was not in fact his cover at all) thus finds itself juxtaposed to Torgovnick's own Chicago cover, in her case Man Ray's 1926 photograph *Kiki* (also called *Noire et blanche*), an egregious example, no doubt, of modernist "primitivism," in its juxtaposition of the oval head of Man Ray's sleeping mistress (Kiki) to the oval African mask with its sightless eyes, both the "white" face, underneath jet black hair, and the black mask, silhouetted against Kiki's naked white arm and shoulder, being rendered as fetishized objects controlled by the male artist-photographer Man Ray. What the Leiris–Man Ray juxtaposition masks, however, is that, unlike Man Ray, whose passionate love life was legendary, Michel Leiris had, by his own account, enormous sexual difficulties. His erotic fantasies of dismemberment, far from being directed outward, say, toward African women who would have to submit to his will, were primarily directed at his own person.

The aim of Torgovnick's chapter, in any case, is to debunk the myth of Leiris as "intellectual hero," a term I have never seen applied to Leiris but which Torgovnick uses a number of times interchangeably with "postmodern ethnographic hero." Although in his famous essay of 1950, "L'ethnographe devant le colonialisme," Leiris "correctly" (the word is Torgovnick's) "notes the colonized would begin to 'speak back' to the once monologic West," and although Leiris "admirably" (again her word) "maintains that the ethnographer's role should be that of facilitating the future that the formerly colonized imagine for themselves" (GP 106), such "admirable" and "correct" ideas are evidently not enough to redeem a writer whose early autobiographical work *Manhood,* when read in conjunction with the ostensibly anticolonialist *African Art* (1967), reveals "a spillage between sexuality and Western interest in African art—a spillage we too often take for granted, and take for granted to our shame" (GP 107).

Let us see what we should be ashamed about. *Manhood,* Torgovnick claims, cannot just be read as an arresting fictionalized autobiography; on the contrary, "the terms Leiris chooses for his exposure of self should be taken seriously and count as facts about his brand of primitivism, even if they are 'invented' or 'constructed' facts" (GP 108). The word *facts* is interesting in this context. One such "fact," evidently, is Leiris's reading of Cranach's *Lucrece and Judith,* a double painting that, so the author tells us, represents the two erotic poles that haunted his adolescence and young manhood. Here, taken out of its context which I shall discuss in a moment, is Leiris's description:

> the first, Lucrece, pressing to the center of her white chest, between two marvelously hard round breasts (whose nipples seem as rigid as the stones decorating a gorget or cuirass at the same place), the narrow

blade of a dagger whose tip is already beaded, like the most intimate gift appearing at the end of the male member, with a few drops of blood, and about to annihilate the effect of the rape she has suffered by a similar gesture: one that will thrust into a warm sheath of flesh, and for a bloody death, the weapon at its maximum degree of stiffness, like the rapist's inexorable virility when it enters by force the orifice already gaping between her thighs, the gentle pink wound that soon after returned the libation in full measure, just as the wound—deeper, wickeder too, but perhaps even more intoxicating—made by the dagger will release, from Lucrece's very heart as she faints or fails, a torrent of blood; the second, Judith, in her right hand a sword naked as herself, its point piercing the ground close to her slender toes and its firm broad blade having just severed Holofernes' head, which hangs, sinister trophy, from the heroine's left hand, fingers and hair mingled in hideous union—Judith, wearing a necklace as heavy as a convict's chain, whose coldness around her voluptuous neck recalls that of the sword close to her feet—Judith, placid and already seeming to ignore the bearded ball she holds like a phallic glans she could have sundered merely by pressing her legs together with Holofernes' floodgates opened; or which, an ogress at the height of her madness, she might have cut from the powerful member of the drunken (and perhaps vomiting) man with a sudden snap of her teeth.[7]

Interestingly, Cranach's paintings have little of the violence and horror that Leiris ascribes to them; his astonishing ekphrasis teases out meanings largely submerged if not absent in the diptych, where the myths are primarily vehicles for the painter's exhibition of the female body in all its sensuous nudity. The reference to Judith's "fingers and [Holofernes'] hair mingled in hideous union," for instance, is a pure invention on Leiris's part, the calm expression on Judith's lovely face all but belying what has just taken place. But Torgovnick pays no attention to these anomalies, concerned as she is with what she takes to be the "repellent" "pornographic violence" of Leiris's description, and concluding that he must have come to ethnography "via sensual associations very much like those which attract him to Cranach's Lucrece and Judith."[8]

Accordingly, when she reads the later, seemingly objective account in *African Art* of the tribal signification of scarification and tattooing, as well as of circumcision and, in the case of young women, excision of the clitoris and the *labia maiora*, Torgovnick detects an ulterior motive. Leiris is not, she argues, writing a disinterested account of African tribal customs; he is enjoying what she calls the "prophylactic effect" inherent in his "ethnographic approach to the primitive" (GP 114). Like Judith and Lucrece, the native women described with seeming scientific detachment cannot "talk back," the male viewer thus being able to gaze at them voyeuristically. "They are object; he is subject. He is in control, empowered, unthreatened" (GP 114). The attraction of Africa for Leiris turns out to be pornographic, a vehicle for his diseased sexual fantasies about women. Such ethnographic work, Torgovnick concludes, is finally "perverse," a model we who are enlightened must abjure. Its "structures of mastery" must give way to those of "mutuality; a reaching out to the natural world as our home and mother, not the exploitation of that world for profit." "Primitive societies," after all, should be "allowed to exist in their own times and spaces, within their own *conceptions of* time and space, not transposed and filtered into Western terms." Indeed, a correct history of primitive societies would acknowledge these societies "as full and valid alternatives to Western cultures" (GP 247).

On what planet, one wonders, do these utopian conditions obtain? Where are the "structures of mutuality," where the "natural world" is "our home and mother," where each society exists "in [its] own time and space"? Not, assuredly, in Leiris's France, a France that during the writer's high school years was engaged in the horrific trench warfare of World War I, a France, moreover, that by the time he published *Manhood* was months away from the Nazi occupation of World War II. In these circumstances, "structures of mutuality" and "full and valid alternatives" (themselves, incidentally, nothing if not Western post-Enlightenment norms) may have seemed just slightly out of reach.

Here is where history comes in, history which is the great absence in the branch of cultural studies practiced by Torgovnick.[9] Her reasoning goes something like this: (1) Enlightened narrative about so-called primitive societies is directly related to "enlightened" personal morality; (2) Leiris, judging from the revelations in his autobiography, revelations that must count as relevant "facts" in any assessment of his "character," had curious sexual obsessions; therefore, (3) even though Leiris later writes explicitly and eloquently against colonialism, his accounts of such matters as African tattoo and scarification rituals are not to be trusted. To put it crudely: anyone so preoccupied with what well may be kinky sex, and who persists in seeing sex in its relationship to death, cannot be the kind of "ethnographic hero" "we" want.

I wish I could say my summary of Torgovnick's argument was simplified, but the fact is that the colonialist Joseph Conrad and the racist D. H. Lawrence, the voyeuristic Bronislaw Malinowski, and even the cowardly Margaret Mead who, despite her own lesbian leanings, "stop[ped] short of explicitly writing against homophobia" (GP 238) — all these are found wanting according to the severe Puritan yardstick applied to them in *Gone Primitive*. How Conrad's representations of the European experience of the Congo in the early century relate to other accounts of the period is considered beside the point, the point being, it seems, that Conrad refused to spell out what lay behind Kurtz's famous phrase, "the horror, the horror," that he ignored "ugly facts, facts like how those heads [of the natives] got on the palisade, facts like the African woman's relation to Kurtz" (GP 152). "Conrad's version of the primitive," declares Torgovnick with great moral authority, "is a cheat" (GP 153).

So, it seems, was the "phantom Africa" of Michel Leiris. Born in 1901, Leiris grew up in bourgeois comfort in Paris, where his father was a banker, seemingly insulated from the Great War, which broke out, let us remember, when he was at the impressionable age of thirteen. Not that *Manhood* is overtly a war book. Indeed, its foreword, "De la littérature considérée comme une tauromachie" (in the English translation, "The Autobiographer as *Torero*" becomes the afterword), begins with the nonchalant reference to its author's coming to legal maturity "four years after the war, which like so many other boys of his generation, he had experienced as scarcely more than a long vacation" (MLM 154; LD 9). But in the very next paragraph, we read, "Now in 1939, when the young men of the post-war period see the utter collapse of that structure of facility which they despaired of trying to invest with not only an authentic fervor but a terrible distinction as well, the author freely acknowledges that his true 'manhood' still remains to be written, when he will have suffered, in one form or another the same bitter ordeal his elders faced." And on the following page, the narrative breaks off abruptly with the following remarks:

> This was the preface I was writing for *Manhood* on the eve of the "phony war." I am rereading it today [evidently 1945] in Le Havre, a city I have often visited for a few days' vacation and to which I am bound by many old ties (my friends Limbour, Queneau, and Salacrou, who were born here; Sartre, who taught here and with whom I became associated in 1941 when most of the writers remaining in occupied France united

against the Nazi oppression). Le Havre is now largely destroyed, as I can see from my balcony, which overlooks the harbor from a sufficient height and distance to give a true picture of the terrible *tabula rasa* the bombs made in the center of the city, as if there has been an attempt to repeat in the real world, on a terrain populated by living beings, the famous Cartesian operation. On this scale, the personal problems with which *Manhood* is concerned are obviously insignificant: whatever might have been, in the best cases, its strength and its sincerity, the poet's inner agony, weighed against the horrors of war, counts for no more than a toothache over which it would be graceless to groan. (MLM 154–55; cf. LD 11)

Such speculations might have led to silence—the "no poetry after Auschwitz" stance. Or they might lead, as indeed they did, to the use of "the toothache over which it would be graceless to groan" and related aches and wounds as synecdoches and analogs for those "horrors of war," and, in a larger sense, horrors of being human, which are, in any case, always seen as paradoxical. "Even in Le Havre," Leiris remarks in the foreword, "things continue, urban life persists. Above the still intact houses as above the site of the ruins there shines intermittently, despite the rainy weather, a bright, beautiful sun" (MLM 155). Just so, the imagery of death, of shame and horror, of the abject which is so prominent in *Manhood* is made poignant by its association with desire and pleasure, with the longing for voluptuous gratification. And to complicate matters further, what makes modern "civilized" urban life so terrifying is that the orderly and familiar rituals of bourgeois family life to which the child is exposed, the boredom of normal everyday existence provide only the flimsiest screen for the violence beneath the surface.[10]

In assessing Leiris's authorial position in *African Art*, read retrospectively in the light of his autobiography, Torgovnick writes "They [the African women] are object; he is subject. He is in control, empowered, unthreatened" (GP 114). Presumably Leiris has this position because he is a white man, describing the tribal mutilation practices of black women.[11] But surely no one is less "in control" and "unthreatened" than the hero of *Manhood*, who, from the opening page of the book, presents himself as having a "head . . . rather large for my body," legs "a little short for the length of my torso," and thin, hairy hands, "the veins distinct; my two middle fingers, curving inward toward the tips, [which] must denote something rather weak and evasive in my character." And further: "Sexually, I am not, I believe, abnormal—simply a man of rather cold temperament—but I have long tended to regard myself as virtually impotent. It has been some time, in any case, since I have ceased to consider the sexual act as a simple matter, but rather as a relatively exceptional event" (MLM 5). Here is the personal predisposition that colors so many of the book's subsequent events and memories.

Take the memory of the boy's first erection, which takes place when he is six or seven on a family picnic in the woods near Paris. "The event which caused my excitement was the sight of a group of children . . . climbing trees barefoot. . . . Much later, it seemed to me that the strange sensation I experienced then came from imagining what must have been both a pleasant and painful feeling for the children in question, the feeling caused by the contact of the soles of their feet and their bare toes with the rough bark" (MLM 13–14). We may consider such confessions as, in Torgovnick's words, "a disturbing reminder of how this linking of sex and violence . . . pervades Western culture and provides a psyche like Leiris's with ready simulacra" (GP 110). Or we may try to understand Leiris's collage of "disturbing" images as by no means "simulacra," but, on the contrary, images with specific reference to a time and place when pretensions of protected childhood and "civilized" behavior, of paternal and church authority and training, of fixed class division and the seemingly incontrovertible gap between masters and servants—when all these cultural formations were playing themselves out against the backdrop of a world war that is a persistent but barely alluded to subtext.

We can see this anomaly most clearly in the short sequence called "Throat Cut," in the chapter "The Head of Holofernes." The incident in question could hardly be more ordinary, and yet the autobiographer, who has presented his childhood self as acquiring his knowledge of violence and tragedy largely from spectatorship, whether at the opera, at the theater, or in the museum, recalls it as "the most painful of all my childhood memories":

> At the age of five or six, I was the victim of an assault. I mean that I endured an operation on my throat to remove certain growths; the operation took place in a very brutal manner, without my being anesthetized. My parents had first made the mistake of taking me to the surgeon without telling me where we were going. If my recollections

are correct, I believed we were on the way to the circus; I was therefore far from anticipating the nasty trick about to be played on me by our family doctor, who assisted the surgeon, as well as by the latter himself. The occasion went off, point by point, like a play that had been rehearsed, and I had the feeling that I had been lured into a hideous ambush. Matters proceeded as follows: leaving my parents in the waiting room, the old doctor led me into another room where the surgeon was waiting for me, wearing a huge black beard and a white gown. . . . I saw various sharp instruments and must have looked frightened, for the old doctor took me on his lap and said to reassure me: "Come here, *mon petit coco!* Now we're going to play kitchen." From this moment on I can remember nothing except the sudden assault of the surgeon, who plunged some kind of sharp instrument into my throat, the pain that I felt, and the scream—like that of a slaughtered animal—that I uttered. My mother, who heard me from the next room, was terrified.

On the way home in the carriage, I did not speak a word; the shock had been so violent that for twenty-four hours it was impossible to get a word out of me; my mother, completely disoriented, wondered if I had become mute. All I can remember about the period immediately following the operation is the carriage ride, my parents' vain attempts to make me speak, and then, back at the house, my mother holding me in her arms in front of the living-room fireplace, the sherbets she had me swallow, the blood I spat up at each mouthful and which mingled with the raspberry color of the sherbets. (MLM 64–65)

"My whole image of life," remarks Leiris, "has been scarred by the incident: the world, full of traps, is nothing but a huge prison or an operating theatre; I am on earth only to become a specimen for doctors, cannon fodder, food for worms" (MLM 65). What justifies this seemingly excessive response is that the incident in question depended on a terrible deception, on the collusion of the narrator's parents with the doctor's "enlightened" view that children are to be manipulated and coerced into acquiescence. But the curious phrase in the above sentence is "cannon fodder" ("chair à canons," LD 112). The world as prison, as operating theater: these classic metaphors emerge naturally from the situation of the tonsillectomy, but the image of "cannon fodder" relates the ordinary childhood incident to the extraordinary circumstance of the war outside the nursery. The child is lured by the promise of the circus just as the young medical student in

Celine's *Voyage au bout de la nuit* is promised adventure and a beautiful uniform only to end up, like little Leiris, in the place of dismemberment, where the red of raspberry sorbets is mixed with blood.

The memory of the throat operation foreshadows another seemingly trivial "suburban" incident:

> One day a cousin whose parents lived in the villa next door to ours was bitten by a dog. One detail made me shudder: I was told that the bite had been so deep "a piece of buttock had remained in the child's underwear." I cannot think of this cousin—who was subsequently killed in the war—without remembering what he was like when the incident occurred: a big, well-built, heavy-set boy whose parents adored him because he represented, from a certain point of view, the ideal of beauty and health, and whose chubby calves were the admiration of almost everyone in the family, except for my mother who said he was a "big softy" and thought her sons "more delicate." (MLM 67)

It is against the backdrop of such incidents that we must understand the attraction-repulsion associated for Leiris with "Lucrece the chaste and Judith the patriot prostitute" as depicted in Cranach's double painting:

> One might . . . suspect that their two apparently distinct gestures were at bottom identical, and that both were supremely concerned to cleanse in blood the taint of an erotic act, the one expiating by her suicide the shame of having been violated (and perhaps of having enjoyed that violation), the other expiating by murder the shame of having prostituted herself to her victim. So that it would not be out of mere caprice, but by virtue of profound analogies, that Cranach painted the two as pendants, both similarly naked and desirable, at one in that complete absence of moral hierarchy which is the necessary concomitant of nakedness, and shown on the verge of committing particularly arousing actions. (MLM 93–94)

"The passage repels most," writes Torgovnick, "by its suggestion that Lucrece enjoyed (must have enjoyed) her rape . . . and its parallel suggestion that Judith castrates Holofernes to punish him for his sexuality, rather than kills him as a political act" (GP 110). The either/or of the latter statement (i.e., it's either politics *or* sex) would be quite alien to Leiris's radius of discourse, but the former, with its very contemporary (and justified) complaint about the still-prevalent male assumption that women who are raped somehow "want" it, is also misconceived. The death of Cleopatra, who represents for Leiris a kind of symbolic union of the Lucrece and Judith prototypes, is apposite here: "on the one hand the murderous serpent, the male symbol par excellence—on the other the figs beneath which [the asp] was concealed, the common image of the female organ. . . . I cannot help noting with what exactitude this meeting of symbols corresponds to what for me is the profound meaning of suicide: to become at the same time *oneself and the other,* male and female, subject and object, killed and killer—the only possibility of communion with oneself." And Leiris relates this image of "the right to love oneself to excess" to "that of Prometheus punished for having stolen fire" (MLM 93).

Leiris is not, then, subscribing to anything so vulgar as the patriarchal belief that woman is the subject who "enjoys" rape. He identifies, after all, not with Lucrece's rapist but with Lucrece; not with Holofernes but with Judith, his case being for the dissolution of gender boundaries in the love act and for the inseparability of eros and thanatos. The issue is not whether this particular vision of human sexuality is "true" or not but whether Leiris's powerful self-examination and pitiless self-critique carries conviction. The aim of *Manhood,* after all, is not to provide moral uplift or to present the reader with "full and valid alternatives," but to depict an especially demonic (because so seemingly placid and bourgeois) world, the world of *entre deux guerres,* in all its excesses and contradictions.

Can a writer of Leiris's kind be a "good" ethnographer and an important source for our understanding of the "primitive"? In the final chapter of *Manhood,* Leiris tells us that in response to a crisis period in his twenties, he decided to engage in "a more strenuous life for a while," and "went to Africa for almost two years, as a member of an ethnographical expedition. After months of chastity and emotional weaning, I fell in love while in Gondar with an Ethiopian woman who corresponded physically and morally to my double image of Lucrece and Judith" (MLM 40). This woman's face, Leiris recalls, was "beautiful but her breasts ravaged"; she was "wrapped in a filthy gray toga, smelled of sour milk, and owned a young Negro slave girl"; he dwells further on the "bluish" tattoos around the neck of this "syphilitic" witch, and notes that "her clitoris extirpated, like all the women of her race, she must have been frigid, at least from a European point of view." "I never," he concludes, "made love to her, but when the sacrifice took place it seemed to me that a relation more intimate than any carnal link was established between her and myself" (MLM 140).

It is interesting to compare this retrospective description of the Gondar woman to the diary version recorded just a few years earlier and published in *L'Afrique fantôme* (1934). Emawayish, as the woman in question was called, was the daughter of Malkam Ayyahou, the charismatic leader of a group of initiates possessed by "zâr" genies. Leiris's entry for 25 August 1932 records a dark mood: "Bitterness. Resentment against ethnography which makes you take so inhuman a position, that of an observer, in situations where it would be best to let go." [12] As James Clifford recounts in his notes to the translation, "Three days later, during an intense possession seance, Emawayish contrives to leave her mother, comes over to the bed on which Leiris is sitting and, in a gesture of apparent intimacy, places his hand under her armpit. The ethnographer is entranced by the songs she sings while possessed and wants her to write them down so that he and his Ethiopian co-worker Abba Jérome can make translations" (S 42). Here is the beginning of Leiris's entry for 31 August:

> During the morning, letter from Emawayish. She would be pleased if I made her a gift of a blanket. Quite a natural wish, following my courtly declarations of devotion. . . . I'll never accuse a native of venality. Just imagine how insanely wealthy a European must seem to such poor people and how they must look obsessively on his smallest objects of comfort, as if they were treasures! (S 42–43)

Leiris now brings Emawayish pens, ink, and a notebook "so she can record for herself—or dictate to her son—the manuscript [of her songs]"; he is upset that another member of the expedition, Lutten, for whom "making love is only a matter of pleasure or hygiene!" wants to sleep with her, whereas he himself finds it "impossible . . . to treat love with nonchalance." Isolated, lonely, unable to find anyone to whom he "can speak from the bottom of [his] heart," he is all but suicidal. When he urges her to record her love songs, Emawayish asks pointedly: *"Does poetry exist in France?"* And then, as if challenging Leiris's manhood: *"Does love exist in France?"* (S 43; AF 359).

The very next entry (1 September) begins: "Very bad night. First insomnia, then, very late, a little sleep," which is haunted by guilt dreams. "During the day," Leiris notes, "though tired and enervated, I feel better. I realize I've been overworked, that I've been too caught up with research in a dangerous area." And he admits his doubts as to the methods of gathering material, the poetry collected "probably not as beautiful as I had thought, the possession states not as intense . . . and also covering up quite a bit of merchandizing. . . . But above all, and in contradiction to all this, an ardent sensation of being at the edge of something whose depths

I will never touch." Then, after describing Emawayish's belief that "one of the spirits inhabiting the head of her mother is capable of killing her son," he remarks sadly that he cannot really enter her spirit world, "imbued whatever I do with a civilization that leads one to give everything a moral rather than a magical tint. And this is the great boundary I will never cross" (S 44; AF 360).

Is this the white man whom Torgovnick takes to be wholly "in control, empowered, unthreatened" in his relation to African women? Who voyeuristically revels in the sight of their naked breasts and colorful tattoos? One wonders what sort of relationship between the Leiris of 1932 and this particular Ethiopian woman critics like Torgovnick would consider acceptable. The West, she asserts, might have developed a "history in which primitive societies were allowed to exist in all their multiplicity, not reduced to a seamless Western fantasy . . . when the majority of Euro-Americans can accept that our nations—for all their present comforts and power—exist on the same plane with other social and political entities" (GP 147). But perhaps this optimistic trust in an "openness" by fiat so to speak, "to alternative conceptions of knowledge and social reality" is itself the ultimate "seamless Western fantasy."

How, asks James Clifford in a critique of Edward Said's 1978 *Orientalism,* "can one ultimately escape procedures of dichotomizing, restructuring, and textualizing in the making of interpretive statements about foreign cultures and traditions?" (JCP 261). If, that is to say, Said presents Orientalism as "a corporate institution for dealing with the Orient," an institution which has, throughout the colonial period that extends from the late eighteenth century to the present, wielded the power of "dominating, restructuring, and having authority over the Orient" (JCP 259), how can his own account avoid the essentialism inherent in the unstated assumption that the "oppressed" Orient is in fact *not* like the one produced by the Orientalist myth? The critique of Orientalism presupposes, in other words, an Orient with such and such specific characteristics, characteristics that have been *misrepresented* by the West. And further: "The Western culture of which Orientalism is an exemplar [is viewed] as a discrete entity capable of generating knowledge and institutional power *over* the rest of the planet. Western order, seen this way, is imperial, unreciprocal, aggressive, and potentially hegemonic" (JCP 272). Against this binary opposition, an opposition Said himself begins to doubt as his argument proceeds, Clifford makes the case for a "West" that is itself "a play of projections, doublings, idealizings, and rejections of a complex, shifting otherness." "Europe," in this case, may be seen as, in its turn, a false stereotype of the Orient, the question being, in Clifford's words, "How . . . is an oppositional critique of Orientalism to avoid falling into 'Occidentalism'"? (PC 259).

There are no easy answers to such questions. That colonialist "fictions of the primitive" have been used for at least a century to bolster the West's own self-image is incontrovertible. But that we can now enter a utopia where we approach "primitive" cultures as "full and valid alternatives" to our own is perhaps an even more dangerous myth. If I have dwelt at such length on the argument of *Gone Primitive,* it is because this well-meaning study epitomizes the wrong turn the new "cultural studies" takes when it ignores both history and common sense. In her attack on Leiris, as on the "primitivism" of Conrad and Lawrence, Freud and Roger Fry, Malinowski and Mead, Torgovnick's root assumption is that a good writer (or ethnographer) is equivalent to a good person, and, concomitantly, that a "good" book is one which is the repository of the "right" cultural values. But, as John Guillory has recently argued, we must beware of equating "the values expressed in a work with the value *of* the work, of assuming that a given work is simply the "container of such and such values":

> The reversion to moralism is determined by the equation of text-selection with value-selection. For this reason much of what passes for political analysis of historically canonical works is nothing more than the passing of moral judgment on them. The critique of the canon moves quickly to reassert absolutist notions of good and evil.[13]

One thinks here not only of a study of primitivism like Torgovnick's but such recent studies of minority writing as Cary Nelson's *Repression and Recovery: Modern American Poetry and the Politics of Cultural Memory 1910–1945* (1989). With its eloquent but ultimately absolutist replacement therapy, the canonical "greats" (Eliot, Pound, Frost, Stevens, Williams, etc.) are swept under the rug to make room for a large body of "neglected" and hence ipso facto "deserving" poets of the period: women, African-Americans, communist activists.

Perhaps a more satisfactory critique of primitivism and its analogs would begin with the recognition that primitivisms, like the modernisms to which they are related, can only be plural. How, to take just one example, does the Russian "neoprimitivism" of the artists Goncharova and Larionov, Tatlin and Malevich, or the poets Khlebnikov and Kruchenykh square with the "primitivism" of Leiris and his colleagues at the Paris Collège de Sociologie? Why does the Russian avant-garde's "primitivist" concern for peasant and folk art, the *lubok* (woodblock) and the icon, and the "primitivist" quest of Khlebnikov, "to find the magic stone for transforming all Slavic words, the magic that transforms one into another without breaking the circle of verbal roots,"[14] take a spiritualist turn, so unlike the erotic "primitivism" of a Picasso, who gives two of his androgynous "demoiselles d'Avignon" African masks for faces?

We cannot hope to address such questions without a consideration of history as well as geography. Khlebnikov, descended from Mongolian Buddhists who inhabited the grassy steppes on the west bank of the Caspian Sea, Khlebnikov the son of a prominent naturalist and ornithologist who studied the biological sciences and mathematics before he ever came to poetry in St. Petersburg, Khlebnikov whose first publication in Petersburg (1908) was an anonymous manifesto posted in a university corridor, a call to defend the Slavic countries of Bosnia and Herzegovina against annexation by Austria, declaring: "Holy War! Unavoidable, approaching, immediate—war for the trampled rights of the Slavs, I salute you! Down with the Hapsburgs! Hold back the Hohenzollerns!"[15]—Khlebnikov was inevitably attracted to a homegrown "primitivism" quite alien to the disillusioned postwar musings of the author of *L'Afrique fantôme*. Yet—and this is the irony—Leiris's surrealist compilation of language games and concrete poems called *Glossaire* is nothing if not Khlebnikovian. Here is one such passage, published in *La Révolution surréaliste* in 1925:

> By dissecting the words we like, without bothering about conforming either to their etymologies or to their accepted significations, we discover their most hidden qualities and the secret ramifications that are propagated through the whole language, channeled by associations of sounds, forms, and ideas. Then language changes into an oracle and there we have a thread (however slender it may be) to guide us through the Babel of our minds.[16]

This might be one of Khlebnikov's descriptions of *Zaum* (transrational) language, were it not that Khlebnikov takes etymology to be the key to *Zaum* language formation, a view that perhaps classifies the Russian poet as more of a "primitivist" than the primitivist Leiris. At the same time, Khlebnikov's primitivism has none of the eroticism central to Leiris's, and it is hard to call it "racist" since the primitive race invoked and "exoticized" is Khlebnikov's own.

But the exotic is, of course, always a contested site. I recall meeting

Margaret Mead once, at a Washington dinner party in the sixties. She was wearing a long colorful cotton dress and lots of wooden jewelry, and she supported herself on a large shepherd's crook, which she tapped emphatically on the floor when she wanted to make a particular point. I found her extremely exotic—a powerful, individual presence. Marianna Torgovnick, however, scolds her for such things as "never fully mingl[ing] with the Samoans" or for "referring routinely to male graduate students as 'men' and females at the same stage of professional life as 'girls'." It seems that the poor Margaret of memoir and historical record is not allowed to dwell, as are the "primitives" toward whom Torgovnick expresses such tolerance, in her "own *conception of* time and space"; nor is hers judged to be one of those "full and valid" alternatives the author wants us to respect. The "full range of human sexual possibilities and variations in belief" (GP 246)—these are evidently available only to the still-exotic Others.

Surely there are more satisfying ways of approaching the Other. I conclude with some lines from "Chapter 217" of Lyn Hejinian's long poem *Oxota: A Short Russian Novel,*[17] which tells the story of the American poet's gradual initiation into the otherness of the then Soviet Union:

> Recognition in itself is a source of great excitement
> I discovered I knew *Tekhnologicheskii Institut* as well as *Ploshad Lenina*
> Deductions are directions
> Truths change, things develop
> I felt a thrill of gratitude—to whom or what it may refer
> Lurking with competence, I was familiar with the future. . . .

3. "Barbed-Wire Entanglements"

The "New American Poetry," 1930–32

January 1931. In the "News Notes" at the back of *Poetry* magazine, Harriet Monroe announced that the February issue would be edited by one "Mr. Louis Zukofsky, who has been for several years a prominent member of a group of writers interested in experiment in poetic form and method. . . . Mr. Zukofsky is recommended on the high authority of Ezra Pound and others whose opinions we greatly respect."[1] But, having "abdicated [her editorial powers] temporarily," Monroe evidently felt betrayed. In the March issue, she wrote an angry response to the "Objectivist" number of *Poetry* called "The Arrogance of Youth." Zukofsky, she insisted, was wrong to "abandon" such big poetry names as E. A. Robinson, Robert Frost, Edgar Lee Masters, and Edna St. Vincent Millay, as well as the "once-revolutionary imagists." And "what," asks Monroe, "are we offered in exchange? A few familiar names get by [she is evidently thinking of William Carlos Williams's "Botticellian Trees"] though often by severely wrenching Mr. Zukofsky's barbed-wire entanglements."[2]

What was the nature of the Objectivist experiment, as represented by Zukofsky's selection for *Poetry*—a selection that included, aside from the obvious names (Basil Bunting, George Oppen, Carl Rakosi, Charles Reznikoff, Zukofsky himself), Robert McAlmon and Kenneth Rexroth, Whittaker Chambers and Henry Zolinsky, John Wheelright and Martha Champion? And in what sense was the work of these poets a departure from that of the "once-revolutionary imagists"? Williams, for one, seems to have been skeptical, even though Zukofsky's *"Objectivists" Anthology* of the following year contains a large selection of his own poems. "Your early poems," he told Zukofsky in a letter of 1928, "even when the thought has enough force or freshness, have not been objectivized in new or fresh observations. But if it is the music, even that is not inventive enough to make up for images which give an overwhelming effect of triteness. . . . The language is stilted 'poetic' except in the places I marked. Eyes have always stood first in the poet's equipment. If you are mostly ear—a newer rhythm must come in more strongly than has been the case so far."[3]

As examples of such "stilted 'poetic'" language, Williams singles out the phrases "all live processes," "orbit-trembling," "our consciousness," and "the sources of being" in what he calls Zukofsky's "Lenin poem," "Memory of V. I. Ulianov."[4] "It may be," he admits, "that I am too literal in my search for objective clarities of image. It may be that you are completely right in forcing abstract conceptions into the sound pattern. . . . It may be that when the force of the conception is sufficiently strong it can carry this sort of thing. . . . Perhaps by my picayune, imagistic mannerisms I hold together superficially what should by all means fall apart" (WCWL 103).

The recognition that "imagistic mannerisms" may well have had their day is echoed by Ezra Pound. Having urged Harriet Monroe to put Zukofsky "at the wheel of the Spring cruise," as he put it in a letter, and having "refused to contribute to Aldington's Imagist mortology 1930," which he dismisses as "20 ans apres [*sic*]," Pound urges Zukofsky to make his special issue "a murkn number; excludin the so different English." Indeed, if Zukofsky does his job, Pound suggests, *Poetry* might once again be "what it was in 1912/13, the forum in which the Zeitideen WERE presented and discussed."[5]

But the "Zeitideen" of 1931 were, as Pound himself was the first to recognize ("Prob[lem] ain't now the same"), no longer those of 1913. For one thing, the relationship between tradition and the new had become vexed. "The number ought to be NEW line up," Pound repeatedly urges Zukofsky. "You can mention me and old Bill Walrus [Williams] in the historic section. . . . I do not think contributions from ANYONE over 40 shd. be included; and preferably it shd. be confined to those under 30" (PZ 51–52). And he notes acutely, "ONE notable difference between yr. position in 1930 and mine in 1910 is that you would LIKE to include several older american authors. Bill, Me and I suppose Possum Eliot, with Cummings an already known name" (PZ 53).

Zukofsky responded defensively. "The only progress made since 1912," writes the twenty-six-year-old poet to his forty-six-year-old mentor, "is or are several good poems, i.e. the only progress possible—& criteria are in your prose works" (PZ 65). And again, "Think I'll have as good a 'movement' as that of the premiers imagistes—point is Wm. C. W. of today is not what he was in 1913, neither are you if you're willing to contribute—if I'm going to show what's going on today, you'll have to. The older generation is not the older generation if it's alive & up. . . . What's age to do with verbal manifestation, what's history to do with it?" (PZ 67). Which Pound shrugs off laconically: "In 1913 les jeunes did not respect their papas. In 1930 there are a few middle-aged bokos that we can afford to let live" (PZ 74). It was fine, in other words, for Zukofsky to reprint, in his preface to the *"Objectivists" Anthology*, Pound's own imagist manifesto in "A Retrospect" (1912), along with his famous division of poetry into three "kinds" (melopoeia, phanopoeia, logopoeia) articulated in "How to Read" (1928), and to quote the opening of the newly completed Canto XXX ("Compleynt, compleynt I hearde upon a day"). And the *Anthology* is dedicated to Pound, who "is still for the poets of our time / the / most important."

A certain sense of belatedness—the belatedness usually associated with our own postmodern ethos—thus haunts Zukofsky's production. But then "make it new!" could hardly be the watchword of a poetic generation that came of age in the Great Depression, a generation that understood that the "new" was by no means equivalent to the true, much less to the good and the beautiful. Just the same, despite Zukofsky's own evident inability to articulate the difference between Pound's aesthetic and that of the *"Objectivists" Anthology* that he had assembled, there really was something new going on in that anthology, as in the little magazines of the early thirties in general. Indeed, with the hindsight of the 1990s, the early 1930s were *anni mirabiles* for poetry, as the magazines that now replaced the *Dial* and *Little Review* (both ceased publication in 1929)—magazines like *Blues, Morada,* the *New Review, Furioso, New Masses*—testify. The *"Objectivists" Anthology,* for that matter, far from being the anomaly Zukofsky and Oppen scholars have often taken it to be, was in fact representative of a larger aesthetic that has been insufficiently distinguished from its modernist past and its postmodernist future. The shift that takes place at the turn of the decade is one from the modernist preoccupation with *form*—in the sense of imagistic or symbolist structure, dominated by a lyric "I"—to the questioning of *representation* itself. Discourse now becomes increasingly referential, but reference does not go hand in hand with the expected mimesis. Rather, the boundaries between the "real" and the "fantastic" become oddly blurred.

The taste for the "natural," as in Pound's insistence that "the natural object is always the adequate symbol,"[6] gives way to artifice and a marked taste for abstraction and conceptualization. In the same vein, irony—so central to modernist poetics—gives way to the parodic, but even parody is often not sustained, with abrupt tonal shifts and reversals in mood becoming quite usual. Indeed, this "time of tension," to borrow Eliot's phrase from his 1930 poem "Ash Wednesday," exhibits a mannerist style as distinct from its modernist antecedents as from the socialist realism to come.

In the discussion that follows, I take as my example a single "little magazine," *Pagany,* which ran for twelve issues between January 1930 and December 1932, thus coinciding with the darkest years of the Depression, from the October 1929 Wall Street crash to the election of Roosevelt and the coming of his New Deal in 1932. It was in *Pagany,* edited by an affluent young Boston litterateur named Richard Johns,[7] that Williams published the first ten chapters of *White Mule* and such famous short lyrics as "Flowers by the Sea" and "The Red Lily"; Stein, the first version of *Before the Flowers of Friendship Faded Friendship Faded;* Pound, Cantos XXX–XXXII as well as critical commentary; and Zukofsky, *"A"*1. In his capacity as informal poetry advisor,[8] moreover, Zukofsky evidently persuaded Johns to publish poems by his "Objectivist" friends Carl Rakosi, Charles Reznikoff, George Oppen, and Basil Bunting, by Kenneth Rexroth and Yvor Winters, Mary Butts and Mina Loy. But *Pagany* also published such early "naturalist" fiction as Edward Dahlberg's *Flushing to Calvary,* Erskine Caldwell's *American Earth* stories, and John Dos Passos's "Eveline" from *U.S.A.*

Johns takes the title of his journal from a work he greatly admired, Williams's autobiographical novel *Voyage to Pagany* (1928). But whereas Williams's Pagany is of course Europe, the "pagan" Old World where American innocents come to be initiated into the complexities of a sophisticated culture, Johns's Pagany, as the journal's subtitle, *A Native Quarterly,* makes clear, neatly reverses this Jamesian contrast between Old and New Worlds. In the announcement on the opening page of the first issue (January–March 1930), Johns explains:

> *Pagus* is a broad term, meaning any sort of collection of peoples from the smallest district or village to the country as an inclusive whole. Taking America as the *pagus,* any one of us as the *paganus,* the inhabitant, and our conceptions, our agreements and disagreements, our ideas, ideals, whatever we have to articulate is *pagany,* our expression.

This *Native Quarterly* is representative of a diverse and ungrouped body of spokesmen, bound geographically. Wary of definite alliance with any formulated standard PAGANY (as an enclosure) includes individual expression of native thought and emotion.[9]

Here, by an odd sleight-of-hand, *Pagany* (Europe) becomes the "diverse and ungrouped body of spokesmen" that is America. From the exotic and corrupt European Other to the cultural diversity of the United States: it is an emblem of the shift from the expatriate 1920s to the American 1930s, a shift that the journal will trace. Interestingly, when foreign writers (the English Mary Butts, the French Georges Hugnet) or artists (the French Eugène Atget) are included, their work is mediated by a specific American sponsor: Butts by Ezra Pound, Hugnet by Gertrude Stein and Virgil Thomson, Atget by Berenice Abbott.[10] The first issue of *Pagany*, for example, contains Mary Butts's short story "The House Party," which gives the Jamesian initiation-into-Europe motif a sardonic twist. The hero Paul is an American "joy-boy," "a cracked little specimen of a gigolo, after a year in prison for something he had not done," who is invited by a worldly Englishman named Vincent to a house party in a "sea-washed, fly-blown, scorched hotel along the coast":

> Under Vincent's wing, a man could stand up a bit. Vincent was English, tender, serious, older than he was. Vincent wanted him to come. Was no doubt cajoling, hypnotizing certain objections. Objections that were always made about him, especially by his own countrymen, the Americans who made a cult of Europe, a cult and a career, not quite perfect in their transplanting and conscious of it.

Like the Zukofsky whom Williams criticized for "forcing abstract conceptions into the sound pattern," Butts produces a prose notable for its calculated imprecision, its verbal and syntactic oddities. "Under Vincent's wing, a man could stand up a bit": the sentence begins with a familiar cliché, only to deflate it with an absurd description: how does one stand up under someone's "wing"? Then, too, "a man could stand up a bit" alludes to Ford Madox Ford's 1926 *A Man Could Stand Up* (the third volume of the *Parade's End* tetralogy), a novel Butts surely knew. Is she saying that Paul's is, in its own way, a life in the trenches not wholly unlike that of Christopher Tietjens? It is hard to tell, Butts's mode being pastiche in Fredric Jameson's sense of "blank parody," parody "devoid . . .

of any conviction that alongside the abnormal tongue you have momentarily borrowed, some healthy linguistic normality still exists."[11] Vincent, we read further, was "no doubt cajoling, hypnotizing certain objections." Again the shift from a Victorian construction ("no doubt cajoling") to the odd application of hypnosis not to persons but to abstract nouns referring to mental states. In a similar vein, the energy of the European hosts is said to be "virgin" and Paul's "adventures" are characterized not by their kind but by their "directions." The simile "his adventures out-numbered theirs as the stars the dim electric light bulbs of the hotel" calls attention to the willed extravagance of Butts's style, her refusal of structural coherence in favor of disjunction and dislocation. As she puts it in the opening of "Brightness Falls," "There is no head or tail to this story, except that it happened. On the other hand, how does one know that anything happened? How does one know?"[12] Or take the opening of "The Warning": "This happened in the kind of house people live in who used not to live in that kind of house, who were taught to have very distinct opinions about the kind of people who lived in them. Yet, now that they have gone to live in them, they are rather different than when the other sort of person lived there" (MB 117).

The similarity to Stein should not be surprising; Butts knew Stein through her close friend Virgil Thomson and had frequented Stein's Paris salon. The first issue of *Pagany,* for that matter, also contains Stein's "Five Words in a Line" (later incorporated into *Stanzas in Meditation,* 1932), which begins:

> Five words in a line.
> Bay and pay make a lake.
> Have to be held with what.
> They have to be held with what they have to be held.
> Dependent of dependent of why.
> With a little cry.[13]

In his essay "The Work of Gertrude Stein," which follows "Five Words in a Line," Williams remarks, "Having taken the words to her choice . . . [Stein] has completely unlinked them from their former relationships in the sentence. . . . The words, in writing, she discloses, transcend everything" (P1, 1:43–44). Most poets, Williams reminds the reader, take the easy way out: "Starting from scratch we get, possibly, thatch; just as they have always done in poetry. Then they would try to connect it up by something like—The mice scratch, beneath the thatch. Miss Stein does away with all that. The free-versists on the contrary used nothing else. They saved—The mice, under the . . ." (PI, 1:42).

Reading Williams's essay, as one normally does, in *A Novelette and Other Prose* (1931) or, together with his "A 1 Pound Stein" (1934), in the *Selected Essays*,[14] one assumes that Stein's was a case wholly exceptional, that no one else at the time was so thoroughly "unlinking" words from their normal syntactic relationships. But reading Williams's essay in the context of *Pagany* suggests that Stein's "unlinkings," like the syntactic oddities, abstractions, and ungainly compoundings (e.g., "orbit-trembling") of Zukofsky, which Williams had called into question, were not all that exceptional in the writing of the early 1930s. Indeed, Stein's free adaptation of Georges Hugnet's Surrealist poetic suite *Enfances,* which appeared in the January–March 1931 issue of *Pagany,* provides an interesting index to the new poetics.

Between the Cracks

Stein's thirty-eight-page text, which prints Hugnet's French poem and Stein's English version on facing pages, has a complicated history that needn't preoccupy us here;[15] suffice it to say that, according to the original plan, *Enfances,* together with Stein's "reflection," as she called her version, was to be published in Paris by Editions Jeanne Bucher, with illustrations by Picasso, Louis Marcoussis, and Pavel Tchelitcheff. But when Hugnet objected that Stein's version could not be considered a translation of his poem, she responded by giving the text printed in *Pagany* the title "Poem Pritten on Pfances of Georges Hugnet."[16] When she brought out the book version later that year, Stein eliminated the French text altogether and called her own poem *Before the Flowers of Friendship Faded Friendship Faded.*

Stein's "free translation" of Hugnet's *Enfances* has been roundly criticized. Richard Bridgman says it "suffers badly in the presence of the original which it purports to reflect. . . . Stein's liberties were so extreme that, did they not emanate from her, one might reasonably conclude that the translator knew too little French to do the job properly. . . . She carefully censored Hugnet's images of death, sex, nudity, and onanism. For a woman who offered lines of fearsomely coy sexual innuendo, Gertrude Stein remained, even in her middle fifties, prudish, or at least evasive." And even Marianne DeKoven, who celebrates Stein's experimental writing, remarks, "Unfortunately, she seems to equate the essence of poetry with the way many poems sound, and instead of illuminating abstraction she achieves only travesty. . . . Much of the painfully unassimilated 'poetic' diction in Stein's poem is the trace of the French original."[17]

Note how similar this charge against Stein is to Williams's complaint about Zukofsky's "stilted 'poetic'" language and his "forcing of abstract conceptions into the sound pattern." It is a modernist-based critique of a new way of writing that came to be known by the curiously inappropriate label "Objectivist." Consider #12 of Hugnet's *Enfances:*

> Ma faim est large, mon appétit démesuré.
> Je peux parler longtemps sans médire
> mais tout me blesse et je sais haïr,
> Ce pays que je vois pour la première fois
> à ma timidité confie les soins du voyage,
> tout ce qu'une absence crée d'incertitude,
> tout ce que la surprise a gagné sur l'amour,
> et c'est si haut que je pense à mon orgueil
> qu'aucun regret de mes humiliations subies pour toi
> n'éxerce mon enfance à redouter la nuit,
> la nuit et ces dons que tu m'as faits,
> ces dons où se tatoua ton indifférence
> sous la forme et le chant d'un regard particulier.
> Enfance, je te nomme au centre du monde,
> au centre de mon coeur tu te nommes toi-même,
> tu te nommes la course à l'exemple de ma faim,
> enfance homicide à l'exemple de ma faim.
>
> (P2, 1:21–22)

> My hunger is great, my appetite without bounds.
> I can speak for a long time without voicing slander
> but everything hurts me and I know how to hate,
> This country which I see for the first time
> entrusts to my timidity the preparations for the trip,
> all that an absence can produce from uncertainty
> all that surprise can do to replace love,
> and it is so great that I think of my pride
> that no regret for the humiliations suffered for you
> can make my childhood fear the night,
> the night and these gifts you have bestowed on me,
> these gifts on which your indifference is tattooed

beneath the shape and the song of a particular look.
Childhood, I place you at the center of the world,
to the center of my heart, you place yourself
you choose the path commensurate with my hunger,
homicidal childhood commensurate with my hunger.

Hugnet's seventeen-line lyric celebrates, in rather melodramatic and strained terms, the secret pleasures of childhood masturbation. Its formal alexandrines, occasionally rhyming, give the poem a Baudelairean cast, even as its theme recalls the self-absorption of Hugnet's friend Jean Cocteau. Stein's "reflection" on Hugnet's "love" poem is wonderfully droll:

> I am very hungry when I drink,
> I need to leave it when I have it held.
>   They will be white with which they know they see, that darker makes it be a color white for me, white is not shown when I am dark indeed with red despair who comes who has to care that they will let me a little lie like now I like to lie I like to live I like to die I like to lie and live and die and live and die and by and by I like to live and die and by and by the need to sew, the difference is that sewing makes it bleed and such with them in all the way of seed and seeding and repine and they will which is mine and not all mine who can be thought curious of this of all of that made it and come lead it and done weigh it and mourn and sit upon it know it for ripeness without deserting all of it of which without which it has been not been born. Oh no not to be thirsty with the thirst of hunger not alone to know that they plainly and ate or wishes. Any little one will kill himself for milk. (P2, 1:21–22)

Contrary to Bridgman's supposition, Stein has obviously read her Hugnet carefully. Indeed, her witty pastiche of his masturbatory lyric takes all his references into account: extreme hunger and despair, the thirst for life punctuated by fear of death, the fidelity to one's ideals and refusal to betray them, the contrast between a virginal white and the red of penetration, the infantile regression to the nursing state. Then, too, Stein makes as much as Hugnet does of repetition and one-ups him at rhyming: "They will be white with which they know they see, / that darker makes it be a color white for me," "when I am dark indeed with red despair / who comes who has to care," and so on. But Stein goes much further: her own poem modulates a complex series of monosyllables containing long and short *is* ("I like to lie I like to live I like to die I like to lie and live and die and live and die and by and by"), creating a singsong nursery-rhyme rhythm that expresses *enfance* via sound rather than imagery. In this playful network, every phoneme counts: "lie" becomes "live" with the addition of one consonant, and the "it" of line 2 ("I need to leave it when I have it held") changes meaning with every new phrase. Finally, the hyperbole of "thirsty with the thirst of hunger" playfully acknowledges Hugnet's "à l'exemple de ma faim," even as parts of speech are unlinked from their normal position ("not alone to know that they plainly and ate or wishes"). And the poem concludes on a commonsense note that truly does characterize infancy: "Any little one will kill himself for milk."

One might object at this point that, whatever Stein's relation to Hugnet and his poetic sequence, her version of #12 should be understood as a characteristic Stein work, one text among many similar ones like *Tender Buttons* or *A Long Gay Book,* both written almost two decades earlier. But however familiar the repetition, reduced vocabulary, and skewed grammar, the Stein of the 1910s and early 1920s was not as given to parody and allusive literary play as is the author of "Poem Pritten on Pfances of Georges Hugnet." The early portraits like "Picasso" and "Mabel Dodge at the Villa Curonia" manifest a care for consistency that we don't find here or in the great poem of this period, "Stanzas in Meditation." Abstraction, intertextuality, the dispersal of the subject, obsessive rhyming, and related sound patterning—these become Stein's signature. Blood, in her scheme of things, is associated not with Hugnet's wound of love but with what are obliquely presented as her preferred domestic activities. Sewing ("the difference is that sewing makes it bleed") modulates slyly via the rhyme "bleed" / "seed" into the onanism Bridgman takes Stein to have ignored. "All the way to seed and seeding and repine and they will which is mine and not at all mine": these words constitute Stein's covert tribute to Alice Toklas and her witty exposure of Georges Hugnet's vaunted self-absorption. "Know it for ripeness," as she archly puts it, "without deserting all of it."

From the vantage point of high modernism, such writing was bound to appear deficient: no "direct treatment of the thing," no objective correlative, no clear visual images. Stein's "deliberate gracelessness"—the phrase is Peter Quartermain's with reference to Mina Loy [18]—may also be linked to the new transgression of conventional gender roles, a transgression that goes hand in hand with the social uncertainties of the early Depression years. The July–September 1931 issue of *Pagany,* for example, contains Loy's "Lady Laura in Bohemia," which begins:

Trained in a circus of swans
she
proceeds recedingly

Her eliminate flesh of fashion
inseparable from the genealogical tree
columns such towering reticence
of lifted chin
her hiccoughs seem
preparatory to bowing to the Queen

Her somersault descent
into the half-baked underworld
nor the inebriate regret
disturb her vertical caste
"They drove 'em from the cradle on the curb"
(P2, 3:125–26)

"Lady Laura in Bohemia" is perhaps best understood as a late modernist send-up of Eliot's "Portrait of a Lady," of Pound's "Portrait d'une Femme," and section 12 of *Hugh Selwyn Mauberley* ("The Lady Valentine"). The swans of Loy's poem are no longer Yeats's "brilliant creatures," drifting mysteriously on Coole lake, but a "circus" of debutantes, "trained" to behave according to the norms of their "genealogical tree." "Trained," the opening word in the poem, places emphasis on social and cultural control, an emphasis underscored by the poem's rhythm, which is much closer to the "sequence of metronome" than to that of the "musical phrase" Pound advocated so strenuously. Take the lines:

> she
> proceeds recedingly
>
> Her eliminate flesh of fashion
> inseparable from the genealogical tree

Here the rhymes "she" / "recedingly" / "tree" are intentionally silly, forcing the reader to stress the last syllable of "recedingly" and run "genealogical" and "tree" together. More important, Loy's structures of modification are characterized by repeated grammatical oddities: Laura "proceeds recedingly," her "flesh" is "eliminate" (rather than "eliminated") and it "columns" a "towering reticence / of lifted chin." In line 12, the abstract noun "regret" is described as "inebriate" or drunk. In line 13, "caste," Lady Laura's "caste" is defined as "vertical," and the quotation in line 14 is not attributed to anyone in particular. It could be Lady Laura's exclamation, but then again it could be that of a bystander in the "Bohemian" night club or even the words of the poet herself.

Once one accustoms oneself to the curious coupling of abstract and concrete words in Loy's poetry, her language begins to resonate. The opening describes the entrance of a well-brought up and aristocratic young woman ("Trained in a circus of swans") into a Montparnasse bar (a later couplet reads "her hell is / Zelli's" [126])—an entrance made "recedingly," with mock unobtrusiveness and tiny, graceful steps. In keeping with the fashion and her "genealogical tree," her flesh is "eliminate"—she is properly sleek and slim. But she carries herself so upright that her "lifted chin" and demure demeanor give her an air of "towering reticence" as she "columns" her way into the room. Drunk though she may be, her "hiccoughs" are beautifully disguised as little bows: she might be curtseying to the queen. Her "descent / into the half-baked underworld" of Bohemia is not so much a fall as a "somersault," which is to say that women of Laura's "vertical caste" always bounce back, no matter how great their "inebriate regret." Her behavior, in other words, is dictated by birth and caste, in sharp contrast to those whose "cradle" has been the "curb."

What Loy has produced, then, is a sardonic cartoon of café society, the poetic equivalent of a George Grosz cabaret scene. Yet it is composed of the most minimal strokes; no visual picture of the characters or the setting ever fully emerges. People are defined by synecdoches: Laura *is* the eliminate flesh of fashion, the column of towering reticence, and so on. And when metaphor is used, it is invariably sardonic, as in the final line of the poem, "She is yet like a diamond on a heap of broken glass" (126). There is nothing diamondlike about this "memorable divorcée," who was "christened by the archbishop of Canterbury"; only in a "heap of broken glass" can she sparkle momentarily. And even this reference has a double entendre, Loy no doubt alluding playfully to the "heap of broken images" in *The Waste Land*. Eliot parodies, for that matter, were common in this period: in the same volume of *Pagany*, Mary Butts has a poem called "Thinking of Saints and of Petronius Arbiter" (the title comes directly from Yeats's elegy for Mabel Beardsley, "Upon a Dying Lady") that contains this parody of "The Hollow Men":

Between the cocktail and the crucifix
Between the prayer and the fear
Lies the sword.

Between the toy and the cigarette
Between the spite and the joke
Lies the imagination. . . .

(P2, 2:89) [19]

Logopoeia: brittle, hard-edged, tough-minded, slightly nasty. For both Loy and Butts, extravagant verbal play is more important than the Poundian demand for accuracy and precision. But what is especially odd is that even the so-called realistic fiction, most of it by men, found in the pages of *Pagany*—a fiction I now turn to—displays a taste for the grotesquerie and self-parody we find in the work of Stein, Loy, and Butts.

From Imagism to Superrealism

The January–March 1931 issue of *Pagany,* for example, opens with a short story, more properly a prose poem, bearing the portentous title "Hours before Eternity." It has fifty-three short sections, each assigned a roman numeral. Here are the first two:

I

In the chill frost of winter I left Memphis and rode on the outside of freight cars all the way to the Atlantic. The nights were so cold that my fingers froze around the iron bars and at daybreak each morning I had to bite them away with my teeth. The joints of my fingers broke sometimes when I bit them from the iron and the flesh cracked to the bone like the deep cut of a sharp knife. When I got to Charleston I worked all night in a dairy and drank the warm foam of the new white milk and all day I sat in my room at the boarding house and waited for the coming of the first blossoms of the magnolia trees.

II

Men who worked with their hands and backs were proud of their male strength when they ran shouting in naked strides to their women but those with soft damp fingers were so ashamed of themselves that they whispered in halting negatives and tried to cover their vulgarity with towels. (P2, 1:1)

Realistic autobiographical narrative in the vein of Sherwood Anderson or Ring Lardner? A naturalistic picture of the seamy side of life in the poverty-stricken rural South? It begins that way, with the references to Memphis and Charleston, the hopping of freight trains and fingers frozen to their iron bars. But the second section, with its distinction between the "Men who worked with their hands and backs," (note the erotic double entendre in the apparently blunt statement) and "those with soft damp fingers" seems oddly gratuitous in the context. The strong and the weak? The studs and the pansies? What, one wonders, does this seemingly homophobic dismissal have to do with the narrator's quest, which leads him to pursue "the quick beauty of a girl's face" seen in a crowd and stunning enough to be blinding. "As soon as I could see again I looked and saw a scar on my eyes. The scar was an etching of the beauty I had seen and when tears had tried but could not wash its lines away I saw it framed in colors like the rainbow"? (P2, 1:2).

The image of the scar across the eyes has a surrealistic cast (one thinks of Max Ernst's 1929 *La Femme 100 têtes*) at odds with the hard-boiled narrative of passages like "I walked into the country again and worked among negroes on a farm. The white man made us sweat from sun-up till dark and he would not let us stop for a drink of water" (XII). A similar equivocation between surrealism and naturalism occurs later:

XV

The negro girl that he told me to bring him would not come to his house and I went back and told him so. He told me to harness a mule and follow him. We went down to the cabin where the girl was and he brought her outside and dropped her in the yard. While he put a trace chain around her waist I backed the mule and hooked the chain to the single-tree. When we were ready to go he kicked the mule in the belly and broke off a hunk of chewing tobacco. The negro girl was dragged behind the mule to the house and when we got there I helped him take her inside. He forged the chain around her and spiked it to the floor. When I went to sleep I could hear the rattling of the chain and when I woke up it was rattling again. The girl cried all the time but he would not let her go home.

XVI

Once that winter one of the negroes said he was too sick to work so we killed him with a shotgun and buried him in the manure pile.

XVII

The man brought another negro girl to the house but she had greased her body with lard and when he took off her clothes he could not hold her. (P2, 1:3)

Such writing has usually been classified as the "literature of social protest," with the horrific narrative providing, in flat, objective manner, a graphic image of white oppression and black victimization. Short declarative sentences, reductive vocabulary, lack of involvement of the speaking subject: these are what one might expect from the author of "Hours before Eternity" who happens to be Erskine Caldwell, the best-selling Southern "naturalist" author of *Tobacco Road* (1932) and *God's Little Acre* (1933), the young communist who went on to visit Russia with his then-wife Margaret Bourke-White and who wrote the text for her book of documentary photographs *You Have Seen Their Faces* (1937). Later he became increasingly conservative, a "sell-out" to Hollywood, relegated today to the company of forgotten white male writers of the period. Even James E. Devlin, who wrote the 1984 Twayne book on Caldwell, concludes:

He is without any question a minor writer, and further, a limited one. Philosophically he is of few ideas and those often inconsistent. He has never decided whether it is the heart or the head to which he owes the greater allegiance. His belief in feeling, intuition, and emotion as God-directed often falters when opposed by the strong pressure of a naturalistic determinism that also guides his thought. About sexual passion he is simultaneously knowledgeable and as innocent as Steve Henderson, the wooden sixteen-year-old of *Summertime Island* (1968).[20]

What, then, is this "minor" "naturalist" writer doing in *Pagany*, alongside Pound, Williams, Butts, Stein, Loy, and Zukofsky, alongside the photographs of Eugène Atget and Berenice Abbott, the Charles Demuth illustrations for Henry James's *Turn of the Screw?* Is it just one of those mistaken links that hindsight can correct?[21] Or can we read the much castigated stylistic inconsistencies somewhat differently?

In a 1935 essay for the *New Republic*, reprinted in *The Philosophy of Literary Form*, Kenneth Burke singles out for comment Caldwell's "Hours before Eternity" and the two related stories that comprise "The Sacrilege of Alan Kent," published in the collection *American Earth* (1931):

They contain a kind of aphoristic rhetoric, except that the aphorisms are less ideas than tiny plots. . . . The swift segments shunt us back and forth between brutality and wistfulness. Perhaps the grandiose, the violent, and the gentle qualities of the piece are all fused in this bit of purest poetry: "Once the sun was so hot a bird came down and walked beside me in my shadow." A section in *Pagany* containing this item was the first thing by Caldwell I ever saw. For days I was noisy in my enthusiasm—but I could not understand how it went with some of his other work.[22]

In trying to understand his own reaction, Burke suggests that Caldwell's "cult of incongruity" (KB 352) results from a "balked religiosity" channeled into "political exhortation," the resulting perspective being not so much complex in the modernist sense as willfully contradictory. His "particular aptitude has been in scrambling or garbling properties," a "deft way of putting the wrong things together" (KB 351–52). For Devlin, such inconsistency is ipso facto a fault, but for Burke, proto-postmodernist that he is, irresolution has a positive side. What he likes about "Hours before Eternity" is that the text "muddl[es] our judgments instead of stabilizing them" (KB 353). Such withholding on the author's part, he posits, "is the subtlest feature of Caldwell's method. Where the author leaves out so much, the reader begins making up the difference for himself. Precisely by omitting humaneness where humaneness is most called for, he may stimulate the reader to supply it" (KB 355). And he concludes, "I have denied that Caldwell is a realist. In his tomfoolery he comes closer to the Dadaists; when his grotesqueness is serious, he is a Superrealist," a poet of "*nonrational* linkages" and "fantastic simplifications" (KB 356–57).

"Fantastic simplification" is a good term, not only for Caldwell's fiction but also for much of the work published in *Pagany* and in such related journals as *Blues* and *Contact*. "Dada" and "Superrealist" (surrealist) may not be quite the defining terms for "Hours before Eternity," for the dadaists would never have produced sentences so sober and realistic as "He handed me a cup of flour and a piece of fat meat and a few potatoes and gave me permission to use his cooking stove" (P2, 1:3), and the surrealists were much more programmatic and Freudian. Rather, Caldwell's "deft way of putting the wrong things together" depends on a curious undercutting of the authority of the subject. The tone is so uncertain, shifting as it does from caricature to pathos, from a racy humor to a grim earnestness, that, in Burke's words, "it muddl[es] our judgments rather than stabilizing them." In a paragraph like section XV above, for example, the curious and confusing use of personal pronouns (thirty-one in nine sentences) distances the reader from the terrible events, "him" and "her" becoming, in one sense, so many counters on a chessboard.

Such distancing superrealism would seem to be a homegrown product, quite appropriate for the pages of a "Native Quarterly." Indeed, the "non-rational linkages" and "fantastic abstractions" Burke speaks of, the predilection for parody, play, contradiction, and the undercutting of mimesis despite referential overload, can be seen as a kind of signature of literary discourse in Depression America. Take Edward Dahlberg's autobiographical narrative "Graphophone Nickelodeon Days," which immediately follows Gertrude Stein's "Poem Pritten on Pfances" in the January–March 1931 issue of *Pagany*.

Like Erskine Caldwell, Edward Dahlberg is now a largely forgotten writer; his name is not even listed in the 1988 *Columbia Literary History of the United States*. If he is remembered at all, it is largely for the role he played as mentor to the young Charles Olson.[23] But again like Caldwell, when read against texts by Stein and Williams in the pages of *Pagany*, Dahlberg emerges as by no means just another documentary realist with socialist convictions. "And yet it all came back, the taste of it, the tang and brine of it, like the windy crispy newspaper afternoon air over the san francisco wharves," the *Pagany* story begins, conventionally enough, its focus on the recording, remembering "I," detached from the "tastes" and "tang" of his childhood. But detachment gives way to penny-arcade jingles, whose rhythms recall Stein's *Before the Flowers of Friendship Faded*:

> call me up some rainy afternoon
> and we'll have a quiet little spoon
> and we'll talk about the weather
> i'll see that my mother takes a walk
> mum's the word, baby dear
> (P2, 1:39)

And these Tin Pan Alley tunes are juxtaposed with manic catalogs in which image is piled on image to create a space at once "real" and yet wholly fantastic in its contours:

> dago bread, cheney watermelon hucksters, lyric moving picture house, open air tents, lawdie lawdie tabernacle sermons, halley's comet, the end of the world, bad rodent dreams in the 8th street flat, bohunk nightmares, blackhand barky trees, pimpish gaslight joints, the midnight ride of a can of beer, *ach du lieber augustin*

the kansas city west bottoms, a wiry and rusty rat trap, the bluffs stale, gone-looking boxcar smoke in the back of his throat, red caboose bonfires, corn-stalk smoking, m.k.t., chicago & alton blakean alfalfa field midnights, *casy jones got another papa,* roundhouse cindery toe-stubbing noons, adobe main street 11 o'clock mornings, armour & swift packinghouse summers, dusty hoofbeaten heifer clouds. . . . hoss swopping piddling saturdays, *pony boy, pony boy, won't you be my tony boy.* . . . (P2, 1:39–40)

Such cataloging is closer to Ginsberg than to Whitman, as is evident if we lineate Dahlberg's passage using as model the strophes of "Howl!" or "America":

> gone-looking boxcar smoke in the back of his throat, red caboose
>   bonfires, corn-stalk smoking, m.k.t., chicago & alton blakean
>   alfalfa field midnights, casy jones got another papa, roundhouse
>   cindery toe-stubbing noons. . . .

As later in "Howl," such passages are melopoeic rather than phanopoeic, with the clustering, heavy stresses, marked alliteration and assonance producing a heightened, surreal rhythm, as in:

$$\textit{al}\text{ton } b\textit{lak}\text{ean } \textit{alfalfa f}\text{ield midnights}$$

where "blakean" is a self-conscious intervention into the otherwise mimetic base, as is the subsequent interjection of the song lyric *"casy jones got another papa."* Williamsian images like "a wiry and rusty rat trap," and "red caboose bonfires" alternate with documentary reference ("armour & swift packinghouse") and surreal phrasing ("the midnight ride of a can of beer"). The text never quite makes up its mind where it wants to go, but this may be precisely its appeal, the very language calling into question the forward linear movement we expect of narrative.

Is the publication in *Pagany* of Dahlberg's prose an anomaly? I think that on the contrary this text, like Caldwell's "Hours before Eternity," provides a matrix for Zukofsky's early "Objectivist" poetry that may well be more telling than the usual placement of that poetry in the Pound-Williams tradition. Take, for example, Zukofsky's "Four Poems" ("Buoy," "Awake," "Blue light is the night harbor-slip," and "Passing tall"), published alongside Dahlberg's "Graphophone Nickelodeon Days," Stein's "Poem Pritten on Pfances," and Butts's "Thinking of Saints." With the exception of "Awake," these poems, written between 1925 and 1931, were included in "29 Poems."[24] Here is "Buoy":

> Buoy—no, how
> It is not a question: what
> Is this freighter carrying?—
> Did smoke blow?—That whistle?—
> Of course, commerce will not complete
> Anything, yet the harbor traffic is busy,
>   there shall be a complete fragment
>
> Of—
> Nothing, look! that gull
> Streak the water!
> Getting nearer are we,
> Hear? count the dissonances,
>
> Shoal? accost-cost
> Cost accounting."
>
>   (CPLZ 23–24)

Williams was surely right in telling Zukofsky that his early poems had not been "objectivized in new or fresh observations." Zukofsky's break with what Burton Hatlen has called a "late Imagist" "poetics of presence," a poetics in which "words remain absolutely faithful to 'things' in their sensory immediacy," is incontrovertible, but I am not sure it follows that "if the seeable is by definition unsayable, then language, rather than giving us Being in its fullness, must reconcile itself to the more difficult task of enacting our endless and endlessly frustrated struggle *toward* Being."[25] For like the Stein of "Poems Pritten on Pfances" or the Loy of "Lady Laura in Bohemia," the Zukofsky of "Buoy" foregrounds the play of the signifier, especially paragram and pun. "Buoy—no, how": the first line puns on "Boy—know how," "know how" being the great trait in thirties technological America. "Boy, what know how!": like George Oppen's frigidaire poem ("Thus / Hides the / Parts"), published in the "Objectivist" number of *Poetry* (January 1931), Zukofsky is examining a world in which coherent natural images—a buoy at sea as a *point de repère* for incoming freighters—have been replaced by floating signifiers. "It is not a question" (line 2) of asking what "this freighter [is] carrying," or even where the smoke is coming from or who blew the whistle. Since "commerce will not complete / Anything," there are no meaningful images, only a "complete fragment"—but "Of" what? Evidently "Of— / Nothing."

The second stanza urges us to "look" at "that gull / Streak the water!" But this is not the world of Hart Crane's "Bridge," composed in these same years, where the "seagull's wings shall dip and pivot him, / Over the chained bay water Liberty." No "apparitional" white gulls as emblems of transcendence. "Getting nearer are we," asks the poet. "Hear?" (again with a pun on "here"). And then, in what is a statement of poetics, we read, "count the dissonances." And dissonances are what we live with. The following question "Shoal?" suggests that there is no coherent picture to be composed of this harbor scene, no line of demarcation between shore or shoal and water can be shown. Images "accost" us, but "accost" contains within it the word "cost," and this in turn suggests the "Cost accounting" of the final line. "Commerce" is what it's really all about; money is the "buoy" or marker around which the "busy" harbor traffic revolves. But— and I think this is important—the poem is not at all polemical about this state of affairs; its focus is on the ironic potential of words to "mean" differently when they are "unlinked" from their usual contexts. No pretty harbor scene with freighters in the distance sailing between the buoys. "Count—cost-accost-account": the cost of accounting, the accosting (accounting) of costs: the play is Steinian in its wit.

Then, too, the lineation of "Buoy" obliquely pokes fun at the imagist free-verse lyric. Much has been made of Zukofsky's musical virtuosity,[26] but it is useful to remember that his soundscapes exist at the micro rather than the macro level of lyric form, a poem like "Buoy" modulating long *o*s ("no," "smoke," "blow") and *iy* diphthongs ("Streak," "nearer," "we," "hear") with great ingenuity, even as its individual lines are purposely flat-footed. "Buoy—no, how": three stresses on monosyllables, separated by punctuation: hardly an attractive line. The next two are similar:

> It is nót a quéstion: // whát
> Is this fréighter cárrying?—

To call these lines "prosaic" would still not convey the oppositional, anti-poetic stance of the young Zukofsky, his aggressive challenge to the reader to "count the dissonances." Surely "Objectivist," with its connotations of materiality, is a curious label for a lyric so uncompromising and so self-destructive.

Figure I. Eugène Atget, *Avenue des Gobelins* (1927).

America First and Last

I have been arguing that the poetics of the early 1930s produced an adversarial literature that called into question the pieties of an earlier, more innocent modernism by means of powerful wit, complex parody, contradiction of formal and emotional registers, and especially the dissolution of the coherent "lyric voice" as controlling presence in the poetic text. The sentimental slides into the cynical and back again. Reference, moreover, does not insure mimetic representation. Nothing is taken for granted; nothing is quite what it seems to be.

This can be seen even in the photographs of the period. In the January–March 1931 issue of *Pagany*, we find, side by side with Dahlberg's fiction and Zukofsky's poetry, four reproductions of Eugène Atget photographs, evidently transmitted to the editor by Berenice Abbott, of whom more

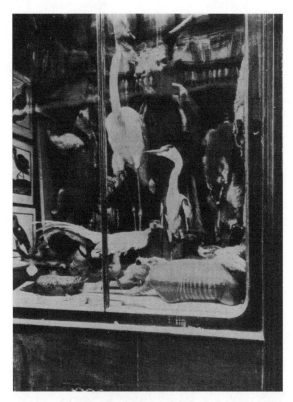

Figure 2. Eugène Atget, untitled
[Window with Stuffed Animals, 1927–30].

in a moment. Atget's astonishing images of shop windows, arcades, door-
ways, and street corners, most of them curiously empty of people, are at
once documentary and surrealistic, their lighting and angle shots endow-
ing the most ordinary scenes—a dressmaker's dummy in a shop window,
a display of stuffed animals, a puppet-theater curtain, or a monkey house
in the park (figures 1–4)—with a dreamlike presence, rather as Zukofsky's
"buoy" or Williams's "back wings of the hospital" become part of a language game. Furthermore, the fabled breakdown of the divide between
"high" and "low" art attributed to postmodernism is taken for granted
in these prints, where the mundane is inseparable from the emphasis on
formal composition.

Thousands of the negatives Atget made prior to his death in 1927, at a
time when his work was virtually unknown, were rescued and printed by
Berenice Abbott, four of whose own photographs appear in the next issue

of *Pagany*. Having returned to America as part of the expatriate exodus from Paris in 1929, Abbott wanted to do for New York what Atget had done for Paris. In particular, she wanted to provide a documentary record of urban transformation: the demolition of old buildings to make way for the new skyscrapers, the surviving neighborhood shops, the relation of technology to nature, stone and steel to sky (figures 5–8). Like Atget's, her images are only superficially instances of documentary realism, their strange placement and surprising juxtapositions of materials creating a landscape as surreal as Caldwell's mysterious southern sites.

The 1931 volume, which featured these photographs as well as Charles Demuth's similarly stylized watercolor illustrations for Henry James's *The Turn of the Screw,* side by side with the poetry of Williams and the fiction of Dahlberg and Dos Passos, was thus a triumph for *Pagany*. But the following year, things began to unravel. True, Richard Johns was still discovering new (or new for him) authors: the January–March 1932 issue had a long poem ("Brown River, Smile") by Jean Toomer, whose *Cane*

Figure 3. Eugène Atget, untitled
[Puppet-Theater Curtain, 1927–30].

Figure 4. Eugène Atget, untitled [Palais des singes, 1927–30].

Johns had long admired, as well as a first appearance ("Electra-Orestes") by H. D. But the journal's financial situation had become precarious.[27] Often Johns couldn't afford to pay his authors, much less the print shop, and the quality of production went down. To make things worse, a number of accidents (including a fire) caused manuscripts to be destroyed. The October–December 1932 issue was thus delayed and didn't come out until February 1933. And this was *Pagany*'s final issue.

The usual explanation for such endings is that the modernist avant-garde could not survive the Depression, that it gave way to a more socially conscious, more politicized "writing on the Left," as it came to be called. In his moving introduction to Stephen Halpert's *Return to PAGANY* (1969), for example, Kenneth Rexroth, whose own poetry was featured in the pages of Zukofsky's *"Objectivists" Anthology* and Charles Henri Ford's *Blues,* as well as in the first issue of *Pagany,* put it this way:

> *Pagany*'s lifetime spanned the breakdown of the international avant garde as the world economic crisis shut down and a quite different kind of literature emerged. . . . Under the pressure of catastrophe, writers and artists all over the world began to turn to attack the specific social evils from which they had thought they had escaped by concentrating on

the underlying, fundamental Lie. Richard Johns was especially sensitive to this great turn, and published some of the earliest and finest writing of the kind that was eventually to be debauched and destroyed by the slogans of falsification — Proletcult and Socialist Realism. (ARP xiii, xv).

But this is not quite the way it happened. For one thing, the poetry of the Objectivists, as of Mina Loy and Mary Butts, and of the Gertrude Stein and William Carlos Williams of the 1930s, was already quite different in mood and rhetoric from the more utopian work of the early modernists. Picasso's *Ma Jolie* (1913), for example, was, for all its cubist fragmentation and complexity, still a highly painterly work, a portrait, after all, of a lady, whereas it isn't clear that Abbott's "documentary" studies of barbershop storefronts, sandwiched between newer steel and concrete structures, are "art" at all. A similar contrast can be found between Joyce's *Ulysses* and

Figure 5. Berenice Abbott, untitled [Manhattan Skyline near 42nd Street, 1930–31].

Figure 6. Berenice Abbott, untitled [The Old Union Square Cigar Store, 1930–31].

Dos Passos's *U.S.A.,* whose "Eveline" sequence appeared in the summer and autumn 1931 issues of *Pagany.*

Second, the umbrella term "social protest literature" obscures some important distinctions. Like Rexroth himself, the Objectivist poets were certainly "writers on the Left" (George Oppen is perhaps the most striking example of a poet who, as a onetime Communist Party member, had to go underground during the McCarthy years), but the Left was itself curiously divided when it came to questions of aesthetic. Consider the July–September 1932 issue of *Pagany,* which features the "First Movement" (to become book 1) of Zukofsky's monumental poem *"A".* The well-known opening, which provides us with the title of the poem, its first word, and the note musicians tune by—all the while using the separation of the indefinite article ("A") from the noun ("round") it modifies to create a pun on the preposition "around"—immediately calls into question the authority of the lyric speaker:

> A
>> Round of fiddles playing Bach—
>> The double chorus.
>>> "Come ye daughters, share my anguish—"

Bare arms, black dresses
"*See Him! Whom?—*"
Bediamond the passion of our Lord
"*See Him! How?—*"

(P3, 3:9)

The scene (we learn further along) is Carnegie Hall, the occasion an Easter
Sunday performance of Bach's *St. Matthew's Passion,* with phrases from
the oratorio punctuating the narrator's account. And even these phrases
become the subject of the poet's play, with "*See Him! Whom?,*" "*See Him!
How?*" referring to the audience's alienation from the Christian ethos
of the *Passion.* "First Movement" now submits these motifs to a complex "musical" development that partly echoes, partly ironizes Bach's own
music, and it ends with bits of conversation overheard on the street after
the concert:

Figure 7. Berenice Abbott, untitled [Barbershop, 1930–31].

Figure 8. Berenice Abbott, untitled [Manhattan Skyline from Downtown, 1930–31].

> "We ran 'em in chain gangs, down in the Argentine,
> *Executive*'s not the word, use *engineer,*
> Single-handed, ran 'em like soldiers,
> Seventy-four yesterday, and could run 'em today. . ."
>
> (P3, 3:13)

This voice (evidently of a wealthy industrialist) is punctuated by the words of the *Passion* ("*Ye lightnings, ye thunders / In clouds are ye vanished?*"), which in their turn modulate into a concluding line—"Open, O fierce flaming pit!"—that refers not only to the oratorio from which it comes but also to the poet's own sense of hell inherent in the contrast between the musical discourse of Bach and the discourse of the city in which his *Passion* is heard, or rather goes unheard.

It is instructive to compare *"A"* to a poem that appears later in the same issue of *Pagany:*

Entreaty at Delphi

We again have come
through muted lanes where shadows were aflame

with lowered voices, 'and where wings were lame
and wide limbs dumb;

we again have seen
the terror muffled with an earthly tread
of inner footbeats travelling where led
into a desert scene

and we have glanced
upon the muffled image of the flower
opening, petal on petal, every hour
and were entranced

to a deep sleep
made up of cast-off visages and days
recalled, and many unenacted plays
where actors weep

and know not why.
O, must the evening find us still unborn
unknowing while our foliage is torn
cruelly from us, here, before we die?

(P3 3:88–89)

Coming upon this after reading Butts and Loy, Stein and Zukofsky, the reader may well be confused. Is this a late poem by Arthur Symons? Ernest Dowson? John Davidson? The voice that speaks in neatly rhyming *abba* quatrains is in total control, able to speak for a larger "we," a "we" who are somehow (how?) "unborn" and "unknowing," waiting for the miracle at Delphi to occur. Predictably the lanes are "muted," their shadows "aflame," their "terror muffled." Everything is vague, shadowy, disembodied, melancholy. But why and how?

The author of this poem, Edwin Rolfe, was a communist activist poet as well as a fiction writer–journalist whose work appeared frequently in *New Masses* and the *Daily Worker*. He was to serve, in 1937, in the Abraham Lincoln Brigade and to write a volume of poems about the Spanish Civil War. "Rolfe," writes Cary Nelson, "is one of the politically committed poets whose work largely meets New Critical standards for producing formally coherent, metaphorically inventive, fully realized, and self-sufficient poems. That he is almost wholly excluded from our cultural memory demonstrates that political—not merely purportedly disinterested aesthetic—

criteria have helped determine what poets we honor in our texts and literary histories."[28]

But it is not clear what Nelson means by terms like "formally coherent," "self-sufficient," or "aesthetic." In point of fact, Rolfe's latter-day Yellow Nineties mode[29] would certainly not meet "New Critical standards," and not because of the poet's political stance; rather, a critic like Cleanth Brooks or Allen Tate would have complained of the laxity of the poem's diction and the self-indulgence of its tone. Indeed, it is time we stopped pitting the ostensible "radicalism" of poets like Rolfe against "New Critical" "conservatism" and compare it instead to the very different Left radicalism of the Objectivists, whose work was at least as neglected by, say, Brooks and Warren as was Rolfe's.

The case of James T. Farrell, whose first appearance in *Pagany* was in the same issue, is similar. Here is the opening of "Twenty-Five Bucks":

Fifteen years is a hell of a long time to live in grease. Fifteen years is a hell of a long time to keep getting your jaw socked. Fifteen years is a hell of a long time for a broken-down, never-was of a palooka named Kid Tucker. Fifteen years stretched back through a reeking line of stale fight clubs, of jeers and clammy dressing rooms, and lousy gyms, and cheap can houses where every bed sheet is filthy with the countless foot marks of nameless customers, of ratty saloons with sawdust floors. (P3, 3:97)

"Use no word," Pound had cautioned in a statement Zukofsky, for one, took very seriously, "that does not contribute to the presentation." But in Farrell's tale of the prizefighter's demise, the opening paragraph is a kind of recycling of Eliot's "sawdust restaurants with oyster shells" but lacks Eliot's irony. Farrell's words, especially his adjectives, are nothing if not predictable: fight clubs are "stale," dressing-rooms "clammy," gyms "lousy," saloons "ratty," and bed-sheets "filthy." And the passage's heavy repetition (the anaphora of "Fifteen years . . .") does not exactly make for a dynamic rhythm.

Oddly enough, then, this vein of "proletarian" writing bypassed modernism, returning to the genteel tradition of a previous generation. The split between the aesthetic and the political, a split that had threatened the life of the avant-garde from the time of its inception in the later nineteenth century, had now widened to a large fissure. The "radical political" wing associated with Edwin Rolfe and James Farrell was quickly co-opted by the Establishment. In the winter of 1934, exactly one year after the last issue of *Pagany* was published, the *Partisan Review* put out its first issue.

Subtitled "A Bi-Monthly of Revolutionary Literature," *Partisan Review* was the official organ of the John Reed Club of New York (a cell of the American Communist Party) until 1937 when, in response to the Moscow Show Trials, the magazine severed its party connections. The editorial in the first issue states:

> We propose to concentrate on creative and critical literature, but we shall maintain a definite viewpoint—that of the revolutionary working class. Through our specific literary medium we shall participate in the struggle of the workers and sincere intellectuals against imperialist war, fascism, national and racial oppression, and for the abolition of the system which breeds these evils. The defense of the Soviet Union is one of our principal tasks. (*Partisan Review* 1, no. 1 [February–March 1934]: 2)

The issue opens with two short stories about social injustice by Grace Lumpkin, but otherwise its contributors (all of them white male) resort to the Poetic Diction I described above. Here again are Farrell (an extract from *Studs Lonigan*) and Rolfe, whose "Poem for May First" is a clarion call urging the comrades to create a brave new world in the image of the new Soviet Union. Here is an excerpt:

> The brain will not deny
> the days that come with verdure nor the eye
> ignore the splendor of the changing year
> invested with surprise: bells clanging in the ear
> with sound that drowns the singing of the birds
> and voices rich with prophecy—the words
> fraught with great deeds.[30]

The language of the people? Or an echo of Longfellow? If, as Henri Meschonnic and Anthony Easthope (both, incidentally, Marxist critics) have argued, the choice of meter is itself an ideological choice,[31] then Rolfe's smooth iambic pentameter couplets have an interesting subtext.

And indeed by 1937 the *Partisan Review* had not only dissociated itself from the John Reed Club but was publishing mainstream modernist and neomodernist works: the December 1937 issue featured Delmore Schwartz's "In Dreams Begin Responsibilities," Wallace Stevens's "The Dwarf," an essay by William Troy called "The Symbolism of Zola," and reviews by Lionel Trilling, Arthur Mizener, Sidney Hook, and Philip Rahv. Within a few years, *Partisan Review* poetry, fiction, and criticism were all but indistinguishable from the poetry, fiction, and criticism of the "conservative" *Kenyon Review,* founded in 1939. The first issue of the *Kenyon Review,* for that matter, included Delmore Schwartz's essay "The Two Audens" and Philip Rahv's "Franz Kafka: The Hero as Lonely Man."

So began the rapprochement between the Left and its supposed enemy, the New Criticism. Meanwhile, the "other" or "aesthetic" radical wing had a harder time of it. "Poor ol White Mule," wrote Williams sadly to Richard Johns in late 1933, "I wish I could go on with it. Not a word have I written on it since Pagany busted" (ARP 511). Not until 1937, when a young publisher named James Laughlin came into the picture, did Williams have the heart to finish his novel, which Laughlin offered to bring out.

The Objectivists and related *Pagany* poets had a harder time of it. Never published in mainstream little magazines like *Partisan Review,* they more or less went underground, not to be revived until the 1960s and 1970s when first the Black Mountain/San Francisco poets and then the Language group took them up. At the "Poets of the Thirties" conference held at the University of Maine in June 1993, there were five sessions on Zukofsky alone and three apiece on Reznikoff, Loy, and Lorine Niedecker, whose Objectivist poetry began to appear shortly after the *Pagany* period. The keynote poetry reading, moreover, was given before a large and reverential audience by the now ninety-year-old Carl Rakosi. The poetic of the 1930s, distinct as that poetic is from the modernism that immediately preceded it, seems finally to be getting its due. At the same time—and perhaps this is why the early 1930s are so fascinating for us—the split that haunts that American decade similarly haunts our own. The argument for "radical" subject matter (never mind its mode of production or materiality) is once again being made, this time no longer for writers identified with a particular political party or movement, but for members of particular ethnic, racial, and gender groups. Now as then, identity politics is often co-opted by what turns out to be a conservative aesthetic—the minority group, its teeth unfanged, turned commodity on the *Bill Moyers Journal* and similar television programs. A real Revolution of the Word, we learn from such publications as the *"Obectivists" Anthology* or *Pagany,* cannot be packaged; it inevitably involves the "barbed-wire entanglements" that made Harriet Monroe extremely nervous, even as she had the courage to give them a hearing.

4. "A Step Away from Them"

Poetry 1956

One of the most acclaimed poetry books of 1956 was Richard Wilbur's *The Things of This World,* published by Harcourt, Brace. Here is the title poem:

> The eyes open to a cry of pulleys,
> And spirited from sleep, the astounded soul
> Hangs for a moment bodiless and simple.
> As false dawn.
> > Outside the open window
> The morning air is all awash with angels.
>
>   Some are in bed-sheets, some are in blouses,
> Some are in smocks: but truly there they are.
> Now they are rising together in calm swells
> Of halcyon feeling, filling whatever they wear
> With the deep joy of their impersonal breathing;
>
>   Now they are flying in place, conveying
> The terrible speed of their omnipresence, moving
> And staying like white water; and now of a sudden
> They swoon down into so rapt a quiet
> That nobody seems to be there.
> > The soul shrinks

From all that it is about to remember,
From the punctual rape of every blessed day,
And cries,

          "Oh, let there be nothing on earth but laundry,
Nothing but rosy hands in the rising steam
And clear dances done in the sight of heaven."

      Yet, as the sun acknowledges
With a warm look the world's hunks and colors,
The soul descends once more in bitter love
To accept the waking body, saying now
In a changed voice as the man yawns and rises,

      "Bring them down from their ruddy gallows;
Let there be clean linen for the backs of thieves;
Let lovers go sweet and fresh to be undone,
And the heaviest nuns walk in a pure floating
Of dark habits,

          keeping their difficult balance.[1]

This much anthologized poem[2] provides us with an interesting index
to Establishment poetics in the mid-fifties. Its thirty lines are divided into
six five-line stanzas, the meter being predominantly iambic pentameter
("Sóme are in smócks: but trúly thére they áre"), with some elegant variation, as when a line is divided into steps (see lines 4, 15, 18, 30), presumably
to create a more natural look. A similar effect is gained by the absence
of end rhyme, although there is a good deal of alliteration and assonance
(e.g., "And *s*pirited from *s*leep, the a*s*tounded *s*oul").

"You must imagine," Wilbur remarked in an interview, "the poem as
occurring at perhaps seven-thirty in the morning; the scene is a bedroom
high up in a city apartment building; outside the bedroom window, the
first laundry of the day is being yanked across the sky and one has been
awakened by the squeaking pulleys of the laundry-line."[3] What interests
me here is the pronoun "one." Indeed, in the opening stanza, the references
are to "The eyes," not "My eyes," to "the astounded soul," not to "my"
astounded soul. The claims the poem will evidently make are for the uni-

versality of the experience described. Or so it struck three poet-critics—Richard Eberhart, Robert Horan, and May Swenson—who responded to Wilbur's poem in Anthony Ostroff's anthology *The Contemporary Poet as Artist and Critic*.[4]

"The important thing about Wilbur's poem," writes Eberhart, "is that it celebrates the immanence of spirit in spite of the 'punctual rape of every blessed day.' . . . The soul, felt as a vision of angelic laundry on awakening, must still be incorporated into the necessities and imperfections of everyday reality" (AO 7). The ideal, for Eberhart and his fellow poet-critics, is the "difficult balance" of the poem's last line, the balance between body and soul, the material and the spiritual, the disembodied angels and the "heaviest nuns walk[ing] in a pure floating / of dark habits." "The modern lyric," declares May Swenson, "is autonomous, a separate mobile . . . an enclosed construct . . . a package individually wrapped" (AO 12). Such an individual package depends on the careful control of tensions and balances. Notice, for example, the tension between words of stress ("pulleys," "hangs," "shrinks," "gallows") and those of rest ("calm swells," "impersonal breathing," "yawns"), between white ("angels," "water," "steam," "linen," "pure") and red ("rape," "rosy," "warm look," "love," "ruddy"). "The whole poem," writes Swenson, "is in fact an epitome of relative weight and equipoise" (AO 16).

The Age Demanded such equipoise, an equipoise, epitomized in 1956, in the poetry world of the *Kenyon Review, Partisan Review, Sewanee Review,* and so on, by metaphysical poetry, especially that of John Donne, and, more immediately for Wilbur, by the Yeats of "Sailing to Byzantium," who referred to the soul as "clap[ping] its hands" and singing. But whereas Yeats's body/soul antinomies are part of a larger and coherent late romantic ontology, Wilbur's laundry-as-angel metaphor strikes me as no more than an elaborate contrivance, characterized by its curious inattention to the "things of this world" of the poet's title. "The incident," writes May Swenson, "is so common that everyone has seen it, and . . . the analogy is . . . fitting in each of its details: a shirt is white, it is empty of body, but floats or flies, therefore has life (an angel)" (AO 13). But if, as Wilbur himself explains it, the scene is outside the upper-story window of an apartment building, in front of which "the first laundry of the day is being yanked across the sky," the reality would be that the sheets and shirts would probably be covered with specks of dust, grit, maybe even with a trace or two of bird droppings. At best, those sheets seen (if seen at all) from Manhattan high-rise windows in the fifties, billowing over the fire escapes under the newly installed television aerials, would surely be a bit on the grungy side.

But of course the awakening poet might not notice this because the laundry is certainly not his concern; the poet, after all, is represented as having been asleep when it was hung out to dry. Richard Eberhart seems to be aware of this aloofness when he remarks that Wilbur's "is a man's poem. Certainly not all women would like a laundry poem which pays no heed to hard work and coarsened hands. They might say, poet, have your ruddy dream, but give us better detergents" (AO 5). A remarkable fifties statement, this, in its assumption that woman is she who has "coarsened hands" from doing the laundry, while man, that ruddy dreamer, can view that same laundry as angelic. Or, to turn the dichotomy around, woman is she who only dreams of better detergents — a dream, by the way, the affluent fifties were in the process of satisfying — whereas man dreams idealistically (and hence hopelessly) of "clear dances done in the sight of heaven," dances that might allow him to escape, at least momentarily, "the punctual rape of every blessed day."

"Punctual rape": it is the alarm clock going off, violating one's delightful daydreams, even as Donne's "busie old foole, unruly Sunne" intrudes, through windows and curtains, on the sleeping lovers in "The Sunne Rising." But in Wilbur's poem the intruding daylight is not chided, evidently because to be alive, however difficult, is to be blessed. The metaphor will not withstand much scrutiny, for here, as in the case of the laundry metaphor, the drive is to get beyond the image that serves as vehicle as quickly as possible, so as to talk about the relation of soul to body, spirit to matter — those great poetic topoi introduced by the Augustine-derived title, "Love Calls Us to the Things of This World." The actual "things of this world," in 1956, it turns out, are studiously avoided. The poem refers to "rosy hands in the rising steam" — no doubt, as Eberhart remarks, an allusion to Homer's "rosy-fingered dawn" (AO 4) — but where are the real hands of those laundresses, hands that Eliot, half a century earlier, had envisioned as "lifting dingy shades in a thousand furnished rooms?"

"Poems," Richard Wilbur remarked in an interview, "are not addressed to anybody in particular. The poem . . . is a conflict with disorder, not a message from one person to another."[5] But the "conflict with disorder" in "Love Calls Us" is carefully removed from any arena where resistance might take place: the bedsheets and alarm clock cannot, so to speak, talk back; indeed, we might say that they really have been "laundered." It is the poet as producer, not the poet inside the poem who is in control, and thus there is no room for deviance, no message from one person to another. Order/disorder: terms that Wilbur's model, John Donne, grounded in the actual scientific and theological circumstances of his day, here become mere counters, uncontested abstract moral categories that can become the stuff of poetic metaphor outside of any specific cultural context.

Such claims for timelessness and universality were characteristic of the mid-fifties moment; indeed, "Love Calls Us to the Things of This World" has interesting affinities to what was billed as the "greatest photographic exhibition of all time," Edward Steichen's *Family of Man*, which was drawing huge crowds at the Museum of Modern Art in 1956 and then traveled around the world. Carl Sandburg, who provided the Preface for the catalog (which became a best-selling book), exclaims:

> Everywhere is love and love-making, weddings and babies from generation to generation keeping the Family of Man alive and continuing. Everywhere the sun, moon and stars, the climates and weathers, have meanings for people. Though meanings vary, we are alike in all countries and tribes in trying to read what sky, land and sea say to us. Alike and ever alike we are on all continents in the need of love, food, clothing, work, speech, worship, sleep, games, dancing, fun. From tropics to arctics humanity lives with these needs so alike, so inexorably alike.[6]

So a photograph of lovers in Italy is juxtaposed to a "comparable" one from New Guinea (see figures 1 and 2), nude women, heavy with child, roaming the rocky steppes of Kordofan (figure 3) are juxtaposed to a blonde pregnant American woman, cosily nestled under a blanket contemplating the pussy cat at her feet (figure 4), and so on. Love-making, marriage, childbirth, death: these basic human activities and rites of passage, we learn from *The Family of Man*, are the same the world over.

Figure 1. *The Family of Man.*

But not everyone subscribed to this cheerful "United Nations" vision of things. In 1955–56, the Swiss-born photographer Robert Frank, who emigrated to the United States from Switzerland in 1947 at the age of twenty-three,[7] took a cross-country trip around the United States courtesy of a Guggenheim fellowship and shot some twenty thousand frames, eighty-two of which were collected in a book called *The Americans,* published by Grove Press in 1959. In his preface, Jack Kerouac exclaims: "The humour, the sadness, the EVERYTHING-ness and American-ness of these pictures! . . . the faces don't editorialize or criticize or say anything but 'This is the way we are in real life.'"[8]

What way is that? The first picture in *The Americans,* captioned *Parade — Hoboken, New Jersey* (figure 5), depicts a plain brick wall, broken by two windows, the right-hand window partly covered by a billowing American flag. Evidently, the figures inside the windows are watching a parade passing by below—perhaps, as the presence of the flag suggests, a Veterans' Day or Memorial Day parade. On the left is an elderly woman with blankly staring eyes; she wears what looks like a flowered house dress, and on her left, all but hidden by a curtain, we see an elbow encased in a sleeve

Figure 2. *The Family of Man.*

Figure 3. *The Family of Man.*

made of the same fabric. Two women, then, in some sort of uniform, perhaps the uniform of inmates of an institution. But the woman in the right-hand window, whose face is covered by the flag, is dressed differently; she wears a loose jacket or coat, and her upper hand looks like a prosthesis. Is the building a prison? A hospital? An old age home? Or just an apartment house? The picture is at once wholly literal and yet enigmatic.

The composition of the picture is divided into three almost equal parts, window, brick wall, window. Further, the horizontal rectangles—bricks, window sills, partially lowered shade in left window, and large billowing flag (which continues the lower border of the left window shade)—cre-

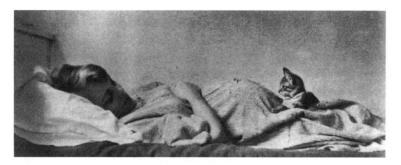

Figure 4. *The Family of Man.*

Figure 5. Robert Frank, *Parade—Hoboken, New Jersey.*

ate a deceptive grid structure, deceptive because although the windows balance one another, they fail to match. The accent is thus on separation—of one body part from another, inside from outside, the flag from the patriotic event it supposely signifies, the viewers from the viewed. The framing, moreover, heightens the sense of confinement suggested by the uniforms—if indeed that is what the matching dresses are. And, with respect to scale, the women in the windows receive much less attention than the texture of the brick wall itself.

Figure 6. Robert Frank, *Ranch Market—Hollywood.*

"Grainy and contrasty," writes John Brumfield, "the photograph is a bit on the harsh side, almost scuzzy, with a sour kind of bleakness emphasized by the immobility of the figures and the monotony of the building."[9] No "warm" and "lovely" *Family of Man* image here, no assurance that "Love Calls Us to the Things of This World." But no anger either: the contrast between the flag and what it "covers," the dreariness of urban poverty, the isolation of the women in the windows—these are presented without comment. And indeed, in the larger scheme of *The Americans,* the Hoboken scene is perhaps no "uglier" than the images of large sleek convertibles in *Drive-in Movie, Detroit* (RFA 101) or than the smiling faces of the hatted, gloved, well-off ladies in *Cocktail Party* (RFA 115). If *The Family of Man* stresses unity, Frank's America is one of emptiness and separation: in *Ranch Market—Hollywood* (figure 6), for instance, a girl stares out from behind the lunch counter, her back to another employee behind her, her face in profile, juxtaposed to the face of a cardboard Santa Claus above her head as well as an ad for "JUMBO SIZE HOT DOG 18¢." Indeed, people are not sharply differentiated from the things in their environment: the juke boxes and coffins, shiny new motorcycles and huge cars with big fins, the mailboxes on wooden poles and trash cans in the parks, the gas pumps rising like a mirage in the desert of Santa Fe, bearing a huge neon sign that says "SAVE" (see RFA 93). As for nature, even the rare grassy hillsides and bushes look as if they are made of plastic (see RFA 87).

When *The Americans* was first published, reaction was largely hostile, for its images did not conform to the ameliorist "one world" vision found in *The Family of Man,* or, for that matter, in the pages of *Life* or *Look.* At the same time, Frank's photos are hardly protest pictures; he is not making a political statement or suggesting that there is a better world elsewhere. Indeed, his purportedly "documentary" mode is intensely concerned with formal values: the way light is used, for example, to relate the curve of chairs in a dingy little cafe to the curve of the electric fan or the square shape of the television to the square table top (*Restaurant—U.S. 1 Leaving Columbia, South Carolina,* in RFA 99). Such formal repetitions subtly underscore difference: in the café shot, the empty restaurant table is contrasted to the "full" television screen, the former devoid of human life, the latter bearing the one human image in the room, but an image made only of pixels. "Robert Frank," says Kerouac, "Swiss, unobtrusive, nice, with that little camera that he raises and snaps with one hand he sucked a sad poem right out of America onto film, taking rank among the tragic poets of the world" (RFA 9).

Excessive as that last claim may be, the linkage of Frank's photography to poetry is useful: in Frank's "poeticized" images of everyday life in the fifties, a new aesthetic was in the making, the representation of a troubled identity, whose fabled "apoliticality" was much more complex than one might assume, judging from the dominant Wilburian aesthetic of the period. The "tranquillized *Fifties,*" Robert Lowell's famous epithet for the decade in his 1959 *Life Studies,*[10] seems to me a misnomer for what Kerouac, thinking of his own work as well as Frank's, refers to as the "sad poem right out of America." As we see in image after image, it has to do with the curious conjunction of the new peacetime affluence, with its promise of cultural as well as material possibility, and the nagging Cold War anxiety that the situation might just be out of control, that the "political" was too remote and too overwhelming to be processed by the individual artist. Indeed, it is the peculiar Hydra-headedness of late-fifties public discourse that defined the tone of its cutting-edge art and poetry.

Culture Shocks

The lead story of the 23 January 1956 issue of *Newsweek* was called "The Eisenhower Era." Although the president had not yet made up his mind to run again (that didn't happen until March), and although the public worried that Ike's failing health would put Nixon, who was generally disliked and mistrusted,[11] just "a heartbeat away from the presidency," Eisenhower was enormously popular. Polls gave his performance a 75 percent approval rating, and no wonder: as *Newsweek* recorded, jobs were up from 61.3 to 65 million, taxes were cut although inflation was down, and 57 percent of Americans owned their own homes as compared to 55 percent in 1952. Ten years after the end of World War II, three years after the end of the Korean War, and a decade before there was full-fledged war in Vietnam, Americans were not fighting anywhere on the globe. And even McCarthyism was losing its force: the senator, stigmatized by the Senate's condemnation motion of December 1954, was to die within the year.

In his introduction to *Colliers*'s new series "The American Tradition," Henry Steele Commager asked, "What has America meant to mankind?" His own answer was:

> It has meant a chance to prove that men could govern themselves, and to show that a vast continent with the greatest diversity of interest and mixture of peoples could nevertheless hold together as a single nation. It has meant an example to the whole world of expansion without imperialism and power without militarism. And it has meant freedom — freedom from tyrannical government, freedom from economic oppression, freedom from ignorance and superstition.
>
> These are all part of the American tradition, and so, too, those less dramatic and quieter things — the land itself, so spacious and various and beautiful, the struggle with the frontier carried on from generation to generation; the spread of plenty and well-being over a large area; the widest experiment in public education in all history, schoolhouses in every village and town, and colleges and universities in every state of the land; the elevation of the status and dignity of woman; philanthropy on a scale never before practiced; the spread of libraries and museums and orchestras and the quickening of pride in the commonwealth. All this, too, is part of the American tradition. (27 April 1956, 21)

From the hindsight of 1996, we tend to read these optimistic and patriotic declarations of '56 with skepticism, if not downright cynicism. But it is important to remember that there was a grain of truth in Commager's article: the creation of new universities, orchestras, libraries, and cultural centers *was* astonishing, as was the affluence that made it possible for, say, the young Allen Ginsberg, arriving in San Francisco in 1954 with only twenty dollars in his pocket, to land "almost immediately" a market research position with Towne-Oller Associates, an elegant firm on Montgomery Street. He had a secretary and was making up to four hundred fifty dollars a month.[12] And when, a few months later, Ginsberg told his psychiatrist that what he really wanted to do was to stop work, write poetry, spend days out of doors, visit museums and friends, and cultivate his own perceptions and visions, Dr. Hicks replied, "Well, why don't you?"—a challenge that Ginsberg quickly accepted, managing (on what?) to produce the poems to be collected in *Howl* (1956).[13] On the other coast, meanwhile, Frank O'Hara, living with a succession of friends and lovers in a succession of wonderfully cheap apartments (at about sixty dollars a month), was able to find work at the ticket booth or card shop of the Museum of Modern Art so as to support his poetic habit. But then of course O'Hara and Ginsberg were hardly members of the working class. They were Ivy Leaguers (Harvard and Columbia respectively), and in the mid-fifties Ivy Leaguers could always get by somehow.

Indeed, the affluence of the Eisenhower years was nowhere more visible than in the booming university culture (thanks to the GI Bill) and arts establishment. It was a time of ardent Francophilia: on Broadway, Julie Harris was starring in *The Lark,* Jean Anouilh's sentimental psychodrama about Joan of Arc, and Giraudoux's version of the Trojan War, *La Guerre de Troie n'aura pas lieu,* was a big hit in Christopher Fry's verse translation, *Tiger at the Gates.* The Comédie Française on tour presented Molière's *Bourgeois Gentilhomme* and Marivaux's *Arlequin poli par l'amour.* Simon and Schuster brought out an English translation of Proust's *Jean Santeuil* (reviewed in the *Nation* by Mina Curtis), Vintage published Montaigne's autobiography, Baudelaire's art criticism (under the title *The Mirror of Art*), Bergson's *Comedy,* Gide's *Strait is the Gate* and his *Journals,* and Camus's *Rebel.* And Harcourt Brace published a new translation of Molière's *Le Misanthrope* by none other than Richard Wilbur. It was still a time, then, when mainstream publishers brought out "serious" literary works, preferably French or at least foreign (but rarely, in this early postwar period, German). And not only literary: Doubleday, today a largely commercial house, published a new translation of Diderot's *Rameau's Nephew,* Ortega y Gasset's *Dehumanization of Art,* Henri Frankfort's *Birth of Civilization in the Near East,* Arthur Waley's *Three Ways of Thought in Ancient China,* and, what was to be a central work for both John Cage and Jackson Mac Low, Suzuki's *Zen Buddhism, Selected Writing.*[14]

But the parameters of the "intellectual," as of the "literary," were rigorously circumscribed. A series of monthly programs on intellectuals, inaugurated by a Pittsburgh television station (WQED) and aided by special funds from the Mellon Educational and Charitable Trust, was called "Wise Men." The first Wise Man of the Month was Robert Frost. "Tapping the top of a high-toe shoe," we read in *Colliers* (27 April), "he says poems simple in sound, profound in thought, and amazes his audience with the range of his knowledge" (42). In Pittsburgh, Frost faced an audience of thousands, and he was interviewed by another Wise Man, Jonas Salk. In response to a question about poetic form, Frost made his famous declaration, "I'd as soon write free verse as play tennis with the net down," a pronouncement few established poets at the time seemed eager to quarrel with.[15] As for the larger function of poetry, Frost declared that "My poems are my adjustment to the world," a revealing statement, for *adjustment* was one of the big watchwords of the psychoanalytic fifties, the drive to be "well-adjusted" dominating so much of the personal life of the period. In Freudian parlance, moreover, "well-adjusted" was a code word for "straight": the "well-adjusted" got married, had families, and lived what were then called "normal" lives.

Perhaps playing tennis with the "net down" seemed so dangerous because the cultural order, impressively artistic and intellectual as it was at one level, could not easily deal with the tensions just beneath the surface. In the mid-fifties, the United States was the richest and most powerful country in the world but also, as one critic puts it, the "most jittery."[16] And no wonder. The Cold War, now a decade old, took a new turn in April 1956, when the new Soviet leader Khrushchev, addressing the Twentieth All-Union Party Congress in the USSR just three years after Stalin's death, denounced the previous near-thirty years of Stalinist rule as a reign of terror. Khrushchev's speech, which sent shock waves through the various European Communist parties as well as the American Left, was discussed in issue after issue of *Look* or *Colliers* or *Newsweek:* articles bear names like "Must our Air Force be Second Best?" (*Look,* 1 May), "Ex-Stalinists of the West," (*New Republic,* 9 April), "The Red Atom" (*Colliers,* 23 November), "Algeria—Can France Hold On?" (*New Republic,* 9 April), "Communism in South East Asia" (*Yale Review,* spring 1956), and so on. Anticommunism became a religion: one of the most startling articles, from the perspective of later developments, is Peter Kalischer's "Upsetting the Red Timetable," in the 6 July issue of *Colliers* (29). "Two years ago at Geneva," writes Kalischer, "South Vietnam was virtually sold down the river to the Communists. Today the spunky little Asian country is back on its own feet, thanks to a 'mandarin in a sharkskin suit,'" who was none other than President Ngo Dinh Diem. "Today," we read, "a republic nine months old, South Vietnam is alive, kicking, and pugnaciously anti-Communist." Or so it was hoped, given that, as early as 1956, according to Kalischer, 53 percent of all U.S. foreign aid was going to buttress the South Vietnamese armed forces.

But the obsession with the Soviet Union's possible and projected acts of aggression, excessive as it may strike us now that the Cold War is over, was by no means a figment of the Pentagon's imagination. For by the autumn of 1956, just two weeks before Eisenhower was reelected in a landslide and despite Khrushchev's protestations of a new era of good will, an event took place that marked a significant turning point in Cold War politics. That event was the aborted Hungarian Revolution. Fighting broke out on 23 October and, by the 28th, the Imre Nagy government had proclaimed a cease-fire, demanded withdrawal of Soviet forces from its capital, reconstituted the pre-1947 democratic parties of workers and peasants, and announced the abandonment of a one-party regime and withdrawal from the Warsaw Pact, and declared political neutrality and free elections. The Soviets hesitated but, when the West made no response, on 4 November they moved in with tanks, brutally crushing the rebellion. Almost two hundred thousand refugees came to the United States within the next few months.

The press devoted a good deal of space to the failed revolution as well as to the Poznan workers' riots that took place almost simultaneously in

Poland. Together with the Suez crisis of July (which signaled the end of British imperialism in the Middle East) and the Egypt-Israeli war that broke out in October, the year that began with such euphoric commentary on American affluence and world peace was ending in a kind of nightmare. No longer could the United States trust in Khrushchev's "revisionist" intentions. Even the *Nation,* which in the earlier months of 1956 had reported enthusiastically about the new Five-Year Plan for consumer goods (Alexander Werth, "Russia's Hopes for 1960: Steel, Power and Food," 18 February), and about the Soviets' good intentions so far as disarmament was concerned (Paul Wohl and Alexander Werth, "New Soviet Blueprint: Challenge to the West," 3 March), was forced to admit that the Russians were not to be trusted.

The difficulties abroad were matched at home by the aftershocks of the Desegregation of the Schools Act of 1954. Indeed, although one would never know it, in reading, say, the *Kenyon Review* or even the *Black Mountain Review,* the race wars were an especially poisonous feature of the discourse of these years. The Montgomery bus boycott, which began in December 1955, came to a head in January 1956 and brought Martin Luther King Jr. to national attention. Media response to these events was typically one of fear and caution. In the 24 September issue of the *New Republic,* L. D. Reddick, then a student at Fisk University, reviewed Robert Penn Warren's little book, *Segregation: The Inner Conflict in the South.* Warren, who was teaching at Vanderbilt, was extremely cautious about integration. It shouldn't, he observed, come too soon, for the Negro was not ready for it. Such caution was the theme of a *Look* special feature (3 April) evaluating the Desegregation Act. The issue begins by reprinting the famous Supreme Court Decision, as expounded by Chief Justice Earl Warren: "We conclude that in the field of public education the doctrine of 'separate but equal' has no place." But this view is countered in Senator Sam Ervin Jr.'s "The Case for Segregation," with its current wisdom that "people like to socialize with their own" (32). And in an ostensibly neutral article called "Fear Underlies the Conflict," William Atwood writes:

Whatever they may tell you, white Southerners are afraid of the Negro in their midst. And they are afraid of him today as never before. For the

Negro no longer behaves like the amiable "dark" who knew his place and did not question the white man's right to give orders.

The fear is partly politieal. In the Black Belt, white men shudder at the prospect of Negro bloc-voting that might put them under the jurisdiction of colored officials. Still haunted by the nightmare of Reconstruction, they now feel that any concession to Negro demands for equality means another surrender, another Appomattox.

The fear is also economic. Industrialization has enabled Negroes to earn wages that are making them independent of an economic order based on discrimination. . . . A negro with money in the bank is no longer at the mercy of the dominant race; he becomes a customer to be catered to.

And the fear is social, with profound sexual undertones. To a white Southerner, classroom integration implies a kind of social equality that does not exist even on an assembly line. He will tell you that sooner or later, some Negro boy will be walking his daughter home from school, staying for supper, taking her to the movies . . . and then your Southern friend asks you the inevitable, the clinching question, "Would *you* want your daughter to marry a Nigra?"

And there is nothing you can say to quiet his fears . . . that mixed schools will "mongrelize" the race. (27)

It may have taken an outsider like Robert Frank to show us what everyday life in the South looked like in 1956 (see *Funeral — Saint Helena, South Carolina*, RFA 121, and *Charleston, South Carolina*, RFA 35). In *Trolley — New Orleans* (figure 7), for example, seven people — up front, a formally dressed white man and, behind him, white woman, in the rear, a shirt-sleeved black man and casually attired black woman, and in the center, two white children, dressed up in what look like party clothes, with their all but invisible black nanny hovering behind them — are placed within a tight grid: windows separated by metal strips, upper rectangular panels, reflecting only dimly what is going by outside the streetcar, and the metal surface below the window, again broken up into rectangles, separated by a studded strip. The grid indicates not only race but gender separation and hierarchy: in all three cases, the man (or little boy) comes first.

Figure 7. Robert Frank, *Trolley—New Orleans.*

None of the passengers look at one another; rather, all are looking out at something—but what? The white man's face is veiled by the reflection of the glass because his window is down, the white woman's head is cropped as is the black woman's elbow. But whereas the whites sit facing front in "normal" position, the children and the black man and women are turned ninety degrees, facing out of the window, the black woman in back looking over her left shoulder. The photograph makes no overt comment on segregation, the faces of the blacks at the rear of the car, for instance, showing no anger. But the image of the jail-like grid is there, startling testimony that the Family of Man, the entity that Sandburg called "one big family hugging close to the ball of Earth for its life and being," is more accurately an aggregate of separate beings placed together in a series of arbitrarily defined spaces that have been assigned to them. "Robert," said Allen Ginsberg in a 1985 piece on Frank's work, "had invented a new way of lonely solitary chance conscious seeing, in the little Leica format. . . . Spontaneous glance—accident truth."[17]

Counterpoetics

"Lonely solitary chance conscious seeing": Ginsberg might have been talking about his own poetry or, for that matter, about the "New American Poetry" as it manifested itself in 1956, the year of *Howl* as well as of some of Frank O'Hara's most important "lunch poems,"[18] and of John Ashbery's *Some Trees,* which won the Yale Younger Poets Prize for 1956. Of these poets, all of whom were gay and hence of necessity outsiders in fifties America, only Ginsberg was, in any overt sense, political, but even for a self-styled counterculture figure like Ginsberg, the meaningful access to a larger public sphere seems to have become increasingly problematic.

A terrifying and ideologically charged war had just been "won," but before the lessons of that war and the Holocaust could in any way be assimilated, much less digested, our former allies, the Soviets, were shown to have committed genocide that rivaled Hitler's—genocide, moreover, against their own people, beginning with the destruction of the peasantry in the course of the collectivization of the farms and culminating in the gulag. The cycle of totalitarianism and death seemed to be starting all over again, this time with the new threat of nuclear weapons. At the same time, the Cold War was just that—cold—which is to say a very distant reality to those who actually lived their everyday lives in the New York or San Francisco of the later fifties. If you were a male white poet, even a gay male white poet in 1956, the reality of everyday life was the reality of possibility: new ballets to see and great Italian movies to go to, new travel possibilities to the art centers of Europe, the Buddhist shrines of Japan and India, the Mayan culture of Uxmal and Palenque; new art galleries showing breakthrough painting and performances of John Cage's "Music of Changes." At the same time, the repressive bourgeois climate of the fifties, with its par-for-the-course white male dominance and homophobia, placed unspoken but very real constraints on the vibrant new arts community.

Social critique, thirties-style, was out of the question, there being no specific "them" to blame for international conditions and no commitment, as yet, to focus on the plight of minorities at home. Better not to think about politics at all and to concentrate, as fifties poetry did with a vengeance, on personal fulfillment. Even Ginsberg's "angelheaded hipsters," after all, were those who, in the words of "Howl," "drag[ged] themselves through the negro streets" (notably not the hipsters' streets but the streets of Harlem) "looking for an angry fix," or "drove crosscountry seventytwo hours to find out if I had a vision or you had a vision or he had a vision to find out Eternity."[19] En route to vision, there was a good deal of contradiction, as in Ginsberg's marvelously comic, marvelously painful ode of 1956 called "America." It begins:

America I've given you all and now I'm nothing.
America two dollars and twentyseven cents January 17, 1956.
I can't stand my own mind.
America when will we end the human war?
Go fuck yourself with your atom bomb.
I don't feel good don't bother me.[20]

Warren Tallmann rightly called "America" "the nearest thing to a purely clown poem Ginsberg has."[21] It's not that the poet isn't genuinely worried about the atomic bomb and the Cold War, but the relationship between public and private has become so fractured that the strongest urge is to opt out. "I don't feel good don't bother me" is a candid admission that he, at any rate, doesn't want to participate.[22] The only way to respond, it seems, is to play the fool:

When can I go into the supermarket and buy what I need with my
good looks?
America after all it is you and I who are perfect not the next world.
Your machinery is too much for me.
You made me want to be a saint.
There must be some other way to settle this argument.

(AGCP 146)

But what is rarely remarked is that the droll self-deprecation we find in "America" is itself a function of affluence. Consider the following lines:

I smoke marijuana every chance I get.
I sit in my house for days on end and stare at the roses in the
closet. . . .
My psychoanalyst thinks I'm perfectly right.
I won't say the Lord's Prayer

I have mystical visions and cosmic vibrations
America I still haven't told you what you did to Uncle Max after he
    came over from Russia. . . .

I'm obsessed by Time Magazine.
I read it every week.
Its cover stares at me every time I slink past the corner candystore.
I read it in the basement of the Berkeley Public Library.
It's always telling me about responsibility. Businessmen are serious.
    Movie producers are serious. Everybody's serious but me.
It occurs to me that I am America,
I am talking to myself again.
Asia is rising against me.
I haven't got a chinaman's chance.
I'd better consider my national resources.
My national resources consist of two joints of marijuana millions of
    genitals an unpublishable private literature that jetplanes 1400 miles
    an hour and twenty-five-thousand mental institutions.
I say nothing about my prisons nor the millions of underprivileged
    who
    live in my flowerpots under the light of five hundred suns.
I have abolished the whorehouses of France, Tangiers is the next to go.
My ambition is to be President despite the fact that I'm a Catholic.
                                                            (AGCP 146–47)

The latter part of this passage acts as an index to the U.S. "concerns" of
the day, as reported in the newspapers—the U.S. obsession with communist China, the flaunting of "national resources," the burgeoning prison
and mental hospital population (Ginsberg knew the latter at first hand),
and the public indifference to the underprivileged "liv[ing] in my flower-
pots" (a foreshadowing of the homelessness to come two decades later).
And Ginsberg is wonderfully deft at weaving together the clichés of press
talk ("Asia is rising against [us]") with ordinary racist cliché ("I haven't got
a chinaman's chance"), memories of personal oppression, as in the reference to Uncle Max, jokes about middle-class morality ("I have abolished
the whorehouses of France, Tangiers is the next to go"—this latter, a ref-

erence to William Burroughs, who went there for the sake of the drug culture), and finally with the common wisdom of the day (*pace* then Senator John F. Kennedy) that a Catholic could not be elected president in the Protestant United States.

But note that Ginsberg's absurdist "holy litany" is predicated on the availability of possessions undreamt of by the citizens of other nations in 1956—plenty of free time, liquor, marijuana, the public library, and money to pay the psychoanalyst—so that the "national resources" he lampoons so brilliantly are also ones he takes for granted. Again, the catalog "America free Tom Mooney / America save the Spanish Loyalists / America Sacco & Vanzetti must not die / America I am the Scottboro boys" and the spoof on anticommunist paranoia in Ginsberg's "cigar-store Cherokee"[23] parody dialect—"The Russia wants to eat us alive. The Russia's power mad. She wants to take our cars from out our garages. . . . Him big bureaucracy running our filling stations" (AGCP 147–48)—is undercut by the campy conclusion:

> America is this correct?
> I'd better get right down to the job.
> It's true I don't want to join the Army or turn lathes in precision
>   parts factories,
>   I'm nearsighted and psychopathic anyway.
> America I'm putting my queer shoulder to the wheel.
>
> (AGCP 148)

Here is a twist to "Love Calls Us to the Things of This World" that Richard Wilbur didn't have in mind. Ginsberg's candor and colloquialism, his pointed imagery (so different from Wilbur's elegant metaphysical conceits), his defiantly antipoetic, nonscannable chantlike verse, his willingness to let it all hang out, his refusal to play the game, his admission of weakness—these were surely a breath of fresh air in the poetic world of 1956. Indeed, the stunning conclusion, with its allusion to Whitman's equally queer if more decorous apostrophes to America, remains a watershed in postwar American poetry. Yet—and this is a signature of the time—no matter how "oppositional" Ginsberg's stance purports to be, its disengagement ("drop out," "get high," "have sex") may strike us as problematic. Unlike its models—Whitman's "Song of Myself" and "I Hear

America Singing," Blaise Cendrars's "Easter in New York," Apollinaire's "Zone," Mayakovsky's "Cloud in Trousers"—poems where personal vision goes hand in hand with serious social critique—here putting one's "queer shoulder to the wheel" is not likely to lead to anything. "I'm in my house for days on end and stare at the roses in the closet": Is this a wise passiveness? or just self-indulgence?

Perhaps the difficulty is that, brilliant as the Ginsberg of "America" was at lampooning media talk and Cold War sloganeering, he didn't himself have any clear idea how government should, in fact, operate. Indeed, the media, like it or not, tended to be the only source of a given poet's knowledge of political events. When, for example, William Carlos Williams introduced the image of the atomic bomb in "Asphodel, That Greeny Flower," [24] he was referring, not to anything he had personally witnessed (as would generally have been the case before the Second World War), but to the image of the mushroom cloud that became almost a logo in the magazines and film clips of the period.

A more workable poetic, then, seemed to be one that avoided political statement altogether. If such a choice sounds like a throwback to a Richard Wilbur "universalist" position, let's consider how the "nonpolitical" works when the lyric "I" is placed in an actual, everyday context. Take Frank O'Hara's "A Step Away from Them":

> It's my lunch hour, so I go
> for a walk among the hum-colored
> cabs. First down the sidewalk
> where laborers feed their dirty
> glistening torsos sandwiches
> and Coca-Cola, with yellow helmets
> on. They protect them from falling
> bricks, I guess. Then onto the
> avenue where skirts are flipping
> above heels and blow up over
> grates. The sun is hot, but the
> cabs stir up the air. I look
> at bargains in wristwatches. There
> are cats playing in the sawdust.

to Times Square, where the sign
blows smoke over my head, and higher
the waterfall pours lightly. A
Negro stands in a doorway with a
toothpick, languorously agitating.
A blonde chorus girl clicks: he
smiles and rubs his chin. Everything
suddenly honks: it is 12:40 of
a Thursday.
        Neon in daylight is a
great pleasure, as Edwin Denby would
write, as are light bulbs in daylight.
I stop for a cheeseburger at JULIET'S
CORNER. Giulietta Masina, wife of
Federico Fellini, *è bell' attrice.*
And chocolate malted. A lady in
foxes on such a day puts her poodle
in a cab.
        There are several Puerto
Ricans on the avenue today, which
makes it beautiful and warm. First
Bunny died, then John Latouche,
then Jackson Pollock. But is the
earth as full as life was full, of them?
And one has eaten and one walks,
past the magazines with nudes
and the posters for BULLFIGHT and
the Manhattan Storage Warehouse,
which they'll soon tear down. I
used to think they had the Armory
Show there.
        A glass of papaya juice
and back to work. My heart is in my
pocket, it is Poems by Pierre Reverdy.[25]

In this famous "lunch poem," public events, political or otherwise, obviously play much less of a role than in Ginsberg's "America." Indeed, the poem's oppositionality would seem to be all on the level of rhetoric. For Wilbur's highly crafted stanzas, O'Hara substitutes a nervous, short, tautly suspended free-verse line;[26] for Wilbur's studied impersonality, O'Hara substitutes the intimate address, whether to a friend or to himself, he describes in "Personism";[27] and for Wilbur's elaborately contrived metaphor, his "I" substitutes persons, places, and objects that are palpable, real, and closely observed.

The poet's lunch-hour walk, presumably from his workplace, the Museum of Modern Art on 53d Street between 5th and 6th Avenues in the direction of Times Square, is full of enticing sights and sounds: cabs hum, laborers in hard hats (whose "dirty / glistening torsos" the gay poet subliminally desires) are eating sandwiches and drinking Coca-Cola, the skirts of girls in high heels (the then proverbial office uniform) "flip" and "blow up over / grates," the myriad cut-rate jewelry shops on 6th Avenue try to outdo each other with "bargains in wristwatches," the huge Chesterfield ad above Times Square blows smoke at the cigarette-friendly pedestrian, a black man, hanging out in a doorway makes eyes at a blonde chorus girl walking by, and the Puerto Ricans on the Avenue are enough to make it, by the poet's dadaesque reasoning, "beautiful and warm." Pleasurable, too, are the absurd contradictions representative of New York life: the "Negro . . . with a toothpick, langorously agitating," the "neon in daylight" and "lightbulbs in daylight," the lunchspots with incongruous names like "Juliet's Corner" that serve cheeseburgers and chocolate malteds, the ladies with poodles who wear fox furs even on the hottest summer day, and so on.

But, as James E. B. Breslin noted in his excellent essay on O'Hara (JEB 210–49), the poet seems to be "a step away," not only from the dead friends (Bunny Lang, John Latouche, Jackson Pollock) he will memorialize later in the poem, but from all the persons and objects in his field of vision. "Sensations," writes Breslin, "disappear almost as soon as they are presented. Objects and people . . . remain alien to a poet who can never fully possess them" (JEB 218). For Breslin, the poet's malaise, his inability to hold on to things, to move toward any kind of transcendence beyond the fleeting, evanescent moment is largely a function of O'Hara's unique psychological make-up. But since, as Breslin himself suggests, O'Hara's fabled "openness is an admitted act of contrivance and duplicity" (JEB 231), we might consider the role culture plays in its formation.

Consider, to begin with, the repeated metonymic displacements of specific metaphors. New York's yellow cabs are compared to bees ("hum-colored"), but their color relates them to the laborers' "yellow helmets," worn to "protect them from falling / bricks, I guess." Yellow helmets, yellow jackets: the poem's brilliance is to connect these disparate items and yet to leave the import of the connection hanging. Is the tentative explanation ("I guess") about "falling bricks" tongue-in-cheek or serious? In the same vein, "skirts" are no sooner seen "flipping / above heels" in the hot air than they are described as "blow[ing] up over / grates," (perhaps an allusion to Marilyn Monroe in *The Seven Year Itch*), even as the sign high up in Times Square "blows smoke over my head." "Blow," for O'Hara, always has sexual connotations, but "blow up," soon to be the title of Antonioni's great film, also points to the vocabulary of nuclear crisis omnipresent in the public discourse of these years. The muted and intermittent sounds of skirts flipping, smoke blowing, cabs stirring up the air, and cats playing in the sawdust give way to the moment when "Everything / suddenly honks: it is 12:40 of / a Thursday." Here sound is illogically related to time: gridlock in the streets, an absolutely ordinary event in midtown Manhattan, somehow makes the poet look up at the big clock above Times Square and have the surreal sense that time is coming to a stop. The connection is momentary (rather like an air-raid siren going off), but it changes the pedestrian's mood. At 12:40, at any rate, lunch hour has passed the halfway point, and now thoughts of the dead come to the fore—or were they already there in the reference to the "sawdust" in which the cats play? The pronoun "I" shifts to the impersonal "one"; "neon in daylight" is no longer such a pleasure, revealing as it does the "magazines with nudes / and the posters for BULLFIGHT," and the mortuary-like "Manhattan Storage Warehouse / which they'll soon tear down," the reference to the armory in the next line linking death with war.

By this time, the "great pleasure" of the poet's lunch hour has been occluded by anxiety. Not the fear of anything in particular: O'Hara's New York is still a long way from the crime and drug-ridden Manhattan of the nineties. On the contrary, the poet's anxiety seems to stem from the sheer glut of sensation: so many new and colorful things to see—new movies starring Giulietta Masina, new Balanchine ballets for Edwin Denby to write about, new editions of Reverdy poems, new buildings going up all over town. Colorful, moreover, is now associated with persons of color: the poet, exoticizing the Other, takes pleasure in the "click" between the "languorously agitating Negro" and "blonde chorus girl" (a sly parody of the scare question being asked with regularity in the wake of the Desegregation Act of 1954, "Would you want your daughter to marry a Nigra?"),[28] and he observes playfully that "There are several Puerto Ricans on the avenue today, which / makes it beautiful and warm." Yet—and here the contrast replicates the juxtapositions found in *Look* or *Colliers*—for every exotic sight and delightful sensation, there are falling bricks, bullfights, blow outs, armories, mortuaries, and, as the name Juliet's Corner suggests, tombs. In this context, ironically, the actual death references in the poem ("First / Bunny died") function almost as overkill.

The "glass of papaya juice" of the penultimate lines sums it up nicely. Papaya, now sold in every large city supermarket, was a new commodity in the fifties; the recent Puerto Rican émigrés (who, for O'Hara, make it "beautiful and warm") were opening juice bars all over Manhattan. Papaya juice was considered not only exotic but healthful, the idea of drinking fruit and vegetable drinks that are good for you being itself a novelty in this period. The juice bar O'Hara frequents on the way "back to work" makes a wonderful contrast to the hamburger joint where he had lunch. Cheeseburger & malted: this all-American meal, soon to be marketed around the globe by McDonald's, gives way to the glass of papaya juice— a new "foreign" import. But the juice the poet ingests is also contrasted to the heart which is in "my pocket" and which is "Poems by Pierre Reverdy." The heart is not in the body where it belongs but in a book, placed externally, in the poet's pocket. And again it is a foreign vintage.

In the postwar economy of the late fifties, such new foreign imports created an enticing world of *jouissance*. But what is behind all those pleasurable "neon in daylight" surfaces and desirable "dirty / glistening torsos" that attract the poet? For O'Hara, there is no anchor, even as the heart is no longer the anchor of the self. If, as a slightly later poem begins, "Khrushchev is coming on the right day!" (FOH 340), "right" refers absurdly, not to any possible political rationale, but, with wonderfully absurd logic, to the fact that the September weather is so invigorating, with its "cool graced light" and gusty winds, and the poet so ecstatic in his new love affair with Vincent Warren, that surely it must be a good day for Khrushchev's visit! The public sphere thus becomes a cartoon backdrop against which the poet's "real" life unfolds. And yet that life, as we see in "Khrushchev" as in "A Step Away from Them," is everywhere imbricated with race and gender politics, with thoughts of dispersal ("New York seems blinding and my tie is blowing up the street / I wish it would blow off") and death. Apolitical? Intentionally, yes, but very much itself a construction of the postwar moment.

Indeed, interiority becomes itself politically charged. When O'Hara's close friend John Ashbery won the Yale Younger Poets prize for *Some Trees* (1956), its seemingly unanchored images, so far removed from the extended metaphysical conceits of Wilbur or the young Lowell, were considered hopelessly hermetic.[29] The poet himself was not available to defend it; he had left the United States for Paris in 1955, not to return for a decade. In a 1988 interview, Ashbery sketches in the 1950s background:

> I couldn't write anything from about the summer of 1950 to the end of 1951. It was a terribly depressing period both in the world and in my life. I had no income or prospects. The Korean War was on and I was afraid I might be drafted. There were anti-homosexual campaigns. I was called up for the draft and I pleaded that as a reason not to be drafted. Of course this was recorded and I was afraid that we'd all be sent to concentration camps if McCarthy had his own way. It was a very dangerous and scary period.[30]

This ex post facto explanation may have more to do with Ashbery's self-positioning in the late 1980s than with the realities of his day-to-day life in 1956. The "danger" and "scariness" that he talks of do enter the poetry, but its mediations are multiple. Here is "Two Scenes," the opening poem of *Some Trees:*

> I
> We see us as we truly behave:
> From every corner comes a distinctive offering.
> The train comes bearing joy;

The sparks it strikes illuminate the table.
Destiny guides the water-pilot, and it is destiny.
For long we hadn't heard so much news, such noise.
The day was warm and pleasant.
"We see you in your hair,
Air resting around the tips of mountains."

II
A fine rain anoints the canal machinery.
This is perhaps a day of general honesty
Without example in the world's history
Though the fumes are not of a singular authority
And indeed are dry as poverty.
Terrific units are on an old man
In the blue shadow of some paint cans
As laughing cadets say, "In the evening
Everything has a schedule, if you can find out what it is." [31]

Ironically enough, this particular poem was first published in the *Kenyon Review* (spring 1956), where it was wedged between two quite conventional poems.[32] Given its title and its "normal" stanzaic appearance (two nine-line stanzas with lines ranging from six to fifteen syllables), the *Kenyon* readership might have glanced at it and concluded that it was just another pictorial poem, with pastoral references to "tips of mountains" and "a fine rain." Those who did actually read it, however, must have been more than a little confused.

"We see us," the poem opens, "as we truly behave." Not as the familiar adage has it, "We see ourselves as others see us," and certainly not "We see ourselves as we truly *are*," but, inconsequentially, given that the other's behavior is the one thing we certainly can "see," "as we truly behave." The assertive opening statement is thus no more than tautology, even as the lines that follow convey perfectly reasonable information that doesn't add up because there is no context that relates "a" to "b." "From every corner comes a distinctive offering": a simple enough sentence and suggestive of formal ceremony: the journey of the Magi or homage to the queen on her birthday, perhaps. "The train comes bearing joy" is equally reasonable, but how do "The sparks it [the train?] strikes illuminate the table"? What table? And in line 4 the expected train conductor or engineer turns out to be a water pilot; perhaps, then, the table of line 3 was a water table. The ominously repeated reference to "destiny" defies explanation, at least at this point in the poem, but clearly the arrival of the boat (which has now replaced the train) is significant: "For long we hadn't heard so much news, such noise." Line 7, in contrast, is straightforward description: "The day was warm and pleasant" sounds like the opening of any standard short story in a high school textbook. But again the statement is undercut: the familiar pop song line "I see you in my dreams" becomes the absurd "We see you in your hair," "hair" now rhyming with the "Air" that opens the next line, a line that recalls a Chinese or Japanese brush painting where air seems to rest "around the tips of mountains." This last statement is in quotations, but who says it?

What, then, is the poem all about? In Scene II, which by no means follows I, the first five lines (the first three are rough hexameters) rhyme on unstressed suffixes of abstract nouns: "machinery," "honesty," "history," "authority," "poverty." The verse lumbers on dully, rather like badly written Skeltonics. Yet this stanza does refer back to Scene I. The fine rain anointing the canal machinery takes us back to the movements of the water pilot; perhaps he is steering his ship down the canal. The destiny that guides the pilot is real enough, since "This is perhaps a day of general honesty / Without example in the world's history / Though the fumes are not of a singular authority / And indeed as dry as poverty." A mock announcement is about to be made but it never occurs. Rather, the poet's camera zeros in on "an old man / In the blue shadow of some paint cans." Picasso (and Stevens's) "man with the blue guitar"? Or just an old house-painter? We can never be sure: "As laughing cadets say, 'In the evening / Everything has a schedule, if you can find out what it is.'"

The last line with its Wittgensteinian twist might serve as an epigraph for any number of Ashbery poems and, for that matter, for the language poems that are their successors. On the one hand, procedure is all—everything has a schedule, a formula, an instruction manual. On the other, you can never "find out what it is." But the "if" ensures that we keep on looking. And, indeed, "Two Scenes" is not at all nonreferential. When we reread it, we note that it foregrounds the basic need to decipher what one sees—to catch that "distinctive offering" coming to us "from every corner."

And the ciphers are indeed tantalizing: the train, the sparks that illuminate the table, the water pilot making his way through the canal in a fine rain, the canal fumes, the blue shadow of the paint cans, the laughing cadets.

One way to decipher these suggestive images is to read the poem as a cultural as well as a lyrical text. The mid-fifties, as we have seen in Henry Steele Commager's paean to America, was a period bloated with patriotic and nationalist slogans. "Destiny guides the water-pilot and it is destiny," surely echoes Roosevelt's ringing "I have a rendezvous with destiny" as well as the Hollywood film *God Is My Co-Pilot.* "This is perhaps a day . . . without example in the world's history" recalls the president's reference to 7 December (Pearl Harbor) as a day that shall live in infamy, even as "general amnesty" punningly and absurdly reappears as "general honesty." At the same time, Ashbery's "story line" alludes to the drive toward epiphany so characteristic of *Kenyon Review* short stories ("The sparks it strikes illuminate the table"), as well as to the relentlessly Freudian master narrative then governing the ways in which "we truly behave." In Ashbery's poem there is not an image that we haven't seen somewhere else (think of all the fifties movies where a train chuffs into town, purportedly bringing "joy"), not a reference that hasn't been recycled from another source, like the pop songs alluded to in "We see you in your hair." And the laughing cadets serve as a reminder of military operations, of the boy soldiers about to be given a schedule, but for what? It seems that even here war is not so far away.

Ashbery's lines are ungainly, his language designedly antipoetic. Allusion, used pointedly and sparingly in poems of the Wilbur tradition, is now the very fabric of the poem — everything alludes to something, if you can find out what it is. Unlike Wilbur, Ashbery makes no claim to know "the things of the world"; indeed, things have become so much "canal machinery," as equivocal as Robert Frank's quite literal but ultimately opaque images. Again, Ashbery does not place himself at the center of the poem. "I" becomes "we" becomes "you": the shifting pronoun suggests that, in Michael Davidson's words, "identity is something that can be manipulated and performed, rather than something that one *is* ontologically." [33] A similar, if less extreme, constructivist version of identity is found in O'Hara (especially in "In Memory of My Feelings"), as well as in the contradictory self-presentations in Ginsberg's "America." We are, in any case, a long way from Robert Frost's "Wise Man of the Month" declarations that characterized the public discourse of 1956, such as it was, on "educational" television.

Ashbery's lyric mode in this, the very first of the texts in his *Selected Poems,* thus has enormous implications for the poetry of our own time. In 1956, as I suggested earlier, public spectacle and political discourse, especially as filtered through the media, had become at once so threatening and yet so remote that the easiest poetic (or artistic) path was to pretend they didn't exist. Better to concentrate, as did *The Family of Man* and "Love Calls Us to the Things of This World," on such "universals" as sexual love and friendship, the relation of body and soul, birth and death. In this context, the poetic choices made by Ashbery, like those of O'Hara, produced an important alternative lyric mode that I would call "hyper-realist." Like Robert Frank's scuzzy, grainy images of juke boxes and drive-in movies, this poetry refuses all idealization and metaphysics in favor of a superliteralist rendition, in which "We see us as we truly behave." In Ashbery's or O'Hara's documentary but mysterious images, the bourgeois world is not rejected; on the contrary, its pop songs, movies, and cultural icons have been so strongly internalized that we can no longer separate their language from the poets' own.

"Counterculture" poetics of the 1950s is thus a far cry from the avant-garde of the early century. Whereas, for example, the Russian avant-garde of the 1910s and 1920s (Khlebnikov, Mayakovsky, Akhmatova) was committed to the overthrow of the old order—to the creation of a new utopian, quite sharply defined society—the "oppositional" poetry of the fifties was cool (the temperature of the Cold War) rather than hot, mordant and witty performance rather than its more contemplative, engaged, and analytical European postwar counterpart, as found in, say, the lyric of Paul Celan or Ingeborg Bachmann. War as actual reality (rather than as newspaper report or television feature on nuclear testing) was very much "a step away from them." Thus, when violent upheavals did occur, as they did in Suez in July or in Hungary in October of 1956, O'Hara, Ashbery, and even the overtly political Allen Ginsberg made no commentary, preoccupied, as they seemed to be, by personal questions. Like Robert Frank, who produced brilliant diagnostic images of blacks in the South but stayed far away from the sit-ins in Montgomery, the poets were literally gun-shy.

Potential war and revolution: these far away cataclysms turned television close-ups were all but impossible to absorb into one's poetic discourse. "Everything," as Ashbery put it in "Two Scenes," "has a schedule if you can find out what it is." The poignancy of this particular moment in our cultural history is that "everything" no longer pointed at anything in particular.

5. Lucent and Inescapable Rhythms

Metrical "Choice" and Historical Formation

What place does "prose"—or what looks like "prose"—have in late twentieth-century poetry? In his recent *Poet's Prose: The Crisis in American Verse,* Stephen Fredman declares: "I have felt for a number of years that the most talented poets of my own postwar generation and an increasing number from previous generations have turned to prose as a form somehow most consonant with a creative figuration of our time."[1] Fredman proceeds to study the special kind of prose used by Williams in *Kora in Hell,* by Creeley in *Presences,* by Ashbery in *Three Poems,* and finally by such experimental contemporaries as David Antin and the younger Language poets. At the same time, others have dismissed what we might call the "prose phenomenon" as merely beside the point. Denise Levertov, for example, sees the prose texts of certain Language poets as no more than "rehashed Gertrude Stein veneered with seventies semantics."[2]

In his *Free Verse: An Essay on Prosody* (1980), Charles O. Hartman takes what is surely the sensible position: he adopts Jeremy Bentham's practical definition that "when the lines run all the way to the right margin it is prose; when this fails to happen it is [verse]." Who can object to such good common sense? "*Verse,*" says Hartman, "*is language in lines. This distinguishes it from prose.* . . . This is not really a satisfying distinction, as it stands, but it is the only one that works absolutely. The fact that we can tell verse from prose on sight, with very few errors . . . indicates that the basic perceptual difference must be very simple. Only lineation fits the requirements."[3]

This definition is adequate enough if we bear in mind that it distinguishes prose and *verse,* not prose and *poetry.* But although Hartman himself does recognize that " 'Prose-poems' exist," most critics take the next step and equate poetry with verse, as Hartman defines it. Here is Richard A. Lanham's account in *Analyzing Prose* (1983):

> To print utterances as prose amounts, in our time, to a fundamental stylistic decision. In prose we expect not only a particular range of topics but a transparent style to express them clearly. . . . But with poetry, just the opposite—all the poetic virtues. The poet need not be grammatically correct, he'll talk about feeling not fact and he'll do so in a self-conscious metaphorical way. We expect to look *through* prose, to the subject beneath, but *at* poetry where the language forms part of the subject.[4]

Lanham very sensibly points out that, as readers, we respond differently to the print format of "prose" than to that of "verse." But notice that the word *verse* is now, quite simply, replaced by the word *poetry,* the implication being that the two are identical. It seems that in a century in which "free verse" has largely superseded all the traditional metrical forms, we must hold onto something to give us a sense that poetry as a mode of discourse survives. Lineation, the creation of discourse that does not run all the way to the right margin, is the saving grace. Not that all lineated texts are good poems, but it is their status as lineated texts that allows them to be considered as poems in the first place.

So much for the common wisdom. A very different view is presented in Henri Meschonnic's monumental study, *Critique du rythme: Anthropologie historique du langage.* "Historically, poetically, and linguistically," declares Meschonnic, "there are differences of degree, not of kind, between *the proses and the verses,*"[5] and, accordingly, all binary models (verse/prose; image-full language/non-image-full language; poetry as ordered language/prose as the absence of order, and so on) are wholly reductive. Even Bakhtin's famous distinction between lyric poetry as monologic and prose fiction as potentially dialogic crumbles, so Meschonnic argues, when applied to say, Ezra Pound's *Cantos.*

Meschonnic gives countless examples from around the world of discourse that may be construed as "prose" or "poetry," as the case may be.

In the ninth century, the word *prose* was used to refer to a liturgical prose sequence structured by the assonance of *as* so as to prolong the sonority of the *Alleluia*. Eventually this recitative was lineated and passed into the realm of "poetry." Or again, Boris Eikhenbaum, studying the "prose" of Gogol's *Overcoat,* discovered that the ratio of accented syllables to total number of syllables was precisely that of contemporary iambic meter, as found in the poems of Mayakovsky (HM 461).

Indeed, free verse à la Mayakovsky (a poet who echoed Pound in his declaration that "one must make verses with all of one's life and not by fishing for trochees and iambs") must, so Meschonnic argues, be construed historically. "Free verse is just a passage, a moment, not only of a cultural situation, but of the unity of discourse which contains it and which is the poem." For "it is the poem that makes the free-verse line, not the line that makes the poem" (HM 605). Further, the prominence of free verse must be understood as part of the modernist destabilization of the notion of the poem as object. But the poet is no more "free" vis-à-vis the alexandrine. These forms are, after all, inscribed in a particular culture; they are givens. As Anthony Easthope puts it, "Just as poetry is always a specific poetic discourse, so line organization [or nonlinear organization] always takes a specific historical form, and so is ideological." [6]

These are, I think, important reminders, for we tend to forget that the poet is, as Meschonnic puts it, inevitably "ventriloquized by his or her tradition." In this context, metrical choice becomes an important indicator of the historical and cultural formation in which it takes place. The question for us, as readers of contemporary poetry, is then not, "Is it a good thing for, say, Lyn Hejinian to have written *My Life* in prose?" but rather, "What does it mean that she chose to do so?"

What I propose to do here is to historicize this question by examining the status of four texts, each of which represent a particular moment in the history, or, so to speak, the geography of poetic form: (1) Goethe's early romantic lyric, "Wandrers Nachtlied" (Wanderer's Nightsong) of 1780, (2) Arthur Rimbaud's prose poem "Les Ponts" (The Bridges) of c. 1873, (3) William Carlos Williams's 1916 free-verse poem, "Good Night," and (4) Samuel Beckett's 1972 composition called "Still." All four refer to what is roughly the same subject matter: a moment of silent contemplation when all the elements of the scene stand out in sudden sharp relief. But between Goethe's "Ruh" and Beckett's "Still," two centuries have intervened: by 1972, when Beckett was composing his text, the poet could not, in John Ashbery's words, "say it that way any more." How and why this is the case is my subject.

"Natural" Metrics

Goethe's "Wandrers Nachtlied" (Wanderer's Nightsong) was written on the night of 6 September 1780 in the mountains at Ilmenau above Weimar, where Goethe had accompanied his master, the young Duke Karl August. It was first recorded, evidently in a moment of inspiration, in pencil on the wall of the mountain hut on the Gickelhahn, where the poet spent the night. The same evening, Goethe wrote one of his nightly letters to his mistress Charlotte von Stein:

> On the Gickelhahn, the highest peak of the range . . . I have taken refuge, so as to escape from the turmoil of the town, the complaints, the demands, the hopeless confusion of mankind. If I could only record all the thoughts I have had today there would be worthwhile things among them.
>
> My dearest, I descended into the Hermmansteiner Cave, to the place where you accompanied me, and found the S, which stands out as sharply as if it had been carved yesterday; I kissed it and kissed it so often that the porphyry seemed to give breath to the scent of the whole earth as if in response. I prayed to the hundred-headed god who has so greatly advanced and changed me and yet has preserved your love and this cliff for me, to let me continue to grow and to make me more worthy of your love.
>
> The sky is quite clear and I am going out to enjoy the sunset. The view is extensive but plain.
>
> The sun has set. It is the landscape of which I made a drawing for you when it was covered with rising mist. Now it is as clear and quiet as a large and beautiful Soul, at its calmest and most satisfied.
>
> If there weren't, here and there, some mists rising from the mines, the whole scene would be motionless.[7]

I shall come back to some key motifs in this letter in a moment. But first a few words about Goethe's situation in 1780. The poet was twenty-six when he came to Weimar in 1775 at the invitation of the then eighteen-year-old Duke Karl August. His attendance at the small court was a means of escape from the narrowly constricting life of Frankfurt and from his impending—and dreaded—legal career. The Weimar of the preindustrial period was a small walled Lutheran city of some seven thousand inhabitants, surrounded by the Thuringian forests and, beyond these, the Harz Mountains. The city itself had neither modern amenities nor means of communication. The unpaved roads were unlit at night, there were no sewers, and coach travel was so precarious that Goethe and his friends generally traveled on horseback. When Frederick the Great died, the news did not reach his niece, the Dowager Duchess Amalia, until a week later. The court circle in what was a strictly stratified society spent its time in theatricals, skating parties, and balls; the model was the French rococo court even though the Weimar version was much cruder, less sophisticated. In the evenings the writers-in-residence, like von Knebel, Herder, and Goethe himself, might read to the company or entertain them with dramatic pieces.

In his early Weimar years, Goethe spent much time with the young duke on hunting trips and wild evening parties in the Harz Mountains. The pleasure-loving duke also had a real concern for his people, and one of his accomplishments was the reopening of the stagnant Ilmenau mines, to which the poet refers in his letter to Charlotte von Stein. The Harz expeditions thus gave Goethe a chance to escape the social routine of Weimar and to dwell in what was still an unspoiled natural world. Yet even in the mountains there were difficult human problems to be encountered: the "turmoil of the town" to which Goethe refers in the letter is not that of Weimar but of the village of Ilmenau, where Goethe had to help the duke in various juridicial and financial matters. The mountain retreat, moreover, kept the poet away from his adored mistress at a time when their affair was at its most intense: in this particular week he often wrote her two or three times a day.

This is the setting of the poem called "Wandrers Nachtlied":

> Über allen Gipfeln
> Ist Ruh,
> In allen Wipfeln
> Spürest du
> Kaum einen Hauch;
> Die Vögelein schweigen im Walde.
> Warte nur, balde
> Ruhest du auch.

Above all the peaks
There is quiet,
In all the treetops
You feel
Hardly a breath;
The little birds keep silent in the forest.
Just wait, soon
You too shall rest.[8]

In this seemingly simple little song, which German schoolchildren learn by heart, the rhythm of recurrence is obviously predominant: the short, principally trochaic lines alternate masculine and feminine rhymes and the vowel harmony of *ü, a, i, u*, and the dipthongs *au* and *ei* create an intricate echo structure, which is supported by the alliteration of liquids and nasals. "The Wanderer's Nightsong" might almost be a folk song.

But not quite. Goethe's poem presents a harmony marked by difference. The very rhyme scheme is irregular, the pattern of the first quatrain, *abab,* not being repeated by the second, *cddc.* More important, the lines are uneven:

Über allen Gipfeln
Ist Ruh

where the falling rhythm of the first suspended line receives an answer from the single iamb of the second, the *u* sound being thus prolonged. The third line, "In allen Wipfeln," would be parallel to the first were it not foreshortened, and the fourth, "Spürest du," begins with a stress and surprisingly rhymes a pronoun with the noun "Ruh," the line being enjambed so that the reader must take a short breath before pronouncing the word "Kaum." The fifth line, "Kaum einen Hauch," is a choriamb as is the eighth, "Ruhest du auch," which rhymes with it, although again the rhyming partners are different parts of speech. But the most peculiar echo effect is reserved for lines 6–7:

Die Vögelein schweigen im Walde.
Warte nur, balde

A nine-syllable line, predominantly dactylic, is complemented by the broken five-syllable line, the chiming "Walde" / "balde" being again suspended since meaning is deferred (what is it that will happen soon ["balde"]?) until the final line.

The "nightsong" thus consists of a series of metrical suspensions and vocalic echoes that move toward the resolution of the final rhyme in one extended breath unit. The key to this echo structure is found, I think, in the use of the familiar second person: substitute "Spüre ich" for the fourth line or "Ruhe ich" in the eighth and the difference becomes clear. The "song" is the poet-wanderer's and he addresses himself—or is it nature that addresses him, nature that tells him, "Warte nur, balde / Ruhest du auch"? Or again, the use of "du" may imply that the wanderer's song is for everyone, for all those who find themselves, as he does, alone in the mountains preparing for the night's rest. The very birds are silent: "schweigen," a verb more properly applied to persons, suggests that the birds are part of the wanderer's world. And further the syntax points to a moment of future rest for mankind in general, perhaps to the final resting place.

Now consider the role in the poem of the speaking subject. The account of what the unnamed "I" sees and feels is presented as reliable, indeed authoritative, the implication being that it *is* possible to record such sensations as breathlessness and the absence of bird song. Further, the second-person address suggests that what is true for the poet is true in general ("you" = "one"), that he is himself at one with the natural world. Nature, for Goethe, always wears the colors of the spirit, or, in this case, the imprint of the hundred-headed god (Vishnu) to whom Goethe refers in the letter to his mistress. We do not need to inform ourselves about Goethe's botanic or anatomic studies, his gradually evolving nature philosophy, to see that here, as in the other poems of the period, the poet is positing the relation of the One to the Many, of microcosm to macrocosm, of the "I" to the "other." In the letter, we recall, Goethe speaks of kissing the porphyry stone in the cave until it seemed to give off the very breath of the earth; just so, the poet feels ("Spürest du") the slightest breath that emanates from the treetops. Again, in the letter, Goethe describes the landscape as a "large beautiful soul at harmony with itself," an image conveyed in the poem by the very verse structure with its vowel harmonies and echoes.

Yet Goethe's is not an innocent vision of a harmonious universe. The cautionary imperative "Warte nur" ("Just wait") suggests that "Ruh" ("rest," "peace," "quiet") is not always possible, that the "Wanderer" is not always alone in his mountain retreat, that the silence is welcome precisely because it is not the norm. On the other side of the forest are the mines at Ilmenau and, beyond the mines, the descent into Weimar. Three days after writing "Wandrers Nachtlied" and still in his mountain retreat near Ilmenau, Goethe writes Charlotte von Stein: "This morning we had all the murderers, thieves, and smugglers brought forward and we questioned and confronted them all. At first I didn't want to go, since I shun that which is unclean" (*Briefe* 317). In this context the "Wanderer's Nightsong" can be read as something of a prayer, a song of longing for escape from that which is unclean.

All these tensions are expressed in the sound structure of the poem. Goethe's central conviction that the landscape is man's natural habitat, his sense of himself as at once unique and yet representative, his view of poetry as the fruit of a particular experience, an experience to be "objectified" and universalized by purging it of the merely personal and by re-creating it in accord with fixed metrical laws—all these come together to create a text that calls attention to itself as a "poem," specifically a "song," by foregrounding sound repetition and stanzaic structure. The stress on the natural is an indirect comment on the artificialities of German rococo poetry of the mid-eighteenth century; at the same time, Goethe's own lyric is, as I have argued, a sophisticated poem that reflects its author's social role and his manifold literary and scientific interests. The rhythm of recurrence is defamiliarized even as the very title, "Wandrer's Nachtlied," is self-conscious in its assumption of rusticity. For, despite its eventual popularity, Goethe's poem is hardly intended as a folk song to be recited or sung by the miners and peasants of Ilmenau. Rather, in what will be a characteristically romantic gesture, "the natural" is transformed into "the poetic" by the equation of the "du" with the poem's reader and by the creation of a formal structure that enacts the "Ruh" of the opening line.

Prose Poem

My second text, Rimbaud's prose poem "Les Ponts" (The Bridges), which appeared in *Les Illuminations,* was written in the early 1870s. We have no hard information about the circumstances of composition of the *Illuminations,* but Rimbaud's editors suggest that "Les Ponts" was inspired by a vision of London, which the poet had visited with Verlaine in the autumn of 1872 and again in the spring of 1873, before the tragic quarrel that led to Verlaine's shooting of Rimbaud (and two-year imprisonment) and to Rimbaud's famous renunciation of poetry at the age of nineteen.[9]

The landscape of "Les Ponts" inevitably reflects a very different world from that of Goethe's Harz Mountains. For one thing, the relation of nature to the city had markedly changed. Charleville, Rimbaud's birth-place near the Belgian border (and hence a battleground during the Franco-Prussian War), was a provincial, unattractive village. The child of small *propriétaires,* mean-spirited, narrow-minded, and pious Catholics, Rimbaud could hardly wait to escape to the City of Light. Yet the Paris of midcentury had become a locus of industrialization, poverty, and pollution as well as of art and culture. In one of his Maxims, Goethe writes, "Nature: we are surrounded and wrapped about by her—unable to break loose from her"; by the time of the Paris Commune in 1871 (an event in which the seventeen-year-old Rimbaud participated), nature had withdrawn in the face of what Engels called, with reference to London, "this colossal centralization, this heaping together of two and a half million human beings at one point . . . the hundreds of thousands of all classes and ranks crowding past each other . . . the brutal indifference, the unfeeling isolation of each in his private interest." [10]

The dialect of the urban and the natural is one of Baudelaire's great themes; for Rimbaud, however, the city becomes unreal, at once beautiful and ugly, mysterious and terrifying, a created world whose "reality" exists only in the self-sufficient language field of the poem. It does not really matter, then, whether the site of "Les Ponts" is London Bridge, whether Rimbaud's "domes" include the dome of St. Paul's, or whether the body of water, "as wide as an arm of the sea," is the Thames. For in the semi-abstract verbal composition which is "Les Ponts," all these locales shed their "realistic" identity. Here is the prose poem:

> Des ciels gris de cristal. Un bizarre dessin de ponts, ceux-ci droits, ceux-là bombés, d'autres descendant ou obliquant en angles sur les premiers, et ces figures se renouvelant dans les autres circuits éclairés du dômes, s'abaissent et s'amoindrissent. Quelques-uns de ces point sont encore chargés de masures. D'autres soutiennent des mats, des signaux, de frêles parapets. Des accords mineurs se croisent et filent, des cordes montent des berges. On distingue une veste rouge, peut-être d'autres costumes et des instruments de musique. Sont-ce des airs populaires, des bouts de concerts seigneuriaux, des restant d'hymnes publics? L'eau est grise et bleue, large comme un bras de mer. — Un rayon blanc, tombant du haut du ciel, anéantit cette comédie.

> Crystal gray skies. A bizarre design of bridges, some straight, some arched, others descending or obliquing at angles to the first ones, and these figures renewed in the other lighted circuits of the canal, but all

so long and light that the banks, laden with domes, sink and diminish. Some of these bridges are still encumbered with hovels. Others support masts, signals, frail parapets. Minor chords criss-cross and flow away, ropes rise from the banks. One makes out a red jacket, perhaps other costumes and musical instruments. Are these popular airs, scraps of manorial concerts, remnants of public hymns? The water is gray and blue, wide as an arm of the sea. —A white ray, falling from the top of the sky, annihilates this comedy.[11]

I have discussed in *The Poetics of Indeterminacy* the semantic undecidability of Rimbaud's prose poems, the contradictory connotations of images and word groups that make it all but impossible to specify what it is that is being described.[12] Here, therefore, let me merely point to such particulars as the instability of the angle of vision from which the scene is recorded. Such phrases as "on distingue" (one makes out) or "peut-être" (perhaps) imply that the speaker is trying to report faithfully what he sees. But the "bizarre design of bridges," at once advancing and receding, is all but impossible to locate in space. The reference to "masures" (hovels), for example, suggests that the observer is close to a particular bridge; yet the references to crystal gray skies, the "design" of arches and angles, and to the "rives, chargées de dômes" (banks, laden with domes), place him at a great distance. The landscape, for that matter, is less that of reality than of a work of art, a protocubist painting, say, by John Marin, even as phrases like "accords mineurs" (minor chords) suggest a musical composition. The theatrical scene, in any case, dissolves when "un rayon blanc, tombant du haut du ciel, anéantit cette comédie." A white magical landscape of curves and domes, frail parapets and hovels, collapses in a lightning flash; the vision or waking dream is over.

But why did Rimbaud choose to present these visions, these "Illuminations," in the form of the prose poem? Again, the verse form must be understood intertextually. If the rules of French versification were not as rigid as they were, the nineteenth-century prose poem, whose first great exemplar is found in Baudelaire's *Spleen du Paris,* might not have come into being. As stress languages, English and German allow for great flexibility in the formation of lines; the French alexandrine however is based on syllable count, and so effective versification becomes a matter of observing certain norms: the caesura dividing the two hemistichs, the avoidance of hiatus, the alternation of masculine and feminine rhymes, and so on.

In his early poetry, Rimbaud, like Baudelaire before him, observed these rules carefully. LeRoy Breunig cites the lines from "Les Etrennes des Orphelins":

> La chambre est pleine d'ombre; on entend vaguement
> De deux enfants le triste et doux chuchotement.
>
> (SBAR 35)

Here the first-line caesura follows "ombre" and the twelve-syllable count includes the mute *és* of "pleine" and "vaguement" but not of "ombre," which is followed by a vowel. Beginning with "Le Dormeur du val," however, Rimbaud, as Breunig has shown, began to dismember the alexandrine by introducing repeated enjambments and misplaced caesuras and by ignoring the prescribed alternation of rhymes. By the time of "Mémoire" and "O Saisons, ô châteaux," his poems were barely recognizable as verse so that the "leap into prose" was a logical, indeed, almost an imperceptible step.[13]

Rimbaud's prose poems should not, however, be construed as emblematic of the poet's renunciation of lyric. If the poet substitutes linear progression for the rhythm of recurrence provided by meter and rhyme, his formal structure is nevertheless "free" only vis-à-vis "les premiers romantiques" like Lamartine and especially Musset, whose work is dismissed in Rimbaud's "Lettres du Voyant" of 1871: "Musset is fourteen times loathsome to us. . . . Of the insipid tales and proverbs! O the *Nuits!* O *Rolla* . . . it is all French, namely detestable to the highest degree; French, not Parisian."[14] Not Parisian, which is to say not like the first great Parisian poet, Baudelaire, "the first seer, king of poets, *a real god!*" And yet Baudelaire too is criticized for having lived in "too artistic a milieu" and for lacking the courage to invent new forms.

The "Lettres du Voyant" were written by a provincial seventeen-year-old *paysan* who fought to clear a poetic space for himself, to escape from the anxiety of influence by being more Parisian than the sophisticated Parisian dandy, Baudelaire. "Trouver une langue" (To find a language) in this context meant to write a prose poem, not narrative or parabolic like Baudelaire's, but visionary. "Prose" was, moreover, in Rimbaud's day the vehicle for patient and "realistic" description — one thinks immediately of the prose of Flaubert. To present the visionary, the magical, the artificial in prose was thus to explode the medium in a way that suited the young poet's need to shock, to be outrageous. And indeed one starts to read a text like "Les Ponts" with the expectations that it will provide a "picture" of something. "Des ciels gris de cristal" — the noun phrase promises a kind of exposition, a coherent visual image, that the text will purposely deflate. Not that the syntax is unusual; the typical unit is the simple declarative sentence: "D'autres soutiennent des mâts, des signaux, de frêles parapets" (Others support masts, signals, frail parapets). But within these "normal" syntactic slots, we find references that make no sense: what riverbanks, for example, are "laden with domes"?

Yet—and this is the curious aspect of Rimbaud's prosody—the *Illuminations* don't really violate the norms of nineteenth-century lyric. As Albert Sonnenfeld puts it:

> It would be plausible and tempting to deduce that the prose poem would, as the enactment of freedom from the formal constraints of prosody, aver itself as resolutely anti-teleological or anti-closural. . . . But . . . the *prose poem,* though it may have thrown off the shackles of a caducous tradition of rhyme and meter, is formally a profoundly conservative and traditional structure in its ceremonials of entrance and exit; no matter how radical its content, how relentless its striving for apparent or real incoherence, the prose poem undergoes the secondary elaboration of syntactical coherence and its boundaries most often are clearly defined and marked.[15]

This is an important point. The meaning of the poet's vision in "Les Ponts" may be undecidable, but formally the syntactically ordered series of sentences ends with the strongly closural statement: "Un rayon blanc, tombant du haut du ciel, anéantit cette comédie" (A white ray, falling from the top of the sky, annihilates this comedy). Those who know the *Illuminations* will recognize this as a typical ending: "Aube" (Dawn) ends with the sentence, "Au reveil il était midi" (At waking, it was noon); "Nocturne vulgaire," with "Un souffle disperse les limites du foyer" (One breath disperses the limits of the hearth); and "Parade," with the assertion, "J'ai seul la clef de cette parade sauvage" (I alone have the key for this wild show).

What does the drive toward syntactical coherence and closure tell us? The Rimbaud prose poem, we might say, is still governed by romantic and symbolist norms in that it posits (1) that poetic language is inherently different from ordinary language; (2) that a poem is the site of lyric vision, of the sacred moment; and (3) that a poem, whether in verse or in prose, is a framed discourse, an object separable and distinct from the encroaching discourses that surround it. In Michel Beaujour's words, "A prose poem is a text where the verse density approaches that of regular metrical forms, while eschewing the anaphoric servitudes of prosody." Its insistence on "an absolute distinction between journalistic cacography and artful writing is purely ideological and does not stand up to linguistic and rhetorical scrutiny: it is all a question of taste, and should ideology so decree, *bad* taste might become axiological king of the castle."[16]

Both Sonnenfeld and Beaujour suggest that the nineteenth-century French prose poem was thus a more conservative form, at least, when read in the light of such later developments as dada. Perhaps it would be fair to say that Rimbaud's brilliant prose poetry, revolutionary as it conceives itself to be and as it is with respect to its ways of signifying, also bears the inscription of the culture in which it was created, a culture that no longer looks to nature as the guardian of its soul, and for whom Art is, accordingly, as distinct from Life as possible. The poem, in other words, is regarded as an artifact, whether it is written in the dense verse of the symbolists or in prose. It was the free verse poetry of Apollinaire and Cendrars, of Pound and Williams, of Mayakovsky and Khlebnikov, that was to challenge this "object" status.

Free Verse

Williams was thirty years old when he began, primarily under the influence of Pound, to write in free verse, but he seems never to have quite understood his own composing processes. In 1913, when the imagist movement was at its height, he wrote an essay called "Speech Rhythm," in which he insisted:

> I do not believe in *vers libre,* this contradiction in terms. Either the motion continues or it does not continue, either there is rhythm or no rhythm. *Vers libre* is prose. In the hands of Whitman it was a good tool. . . . [He] did all that was necessary with it. . . .
>
> Each piece of work, rhythmic in whole, is then in essence an assembly of tides, waves, ripples. . . . for me the unit is of a convenient length, such as may be appreciated at one stroke of the attention. . . .
>
> The rhythm unit is simply any repeated sequence of lengths and heights. Upon this ether the sounds are strung in their variety.[17]

Here we must read between the lines or, I should say, the sentences. *Vers libre* was a term first used by Gustave Kahn and his symbolist cenacle in the 1880s; the early *vers librists,* such as Kahn himself, Jules Laforgue, Jean Moréas, and Henri de Regnier, wrote a slow, stately verse, characterized by phrasal and clausal repetition and heavily end-stopped lines. It is this form of free verse that was adopted by the British imagists of the 1910s, a form undoubtedly too formal, too restrained, and too "foreign" for a poet like Williams, whose verse was to be more fluid, its "waves" and "ripples" being less a matter of sound repetition or even of speech rhythm than of sight. "Stanzas you can't quite *hear*," as Hugh Kenner has put it.[18] Here is the first such stanza of a poem called "Good Night," originally published in the New York magazine *Others* in 1916:

> In brilliant gas light
> I turn the kitchen spigot
> and watch the water plash
> into the clean white sink.
> On the grooved drain-board
> to one side is
> a glass filled with parsley—
> crisped green.
>   Waiting
> for the water to freshen—
> I glance at the spotless floor—:
> a pair of rubber sandals
> lie side by side
> under the wall-table
> all is in order for the night.[19]

Since this poem is paradigmatic of so much that is to come in American poetry, its verse form demands careful attention. First, there is no rhyme scheme or stanzaic structure, no fixed stress or syllable count. The stresses range between one ("Wáiting") and four ("ínto the cleán whíte sínk"), the syllables between two ("Waiting," "crisped green") and eight ("all is in order for the night"). By definition, then, "Good Night" is written in free verse, however much Williams may have protested against the term.

What is the ideology embodied in Williams's choice of free verse? Commenting on "Good Night," Allen Ginsberg remarks:

> The mundaneness is interesting to me, because it sees so clearly that it becomes crisp in meaning, still and shining. The water glass suddenly is a totemic object. It becomes a symbol of itself, of his investment in his attention in that object. . . . Because he sees it so clearly, he notices . . . what's particular about the object that could be written down in a word—he sees the object without association. That's characteristic of

visionary moments. . . . You are not super-imposing another idea of another idea or another image on the image that's already there.[20]

Direct treatment of the thing, the absence of imposed symbolism, the act of attention that perceives the radiance in even the most mundane of objects—these are qualities everyone has noted in Williams's poetry, but an account like Ginsberg's does not tell the whole story. As a genuinely democratic American poet, a physician in contact with the daily life of a lower-class ethnic community, Williams obviously focuses, as no poet had since Whitman, on the everyday, the seemingly trivial, the communal, and as such, the argument usually goes, he had to cast off the shackles of conventional metrical forms—forms he himself used in his earliest poetry—and invent a form that would be "free," "natural," and capacious.

The problem with this argument is that Williams's poetry is not, in fact, "natural" and lifelike. Try, for example, to imagine an occasion when someone would say: "In brilliant gas light I turn the kitchen spigot and watch the water plash into the clean white sink. On the grooved drainboard to one side is a glass filled with parsley, crisped green." To whom would one say this and in what voice? Hugh Kenner is surely right when he says, of the related poem, "The Red Wheelbarrow," "Not only is what the sentence says banal, if you heard someone say it, you'd wince. But hammered on the typewriter into a *thing made,* and this without displacing a single word except typographically, the . . . words exist in a different zone" (HK 60).

"Hammered on the typewriter"—this is, I think, the key to Williams's prosody: "A poem," as he puts it in the introduction to *The Wedge,* is "a small (or large) machine made of words."[21] Here Williams gives voice to a poetic that owes much to the avant-garde artists, many of them expatriates, who came to New York during World War I. I have suggested elsewhere (MPPI 86) that Picabia's "machine drawings" for *Camera Work* and *291*—for example, his witty homage to Stieglitz (*Ici C'est Ici Stieglitz/Foi et Amour*)—are in many ways the visual counterparts of Williams's poems, in that ordinary objects like cameras and spark plugs are transformed into semiabstract, simplified geometric forms having an erotic life of their own. Again, Williams's minimal poems like "The Red Wheelbarrow" and the later "Between Walls" have much in common with Duchamp's readymades: in both cases it is a matter of lifting the saying out of the zone of things said, of framing the given object, glass of water or snow shovel, rubber sandals or bird cage, in a new way.

Such framing or re-presenting has everything to do with the technology of the early century: Williams is one of the first poets to have composed directly on the typewriter (often in moments snatched between patients); but the typewriter is only a small part of the technology that includes the automobile (which figures in so many of Williams's poems), the airplane, the telephone ("They call me and I go"), the billboard, the newspaper headline. That technology was a threat to the environment—a frequent theme of Williams—doesn't change the fact that the actual composition and dissemination of the poetic text itself could now become technologized, a process that has gone much further in our own time as a result of tape recordings, copying machines, computer printouts, video screens, and so on.

The immediate impact of technology on the Williams of 1916, in any case, was a new form of typography and lineation. In the case of "Good Night," it is lineation rather than the pattern of stresses that guides the reader's eyes so that objects stand out, one by one, as in a series of film shots: first the gas light, then the spigot, then the plash of water, and finally the "clean white sink" itself. The eye moves slowly so as to take in each monosyllable (all but four of the nineteen words in the first four lines, all but twelve of the sixty-seven words in the whole verse paragraph): "in," "gas," "light," "turn," "the," "and," "watch." . . . The sixth line is suspended: it asks, what is it that is located "to one side"? But what does the parsley look and feel like? Again a new line:

crisped green.

Next there is a wait as the water runs from the tap, and so "Waiting" gets a line to itself, and a prominent line at that, because it is moved over toward the jagged right margin of the poem. Notice that the poem would sound exactly the same if "Waiting" were aligned with "crisped" and "for" at the left margin; the effect, in other words, is entirely visual. And again, the ensuing lines are characterized by suspension: a "pair of rubber sandals" (line 12) do what? They "lie side by side" (line 13). But where?

under the wall-table

As in Picabia's drawings, everyday objects are here granted a curious sexual power: the "pair of rubber sandals / under the wall-table" anticipating the final line of the poem, "I am ready for bed." And yet the poet's separateness is stressed: he does not participate in the life of the young girls seen earlier that evening at the opera, the girls described in stanza 2 as "full of smells and / the rustling sounds of / cloth rubbing on cloth and / little slippers on carpet." Rather, like the "Parsley in a glass, / still and shining," he "yawn[s] deliciously" to himself, knowing that he will be alone in bed.

Indeed, there is nothing inherently "free" about this natural "free verse" poem, which is less a vision of the mundane-turned-radiant than the creation of a field of force, set in motion by the poet's desire. Thus the sounds of the poem do not quite chime: "light" in line 1 receives what is almost a response from "spigot" in the next line, and when the full response comes in the "white" of line 4, the rhyme is internal, its harmony offset by the next word, "sink." Again, vowel repetition is something of a tease, visual chiming not always being matched by aural equivalence. The letter *i*, for example, appears ten times in the nineteen words of the first sentence, but the phoneme may be /i/ or /ay/ or even a /y/ glide as in the second syllable of "brilliant." Still, if one waits long enough, the "brilliant gas light" of the opening line is greeted by the rhyme of "night" in line 15. Each line, for that matter, waits for its fulfillment from the next, with "Waiting," coming, as it does, after "crisped green," exerting the central pull. When, at the end of the poem, the parsley image recurs—

> Parsley in a glass,
> still and shining,
> brings me back—

it is treated to characteristic Williams deflation: being "brought back" is one thing, but life goes on:

> I take a drink
> and yawn deliciously.
> I am ready for bed.

And of course that's what the title has told us to begin with. "It isn't what [the poet] *says* that counts as a work of art, it's what he makes, with such intensity of perception" (WCWE 257). "Good Night" is, in the best sense, a small machine made of words.

The Third Rhythm

Williams's poetry did not gain a wide readership until the last decade or so of his life. Since then, it has become increasingly popular even as, ironically enough, the drive that brought into being Williams's marvelous "suspension-systems" has lost much of its force. A second world war, a growing distrust of technology, as well as the public acceptance of free verse as, quite simply, *the* poetic form of the dominant culture, meant that defamiliarization had to come from new sources. In the later nineteenth century, the chief source of renewal was, I have argued, prose—the prose of novelists like Stendhal and Flaubert—that modernists from Rimbaud to Robert Lowell called on as a source of inspiration. A hundred years later, a similar turn toward prose has occurred, but the "prose" in question is less that of the novel (a form also put in question) than that of philosophy. By the early seventies, American students were eagerly citing Heidegger's definition of poetic speech: "The more poetic a poet is—the freer (that is the more open and ready for the unforeseen) his saying—the greater is the purity with which he submits what he says to an ever more painstaking listening, and the further what he says is from the mere propositional statement that is dealt with solely in regard to its correctness or incorrectness."[22] In equating the "poetic" with a mode of receptive listening and active speaking, rather than with any formal features, Heidegger paves the way for a notion of "poeticalness" that regards genre and, by extension, the question of meter and lineation, as irrelevancies. From the standpoint of poststructuralist theory, poetry is no longer any one thing (the lyric, the language of tropes, metered language, and so on) but rather that species of writing that foregrounds the materiality of the signifier, the coincidence between enunciation and enounced.[23]

Such coincidence cannot be achieved, so the argument goes, by imposing on language an abstract pattern like the iambic pentameter. But since free verse has itself become conventionalized and subject to a number of abstract paradigms, the "rhythm of recurrence" has reared its head in new guises. Consider Beckett's short texts, known as "residua" (his own term), or "lyrics of fiction" (Ruby Cohn's), or "monologues," or, perhaps most commonly, "pieces." Here is the opening page of *Still*, written in 1974 for Stanley William Hayter, who illustrated it with a series of etchings (see figure 1) and printed the verbal-visual text in his celebrated *Atelier 17* in Paris.

Bright at last close of a dark day the sun shines out at last and goes down. Sitting quite still at valley window normally turn head now and see it the sun low in the southwest sinking. Even get up certain moods and go stand by western window quite still watching it sink and then the afterglow. Always quite still some reason some time past this hour at open window facing south in small upright wicker chair armrests.

Figure 1. Stanley William Hayter, etching from
Still by Samuel Beckett.

Eyes stare out unseeing till first movement some time past close though unseeing still while still light. Quite still again then all quite quiet apparently till eyes open again while still light though less. Normally turn head now ninety degrees to watch sun which if already gone then fading afterglow. Even get up certain moods and go stand by western window till quite dark and even some evenings some reason long after. Eyes then open again while still light and close again in what if not quite a single movement almost. Quite still again then at open window facing south over the valley in this wicker chair though actually close inspection not still at all but trembling all over. Close inspection namely detail by detail all over to add up finally to this whole not still at all but trembling all over.[24]

This is approximately a third of the single seamless paragraph that is *Still,* a paragraph that culminates with the sentence, "Leave it so all quite still or try listening to the sounds all quite still head in hand listening for a sound." From "still" to "sound"—how does Beckett's text proceed and how shall we characterize it?

We may note, to begin with, that Beckett's syntactic units are not proper "sentences" at all. Practically speaking, we associate the sentence with a model of wholeness and completeness. The typical sentence, so to speak, enacts a plot: "Pass the sugar, please!" or "We were in class when the headmaster came in, followed by a new boy, not wearing the school uniform, and a school servant carrying a large desk" (*Madame Bovary*). The sentence, says Stephen Fredman commonsensically, "is a primary unit of writing whose purpose is to organize language and thought upon a page. . . . The period posits closure to a string of words; it asks us to regard the words between itself and the preceding period as a unit" (SFPP 29–30). Thus the opening sentence of *Madame Bovary,* which I cited above, is followed by the second sentence, "Those who had been asleep woke up, and everyone rose as if just surprised at his work." Indeed a unit.

But now look at the first two sentences of *Still:* "Bright at last close of a dark day the sun shines out at last and goes down. Sitting quite still at valley window normally turn head now and see it the sun low in the southwest sinking." When this is read aloud (and I have heard it read by the actor Alec McGowran), it sounds like this:

> Bríght at lást
> clóse of a dárk dáy
> the sún shînes oút at lást and gôes dówn.
> Sítting quîte stíll at válley wíndôw
> nórmally túrn heád nôw and sée ît
> the sún lów in the soúthwêst sínking.

The unit of rhythm here and throughout *Still* is a short phrase of irregular length and primitive syntax ("nórmally túrn heád nôw and sée ît"), a phrase heavily accented, discontinuous, and repetitive—a kind of shorthand by means of which the human consciousness tries to articulate what it perceives and remembers. Indeed, this version of what Henri Meschonnic calls the "third rhythm" is no closer to prose than to verse: "The prose of the poem moves in a direction that is, despite all appearances, the opposite of the prose poem. The prose of the poem . . . is the *mise à nu* of the subjective character of rhythm, the rapport between the rhythm of discourse and the speaking subject" (HM 610–11).

This is not to say that the "third rhythm" is another name for the stream of consciousness. In the twenty-one line unit before us, the word "still" appears eleven times in a complex series of permutations: "quite still" (three times), then "unseeing still while still light" (where the monosyllabic word can be adjective ["silent," "motionless"] or adverb ["yet"]), then "Quite still again," and so on. At the same time the words modifying "still" gradually become nodal points, as when "Quite still again" modulates into "quite quiet apparently," or when "Eyes that open again while still light" becomes "Quite still again then at open window."

But further, *Still* is, in Enoch Brater's words, "a verbal journey in disorienting repetition highlighting inversion, opposition, and indeterminacy." [25] That which is "still" is "not still at all" or "trembling all over." Or again, we meet the oppositions "see"/"unseeing," "rise"/"fall," "far"/"near," "western"/"eastern," "sunrise"/"sunset," "quite"/"not quite," and so on. Verbal slippage is likely to turn "quite" into "quiet," "end of rests" into "rest on ends," "quite still" into "till quite." "Stillness," in other words, is anything but "still": everything in this texts moves, shifts, changes before our very eyes and ears.

But *Still* is by no means an exercise in abstraction. It is "about" a person sitting at a window, who watches the sun set. Although the figure's gender is not specified, there are references to eyes, a skull, head, cheekbone, nape, breast, forearms, arms, elbow, hands, thumb, index, fingers, trunk, knees, and legs. But there is no indication as to how these "spare parts" relate to one another or to the body in the "small upright wicker chair armrests" to which they presumably belong. As in Hayter's illustration, the figure's position is viewed mathematically rather than in human, let alone individual terms. We know only that, in the course of the narrative, it is becoming darker (though not dark) and that the "right hand" is finally raised in a motion that seems to mimic the circle of the sun "till elbow meeting armrest brings this last movement to an end and all still once more."

But whose is the voice that tells us these things? The text gives us contradictory signals. "Bright at last close of a dark day the sun shines out at last and goes down": the voice that utters these words is not identifiable; it could be that of the figure in the wicker chair or that of a companion or again of an impersonal narrator. In the next sentence, "normally turn head now" suggests that the speaker is the person in the chair, but "Always quite still some reason" (sentence 3) implies the opposite in that the reason is not known. In sentence 4, the phrase "Eyes stare out unseeing till first movement" positions the observer outside the subject of the discourse, as does "quite quiet apparently" in the next sentence. But the angle of vision continues to shift: there is, in fact, no identifiable narrator who can bring these disparate references together for us.

In Goethe's "Wandrers Nachtlied," we find an "I" aware of itself and of its feelings, a coherent "I" in control of the situation. When the poet declares "Die Vögelein schweigen im Walde," the reader accepts the statement as valid, given the particular context of the speech. In Rimbaud's "Les Ponts," the relationship between the "I" and the "other" becomes more problematic: it is not clear, say, whether the minor chords that crisscross and flow away are *outside* the self or are part of its mental landscape. This disappearance of the distinction between subject and object is equally marked in Williams's "Good Night," in whose field of copresence the "I" and the sprig of parsley in the glass become one.[26] But in Beckett's *Still*, the question of copresence gives way to a doubt as to the very existence of a unitary represented speaker. The inflections of the speaking voice, coming to us in short repetitive phrases, each permutating what has come before, give us no hint as to a controlling presence. To whom, for example, do we attribute the words "Arms likewise broken right angles at the elbows"? To the narrator? The person in the chair? Or are these one and the same? Under such circumstances, the subject position, no longer granted to an identifiable or consistent speaker, can only be assumed by the reader.

In this context, we can see more clearly the function of the "third rhythm" in this and related texts. *Still* is a single paragraph because for Beckett there is no separation between different voices or different levels of discourse. Beckett's composition cannot avail itself of such imposed patterns as meter or stanzaic structure; even lineation may seem too restrictive a device, although the fact is that many poems that make use of the associative of third rhythm are lineated: the "prosaic" rhythms of John Ashbery, not essentially different from the rhythms of his prose work *Three Poems*, are a case in point. Consider the following examples:

(1) It was only much later that the qualities of the incandescent period became apparent, and by then it had been dead for many years. But in recalling itself it assumed its first real life. That time was for living without the reflection that gives things and objects a certain relief, or weight; one drank the rapture of unlived moments and it blinded one to how it looked from outside . . .

(2) All that we see is penetrated by it—
    The distant treetops with their steeple (so
    Innocent), the stair, the windows' fixed flashing—
    Pierced full of holes by the evil that is not evil,
    The romance that is not mysterious, the life that
                is not life,
    A present that is elsewhere.

The first passage comes from Ashbery's *Three Poems;* the second is the opening stanza of the title poem of *As We Know.* [27] Both deal with the nameless "it" that haunts our experience, the privileged moment that we await even as we doubt that it exists. The first passage is in prose, the second in a purposely "prosaic" free verse, the rhythms almost coalescing into blank verse in line 2, only to be dispersed, by the time we reach line 5, into a kind of poulter's rhythm carried through sixteen syllables. Indeed, the "verse" of "As We Know" is surely closer to the "prose" of *Three Poems* than it is, say, to the verse of Williams's "Good Night," not to mention Goethe's "Wandrers Nachtlied." To articulate a line like "Áll that we sée is pénetráted bý it," with its clumsy shift, in the sixth syllable from iamb to trochee and then back again, is to imply that a larger harmony is no longer a meaningful possibility. The same "point" is made in Charles Bernstein's "The Klupzy Girl":

> Poetry is like a swoon, with this difference:
> it brings you to your senses. Yet his
> parables are not singular. The smoke from
> the boat causes the men to joke. Not
> gymnastic: pyrotechnic.[28]

Not pretty, we might paraphrase this, ugly, with the line being a yardstick produced only to violate it.

It is one of the ironies of contemporary poetic discourse that the associative rhythm, the rhythm derived from speech, should become pervasive at the very moment when poets like Beckett and Ashbery, and especially language poets like Bernstein, are positing what we might call the absence of the pronoun, at the moment when it is often impossible to decide whether the speaker is a "he" or an "I" or a "you," much less what the "I" or "you" might be like. Perhaps it is the poet's sense that at a time when the spoken and written word are more pervasive than ever, when our visual fields are bombarded by billboards and manuals, and our aural fields by overheard snatches of conversation and catchy television jingles, the individual voice can no longer be In Charge. Rather, the text gives the impression that the story is telling itself, that it is available for communal use—a kind of score that we endow with meaning by "speaking it" ourselves.

Here an anecdote is apposite. In October 1969, when the Nobel Committee awarded Beckett that year's prize, the writer and his wife were vacationing in the tiny Tunisian village of Nabeul. Before they could be located, the frantic editor of a Norwegian newspaper contacted the *Irish Times* and tried to get information about the writer, but since Beckett had not lived in Dublin for years and was a resident of Paris, the editor got nowhere. The situation was not much better in Paris, where many reporters could not even find Beckett's address. While this scramble for news was going on, heavy rainstorms in Tunisia cut off the ocean village from the desert mainland. In the French press, Beckett was accordingly dubbed "un inconnu célèbre." [29]

"Un inconnu célèbre." The Unnameable is a far cry from the Goethe of 1780 who explains to Charlotte von Stein the precise thoughts and feelings that animate his poems, poems that will be read, in Weimar and beyond, as versions of his own life. Yet just as Goethean lyric gives expression to a particular view of natural process, so Beckett's *Still* employs a rigorous structure of sound repetitions and permutations that convey the tension between "still" and "trembling all over," between silence and the awaited sound, between the short *i* of *Still* and the long *i* of "light" as in the construction "unseeing still while still light." Or consider the following sound chiming found in the first five sentences alone:

bright — shines — quite — upright — eyes — while — light — last — still — stand — still — past — armrests — stare — past — close — goes — go — low — afterglow — open — close — sitting — still — it — window — still — it — still — in — window — wicker — till — still — still.

This chiming continues throughout the text. Indeed, at the climactic moment when the hand of the unknown person is raised in the air, Beckett introduces what can be transcribed as two lines of blank verse:

> till mídway tó the heád it hésitátes
> and hángs hâlf ópen trémbling ín mîd aír.

But no sooner are we lulled by the familiar meter than it is replaced by the choppy rhythms of:

Hángs thêre
as if hálf inclíned to retúrn
thát îs
sínk bâck slówly

and then by the sober scientific discourse of "thumb on outer edge of right socket index ditto left and middle on left cheekbone." Only when we come to the end of the text do we realize that we have all along been "listening ["list" is an anagram for "still"] for a sound" — a sound we can only imagine because none has been described in the text.

Beckett's principle of exclusion is thus rigorous: no colors, no dialogue, no specifiers, no identifiable sounds. Perhaps for that very reason, the final statement of desire comes across as deeply poignant:

Leáve it só
áll quíte stíll
or trý lístening to the soúnds
áll quíte stíll
heád in hánd
lístening for a soúnd.

"The same sound," in Wallace Stevens's words, "in the same bare place." [30] Isn't Beckett's "song," after all, a late twentieth-century version of

Die Vögelein schweigen im Walde.
Warte nur, balde
Ruhest du auch?

Yes and no. Yes, in the sense that there is, of course, no new subject matter, only the old subject matter rendered in new ways. But to call a poem a new "version" of an earlier one is also to admit that it has become something else. In the late twentieth century, to write, for example, a straightforward "Ubi sunt" poem on the medieval model is hardly an available option, even as poets will continue to spin ironic and parodic fantasies on this time-honored topos.

By the same token, we must realize that the choice of verse form is not just a matter of individual preference, a personal decision to render a particular experience as a sonnet rather than a ballad, a prose poem rather than a free verse lyric, and so on. For the pool of verse and prose alternatives available to the poet at any given time has already been determined, at least in part, by historical and ideological considerations. "A mythology," as Stevens put it, "reflects its region." [31]

6. After Free Verse

The New Nonlinear Poetries

What is generally called *free verse* is now more than a century old. It was in 1886 that Gustave Kahn's Paris *La Vogue* published Rimbaud's "Marine" and "Mouvement" (both written in the early 1870s), translations of some of Whitman's *Leaves of Grass* by Jules Laforgue, ten of Laforgue's own free-verse poems, and further experiments by Jean Moréas, Paul Adam, and Gustave Kahn himself.[1] On the other side of the Channel, *vers libre* was soon picked up by the Imagists: in the March 1913 issue of *Poetry*, Pound put forward his famous Imagist manifesto, whose third principle was "As regarding rhythm: to compose in the sequence of the musical phrase, not in sequence of a metronome."[2]

Even as he made this pronouncement, however, Pound remarked that "*vers libre* has become as prolix and as verbose as any of the flaccid varieties that preceded it. . . . The actual language and phrasing is often as bad as that of our elders without even the excuse that the words are shovelled in to fill a metric pattern or to complete the noise of a rhyme-sound" (LEEP 3). And his friend T. S. Eliot, who was to declare in "The Music of Poetry" (1942) that "no verse is free for the man who wants to do a good job,"[3] observed in his 1917 "Reflections on *Vers Libre*," that "there is only good verse, bad verse, and chaos." How to avoid the latter? "The most interesting verse which has yet been written in our language has been done either by taking a very simple form, like iambic pentameter, and constantly withdrawing from it, or taking no form at all, and constantly approximating to a very simple one. It is this contrast between fixity and flux, this unperceived evasion of monotony, which is the very life of verse." And in a formulation that was to become a kind of first rule in poetry manuals, Eliot declares, "the ghost of some simple metre should lurk behind the arras in even the 'freest' verse; to advance menacingly as we doze, and withdraw as we rouse. Or, freedom is only truly freedom when it appears against the background of an artificial limitation." [4]

Eliot's formulation, which was, of course, based on his own practice, still governs most discussions of free verse. As recently as 1993, in a book called *The Ghost of Meter,* Annie Finch treats contemporary free verse as essentially a fruitful quarrel with meter, especially iambic pentameter, and tries to show how in the lyric of poets as diverse as Charles Wright and Audre Lorde, "anger at the pentameter and exhilaration at claiming its authority engender much poetic energy." [5] Derek Attridge's *Poetic Rhythm: An Introduction* (1995) characterizes free verse by citing poems like Adrienne Rich's "Night Watch," which "derives its rhythmic quality from its existence on the borders of regular verse." [6] And in recent years the New Formalists have gone further, arguing that "free verse" has been no more than a temporary aberration, given that, in the words of Timothy Steele, "poetry was always, before the modern period, associated with meter." [7] Indeed, in a 1996 review of the Library of America's newly edited *Collected Poems of Robert Frost,* Helen Vendler cites approvingly Frost's dismissal of free verse ("Let chaos storm! / Let cloud shapes swarm! / I wait for form"), and remarks:

> There used to be a critical orthodoxy (still prevalent in a few backwaters) that anyone practicing rhymed and metered verse was a reactionary and no Modernist; we now understand, having seen many later writers (Merrill, Lowell) alternating metered and free verse, that both forms and free verse are neutrally available to all. [8]

The implication of this claim for "neutral availability" is that verse forms, whether free or otherwise, are independent of history as well as of national and cultural context and that metrical choice is a question of individual predilection. And further: that free verse is some kind of end point, an instance of writing degree zero from which the only reasonable "advance" can be, as Steele suggests, a return to "normal" metrical forms. At the risk of allying myself with those "backwater" forces Vendler refers to so dismissively, I shall want to argue here that there are indeed other possibilities and that verse, like the materials used in any art medium and like the clothes we wear and the furnishings in our houses, is subject to historical change as well as cultural and political constraint. But before I consider the large-scale transformations "free verse" is now undergoing in America (and, for that matter, in the poetry of most other nations as well), some definitions and clarifications are in order.

What *is* free verse anyway? However varied its definitions, there is general agreement on two points: (1) the sine qua non of free verse is *lineation*. When the lines run all the way to the right margin, the result is prose, however "poetic." The basic unit of free verse is thus the line. But (2), unlike metrical or strong-stress or syllabic or quantitative verse, free verse is, in Donald Wesling's words, "distinguished . . . by the lack of a structuring grid based on counting of linguistic units and/or position of linguistic features" (EPP 425). As Derek Attridge explains:

> Free verse is the introduction into the continuous flow of prose language, which has breaks determined entirely by syntax and sense, of another kind of break, shown on the page by the start of a new line, and often indicated in a reading of the poem by a slight pause. When we read prose, we ignore the fact that every now and then the line ends, and we have to shift our eyes to the beginning of the next line. We know that if the same text were printed in a different typeface, the sentences would be broken up differently with no alteration in the meaning. But in free verse, *the line on the page has an integrity and function of its own.* This has important consequences for the movement and hence the meaning of the words. (DA 5, my emphasis)

The implication of free-verse writing, Attridge adds sensibly, is that poetry "need not be based on the production of controlled numbers of beats by the disposition of stressed and unstressed syllables." A more accurate name, Attridge suggests, would be "*nonmetrical verse,* which, as a negative definition, has the advantage of implying that this kind of verse does not have a fixed identity of its own, whereas 'free verse' misleadingly suggests a single type of poetry" (DA 167–68). But the adjective *nonmetrical* is somewhat misleading, given that the item counted may be the number of primary stresses (no matter how many syllables per line), as in Old English and much of Middle English poetry, the number of syllables per line, regardless of the number of stresses, as in the syllabics of Marianne Moore, or the number of long vowels per line, as in classical quantitative verse, and so on. Charles O. Hartman's definition is thus more accurate: "*the prosody of free verse is rhythmic organization by other than numerical modes.*"[9] Free verse retains the linear *turn* inherent in the etymology of the word *verse* (Latin, *versus*), but there is no regularly recurring counted entity.[10]

Once we try to go beyond these basics, there is little unanimity as to the features of free verse. For Donald Wesling, free verse has its roots in the oral forms of ancient cultures—Sumerian, Akkadian, Egyptian, Sanskrit, and Hebrew—none of which have meter (EPP 425). The speech-base of free verse is also accepted by Northrop Frye, who defines it as "the associative rhythm"—that is the rhythm of ordinary speech, with its short, repetitive, irregular, often asyntactic phrasal units—"strongly influenced by verse," which is to say by by lineation.[11] And Robert Pinsky observes that "the line in contemporary practice seems to fall roughly into two overlapping kinds: a rhetorical indicator for the inflections of speech . . . and a formal principle varyingly intersecting the inflection of speech."[12]

But "inflection of speech" doesn't in fact distinguish free verse from its metrical counterparts. On the one hand, there are those like Derek Attridge who argue that *all* verse is speech-based;[13] on the other, those who hold that free verse is distinguished primarily by its visual form, its typographical layout, and that indeed the line break creates verbal and phrasal units quite unlike those of speech.[14] But the link between free verse and visual formation is by no means essential. For the majority of free-verse poems—say those one finds in any issue of *Poetry* or *American Poetry Review*—retain the justified left margin, some form of stanzaic structure, and lines of similar length, so as to produce visual columns not all that different from their metrical counterparts.

If, then, free verse cannot be definitively distinguished, whether aurally, visually, or, for that matter, syntactically,[15] from, say, blank verse, this is not to say that there isn't what we might call a free-verse culture that occupies a particular place in twentieth-century literary history. In *Critique du rythme* (1982), Henri Meschonnic works from the premise that "the aim [of prosodic theory] is not to produce a conceptual synthesis of rhythm, an abstract, universal category, an *a priori* form. Rather, an organized understanding of historical subjects."[16] As he explains:

It is not a question of opposing form to an absence of form. Because the *informe* [formless] is still form. If we want to provide a proper base for the critique of rhythm, we must pass from imperious abstractions to the historicity of language. Where freedom is no more a choice than it is an absence of constraint, but the search of its own historicity.

In this sense the poet is not free. He is not free in confronting the alexandrine, any more than in confronting free verse. *Not free of being ventriloquized by a tradition*. . . . One doesn't choose what one writes, nor to write. No more than one chooses to be born into one's language, there and then.[17]

The so-called freedom of free verse must be understood in this context. When Pound declares in Canto LXXXI, "To break the pentameter, that was the first heave," he is speaking to a particular situation in late-Victorian "genteel" verse, when meter stood for a particular collective attitude, a social and cultural restriction on the "freedom" of the subject. Vladimir Mayakovsky, coming out of an entirely different tradition but in the same time period, makes a similar gesture when he declares in 1926, "Trochees and iambs have never been necessary to me. I don't know them and don't want to know them. Iambs impede the forward movement of poetry" (cited in HMC 528).

Such statements, Meschonnic points out, are neither true nor untrue; rather, they must be understood as part of the drive toward rupture characteristic of the early twentieth-century avant-garde. And the form Pound's own prosody took—the "ideogrammizing of Western verse," in Meschonnic's words—had everything to do with the revolution in mass print culture, a revolution that bred what Meschonnic calls the "theatre of the page." "If we were to talk about practices rather than intentions," he says, "every page of poetry would represent a conception of poetry" (HMC 303). Blank spaces, for example, would become just as important as the words themselves in composing a particular construct (HMC 304–5). Thus, the structuralist argument that lineation in and of itself guarantees that a text will be read and interpreted as a poem[18] is based on two misconceptions. First, it ignores the active role that white space (silence) plays in the visual and aural reception of the poem: the line, after all, is anchored in a larger visual field, a field by no means invariable. Second, and more important, the response to lineation must itself be historicized. In a contemporary context of one-liners on the television screen and computer monitor as well as lineated ads, greeting cards, and catalog entries, the reader/viewer has become quite accustomed to reading "in lines." Indeed, surfing the Internet is largely a scanning process in which the line is rapidly replacing the paragraph as the unit to be accessed.[19]

How lineation as device signifies thus depends on many factors—historical, cultural, and national. The history of free verse in English remains to be written: when it is, it will be clear that the dominant example has been, not that of Ezra Pound, whose ideographic page has only recently become a model for poets, but that of William Carlos Williams, whose verse signature is still a powerful presence.[20] But since my concern in this essay is with the current situation in poetry, I shall confine myself to the postwar era, using as my example two representative anthologies, both of them cutting-edge at their respective postwar moments. The first is *Naked Poetry: Recent American Poetry in Open Forms,* edited by Stephen Berg and Robert Mezey for Bobbs Merrill in 1969 (but including poems from the early fifties on); the second, *Out of Everywhere: Linguistically Innovative Poetry by Women in North America & the U.K.,* edited by Maggie O'Sullivan for Reality Street Studios in London in 1996.[21]

"An Echo Repeating No Sound"

In their foreword to *Naked Poetry,* Stephen Berg and Robert Mezey tell us that they had a hard time finding "a satisfactory name for the kinds of poetry we were gathering and talking about":

> Some people said "Free Verse" and others said "Organic Poetry" . . . and we finally came up with Open Forms, which isn't bad but isn't all that good either. And we took a phrase from Jiménez for a title which expresses what we feel about the qualities of this poetry as no technical label could do. *But what does it matter what you call it?* Here is a book of nineteen American poets whose poems don't rhyme (usually) and don't move on feet of more or less equal duration (usually). (NAK xi, my emphasis)

The assumption here is that there *is* an "it," alternately known as *free verse, organic poetry, open form,* or whatever, but that this "it" cannot be defined "technically," which is to say, materially. And indeed the editors quickly go on to add that "Everything we thought to ask about [the poets'] formal qualities has come to seem more and more irrelevant, and we find we are much more interested in what they say, in their dreams, visions, and prophecies. Their poems take shape from the shapes of their emotions, the shapes their minds make in thought, and certainly don't need interpreters" (NAK xi). Not "form," then, but "content" is what matters. Still, the choice of free verse is central because "We began with the firm conviction that the strongest and most alive poetry in America had abandoned or at least broken the grip of traditional meters and had set out, once again, into 'the wilderness of unopened life' " (NAK xi).

This is a perfectly representative sixties statement about poetry. It takes off from Charles Olson's "Projective Verse" (1950), with its strong dismissal of "closed" verse and concomitant adoption of the line as coming "from the breath, from the breathing of the man who writes, at the moment that he writes." It is the "LINE" that speaks for the "HEART," even as the syllable does for the "HEAD": "the LINE that's the baby that gets, as the poem is getting made, the attention." [22] Interestingly, Berg and Mezey, who were by no means disciples of Olson, here give a curious twist to the famous Olson credo that "FORM IS NEVER MORE THAN THE EXTENSION OF CONTENT." [23] Whereas Olson demanded that form take its cue from the semantic structure of a given poem, Berg and Mezey take the aphorism one step further, dismissing "formal qualities" as more or less "irrelevant," entirely secondary to "what [the poets] say, in their dreams, visions, and prophecies." Indeed, if poems "take shape from the shapes of their emotions," from "the wilderness of unopened life," then "free verse" is effective insofar as it tracks the actual movement of thought and feeling, refusing to interfere with its free flow, to inhibit its natural motion. Or so, at least, the poem must appear to be doing, no matter how much "craft" has gone into it.

Naked Poetry includes nineteen American poets, born between 1905 and 1935, the largest cluster of them born between 1926 and 1930. In chronological order, they are: Kenneth Rexroth, Theodore Roethke, Kenneth Patchen, William Stafford, Weldon Kees, John Berryman, Robert Lowell, Denise Levertov, Robert Bly, Robert Creeley, Allen Ginsberg, Galway Kinnell, W. S. Merwin, James Wright, Philip Levine, Sylvia Plath, Gary Snyder, Stephen Berg, and Robert Mezey. Despite the paucity of women (two out of the nineteen) and the absence (characteristic for 1969) of minority poets as well as poets writing outside the United States,[24] the editors have clearly made an effort to transcend schools and regional affiliations by including representatives of Beat (Ginsberg, Snyder), Black Mountain (Creeley, Levertov), Deep Image (Bly, Kinnell, Wright), Northwest (Roethke, Stafford), and East Coast Establishment (Lowell, Berryman, Merwin, Plath) poetry.

So what do the poems in this anthology look and sound like? Consider the following five poems (or parts of poems), for which I have supplied scansions:[25]

1   A headless squirrel, some blood →

oozing from the unevenly →

chewed-off neck

lies in rainsweet grass

near the woodshed door.

Down the driveway

the first irises   →

have opened since dawn,

ethereal, their mauve →

almost a transparent gray,

their dark veins

bruise-blue.

(Denise Levertov, "A Day Begins," NAK 140)

(2)   The sun sets in the cold without friends

Without reproaches after all it has done for us

It goes down believing in nothing

When it has gone I hear the stream running after it

It has brought its flute it is a long way

(W. S. Merwin, "Dusk in Winter," NAK 255)

(3)   In the depths of the Greyhound Terminal

sitting dumbly on a baggage truck looking at the sky waiting for

the Los Angeles Express to depart

worrying about eternity over the Post Office roof in the night-time

red downtown heaven,

staring through my eyeglasses I realized shuddering these thoughts

were not eternity, nor the poverty of our lives, irritable

baggage clerks,

nor the millions of weeping relatives surrounding the buses waving

goodbye,

nor other millions of the poor rushing around from city to city to

see their loved ones. . . .

(from Allen Ginsberg, "In the Baggage Room at Greyhound,"
NAK 194–95)

(4) Down valley a smoke haze

Three days heat, after five days rain

Pitch glows on the fir-cones

Across rocks and meadows

Swarms of new flies.

I cannot remember things I once read

A few friends, but they are in cities.

Drinking cold snow-water from a tin cup

Looking down for miles

Through high still air.

(Gary Snyder, "Mid-August at Sourdough Mountain Lookout,"
NAK 330)

(5) The ice ticks seaward like a clock.

A Negro toasts →

wheat-seeds over the coke-fumes →

of a punctured barrel.

Chemical air →

sweeps in from New Jersey,

and smells of coffee.

Across the river,

ledges of suburban factories tan →

in the sulphur-yellow sun →

of the unforgivable landscape.

(from Robert Lowell, "The Mouth of the Hudson," NAK 110–111)

The five poets cited are by no means alike: the conventional wisdom would be to oppose the "raw" Allen Ginsberg to the "cooked" Robert Lowell, or the Black Mountain–based Denise Levertov to the more mainstream *New Yorker* favorite, W. S. Merwin, and so on. Indeed, there are real prosodic differences in the above examples. Certainly Ginsberg's strophes, made up of two or more lines, characterized by their emphatic, predominantly trochaic and dactylic rhythm, each strophe emphatically end-stopped, are a far cry from Levertov's minimal, lightly stressed (two or three stresses per line), frequently enjambed lines, arranged in open tercets. For Ginsberg, repetition, whether clausal or phrasal, is the central sonic and syntactic device; for Levertov, whose poem charts minute differences of perception, repetition is studiously avoided. Again, Levertov's "A Day Begins" differs from Snyder's "Mid-August," whose two five-line stanzas are notable for their monosyllabic base (seven of the poem's fifty-seven words are mono-syllables), which insures strong stress on almost every word in a loosely trochaic sequence. Unlike Levertov, Snyder does not run on his lines; neither, for that matter, does Merwin, whose lines are evenly paced to the point of intentional monotony, the avoidance of secondary and tertiary stresses heightening the epiphany of the final line in which two sentences are unexpectedly run together, culminating in the pyrrhic-spondee pattern of "ìt is (a) lóng wáy." And finally in Lowell, whose free verse most closely follows Eliot's prescription that the ghost of meter must lurk behind the arras, the frequent enjambment (as if to say, look, I am writing free verse, using open form!) is offset by the underlying iambic rhythm, as in "The íce tîcks séawârd líke a clóck" and "A négro toásts," as well as by the repetition of identical stress contours, as in the two-stress lines "and smélls of cóffee," "Acróss the ríver."

But despite all these differences—and who would mistake the sound and look of a Ginsberg poem for that of a Lowell or Levertov one?—there is a period style, a dominant rhythmic-visual contour that distinguishes the lyric of *Naked Poetry* from that of a recent anthology like *Out of Everywhere*. Consider the following features:

(1)The free verse, in its variability (both of stress and of syllable count) and its avoidance of obtrusive patterns of recurrence, tracks the speaking voice (in conjunction with the moving eye) of a perceptive, feeling subject, trying to come to terms with what seems to be an alien, or at least incomprehensible, world. Thus Levertov's "A Day Begins" follows the motion of the eye, taking in the frightening sight of the bloody headless squirrel, its location being specified only in the second tercet and in turn juxtaposed to the next thing seen, "the first irises" [that] "have opened since dawn," the poem moving, in the final line, to the "bruise-blue" conjunction between these seeming dissimilars. The same temporal tracking characterizes Merwin's "Dusk in Winter": in line 1, the sun is seen setting; in lines 2–3, the poet responds to the resulting "cold"; in lines 4–5, the sense of loss gives way to renewal as the stream is metaphorically perceived as "running after" the sun, its sound like flute song. In Ginsberg's "In the Baggage Room," the first line sets the scene "in the depths of the Greyhound Terminal," and each subsequent strophe adds an element of perception or cognition. In Snyder's "Mid-August at Sourdough Mountain Lookout," the patient description of the valley in the first stanza triggers the step-by-step withdrawal into the self in the second. And Lowell's eleven-line conclusion to "The Mouth of the Hudson" focuses on the bleakest and ugliest items in sight as representation of the interior "unforgivable landscape" which is the poet's own.

(2) Free verse is organized by the power of the image, by a construct of images as concrete and specific as possible, that serve as objective correlative for inner states of mind. Surely it is not coincidental that the origins of free verse coincide with French *symbolisme* and Anglo-American imagism. From William Carlos Williams's "Good Night" (see essay 5) and "As the cat" to Snyder's "Mid-August at Sourdough Mountain Lookout" and Levertov's "A Day Begins," the free-verse line presents what are often unmediated images, as they appear in the mind's eye of the poet: "A headless squirrel, some blood / oozing from the unevenly / chewed-off neck" (Levertov); "The sun sets in the cold without friend" (Merwin); "In the depths of the Greyhound Terminal / sitting dumbly on a baggage truck looking at the sky" (Ginsberg); "Down valley a smoke haze" (Snyder);

"The ice ticks seaward like a clock" (Lowell). Perception, discovery, re-action: free-verse is the form par excellence that strives toward mimesis of individual *feeling*, as that feeling is generated by sights, sounds, smells, and memories.

(3) Although free verse is speech-based, although it tracks the move-ment of the breath itself, syntax is regulated, which is to say that the free-verse "I" generally speaks in complete sentences: "the first irises / have opened since dawn," "When it has gone I hear the stream running after it," "staring through my eyeglasses I realized shuddering these thoughts were not eternity," "I cannot remember things I once read," "Chemical air / sweeps in from New Jersey, / and smells of coffee." If, these poems seem to say, there is no metrical recurrence, no rhyme or stanzaic struc-ture, syntax must act as clarifier and binder, bringing units together and establishing their relationships.

(4) A corollary of regulated syntax is that the free-verse poem *flows;* it is, in more ways than one, *linear*. Again, the stage for this linear move-ment was already set in a poem like Williams's "As the cat," which moves, slowly but surely, "into the pit / of the empty / flowerpot." Even Gins-berg's complicated patterns of repetition (of word, phrase, clause) move toward the closure of "Farewell ye Greyhound where I suffered so much, / hurt my knee and scraped my hand and built my pectoral muscles big as vagina." In Levertov's "A Day Begins" the perception of death (the view of the blood-soaked squirrel) modulates into one of renewal (the opening irises), the epiphany coming in the final line with the compound "bruise-blue," tying the two together. Merwin's "Dusk in Winter" moves from its quiet, anapestic opening, "The sún séts in the cóld withoût friénds," to the markedly divided final line with its two "it" clauses ("It has," "It is") and concluding spondee, "lóng wáy." In Lowell's "The Mouth of the Hudson" every image from the ticking ice to the "sulphur-yellow sun" sets the stage for the reference to the "unforgivable landscape" of the last line. And even Snyder's "Mid-August," which does not push toward such neat closure, moves fluidly from line to line, culminating in the three strong stresses of "hígh stíll aír."

(5) As a corollary of (4), the rhythm of continuity of which I have been speaking depends on the unobtrusiveness of sound structure in free verse, as if to say that what is said must not be obscured by the actual saying. In this sense, free verse is the antithesis of such of its precursors as Ger-ard Manley Hopkins's sprung rhythm, with its highly figured lines like "I caught this morning morning's minion, king- / dom of daylight's dau-

phin, dapple-dawn-drawn Falcon, in his riding." Not that the free-verse passages cited above aren't very much "worked," organized as they are by internal sound patterning, repetition of stress groups, and the counterpoint that arises from the isolation-by-line of units that otherwise form part of a larger sequence. In Levertov's poem, for example, "oozing from the unevenly / chewed-off neck," produces a sonic disturbance by means of the "uneven" line break and the jagged rhythm (only two full stresses in eight syllables) of the line "oózing from the unévenly." Or again, end stopping and strong stressing on monosyllabic units produces special effects as in Snyder's "Pítch glóws ón the fír-cónes," where "cones" picks up the long *o* sound of "glows" and has an eye rhyme with "on." At the same time, Snyder is wary of the sound taking over: hence the casual quiet lines like "I cannot remember things I once read."

(6) Finally—and this accords with the unobtrusiveness of sound— the free-verse lyric of the fifties and sixties subordinates the visual to the semantic.[26] Levertov's open tercets, Snyder's five-line stanzas, Ginsberg's strophes, Merwin's minimal linear units, and Lowell's loose verse paragraphs—none of these do much to exploit the white space of the page or to utilize the material aspects of typography. Except for Ginsberg's Whitmanesque long lines, all the examples above have columns of verse centered on the page, with justified left margins, and only minimally jagged right margins, line lengths being variable only within limits.[27] The look of the poem is thus neither more nor less prominent than in metrical verse.

Interestingly, the six features I have discussed here—all of them, of course, closely related—turn up in the poets' own statements of poetics included in *Naked Poetry*. "The responsibility of the writer," says William Stafford, "is not restricted to intermittent requirements of sound repetition or variation: the writer or speaker enters a constant, never-ending flow and variation of gloriously seething changes of sound" (NAK 82). "Page arrangement," Ginsberg observes of "Wichita Vortex Sutra," "notates the thought-stops, breath-stops, runs of inspiration, changes of mind, startings and stoppings of the car" (NAK 222). "Organic poetry," writes Levertov in her well-known "Some Notes on Organic Form," "is a method of apperception": "first there must be an experience, a sequence or constellation of perceptions of sufficient interest, felt by the poet intensely enough to demand of him [sic] their equivalence in words: he is brought to speech" (NAK 141). And Merwin seems to speak for all the poets in the anthology when he says:

In an age when time and technique encroach hourly, or appear to, on the source itself of poetry, it seems as though what is needed for any particular nebulous unwritten hope that may become a poem is not a manipulable, more or less predictably recurring pattern, but *an unduplicatable resonance,* something that would be like an echo except that it is repeating no sound. Something that always belonged to it: its sense and its information before it entered words. (NAK 270–71, my emphasis)

An unduplicatable resonance: from its inception, this is what most free verse has striven to be. "For me," says Snyder, "every poem is unique. . . . A scary chaos fills the heart as 'spir'itual breath—in'spir'ation; and is breathed out into the thing-world as a poem" (NAK 357).

But there is one (and I think only one) exception to this poetics in the Mezey-Berg anthology, and it marks a useful transition to the poetry in *Out of Everywhere.* That exception is the poetry of Robert Creeley. Although Creeley's own "Notes apropos 'Free Verse'" make much of Olson's field composition and the use of breath, it also contains the following statement:

I am myself hopeful that linguistic studies will bring to contemporary criticism a vocabulary and method more sensitive to the basic *activity* of poetry. . . . Too, I would like to see a more viable attention paid to syntactic environment, to what I can call crudely "grammartology." (NAK 185)

And he talks about his own interest in "a balance of *four,* a four-square circumstance, be it walls of a room or legs of a table . . . an intensive variation on "foursquare" patterns such as [Charlie Parker's] "I've Got Rhythm" (NAK 186–87).

The "foursquare" jazz-based pattern Creeley talks of here may turn up as a four-line stanza (e.g., "A Form of Women," "A Sight") but also as the number of words per line, as in part 4 of the sequence called "Anger":

> Face me, $\longrightarrow$
> in the dark,
> my face. See me.
>
> It is the cry $\longrightarrow$
> I hear all $\longrightarrow$
> my life, my own $\longrightarrow$

voice, my $\longrightarrow$
eye locked in $\longrightarrow$
self sight, not $\longrightarrow$

the world what $\longrightarrow$
ever it is
but the close $\longrightarrow$

breathing beside $\longrightarrow$
me I reach out $\longrightarrow$
for, feel as $\longrightarrow$

warmth in $\longrightarrow$
my hands then $\longrightarrow$
returned. The rage $\longrightarrow$

is what I $\longrightarrow$
want, what $\longrightarrow$
I cannot give $\longrightarrow$

to myself, of $\longrightarrow$
myself, in $\longrightarrow$
the world.
(NAK 182–83)

To call such poetry "free verse" is not quite accurate, for something is certainly being counted in these little blocklike stanzas, even if it is neither stress nor syllable but word. The pattern is 2-3-4, 4-3-4, 2-3-3, 3-3-3, 4-4-3, 2-3-4, 3-2-4, 4-3-2, the final stanza reversing the word count of the first. So short are the line units and so heavily enjambed (twenty of twenty-four lines) as well as broken by caesuras (see lines 3, 18), so basic the vocabulary, made up as it is of prepositions, pronouns, and function words, that each word takes on its own aura and receives its own stress, as in:

vóice, mý

éye lócked ín

sélf síght, nót

And the stresses are further emphasized by the internal rhyme ("my / eye", also echoing "cry" "my" in the preceding tercet), overriding the line break, and the pulling of "sight" in two directions: one toward "self" via alliteration and the second toward "not" via consonance.

Indeed, although Creeley's tercets superficially resemble Levertov's, the features of free verse I listed above hardly apply. This poem does not present us with a mimesis of speech, tracking the process of perception. The first-person pronoun ("I" / "my" / "me" "myself") is used twelve times in the space of seventy-five words, and yet that "I" is less speaking voice than a particle that passively submits to external manipulation:

> is what I
> want, what
> I cannot give

where "want" and "what," separated by a single phoneme, occlude the "I's" halting presence. Again, monosyllabic lines like "is what I" refer neither to sun and stream, as in Merwin's poem, or to rocks and meadows, as in Snyder's. There is no image complex to control the flow of speech; indeed the shift from line to line is by no means linear: "See me," does not follow from "Face me." The normal syntagmatic chain is broken, the first tercet, for example, calling attention to the play of signifiers in "Face me" / "my face" rather than to that which is signified. And when we come to line 4, "It is the cry," the normal flow of free verse is impeded because the unspecified pronoun "It" returns us to the previous tercet as we try to make out what "It" might refer to. Or again, in line 7, "voice, my" means differently *within* the line than in the larger structure of "my own / voice, my eye locked in / self sight."

The syntactic ambiguity of lines like "for, feel as" and "want, what," coupled with the insistent word-stress, produces a rhythm of extreme weight and fragmentation—a kind of aphasic stutter—that is both heard and seen on the page. Each word, to cite Gertrude Stein, is as important as every other word. Sound becomes obtrusive ("me I reach out") as does the creation of paragrams, formed by cutting up complete sentences or clauses. Thus, although at first glance, the look of Creeley's poem on the page is not all that different from, say, the Snyder counterpart, the consistent detachment of words from their larger phrasal or clausal environment—a practice that goes way beyond what is known as enjambment—creates a very different physical image.

Postlinears and "Multi-Mentionals"

If the unit of free verse is, as all theorists agree, the line, then the unit of Creeley's poem might more properly be described as what the Russian futurists called "the word as such." Indeed, just as early free-verse poets called metrical form into question ("To break the pentameter, that was the first heave"), what is now being called into question is the line itself. As Bruce Andrews puts it in his and Charles Bernstein's symposium "L=A=N=G=U=A=G=E Lines":[28]

> 1. Lines linear outline, clear boundaries' effect, notice the package from its perimeter, consistency, evenness, seemingly internal contours which end up packaging the insides so that they can react or point or be subordinated to a homogenized unit, to what's outside. . . . Boundary as dividing—"you step over that line & you're asking for trouble." . . . Territorial markers and confinements, ghost towns, congested metropolis on a grid. . . .
> 3. Better, constant crease & flux, a radical discontinuity as a lack, jeopardizes before & after, stop & start, a dynamic in fragments, suggesting an unmappable space, no coordinates, troubling us to locate ourselves in formal terms. (LIP 177)

Who would have thought that less than forty years after Olson celebrated the "LINE" as the embodiment of the breath, the signifier of the heart, the line would be perceived as a boundary, a confining border, a form of packaging? "When making a line," writes Bernstein in the mock-romantic blank verse poem "Of Time and the Line" that concludes the symposium, "better be double sure / what you're lining in & what you're lining / out & which side of the line you're on" (LIP 216). Similarly, Johanna Drucker talks of "Refusing to stay 'in line,' creating instead, a visual field in which all lines are tangential to the whole" (LIP 181). Peter Inman refers to Olson's sense of the line as unit of poet's breath "too anthropomorphized." "The general organizational push to my stuff," says Inman, "becomes page-specific I tend to write in pages . . . not in stories or poems" (LIP 204). And Susan Howe remarks that in *The Liberties,* she wanted to "abstract" the "ghosts" of Stella and Cordelia from "masculine" linguistic configuration." "First," says Howe, "I was a painter, so for me, words shimmer. Each has an aura" (LIP 209). And as an example of a "splintered sketch of sound," Howe produces a page from *The Liberties* (LIP 210).

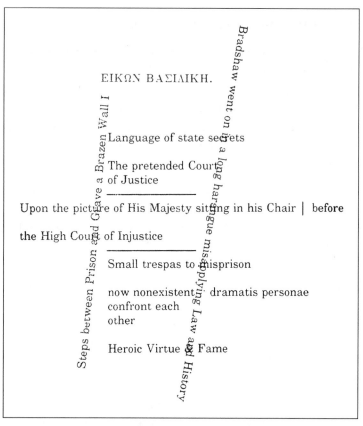

Figure 1. Susan Howe, from *A Bibliography of the King's Book,*
or *Eikon Basilike.*

Howe's own long verbal-visual sequence *Eikon Basilike* (see figure 1),
which is the opening selection in Maggie O'Sullivan's new anthology *Out
of Everywhere,* forms an interesting bridge to what Wendy Mulford calls, in
her "After. Word," the "multi- and non-linear" writing of younger women
poets in the United States, United Kingdom, and Canada. Howe's use of
cut-ups and found text (or invention of a found text, since her version of
the *Bibliography of the King's Book* or *Eikon Basilike* is a complex refiguring
of the ostensible forgery of Charles I's own writings)[29] come out of the
concrete poetry movement, but her typographical devices (mirror images
of lines, overprints, broken fonts) are designed to question the authority
of the historical document, even as she selects certain passages and, so
to speak, overstresses them, as in the lineated text "ENGELANDTS MEMO-
RIAEL," where every word has the "aura" Howe speaks of in her statement
on the line:

Laud Charles Í Fairfax

in which even the number "I" (as in Charles the First) is given a full stress.[30]

According to conventional criteria, the material forms used by the thirty poets in *Out of Everywhere*[31] can be classified as "verse" (e.g., Rae Armantrout, Nicole Brossard, Wendy Mulford, Melanie Neilson, Marjorie Welish), "prose" (e.g., Tina Darragh, Carla Harryman, Leslie Scalapino, Rosmarie Waldrop), or some variant on concrete poetry (e.g., Paula Claire, Kathleen Fraser, Susan Howe, Maggie O'Sullivan, Joan Retallack, Diane Ward). The collection also contains short plays or scenes by Lyn Hejinian, Caroline Bergvall, and Fiona Templeton. But such classifications obscure what is also a common impulse. Consider the following examples:

(1) Although you are thin you always seemed to be in front of my eyes, putting back in the body the roads my thoughts might have taken. As if forward and backward meant no more than right and left, and the earth could just as easily reverse its spin. So that we made each other the present of a stage where time would not pass, and only space would age, encompassing all 200,000 dramatic situations, but over the rest of the proceedings, the increase of entropy and unemployment. Meanwhile we juggled details of our feelings into an exaggeration which took the place of explanation, and consequences remained in the kind of repose that, like a dancer's, already holds the leap toward inside turning out.

Figure 2. Rosmarie Waldrop, from *Lawn of Excluded Middle*.

In *Rational Geomancy,* Steve McCaffery and bpNichol remind us that in standard prose as well as in the

visually continuous poem (Milton's *Paradise Lost* for instance) the page has no optical significance. . . . Being to a large extent a working out of information through duration, prose structures tend to be temporal rather than visual. . . . In extended prose or poetry the page becomes an obstacle to be overcome. [Whereas in poetry] the left-hand margin is always a starting point, the right-hand margin a terminal, neither of which is determined by the randomness of page size but rather by the inner necessity of the compositional process. (RGEO 61)

It is this "inner necessity" that may be noted in the four examples. Whether ostensibly "prose" (Rosmarie Waldrop) or "verse" (Karen Mac

Multi-Mentional

That line's running-board basics

sidereal on all fours

preen

exploitation of perfect timing

renew

maximum syncopation

temperature tantrums clever yes

but mongrel

statistics are with us.

Head up in arms

pieces of time at regular intervals

if the ring fits answer the phone

non-commital background

indications assume no one's perfect

telepathy

soft patience or landslide afloat

the birds not flying pinpoint

a simile swerving away.

Figure 3. Karen Mac Cormack, "Multi-Mentional," from *Marine Snow.*

Cormack), these poems are first and foremost page-based: they are *designed* for the eye rather than merely reproduced and reproducible, as I found when I tried to type them up leaving the original spacing and layout intact. In these visual constructs, the flow of the line as the individual's breath as well as of the simulation of the eye's movement from image to image, observation to observation, is inhibited by any number

A Lesson from the Cockerel

POPPY THANE. PENDLE DUST. BOLDO SACHET GAUDLES
GIVE GINGER. GIVE INK. SMUDGE JEEDELA LEAVINGS,
TWITCH JULCE. WORSEN. WRIST DRIP. SKINDA. JANDLE.
                      UDDER DIADEMS INTERLUCE.
                      ICYCLE OPALINE RONDA.
CRIMINAL   CRAB RATTLES ON THE LUTE.
CONSTITUENTS   BLINDINGLY RAZOR-GUT.
                      SHOOKER — GREENEY CRIMSON
                      NEAPTIDE COMMON PEAKS IN THE
                      SWIFT PULLERY. TWAIL,
                      HOYA METHODS: SAXA ANGLAISE
SKEWERED SKULL INULA.

Figure 4. Maggie O'Sullivan, "A Lesson from the Cockerel," from *Unofficial Word*.

of "Stop" signs. This is the case even in Waldrop's prose passage, which opens with the sentence: "Although you are thin you always seemed to be in front of my eyes, putting back in the body the roads my thoughts might have taken." Syntactically, this sentence is normal enough, but the reader/listener must stop to consider what the conditional clause can possibly mean here. What does being "thin" have to do with inhibiting one's partner's "thoughts," except that the two words alliterate? And does one really "put" those "thoughts" back into the body, as if one is stuffing an envelope? Robert Frost's famous "The Road Not Taken," which is alluded to in Waldrop's sentence, moralizes its landscape, turning the two divergent, but quite similar, roads into emblems of the futility of the choice-making process. But in Waldrop's *Lawn of the Excluded Middle, paysage moralisé* gives way to a curious collapsing of the distinctions between mind and body, space and time, inside and outside. On this new "stage," "only space would age" (notice the rhyme) and "exaggeration . . . took the place of explanation." What looks like prose is in fact highly figured: take the "increase of entropy and unemployment" which characterizes these proceedings. Denotatively, the words are unrelated, although both refer to states of negativity. But visually and aurally, the second is almost an anagram of the first, the only unshared letters being *r, u,* and *m.* The dancer's "leap toward inside turning out" of the last line thus enacts the verbal play we have been witnessing—a play in which "you" and "I," "juggl[ing] the

(4)

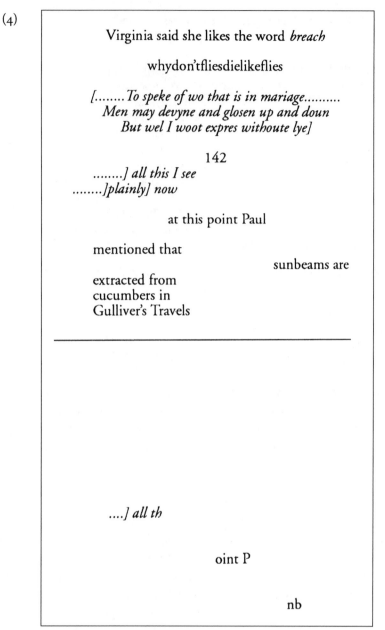

Virginia said she likes the word *breach*

whydon'tfliesdielikeflies

[........To speke of wo that is in mariage..........
Men may devyne and glosen up and doun
But wel I woot expres withoute lye]

142

........] all this I see
........]plainly] now

at this point Paul

mentioned that

sunbeams are

extracted from
cucumbers in
Gulliver's Travels

....] all th

oint P

nb

Figure 5. Joan Retallack, from "Afterrimages," in *Afterrimages.*

details of our feelings," find momentary rest as the voiced stop (*t*) culminates in the silence of the blank space.

If Waldrop's "sentences" are thus more properly "nonsentences," the lines in Karen Mac Cormack's "Multi-Mentional" open like an accordion and close down again, putting pressure on isolated centered words like "preen," "renew," and "telepathy." The relation of space to time, which is central to Waldrop's text, is intricately reconceived here. "Multi-Mentional" signifies "multi-dimensional" but also the "multi" things "mentioned" or worth mentioning in discourse about space-time. On the one hand, we have the "line's running-board basics," those reliable "straight-line" ledges beneath the car door that help the passengers to "get out." What with "perfect timing," "maximum syncopation," and "pieces of time at regular intervals," linear motion should not be impeded. But the "line's running-board basics" are countered by a motion that is "sidereal on all fours." Does planetary influence control our ordinary moves, and why are they on "all fours"? And why are the statistics we should rely on "mongrel"? No use, in any case "preen[ing]" in this situation, a situation in which tantrums are ominously "temperature tantrums" (is something going to explode?) even as being "up in arms," gives way to a case of "Head up in arms," which sounds like a military or calisthenic routine. How, Mac Cormack asks, delimit word meanings? "If the ring fits answer the phone," initially sounds absurd only because we are looking for a finger, but the adage actually makes good sense. If the ring fits (if you recognize the ring as being that of your phone), answer it. Or has the caller already been recognized by "telepathy"? In Mac Cormack's "multi-mentional" world, "patience" is "soft" (which implies there's a hard patience as well), landslides "float," and the location of birds in flight can never be "pinpoint[ed]," any more than "similes" (*a* is like *b*) can measure the "multi-mentional."

The progress from line to line here is thus reversed and spatialized (another "multi-mentional"): "renew," for example, points back to "preen," which has all its letters except the *w*. The heavily endstopped "témperature tántrums cléver yés" jumps ahead to "telepathy." Indeed, going into reverse seems to be the mode of operation in Mac Cormack's poem. Secondary stressing, so central to the poetry of Ginsberg or Snyder (e.g., "Pítch glóws ôn the fír-cônes"), as the representation of an actual voice contour, the flow of speech, is avoided as is ellision so that each morpheme receives attention, as in the guttural "Thát líne's rúnning-bóard's básics," which is almost a tongue-twister. Sounds cannot coalesce into rhythmic units, as they do in Snyder's "Sourdough Mountain," for then their "multi-mentional" quality would be lost. Which is to say that in the ear as on the page, the language act becomes central. "Word order = world order" (RGEO 99).

Maggie O'Sullivan's medievalizing moral tale "A Lesson from the Cockerel" performs similar operations on the catalog poem. From Pound to Zukofsky to Ginsberg, cataloging has been a popular poetic device, but here the list is, so to speak, blown apart by spatial design: the first three lines in capital letters are followed by a rectangular box containing, in a row, the words "CRIMINAL" and "CONSTITUENTS," with a word column along the right margin, and the line "SKEWERED SKULL INULA" (reminiscent of Pound's "Spring / Too long / Gongula"),[32] placed beneath the bottom border. The cataloged items, many of them archaic or obscure, like "BOLDO" and "INULA," both of them bitter alkaloid plant extracts used as drugs, and the many neologisms like "JULCE" and "SHOOKER," are part of an elaborate roll-call of exotic narcotics, a kind of postmodern "Ode on Melancholy," in which the address to the "POPPY THANE" or opium lord becomes a drum call heightened by its Anglo-Saxon and pseudo–Anglo-Saxon ("SAXA ANGLAISE") word particles — "PENDLE DUST," "WRIST DRIP," "NEAPTIDE COMMON PEAKS," "SWIFT PULLERY. TWAIL." Lines like "GIVE GINGER,|| GIVE INK,|| SMUDGE JEEDELA LEAVINGS" exploit the rhythm, alliteration, and assonance of the football cheer or political chant, but the captions inside the empty box mark all this chanting as "CRIMINAL / CONSTITUENTS," and label the "frame" as so much "SKEWERED SKULL."

Is "A Lesson from the Cockerel" free verse? Yes, if we mean by free verse the absence of meter, stress, syllable count, or quantity. But, strictly speaking, O'Sullivan's verse units are closer to the Old English alliterative line, as in

$$\acute{P}OPPY\ TH\acute{A}NE,\ ||\ P\acute{E}NDLE\ D\acute{U}ST$$

or to such Poundian variations on that line as "líons lóggy || with Círce's tísane" (Canto XXXIX), than to nonnumerical linear verse, and, in any case, the visual layout calls attention to itself as what looks like a computer printout, a set of headlines, a sheet of advertising copy coming through the fax machine. As in Mac Cormack's poem, secondary sound features (rhyme, assonance, consonance, alliteration) take precedence over the recurrence of stresses. Phrases like "UDDER DIADEMS INTERLUCE" or "CRAB RATTLES ON THE LUTE" perform at a sonic level before their semantics are fully grasped. The visual/vocal dimension of the words is more prominent than their actual referents. And this too is a time-honored tradition in poetry, however far free-verse poetry, the poetry of the voice and the image, has gotten away from it.

Not images, but "afterrimages," as Joan Retallack's sequence by that title makes clear. "We tend to think," says Retallack in the frontispiece of her book, "of afterimages as aberrations. In fact all images are after. That is the terror they hold for us." "I do not know which to prefer," writes Wallace Stevens in "Thirteen Ways of Looking at a Blackbird," "The beauty of inflections / Or the beauty of innuendoes, / the blackbird whistling / or just after." In Retallack's scheme of things, this becomes "*After* whistling or just _____": in our fin-de-siècle world, every image, event, speech, or citation can be construed as an "afterthought" or "aftershock" of something that has always already occurred.

One form of "afterrimage" Retallack uses is found text: the poem before us draws on Chaucer (the opening of "The Wife of Bath's Tale") and Swift (book 3 of *Gulliver's Travels*) among other "literary" sources; it begins in medias res with someone's advice that there is a "need to give latitude which is often silence," followed by the typographical convention of "and/or." In keeping with this choice, no given line follows from the preceding one, at least not in any normal sequence, the text incorporating reportage, question, number, iambic pentameter citation (lines 4–6), and narrative fragment. The last six lines recall Creeley's strategy of counting words rather than feet, stresses, or syllables. The pattern is 4 (at center), 2-2 (left and lowered right), and then a 2-2-2 tercet. And now come the "afterrimages," chosen, Retallack tells us, by chance operation: thirteen characters or spaces from line 8, six from line 10, two from line 12. These tiny morphemic particles are living proof of what a difference a single letter can make. The ellipsis preceding "*all this I see*" becomes the mere stutter of *all th*; "point" loses its *p*, only to regain it from the capital *P* of "Paul" that follows; the loss opens up the text so that we think of "joint" or "anoint," the latter certainly being appropriate for Saint Paul. And the afterimage of "sunbeams," the meaningless vocalization *nb*, is a witty comment on the activities of Swift's Laputa. Not only, the poem implies, can sunbeams not be extracted from cucumbers, the word "sunbeams" doesn't break down neatly into *sun* + *beams* or even into neatly arranged vowels and consonants, but into the difficult-to-pronounce *nb*, followed by an exhalation of breath, or visual blank which is so to speak, "silence and/or." The final stop (*b*) is the voiced equivalent of the preceding *p*. Retallack's is thus an artifactual, wholly composed meditation on what can and cannot be "extracted from" language.

Susan Howe, I noted above, has referred to her typographical experiments as "abstractions" from "masculine linguistic formations," and many of the poets in *Out of Everywhere* would concur that such deconstruction has been central to their work. But it is also the case that their poems have many counterparts in the work of Clark Coolidge and Steve McCaffery, Charles Bernstein and Bob Perelman, Bruce Andrews and Christian Bök, and my own sense is that the transformation that has taken place in verse may well be more generational than it is gendered. We have, in any case, a poetics of nonlinearity or postlinearity that marks, not a return to the "old forms," because there is never a complete return, no matter how strongly one period style looks back to another, but a kind of "after-rimage" of earlier soundings, whether Anglo-Saxon *keenings,* formally balanced eighteenth-century prose, or Wittgensteinian aphoristic fragment. The new poems are, in most cases, as visual as they are verbal; they must be *seen* as well as heard, which means that at poetry readings, their scores must be performed, activated. Poetry, in this scheme of things, becomes what McCaffery has called "an experience in language rather than a representation by it." [33]

I have no name for this new form of sounding and perhaps its namelessness goes with the territory: the new exploratory poetry (which is, after all, frequently "prose") does not want to be labeled or categorized. What can be said, however, is that the "free verse" aesthetic, which has dominated our century, is no longer operative. Take a seemingly minor feature of free verse like enjambment. To run over a line means that the line is a limit, even as the caesura can only exist within line limits. To do away with that limit is to reorganize sound configurations according to different principles. I conclude with a passage from Caroline Bergvall's "Of Boundaries and Emblems"

> By Evening We're Inconsolable. Having Reached This Far, Bent Over Tables Of Effervescence Within The Claustrophobic Bounds Of The Yellow Foreground: Art Has Kept Us High And Separate, Hard In Pointed Isolation, Forever Moved By The Gestures Of Its Positions And The Looseness Of Even That: Now Vexed And Irritated, Still Plotting Endless Similitudes: We Trip Over Things: Strain To Extricate Ourselves From Closing Borders:
>
> (OOE 206)

Is this prose or some kind of kind of alphabet game, using majuscules and justified margins? The question is falsely posed: whether "verse" or "prose," Bergvall's is first and foremost a performance, an activation, both visual and aural, of a verbal text, whose every stress, "Hard In Pointed Isolation," seems to reverberate. No wonder those "Closing Borders" in the last line above are followed by a colon: a signature, as it were, of things to come.

7. What We Don't Talk about When We Talk about Poetry

Some Aporias of Literary Journalism

The reviewing of poetry or poetry criticism in the leading newspapers and journals has a curious relationship to reviews in related humanistic disciplines. Take, for example, two recent reviews that appeared just a few months apart in the *Times Literary Supplement*. The first is a review by Richard Sennett of four books on contemporary architectural theory (18 September 1992, 3–4), the second, one by Glyn Maxwell of eight books on contemporary poetics (29 January 1993, 9–10).

Richard Sennett is a well-known social critic (currently professor of sociology and humanities at New York University) whose most recent book *The Conscience of the Eye* (1991) is subtitled *The Design and Social Life of Cities*. The books under review in this, a special issue titled "Cities" (which also featured articles by Gavin Stamp, David Rieff, and Saskia Sassen), were Jean-Louis Cohen's *Le Corbusier and the Mystique of the USSR: Theories and Projects for Moscow, 1928–1936* (Princeton, 1991), Robert Harbison's *The Built, the Unbuilt, and the Unbuildable* (Thames and Hudson, 1992), Beatriz Colomina's collection, *Sexuality and Space* (Princeton, 1992), and Anthony Vidler's *The Architectural Uncanny* (MIT, 1992). Sennett wrote about these books as an informed insider: he has himself been active in the symposia held at the Princeton University School of Architecture, where some of the material in question had been aired. His essay takes it as a given that urban spaces are now largely disaster areas but argues that architects neither are to blame for this state of affairs nor can be expected to come up with blueprints for some kind of utopian renewal. Rather, he suggests, in sympathy with the theorists under review, that what is needed at the moment is perhaps a better understanding of how these spaces actually work, how buildings, streets, and open spaces relate to the human body.

Cohen's book on Le Corbusier supplies Sennett with his historical frame, for it details the great architect's design for the proposed Palace of the Soviets in Moscow, a design based on the attempt to integrate inside and outside, the built form to its surrounding space so as to downplay ceremony and create a truly popular architecture. The rejection of the plan by the authorities in 1932 "in favor of a standard-issue monument in neo-Palladian style by Zhotovsky" is taken, both by Cohen and by Sennett, as emblematic of the difficulties of trying to invent a genuinely "popular" form of architecture. Perhaps, then, as Robert Harbison and the contributors to *Sexuality and Space* argue, the best that buildings can do is to create what Harbison calls "fictions of value." Harbison "sees the experience of industrial ruin as inviting a radically innovative response"; in the case of Richard Rogers's Lloyds Building, for example, the elaborate "mock-ruins" unexpectedly built from steel and glass have a curious way of altering our sense of time. And Anthony Vidler's *Architectural Uncanny* (a book that has since become celebrated in discussions of the postmodern arts) carries this notion one step further. To counter the deadness of contemporary neutralized urban spaces, Vidler suggests, one must open oneself to the "uncanny" of crossings, must try to break down the existing borders between suburb, strip, and urban center and see what their intersection will produce. Loss, dislocation, invasion: these become positive values.

Another reviewer might have been less sympathetic to those under review than Sennett, but I think most readers would agree that his is an interesting, sophisticated, well-informed review that helps one to understand what's going on in recent urban theory. And Sennett's knowledge of the social context, his own participation in the debate on what to do with urban spaces, makes him an excellent expositor.

Glyn Maxwell sees his role rather differently. The books that he was assigned to review are, in fairness to him, as curious an assortment of apples and oranges as one can imagine.[1] First, two critical studies of established poets: *The Art of Derek Walcott,* a collection of essays edited by Stuart Brown (Seren, 1989) and James Booth's monograph *Philip Larkin, Writer* (Harvester, 1992). Next, a biography, A. T. Tolley's *My Proper Ground: A Study of the Work of Philip Larkin and Its Development* (Edinburgh, 1992).

These were followed by three more theoretical works: Linda Reinfeld's *Language Poetry: Writing as Rescue* (Louisiana, 1992), Charles Bernstein's *A Poetics* (Harvard, 1992), and Anthony Easthope and John O. Thompson's *Contemporary Poetry Meets Modern Theory* (Harvester, 1991). These three books are related: the poet Charles Bernstein's manifestos, theoretical prose poems, and cultural explorations collected in *A Poetics* stand behind Linda Reinfeld's analytical history of the Language Poetry movement in the United States; Easthope and Thompson, for their part, have brought together a variety of critics who hold the common view that the more radical poetries today have much in common with poststructuralist theory. The three, in any case, have nothing in common with the Walcott and Larkin studies, on the one hand, or with Robert Pack's *The Long View: Essays on the Discipline of Hope and Poetic Craft* (Massachusetts, 1991), on the other. Pack is an American poet who has been around for a long time and is best known as an anthologist. His essays are avowedly personal, impressionistic, and casual. Finally, the review includes a study of Emersonian-Jamesian poetics, *Poetry and Pragmatism* (Faber, 1992), by one of the distinguished academic critics in the United States, Richard Poirier.

Unlike the four books reviewed by Sennett, which are closely related, both historically and ideologically, Maxwell's list thus has no rationale, except that somehow all eight books (published, incidentally, over a four-year period) have some bearing on contemporary poetry, whatever that is. One should note that Maxwell was given some four columns to cover eight books, as against the six columns allotted to Sennett. More important: whereas Sennett is on a par with the authors he reviews, having written comparable books and essays as a fellow worker in the field, Maxwell seems to have been assigned this review in his capacity not as a published poetry critic or scholar or theorist (none of which he is) but as a poet. Indeed, it has become increasingly common in literary journalism for theoretical and historical studies of poetry like Reinfeld's and Poirier's to be reviewed—when they are reviewed at all—by certified poets. (A certified poet is one who has published a book or two of poems with a mainstream publisher and has received a few respectful reviews in the mainstream press.) The parallel, in the case of the architecture books, would be to have an architect, perhaps a partner in a respected firm that specializes in office buildings on Park Avenue or in suburban tract housing, review Anthony Vidler's *Architectural Uncanny*.

Maxwell begins with a set of assumptions: (1) the "great poem" induce[s] strong, conflicting emotions in every reader who reads it in its language; (2) "it is always instantly memorized"; (3) once its author is dead, it quickly gets overinterpreted, has meanings read into it, and a myth of its author comes into being that threatens to displace the "authentic" poet who wrote it; (4) "poets know what is worth saying about other poets"; and (5) the concept of "schools" is "especially unhelpful." All these theorems are put before us as if they were simply a matter of common sense, even though critical theory of the past half century has dismantled, step by step, the notion of the authentic "ur-poem," destroyed by later misreadings, the poem as catharsis of "conflicting emotions" (shades of I. A. Richards), best understood by other poets. As for the memorability criterion, which Maxwell puts forward as if it were the second law of thermodynamics, this criterion does not allow for free verse (hard to memorize), prose poetry or visual poetries—all of them very prominent and exciting today. Memorability depends, of course, on rhyme and meter; it's much easier to memorize *Don Juan* than *The Prelude,* Emily Dickinson's short hymn stanzas than Whitman's long poems, Robert Frost than William Carlos Williams. And how would one "memorize" Ian Hamilton Finlay's poetic compositions? Or Susan Howe's?

Maxwell doesn't worry about such thorny issues. He knows what he likes, and the books on Walcott and Larkin are deemed worthy, not because their contributors are doing anything special, but because Walcott and Larkin are worthy. The reviewer doesn't worry much about them, nor about Pack and Poirier (the latter gets rather short shrift), his witty barbs being reserved for the so-called language poets discussed by Linda Reinfeld, by some of Anthony Easthope's contributors, and by Charles Bernstein, himself one of the founders of the movement. Maxwell doesn't like the concept of the movement or school, which animates Reinfeld's discussion of language poetry, but he never bothers to investigate if the poets in question—Bernstein, Howe, Michael Palmer, Lyn Hejinian, Clark Coolidge, Ron Silliman—do, in fact, constitute one. Never mind: the main thing is that these, to Maxwell, self-evidently worthless poets continue to write about each other "long after the magazine that gave them their name [$L=A=N=G=U=A=G=E$] has disappeared, along with any likelihood of anyone else taking an interest." And further: theirs is a poetry of "complete and deliberate impenetrability," a poetry that "jettison[s] the notion that language can communicate." The twin goals of poetry—to teach and to delight—are thus totally violated.

Unlike Richard Sennett, then, Glyn Maxwell has no commitment to the approaches taken by his subjects. On the contrary, he gives no evidence that he has ever *read* a single poem by Charles Bernstein or the other poets Reinfeld discusses; indeed, it is doubtful that he has so much as looked at *A Poetics,* since Bernstein's arguments are cited only from Reinfeld's book, as if her account, which is after all an interpretation of Bernstein's theory, were simply equivalent to it. As for the Easthope-Thompson volume, I can testify to the fact that he hasn't read my own essay in that collection, of which he writes, "Elsewhere, Marjorie Perloff celebrates the brick wall of Steve McCaffery's work by invoking Ezra Pound—odd how these radical, dethroning writers will gulp whole the dicta ('Make it new!') of an old apologist for fascism." Period. My essay on McCaffery's *Lag* never mentions Pound's name nor do I say anything in it about "Make it new!" But even if I did, the assumption that a Pound echo in McCaffery would somehow link this poet to fascism takes one's breath away. And, incidentally, how and why is McCaffery's poem a "brick wall"? Is it enough merely to so pronounce?

Maxwell's is thus a review that blithely ignores the facts, not to mention the poetic principles involved. The reviewer's assertion that "no one" takes an interest in the language poetry movement is belied by so many articles, books, and symposia, not only in the United States but also in the United Kingdom (as well as in France, China, Japan, and Australia), that the statement hardly warrants serious rebuttal. Indeed, this review would hardly be worth talking about, were it not so typical. For the fact is that whereas *TLS* reviews of books on architectural theory, on feminist studies, on the Elizabethan theater, or on philosophy (the same issue included a brilliant, excoriating piece by Arthur Danto on Mark Taylor's *Ethics of Authenticity*) are largely responsible pieces, written by experts in their various fields, the journal's discourse about contemporary poetry (perhaps about contemporary literary forms in general) is largely impressionistic, uninformed, and philistine. And the *TLS* is by no means the worst offender.

Here, for example, is Anthony Libby, a poet-critic who teaches at Ohio State University, on Stephen Dunn's *New and Selected Poems: 1974–94* (Norton, 1994) and Stephen Dobyns's *Velocities: New and Selected Poems, 1966–1992* (Viking-Penguin, 1994) in the *New York Times Book Review* for 15 January 1995:

> Are all the best poems about loss? They are not, probably, about happiness or love's sweet contentment, and the poet who aims to traverse those pleasant territories takes a hard road. . . . The heart of [Dunn's] collection records a long struggle to develop a voice true to

Mr. Dunn's simple affirmations and proof against the cynical reader's resistance. . . . [As for Dobyns], his is a more traditional style of masculinity, somewhat cool or repressed, angry, torn by constant awareness that "we are the creatures that love and slaughter." . . . The triumph of Stephen Dobyns's poetry may be that it keeps that sense of play intact, without denying horrors. . . . His quirky imagination affirms by celebrating itself, if not the dark and clouded world.[2]

What is this supposed to mean? Why should the "quirky imagination" of our time "celebrate itself"? Why do we want poetry that conveys a "somewhat cool or repressed masculinity"? And do we in fact need poetry to tell us that "we are creatures that love and slaughter"?

Or, to take a third example, consider the poet David Kirby's review of Marilyn Hacker's *Selected Poems, 1965–1990* (Norton, 1994), again in the *New York Times Book Review* (12 March 1995, 6). Kirby begins by announcing, "The history of recent literature is the history of the phrase 'Only connect.' Writers and readers have taken these words from E. M. Forster's *Howard's End* as an exhortation, with 'only' meaning 'merely' or perhaps 'exclusively.'" Those of us who don't quite subscribe to the notion that American poetry in the 1990s is written under the sign of E. M. Forster needn't worry. The reference functions merely as an acceptable literary lead-in, and Kirby quickly moves on to his more personal impressions: "At a time when so many writers seem to be measuring life from a considerable remove, it is invigorating to watch Marilyn Hacker glad-handing her way through the world with a warm facility. And a formalism so colloquial as to undo any readerly stereotypes."

The *New York Times Book Review* has been castigated for not devoting enough space to poetry. For the period January–June 1995, of approximately five hundred reviews, only five—1 percent—deal with new poetry. But quantity is not the answer. Indeed, if journalistic discourse on poetry can't be better than these examples, one might prefer a moratorium on the halfhearted attempt to include, for the sake of some residual notion of "culture," the occasional poetry review along with the occasional poem, the latter invariably presented inside a box as if to cordon it off from more important matters. But my modest proposal is not as pessimistic as it may sound. For I also want to suggest that the abysmal state of poetry reviewing is not, paradoxically, hurting the cause of poetry itself, which is, to my mind, extraordinarily healthy at the moment. Rather, there seems to be a mechanism at play that is making "literary journalism" irrelevant so far as contemporary literary production is concerned. It is this mechanism I want to explore.

History Lessons

Was poetry reviewing better in the Good Old Days? Is it only in recent years, thanks to the increasing commodification of our culture, that poetry has seemed to have no place in the public arena? Conservative critics like Dana Gioia would have us think so,[3] but a statistical survey of actual book reviewing tells us otherwise. My examples here are taken from what are generally regarded as the two leading book reviews in the United States: the *New York Times Book Review,* at this writing exactly a hundred years old, still the review that can make or break a book so far as sales are concerned, and the *New York Review of Books,* which began publication in 1963 in response to the extended strike at the *New York Times* and quickly established itself as the intellectuals' book review of choice.

The first issue of *New York Times Book Review* (subsequently cited as *NYTBR*) appeared on 10 October 1896 as what was then called the *Saturday Book Review Supplement.* Its avowed purpose, according to the introductory essay for the Arno Press Reprint (1968) by the then book review editor Francis Brown, was "to bring to readers news of books, news of authors, news of publishing, literary news of all kinds."[4] In 1896, this last category included such things as "reports on the state of Oscar Wilde in Reading Gaol." Indeed, there are continuing reports, throughout 1897, on Wilde's condition, which is declared "beyond human endurance," and his consequent turn to spirituality (see Rowland Strong in the 12 June 1897 issue). Reviewing was thus a form of reporting, its avowed aim being, as Brown puts it, "to help the reader and buyer, not the writer or publisher." The reviewer, Brown suggests, had the interests of the non-specialist reader in mind; he (the pronoun is used generically) functions as "his reader's guide, philosopher and friend. It is his business to say of new books what there is in them in such wise that his reader may learn whether the book under notice will probably interest him. Knowledge, equity and candor are the chief elements in the equipment of the book reviewer."

Two assumptions govern these and related statements. First, it was assumed that objective judgments on books could be made by more or less anonymous professional reviewers. (In the early years, the front page leader was in fact anonymous.) And second, it was taken for granted that a review of "literature" was just that—a review of novels, poems, plays, perhaps belles-lettres, not, as is prevalent today, primarily books on political, historical, psychological, anthropological subjects, on current events, or biographies and memoirs. Reminiscing about the pre–World War I years, Brown writes:

> In retrospect these were great literary years, these years before World War I. In verse, names were being made that would dominate for a long time to come: Yeats and Masefield, Ezra Pound, William Carlos Williams, Edward Arlington Robinson. In the novel it was the age of Conrad and Thomas Mann, Galsworthy, Anatole France, the still un-appreciated Dreiser. Willa Cather wrote "O Pioneers", D. H. Lawrence, "Sons and Lovers", and there was always Mrs. Wharton. Kipling in 1907 received a Nobel Prize at 42. (Introduction, unpaginated)

The canon would not be described all that differently today. And Brown is also proud to note that in 1922 *NYTBR* pronounced Joyce's *Ulysses* "the most important contribution that has been made to fictional literature in the twentieth century," and that Proust's *Swann's Way* received high marks. In the 6 February 1897 issue, Paul Lawrence Dunbar's *Lyrics of Lowly Life,* published by Dodd, Mead with an intoduction by W. D. Howells, received extravagant (and anonymous) praise for its wit, keen satire, subtle humor, and "rich colors." Richard Le Gallienne, review-ing Dunbar's *Complete Poems* on 18 January 1914, went even further: the poems, he declared, "have a certain classical rank in American literature by virtue of an excellence which is in need of no allowances on account of the poet's race." Dunbar's is an "authentic achievement which must give him a high and permanent place among the dialect poets of the world," and such poems as "The Debt," written in standard English, are also singled out for praise and cited in full. One would be hard put to find an African-American poet today who has received this sort of attention in the *Times.*

But lest we wax nostalgic, it was also true that reviewing as spreading-the-word (more blurb than critique) ran into trouble as the volume of books increased sharply after World War I. Indeed, the increase was not just in volume but variety. In 1909, after all, F. T. Marinetti had managed to get his first Futurist manifesto published on the front page of the Paris *Figaro,* where its competition was little more than the racetrack news, the stock market quotations, and the society news. After the war—a water-shed for book reviews as for so much else—a larger literate (and voting) population demanded more political, historical, and social coverage, in reviews as in news articles and editorials. At the same time, the new modernist poetry was often intentionally difficult and demanding. *The Waste Land* (1922), for example, could not be processed as readily as could the collections of short lyric poems to which audiences were accustomed, even if those poems were, like Dunbar's, by a black man. Eliot's long collage-poem, with its foreign phrases and fussy footnotes, was not reviewed at all in *NYTBR*. By this time, in any case, "books" no longer meant just literary books. On 6 January 1924, for example, the front page of the now larger (thanks to increasing advertising space) book review was devoted to a French memoir, the former premier and war minister Paul Painlévé's *Comment j'ai nommé Foch et Pétain*. The same issue has a review of Count Burian's memoir of Kaiser Franz Joseph and of Bertrand Russell's *ABC of Atoms*. And by the early 1930s, the basic blueprint and layout that characterizes the *NYTBR* to this day was in place. The lead article (on the cover, usually with a large photograph at the center) tended to be a review of a "major new novel" or of a large-scale historical/social critique. On 14 January 1934, for example, the leader is a review of Pearl Buck's *The Mother;* on 28 January, Sinclair Lewis's *Work of Art;* on 4 February, Phyllis Bentley's *A Modern Tragedy* (with the headline "A Novel That Clarifies Our Age"); and on February 11, Oswald Spengler's *Hour of Decision.*

Big novels, big ideas! What happens to poetry or to the more avant-garde literary productions in this context? Poetry could hardly be eliminated, a neo-Victorian, neoromantic culture continuing to demand its "higher" presence, even as it does in today's *New Yorker, New Republic,* or *Atlantic.* But as slender books of poems continued to proliferate, the group review became normative, one of the reviewer's chief tasks thus being to find a common thread like Kirby's "only connect." The reviewers tended to be themselves minor poets or, as in the founding days of *NYTBR,* professional journalists. Certainly there was no precedent for asking a poetry specialist (e.g., an academic critic or theorist) to review these books. For poetry—and this bias is still with us—had come to be considered a category of writing to which the usual questions of expertise did not apply. As Pierre Bourdieu has demonstrated in his study of literary reception:

> Poetry, by virtue of its restricted audience . . . the consequent low profits, which make it the disinterested activity *par excellence,* and also its prestige, linked to the historical tradition initiated by the Romantics, is destined to charismatic legitimation. . . . Although the break between poetry and the mass readership has been virtually total since

the late nineteenth century . . . poetry continues to represent the ideal model of literature for the least cultured consumers.[5]

Jimmy Carter's recent poetry venture is a case in point. "I have always found it possible," said Carter on the publication of his best-selling *Always a Reckoning* (1995), "to say things in my poems that would have been impossible to say in prose." Things like how sad he was to have to kill his aged dog:

> Yesterday I killed him. I had known
> for months I could not let him live. I might
> have paid someone to end it, but I knew
> that after fifteen years of sharing life
> the bullet ending his must be my own.[6]

Try saying that bit of blank verse in prose! The newspaper reviewers, evidently impressed by the sheer disinterestedness of the former president's efforts, did not wish to be harsh. And soon Jimmy Carter was embarking on a book tour around the United States and to Dylan Thomas's Wales.

The 14 January 1934 issue (the one with J. Donald Adams's review of Pearl Buck's *The Mother* on the cover) typically has a full-page article on "Six New Books of Verse by a Diversity of Poets." Among the poets are Kimi Gengo, Adelaide Love, C. Arthur Coan, and Mary Owens Lewis. The reviewer, Percy Hutchinson, praises the poems in Adelaide Love's *The Slender Singing Tree* (its "highly engaging title" is remarked upon) which are "written with skill against a background of deep thought." He cites "The Lien":

> Relentless press of little things;
> Eternal haste to do them all;
> The prior claim upon our days
> Relinquished to the trivial.
>
> Our obligations never paid
> But endless and imperative.
> O life, why must you always leave
> So little time to live?

"Somehow," remarks Hutchinson, "this seems to us the possible utterance of a disciplined Emily Dickinson. Not, of course, that the real Emily could ever have been disciplined, either as to thought or poetic utterance. . . .

But . . . the Amherst spinster-poet must ever stand symbolically for her sex's expression of itself in poetry. Thus it seems to us that Adelaide Love carries on what might be termed the Emily Dickinson tradition, that is, she expresses herself fragmentarily while seeing with inclusive vision, and plucks at the heart-strings, but always with the most gentle touch, perceiving and transferring beauty" (14).

From our vantage point sixty years later, we can laugh at the very idea of Adelaide Love's little jingle being favorably compared to the work of the, alas, "undisciplined" Emily Dickinson. But the problems of poetry reviewing confronting Percy Hutchinson were not all that different from those experienced by David Kirby in his review of Marilyn Hacker or even by Glyn Maxwell in his omnibus piece for the *TLS*. The mandate—to say something telling and original about five or ten unlike and generally unexceptional volumes of short personal lyrics—is not easy to fulfill. We can see this even in the more specifically literary journals like the *Georgia Review* or the *Hudson Review*. Consider an article in *PN Review* 80 (1991), in which T. J. G. Harris discusses Michael Hulse's *Eating Strawberries in the Necropolis* and Andrew Motion's *Love in a Life,* along with the first book, *Tale of the Mayor's Son,* by the very same Glyn Maxwell, who, being the newcomer in this group, gets one long paragraph:

> Glyn Maxwell combines strictness of form with abrupt arbitrariness, a kind of headlong, thrown-together, jagged improvisation that, if it often has small attraction for the ear, certainly has, as Joseph Brodsky remarks on the back of the book, a "propulsion . . . , owing in part to his tendency to draw metaphor from the syntax itself." But the propulsion is not so often real as apparent, and one has the frequent impression that a device (a tricky self-reference or address to the reader, a drawing of metaphor from syntax, a blatant obscurity of one kind or another—of which there are far too many) has been thrown in not so much to keep something going as to stop it from flagging. The "propulsion" also makes reading this book, which would have been better shorter, a wearying—and not, as it should be, an exhilarating— experience, since everything starts sounding the breathless, edgy same as it whoops and echoes in the ear's labyrinth. Maxwell needs an editor. But he is good at creating an atmosphere of arbitrary urban or suburban menace, and he can be funny. One senses a definite and characteristic style coming clear in this, his first book.[7]

This may have a more sophisticated patina than a comparable review in *NYTBR,* but what is it we really learn about Glyn Maxwell from Harris's review? Primarily that the book has the imprimatur of Joseph Brodsky, which probably accounts for its having been published by Bloodaxe in the first place. What else does Harris tell us? Well, that Maxwell uses "strict" forms (presumably rhyming metrical stanzas) to contain his "jagged improvisation." But since "improvisation" is by definition a form of extempore composition, designed to look natural and unrehearsed, why is it better served by "strictness of form" than by, say, free verse or Marinettian *parole in libertà?* Further: if Maxwell is, as Harris implies, tricky and needlessly obscure, how and where is he "funny"? But the most gratuitous phrase in this review is the reference to that "atmosphere of arbitrary urban or suburban menace," which Maxwell is evidently so "good at creating." Does this mean he is not good at creating an atmosphere of rural menace? Lambs stolen by vicious vagrants? Cows on speed, jumping over fences? Or does he mean that Maxwell does not take on the menace of wild, untrammeled nature? Of fire and flood and earthquake? But then what English poet today does write about these subjects? Urban *or* suburban—that about covers the menace most of Maxwell's readers are likely to have experienced.

The fault here is not, of course Maxwell's, nor is it strictly speaking that of his reviewer, T. J. G. Harris. It is the assignment, the demand for the one telling paragraph, that is the problem. The reviewer simply doesn't have space to define his or her terms. Even in somewhat longer reviews, this haziness of vocabulary, coupled with the need to make definitive judgments, poses problems, as when Katha Pollitt, in a full-page review of Robert Pinsky's *The Figured Wheel: New and Collected Poems, 1966–1996* for *NYTBR* (18 August 1996, 9), praises the long poem "Essay on Psychiatrists" because it "really is an essay, that moves from a group portrait of psychiatrists as a bourgeois social type . . . to a large and fully earned conclusion: 'But it is all bosh, the false / Link between genius and sickness.'" Like Harris's "urban or suburban," this assessment cannot withstand scrutiny. For why do we want a poem "really" to be an "essay"? Surely we have enough essays around. And second, if an essay really came to the "it is all bosh" conclusion cited above, wouldn't most readers find the analysis rather facile, given the large library of works that have probed the relation of genius to madness?

The New York Review of Books, (henceforth *NYRB*), to which I now turn, does not go in for this sort of empty impressionism. Its own solution (and that of the *London Review of Books* is similar) is to limit the list of reviewable poets, confining itself to a very small circle and then devoting long, individual reviews to its members. From its inception in 1963, *NYRB* has limited itself largely to the poetry of Robert Lowell (the then-husband of Elizabeth Hardwick, one of *NYRB*'s founding editors) and to the Lowell circle that includes John Berryman, Elizabeth Bishop, Randall Jarrell, Sylvia Plath, and James Merrill. Auden is an elder statesman who belongs to the group as is, at the other end of the age scale, Adrienne Rich. A few British poets—Seamus Heaney, Philip Larkin, Thom Gunn, later James Fenton—have been invited to join the club along with Americans on the circle's fringes like Theodore Roethke, W. S. Merwin, and Howard Nemerov. Helen Vendler, a regular *NYRB* reviewer, has tried to bring John Ashbery into the fold, but Ashbery seems not to be taken very seriously by such other *NYRB* poetry reviewers as Denis Donoghue and Frank Kermode; a number of his recent books have not been reviewed in *NYRB* at all.

However this parochialism may have been justified in the 1960s and 1970s, when, incidentally, the *NYRB* ignored the Objectivists (Louis Zukofsky, George Oppen, Carl Rakosi, Charles Reznikoff, Lorine Niedecker), the Beats, the Black Mountain and San Francisco poets, as well as John Cage, Ian Hamilton Finlay, and any number of Dada, Surrealist, and Fluxus poets, it has become, in the mid-nineties, a way of denying poetry its very life. For most of the above are now safely dead, and where are the young who should replace them? Has time simply stopped so that "poetry" can mean no more than a review of Elizabeth Bishop's posthumously published letters or an obituary essay about James Merrill? Much of today's "literary journalism" would have us believe so. In a recent article in the *Economist* (8 July 1995, 82), for example, we are told that "[America']s poetic voice has shrunk to a whisper," that "since the death of Robert Lowell in 1977, America seems to have lacked a major poet. In fact most people are not even aware of the concerns of American poets these days. It has declined into a minor art, subsidized principally by universities." The occasion for these ruminations is the publication by prestigious Faber and Faber of three younger (actually not so young) American poets: Charles Simic, Chase Twitchell, and August Kleinzahler. But since these are (rightly, to my mind) discovered to be not all that remarkable, the anonymous *Economist* writer feels the point has been proved.

The reasoning here is purely circular. If Chase Twitchell "represents" the

New American Poetry, then the New American Poetry can't be very good. And since many of us would argue that even Robert Lowell can't represent great American poetry quite as convincingly as did Walt Whitman or Emily Dickinson or T. S. Eliot, things must be really bad. Thus, while the *New York Review of Books* and *TLS* pay careful attention to the New Historicism, the New Gender Criticism, or the New Cultural Studies, they pay no comparable attention—indeed, no attention at all—to the New Poetics. Let us consider why this is the case.

Poetry Degree Zero

Suppose a reviewer is assigned to write a piece on Renaissance New Historicist studies. He or she knows (or quickly learns) that the founding father of this movement is Stephen Greenblatt, a professor at Berkeley, whose new book is to be discussed in the review along with others by Thomas Lacqueur, Richard Helgerson, and Nancy Vickers. The reviewer reads background material, considers opposing views, and is ready to write the piece. A similar process takes place when a reviewer takes on, say, the most recent book by Jean-François Lyotard or Hélène Cixous.

But—and here's the rub—what *is* poetry anyway? Does anyone have a clear idea? The problem is not insurmountable if the review is to be of studies of Milton or Eliot or even H.D., for these canonical authors at least partially provide the aesthetic norms against which books about their oeuvre have been and will be judged. But Charles Bernstein? Charles Wright? Charles Simic? Who knows what is to be looked for in the case of their books?

A further complication has been produced by the relative positioning of poetry and theory in the university curriculum of the past few decades. We expect graduate students in English or comparative literature to be familiar with Saussure's distinction between signifier and signified, Roman Jakobson's distinction between metaphor and metonymy, with Lacan's elaboration on that distinction, and Paul de Man's related discussion of irony and allegory. The "death of the author," as defined by Barthes and Foucault, is now a common topic of discussion. Judith Butler's notions of "gender performativity" are regularly cited, as are Fredric Jameson's interpretations of consumer culture and Homi K. Bhabha's theories on the hybridity and porosity of nations. But when the book to be discussed is a book of poems, the reader suddenly seems to forget everything he or she has learned about *literariness,* about the cultural construction of the subject, the naturalization of ideology, or the relation of genre to gender. The fairly simple principle that the choice of verse form is never merely arbitrary, that one doesn't just "at will" write sonnets on Monday, fragmented free verse on Tuesday, and prose on Wednesday is largely ignored, as is the twin question of why poet X—say, Philip Larkin—never wrote prose poetry. And beyond the individual poet, what about period style? National or ethnic styles? Are the "affirmations" of a "quirky imagination" the same in 1990 as they were when Wordsworth wrote "Resolution and Independence"?

A sense of history and a sense of theory: these are the twin poles of criticism missing from most poetry discourse today and hence missing in the typical poetry review. Poet X, we read regularly, "has found his voice." But is his voice one worth finding? Poet Y never lets her formalism get in the way of the colloquial. But why do we want poetry to be colloquial? "There is a distinct world in Michael Longley's poetry," writes his fellow poet Eavan Boland, "He has created it from a sense of lost values, out of lyric irony, and with a considerable fortitude." [8] But in most discourses today the very idea of a "distinct world" is suspect, and as for those "values" to be recovered with "considerable fortitude," maybe it would be better if they were "lost."

The poetry review (one poet reviewing another) comes, directly or indirectly, out of the poetry workshop, and the poetry workshop (or, for that matter, the creative writing workshop in general) is still dominated by a regressively romantic concept of the poet as a man speaking to men (or woman speaking to women—the principle is the same), by the notion that poetry is emotion recollected in tranquillity, the poet speaking for all of us—only more sensitively, perceptively, and expertly. And how could the workshop be otherwise without going out of existence? How could it not be based on the assumption that a given student just might have "talent," that that talent needs to find a conduit of expression and then he or she can become a certified poet? One writes on a given subject or uses a given verse form, the instructor and one's fellow students provide constructive criticism and, if one is diligent and lucky, poems are born—and published in *American Poetry Review*.

Ironically this workshop/journalism discourse is wholly at odds, not only with the discourses of architecture, anthropology, social science, and philosophy, but also with the amazing body of writing on poetics (often by poets themselves) throughout our century. From Roman Jakobson's brilliant study of Khlebnikov called *New Russian Poetry* (1921), Ezra Pound's "How to Read" (1928), and Gertrude Stein's *How to Write* (1931), to the concrete poetry manifestos of the 1950s, produced by the Noigandres group in Brazil, to John Cage's *Silence* (1962) and *A Year from Monday* (1969), Ingeborg Bachmann's *Wir müssen wahre Sätze finden* (1983), and Susan Howe's *The Birthmark* (1993), we have an exciting body of poetics, a discourse on poetry impressive in its richness and excitement. This is not to say that there is large-scale agreement between individual poet-theorists, but what can be said is that, from Futurism and Dada on down, the international poetic impetus has been constructivist rather than expressivist: it is committed, in other words, to the basic theorem that poetry is the language art, the art in which the "what" cannot be separated from "how," in which the said exists only in the saying. In his widely discussed "Artifice of Absorption" (reprinted in *A Poetics*), Charles Bernstein calls this quality the "non-absorbability" of poetic discourse. But then Yeats had already said as much when he declared that "Our words must seem to be inevitable." At the same time—and here is a corollary principle about which there is little disagreement in the arena of poetics (as compared to the arena of poetic journalism)—poetic language is never simply unique, natural, and universal; it is the product, in large part, of particular social, historical, and cultural formations. And these formations demand study.

There is, then, no good intellectual reason why poetry reviewing in, say, the *TLS*, couldn't be just as useful and interesting as reviews of urban or gender studies. But—and here we have to consider the larger cultural landscape—that is not likely to happen in our culture because, to put it bluntly, there isn't enough at stake. As long as self-proclaimed poets appear on the scene in every city and small town in Britain or America—and, oddly enough, poetry still has enough cultural capital for this to be the case[9]—as long as the editors of *NYTBR, NYRB, TLS,* and so on have to choose books to be reviewed from a wide variety of disciplines and areas, there is no way to weed out the dross, which is about 90 percent of so-called poetry publication. Who, we say democratically and bravely, is to decide which of the countless poets now plying their trade are worthy of attention? And why is one set of poetic principles—say, the ones I've just adumbrated above—any more "valid" than another?

Notice we never say this about historians or anthropologists—or even architects, perhaps because certification in these fields is a complex process. A given architect or architecture critic might, for example, personally dislike the work of Frank Gehry or of Denise Scott-Brown. But that work won't be dismissed by reviewers as simply unimportant or irrelevant. In poetry journalism, however, it happens all the time: witness James Fenton's

"Getting Rid of the Burden of Sense," a review of John Ashbery's *Selected Poems* (1985) in *NYTBR* (29 December 1985, 10). The poet, declares Fenton, "ask[s] of the reader impossible feats of attention . . . yielding only a minimum of reward." And he confesses that "there were times during my reading of this 'Selected Poems' [a gathering from thirty years' work] when I actually thought I was going to burst into tears of boredom."

New Thresholds, New Anatomies

What, in the face of such arbitrary and subjective judgment, can be done to strengthen critical writing about poetry? A lot, actually, but perhaps no longer in the popular literary press. In the last decade or so, thanks to the world of the internet and hyperspace, of desktop publishing and small press production, poetry, as even the newspapers keep telling us, is once more a widely practiced and popular art form, and the discourse about it is becoming much more interesting. A case in point is a large, glossy-paged volume called *Exact Change Yearbook No. 1: Yearbook 1995*, edited by a young poet named Peter Gizzi, who received his training in the Buffalo Poetics Program from Charles Bernstein, Susan Howe, and Robert Creeley, and is copublished by Exact Change in Boston and Carcanet Press in the United Kingdom.[10] Its elegant and perhaps too extravagant layout has been executed by a team of production assistants and printed in Hong Kong. *Yearbook 1* features Michael Palmer, glamorously pictured on the book's cover and represented by an excellent interview with Peter Gizzi and a twelve-page selection from his work. And—sign of the times—the *Yearbook* includes a compact disc of readings by twelve poets from Palmer to Ted Berrigan.[11]

In their prefatory "Publishers' Note," Damon Krukowski and Naomi Yang (who doubles as the book's designer) write that they wanted to replace the now defunct New Directions annual (edited for some forty years by James Laughlin) with "a large miscellany of avant-garde work, both contemporary and historical, chosen less to represent a particular 'school,' and more in the spirit of learning what's out there." To this end, the publishers asked Gizzi "to help us find a range of contemporary work that draws on the tradition we publish in our books of Surrealist and other early twentieth-century experimentation. . . . To what came back we added work by Exact Change authors [Stein, Cage, de Chirico, Aragon], as well as a few other discoveries we were eager to share."

What makes the project unusual is that it juxtaposes avant-garde poets and artists from the *United States* (ranging chronologically from the *Imaginary Elegies* of the late Jack Spicer and Fanny Howe's presentation of extracts from John Wiener's very moving journal *707 Scott Street* to a "gallery" of younger largely unknown poets like Paul Beatty, Tory Dent, and Jennifer Moxley) with their counterparts abroad—specifically, in Britain, France, Germany, China, Russia—and, closer to home, in the Caribbean and Canada. And as if these juxtapositions weren't enough, we can also read, say, Clark Coolidge or Susan Howe against Gertrude Stein's *Before the Flowers of Friendship Faded Friendship Faded,* which is reprinted for the first time (as Julianna Spahr explains in her headnote) together with Stein's source text, Georges Hugnet's "Enfances," in exactly the form in which they were originally published in the journal *Pagany* (1930). Or again, we can read Barbara Guest's lecture "Poetry the True Fiction" against Hugo Ball's "Grand Hotel Metaphysics," the "Radio Happenings" of John Cage and Morton Feldman against Erik Satie's "Dried Embryos," Michael Palmer against Louis Aragon's "Peasant's Dream" or the "Fragments" of de Chirico.

Such collaging gives, me at least, a sense of—forgive the taboo word—transcendence. For instead of the usual anthology wars (who's in, who's out, which editor is sufficiently multicultural?), the *Exact Change Yearbook* offers the most convincing evidence I've seen to date that our own radical poetries are not (as Maxwell or Fenton would have us think) some kind of local aberration—spawned by a bunch of theory-crazed, left-wing poets in New York and San Francisco and perpetrated by *les jeunes* at Buffalo and other out-of-the-way stations—poetries that deserve simply to be ignored. Indeed, what Gizzi's juxtapositions of U.S. and foreign portfolios suggest is that the attention to the materiality of language of which I spoke above, to syntactic disjunction and visual constellation, and especially to the reconfiguration of lyric as speaking, once again, not for the hypothetical "sensitive" and "authentic" individual ("Here's a vision I had as I was weeding the garden yesterday") but for the larger cultural and philosophical moment—that all these are now characteristic of poetries produced around the globe.

Take Jeff Twitchell's portfolio of the "Original Chinese Language Group." As Twitchell explains, "Original, not in the sense of unique, but because of their interest in the earlier meanings and associations that can be read in the Chinese written character. . . . So, too, the recuperation of the original impetus of poetry as the play in language." The Original poets, Twitchell notes, go beyond their predecessors, the so-called Misty (because branded "obscure" by the official critics) poets of the late 1970s, of whom the best known in the United States is Bei Dao. The 1988 Original manifesto, reproduced here, comes out strongly against the localism, ethnocentrism, and nationalism that bedeviled communist China until quite recently. The aim is to make contact with "modern Western art," and the vehicle for such contact, the manifesto declares, is the written character, which, compared to spoken language, is "less polluted and pre-judged." "We do not avoid," they declare, "the phrase 'word games' which already has aroused great misunderstanding. We even like it. 'Game' [*yóuxi*] is a word, connoting the profound, eerie spirit of art and philosophy." And the text gives way to the visual image of a large black cross which represents the intersection of "swim" [*yóu*] — to get in touch with reality — and "play" [*xì*].

Twitchell's portfolio is taken from the selection that appeared in the British journal *Parataxis* (#7, 1994), edited by the poet Drew Milne. In translation, the poems themselves — by Che Qian-Zi, Zhou Ya-Ping, Yi Cun, Huang Gan, Xian Meng, and Hong Liu (the one woman in this group) — don't quite live up to that manifesto.[12] "Word games," in the sense of Steve McCaffery's or Charles Bernstein's paragrammatic play, are less common than neosurrealist imagery and the casting of a sharp eye on the "direct treatment of the thing," in the Poundian imagist sense. Just as Pound's fabled "invention of China" turns out to have little to do with the classical Chinese models that were his source, so the Original poets' version of Language poetry is more graphic and precisionist than, say, Lyn Hejinian's or Bob Perelman's. Here, for example, is part 3 of Zhou Ya-Ping's "Vulgar Beauty":

> An afterbirth is unfolded, taking the shape of an umbrella.
> The ridges of an umbrella along yellow lines.
> A fetus like a coal cinder has long been reared in it,
> Lit by me, it will give off light.
> A white crane, unexpectedly covered by a black string-net
> A snake, bound with a copper wire, body
> Like a tightening spring, soft parts flashing.

We must remember that in the Chinese, as J. H. Prynne notes in his afterword, the "iconic deployment [of the language] by stroke play and contexture makes a traffic with the eye worked by a different ground-plan." At one point, the translators planned to include some of the Chinese text so as to show how the tactile element works, but the Originals themselves countered this idea because, as Prynne puts it, "it would suggest exoticism or extraneous willow-pattern ornament; to them, we are the exotics, with our credit-card view of the speech act."

That "credit-card view"—poetry as the spending of words that aren't backed up by real currency—is satirized in Prynne's own poems in *Bands around the Throat,* the entire chapbook, originally published in Cambridge in a limited edition, reprinted in the *Exact Change Yearbook.* And Tom Raworth's "Anglo-Irish Alternative," a portfolio printed elsewhere in the anthology, provides a rich context in which to understand Prynne's work. Such contextualizing (one should certainly read Rosmarie Waldrop's Berlin portfolio against Raworth's) provides a kind of information that is absent from the short review, however elegant, of the individual poet. And Gizzi's juxtapositions have their counterpart in a number of recent anthologies. Since 1993 alone, the following have appeared: Eliot Weinberger's *American Poetry Since 1950: Innovators and Outsiders* (Marsilio, a best-seller in Mexico in a Spanish edition), Paul Hoover's *A Norton Book of Postmodern Poetry* (Norton), Douglas Messerli's *From the Other Side of the Century: A New American Poetry 1960–90* (Sun & Moon), volume 1 of Jerome Rothenberg and Pierre Joris's *Poems for the Millennium* (California), and, most recently, Maggie O'Sullivan's *Out of Everywhere: Linguistically Innovative Poetry by Women in North America & the UK* (Reality Street Editions). Some of these anthologies have barely been reviewed, and yet, in what is a surprising development, they are already being assigned for classroom use and discussed at conferences. Romana Huk, a professor at the University of New Hampshire, for example, organized an international poetry festival called "Assembling Alternatives" (September 1996), largely based, in the case of Anglo-American poetry, on such not-yet-reviewed anthologies and small press books, many of which she came across during a fellowship year in the United Kingdom.

But how, it will be asked, is such work disseminated if not via reviews in the major papers? Here is where electronic discussion groups and the internet come in. On the Poetics Discussion Group sponsored by the Poetics Program at the State University of New York at Buffalo and open to anyone who hears about it by word of mouth and cares to join, the daily conversation now contains an average of twelve hundred lines and includes postings from all over the world. Much of the "talk" is trivial: who said what to whom where, what X meant when she said Y, and so on. But there have lately been extended conversations on the nature of free verse, on "close reading" (Peter Quartermain began this one when he asked, on the net, "Why the animus against close reading? Do we want distant and/or careless reading?"), and on the relation of language poetry to other contemporary movements. Bob Perelman's new critical book *The Trouble with Genius: Reading Pound, Joyce, Stein, and Zukofsky* (California, 1995) has been discussed in a series of postings; indeed, the argument as to what Perelman's book *does* and what its implications might be, acts as a kind of *supplement* (in the Derridean sense of substitute as well as addition) to the more conventional book review.

Buffalo also sponsors the Electronic Poetry Center where one can call up, say, an "Authors" file and access an impressive list of poets, each one represented by a photograph, followed by selected poems, prose writings, bibliography, and so on. Then, too, the Electronic Poetry Center publishes its own journal, *Rif/t,* which contains poems, fictions, critical essays, and reviews, as does the on-line *Postmodern Culture,* published at the University of Virginia. A new group has just been formed in San Francisco that discusses concrete poetry, visual poetics, and language-art relationships; this one is called *Majordomo* and is accessed by subscribing to something called *Wr-eye-tings;* a related group is *Silence,* devoted to the work of the late John Cage; this group is extremely active, sharing information about Cage scores, recordings, musical interpretations, poetic texts, and so on. James Pritchett's recent book on Cage's music (Cambridge, 1994) was discussed and debated in a series of postings.

The "reviewing" that occurs on such lists and in the new e-zines is by no means ideal. Internet reviewers are not as accountable as are their counterparts in the print media, and editors are not likely to ask for a lot of revisions and fact checks. The immateriality of the digital medium controls the discourse: one flick of the finger—and this is a very easy mistake to make—and the text disappears from the screen, perhaps not to be found again. Then, too, on-screen discussion of poetry and poetics is designed for a limited (and largely younger) audience that is at home with the new technologies.

And this raises the specter of the nominal "public" that, for the past hundred years, has ostensibly depended on reviewers to help it decide what poetry books to read. Doesn't a weekly paper like *TLS* owe something to this nonprofessional public, and isn't it therefore better to "cover" a range of books, even as Glyn Maxwell does in his omnibus piece? Two books on Larkin, one on Walcott, some theoretical treatises from the United States: why not let the reader decide which ones are worth her while?

My own sense is that this middle-class poetry public no longer exists, that poetics is now at least as specialized as is architectural discourse; indeed, the latter actually speaks to a much wider audience than does poetry, given that everyone lives and works in specific buildings and hence takes an interest in the look and feel of the built environment. In the case of poetry, however, the rapprochement with the university may well be a fait accompli.[13] And thus it is that the *TLS* or *NYRB* poetry review may well be on its way toward becoming obsolete.

Take the case of Charles Bernstein's *A Poetics,* the book Maxwell dismissed so offhandedly. This 1992 collection of "essays" (the first and longest piece "Artifice of Absorption" is, strictly speaking, a verse treatise, written in what is predominantly iambic pentameter) was reviewed neither in *NYTBR* nor in *NYRB,* nor in the *New Republic,* the *Village Voice Literary Supplement,* or the *Washington Post Book World,* to mention just the most obvious daily and weekly papers. Yet within two years of its publication, it appeared on course syllabi across the United States (and in the United Kingdom and Australia as well), has become a popular item on doctoral qualifying exams, and is cited, along with Bernstein's earlier collection of critical prose, *Content's Dream* (Sun & Moon, 1986), with increasing frequency. The relation of "absorption" to "antiabsorption" in poetry is discussed in learned journals. And *A Poetics* has now sold some five thousand copies and has gone through two printings and numerous translations.

How does the process of dissemination work in a case like Bernstein's? How is the readership for such a book constructed? Can the Electronic Poetry Center and other *e-zines,* together with the more traditional scholarly journals and small poetry magazines in which *A Poetics has* been reviewed,[14] really make the difference? Or is distribution dependent on word-of-mouth on the campus and at the everburgeoning number of conferences? Or controlled by a particular group of fellow-poets, professors, and editors? These are questions I can't yet answer satisfactorily. But what I can say is that literary journalism, as we used to know it and as many of us still practice it, has had nothing to do with the case.

*

Cases

8. English as a "Second" Language

Mina Loy's "Anglo-Mongrels and the Rose"

"These girls," wrote Ezra Pound in the *Little Review* (1918), referring to Marianne Moore and Mina Loy, "have written a distinctly national prod-uct, they have written something which would not have come out of any other country."[1] A rather surprising statement, at least about Loy, given that this "girl" wasn't American at all. Born in England in 1882 as Mina Gertrude Löwy to a Hungarian Jewish father who had emigrated to En-gland as a young man, and an English mother, Julia Bryan, Loy grew up in London, studied art in Munich (1899–1901), and then, with her English husband, a fellow art student named Stephen Haweis, lived first in Paris (1903–06) and then in Florence (1906–16), where her two children Giles and Joella were born.[2] After her marriage to Haweis broke up in 1914, Loy took part in the Futurist movement; she wrote manifestos, participated in art exhibitions, and during 1914 had brief affairs with both the Futur-ist *chef d'école* Marinetti and the poet Giovanni Papini. She also began to publish poems in *Camera Work* and *Trend*. In 1916, at the height of the war, she left Europe for the United States (her children remained in Italy) and became as active on the New York Dada scene as she had been on the Italian Futurist one. And it is here, in Walter Arensberg's studio, that she met the great love of her life, the Dada poet-boxer Arthur Cravan, whose real name, Loy was thrilled to discover, matched her own, being Fabian Avenarius Lloyd. Or rather it matched her own creation: Loy, let us recall, was the shortened and Anglicized form of Löwy that Mina adopted when she first came to Paris in 1903.³ *Loy/Lloyd:* to make things even more aesthetically compatible, Fabian Lloyd was a nephew of Oscar Wilde's wife Constance Mary Lloyd.

The U.S. stay lasted from October 1916 to January 1918 — a little over a year — but it is during this year that the entire sequence *Songs to Johannes* was published as a special issue of *Others* (April 1917) and brought Loy to the attention of Pound and Eliot. In 1918 she followed Arthur Cravan to Mexico; a year later, after a long drawn-out idyll, Loy, penniless and pregnant, sailed for England to have her baby. Cravan, who was to follow shortly, disappeared mysteriously; his body was never recovered. Their child Fabi was born in London in 1919. Loy returned to Italy for two years and then settled with her two daughters (her son Giles had been kidnapped by her former husband and was to die soon thereafter) in Paris, where she lived from 1923 to 1936. Her long poem "Anglo-Mongrels and the Rose" and her unfinished novel *Insel* date from this period. It is only in 1936, at the age of fifty-four, that Loy moved to the United States where she remained, first in Manhattan's Bowery and then with her daughters in Aspen, Colorado until she died in 1966. In these later American years, she published very little and all but disappeared from sight.

Loy would thus seem to be the prototype of the deracinated cosmopolite, the sort of expatriate figure Eliot (who praised her poetry in the *Egoist*)⁴ must have had in mind when he had the *Waste Land*'s Marie say, "Binn gar keine Russin, stamm' aus Litauen, echt deutsch." Fluent in French, Italian, and German as well as in her own late Victorian English, she lived in New York for only one of her first fifty-four years. How, then, could Pound call her work a "distinctly national product" — an oeuvre that couldn't "come out of any other country"? And how is it that Virginia Kouidis would call her book on Loy (the only book-length critical study to date) *Mina Loy: American Modernist Poet?*⁵

Kouidis herself gives three reasons. First, she argues, Loy was "aware that the subjects and structures of English poetry in 1910 were inadequate to experience" (VK 135), and that she must therefore, like her fellow Americans Eliot and Pound, draw on French models. Second, Loy's *logopoeia* (Pound's term, of which more below) is characteristically American: "she employs a compressed diction that abandons the poetic commonplace. . . . This diction reflects modes of perception and utilizes the spoken language" (VK 136). Here Kouidis is thinking of William Carlos Williams and Wallace Stevens, Marianne Moore, and especially of Gertrude

Stein. And third, "Mina Loy is linked to the Americans by her translation into poetry of the techniques and structures of modern European painting, especially Futurism and Cubism" (VK 137). Again, Stein and Moore, Stevens and Williams are cited as parallels.

Two of the three traits here cited are largely negative: Loy is judged to be American by her borrowings from French poetry (Laforgue) as well as French and Italian art forms (Cubism, Futurism). As for the third, the purported adoption of an American speech idiom, the fact is, as we shall see, that Loy's language is anything but direct, colloquial, or idiomatic—what Eliot called the "return to common speech," or Ezra Pound, "direct treatment of the thing."[6] All the same, Pound was on to something important when he declared that Loy's poetry couldn't come out of any other country but the United States. For what does make Loy, like her friend Gertrude Stein, so curiously "American," I shall suggest here, is her invention of an intricately polyglot language—a language that challenges the conventional national idiom of her British (as well as her French or Italian, or, paradoxically, even her American) contemporaries.

It is significant that, from the beginning, it was the United States, not England, whose little magazines—*Camera Work, Trend, Rogue, Blind Man, Others,* and *Dial*—were receptive to Mina Loy's writing. The first two installments of "Anglo-Mongrels and the Rose" came out, very appropriately as we shall see, in the "Exile" issue (1923) of the *Little Review;* the third, in Robert McAlmon's Paris-based *Contact Collection of Contemporary Verse* (1925). As an "exile" in New York, Loy was linked to the Arensberg circle and, later, to the American expatriate circles in Paris. When Alfred Kreymborg came to write his survey of American poetry called *Our Singing Strength* (1929), he placed Loy in his chapter on "Originals and Eccentrics," grouping her with Marianne Moore, Lola Ridge, and Adelaide Crapsey, as well as with Mardsen Hartley, Pitts Sanborn, Helen Hoyt, and Emmanuel Carnevali. "During the war," we read in Kreymborg, a "curious woman, exotic and beautiful, came to New York from foreign shores: the English Jewess, Mina Loy, [whose] clinical frankness and sardonic conclusions, wedded to a madly elliptical style scornful of the regulation grammar, syntax, and punctuation, horrified our gentry and drove our critics into furious despair." Her work as well as her personality, Kreymborg reports, "created a violent sensation."[7]

But in what sense, if any, is the "elliptical style" of this "English Jewess," who spent so little time in America before her fifty-fourth year, identifiable as "American," especially since, overtly, it has little in common with the "American" styles (and settings) of such of her contemporaries as Stevens and Williams? To answer this question, I propose to examine Loy's remarkable long (and still almost unknown) poem "Anglo-Mongrels and the Rose" (1923–25). For here, in this allegorical, parodic, often disjointed pseudonarrative of the poet's ancestry, birth, childhood, and coming of age, we have Loy's most compelling representation of her "mongrelization"—the "crossbreeding" of the English and Hungarian-Jewish strains that produced, so the author herself seems to feel, a form of mental and emotional gridlock that could be overcome, in life as in art, only by large doses of the transnational avant-gardism of the interwar period.

The Mongrel-Girl of No-Man's-Land

What Pound rightly called *logopoeia*, "the dance of the intellect among words," as he put it in "How to Read," aptly characterizes Loy's poetics. Whereas *melopoeic* poetry is one in which "the words are charged, over and above their plain meaning, with some musical property," and *phanopoeia* is "a casting of images upon the visual imagination," *logopoeia* "employs words not only for their direct meaning, but it takes count in a special way of habits of usage, of the context we *expect* to find with the words, its usual concomitants, of its known acceptances, and of ironical play."[8] Kenneth Rexroth seems to have these qualities in mind when, in a 1944 appreciation, he suggests that Loy's neglect is probably "due to her extreme exceptionalism. Erotic poetry is usually lyric. Hers is elegiac and satirical. It is usually fast paced. Hers is slow and deliberately twisting. If it is bitter and dissatisfied, it is at least passionate." And Rexroth adds, "Her virtues are self-evident. She is tough, forthright, very witty, atypical, anti-rhetorical, devoid of chi-chi."[9]

Now consider the opening section of "Anglo-Mongrels and the Rose" called "Exodus," in which the impersonal narrator tells the tale (in the present tense and in swift, cartoonish strokes) of her father's childhood in "Buda Pest," his coming to the "cancelled desert of the metropolis" which is Victorian London, his youthful employment as "highest paid tailor's / cutter in the City," his lonely boardinghouse life and sexual fantasies, and his, to her mind, ill-fated meeting with the "English Rose" who is to be Loy's despised Protestant, virginal, bourgeois, cold and prudish mother. Here is a passage about fifty lines into the narrative:

The arid gravid
intellect   of Jewish ancestors
            the senile juvenile
            calculating prodigies of Jehovah
            crushed by the Occident ox
            they scraped
            the gold gold golden
            muck from its hoofs

moves Exodus   to emigrate
            coveting the alien
            asylum   of voluntary military
            service   paradise   of the pound-sterling
            where the domestic Jew   in lieu
of knouts   is lashed with tongues[10]

This passage makes an interesting contrast to the work of a poet closely linked to Loy—Williams, whose *Spring and All* was published by Contact the same year as "Anglo-Mongrels." Here is the opening of section 8 of the title poem:

The sunlight in a
yellow plaque upon the
varnished floor

is full of a song
inflated to
fifty pounds pressure

at the faucet of
June that rings
the triangle of the air

pulling at the
anemones in
Persephone's cow pasture— [11]

Williams's verse is at once "free" (the lines range from three to seven syllables and from two to four primary stresses) and yet highly structured. The lines are suspended, breaking at odd junctures, as in "a / yellow plaque upon the / varnished floor." But visually these lines are gathered into neat tercets of roughly equal size. And the language of these tercets is concrete and particular, the poet's response to the natural world being conveyed without commentary by means of image and metaphor. The sharply visualized "yellow plaque" of sunlight on the "varnished floor" is described synesthetically as a "song / inflated to / fifty pounds pressure / at the faucet of / June," and then, in terms of myth, as "anemones" lighting up "Persephone's cow pasture."

In contrast, Loy's "stanzas" are intentionally ungainly, syllable and stress count, line length, spacing, and stanza length being much more variable than Williams's. Indeed, Loy's is not so much "free verse," in the usual sense of the term, as it is a variant on *Skeltonics* (so named for the Tudor poet John Skelton), that is, "a distinctive shortlined meter [in which] typically the lines carry only 2–3 stresses in 3–6 syllables (though longer lines are not uncommon), and there are frequent short runs of monorhyme called 'leashes' [and] parallelism is a major rhetorical device."[12] In Loy's version, these "leashes" often come within lines, as in "arid gravid," "senile juvenile," or "Occident ox." What holds these stanzas together is not a larger rhythmic contour or consistent image pattern as in *Spring and All*, but a network of elaborate rhyming, chiming, chanting, and punning, as in the sequence "Jewish—juvenile—prodigies—Jehovah," where *jew* is found in every word, or in the rhyming and chiastic linkage between "*Occ*ident *ox*" and "*Exo*dus." "Crushed by the Occident ox," Exodus" naturally "covet[s] the alien / asylum of voluntary military service paradise of the pound-sterling." "Voluntary"—"military": doesn't this sound like a contradiction in terms? And what sort of "asylum" is "alien"? Yet these tightly packed lines make perfectly good sense: to join the British army voluntarily provides Exodus with the "alien" (to him) "asylum" of the "paradise of the pound-sterling." Once "domesticated," in his new country, the "Jew in lieu / of knouts is lashed with tongues." Not lashed with the whip as were his ancestors in Hungary, just "lashed with tongues." And the rhyme "Jew" / "lieu" suggests that the Jew can never be more than a substitute in English society, a kind of simulacrum, "in lieu" of the true blue Englishman.

Mina Loy's debt to Futurism (as well as her critique of her male Futurist mentors) has been frequently discussed,[13] but what has gone unnoticed is that Loy's very diction and syntax constitute a sharp critique of Marinetti's famed *parole in libertà*. In the "Technical Manifesto of Futurist Literature" (1912), Marinetti had defined poetry as "an uninterrupted sequence of new images" or rather image-bearing nouns in apposition.

"Every noun," he declared, "should have its double; that is the noun should be followed, with no conjunction, by the noun to which it is related by analogy. Example: man-torpedo-boat, woman-gulf, crowd-surf, piazza-funnel, door-faucet." At the same time "One must abolish the adjective, to allow the naked noun to preserve its essential color," and again "One must abolish the adverb, old belt buckle that holds two words together." A sequence of naked nouns, tactile, concrete, imagistic, and often, as in *Zang Tumb Tuum,* onomatopoeic: here is the source of *immaginazione senza fili* (imagination without strings).[14]

In "Anglo-Mongrels and the Rose," Loy turns this aesthetic on its head. Her nouns are abstract, not concrete—*intellect, ancestors, prodigies, asylum*—and they are modified by adjectives that often overwhelm (and even contradict) her nouns as in "the senile juvenile / calculating prodigies," or in "coveting the alien / asylum of voluntary military / service." Not *parole in libertà* but conceptual words and phrases (whatever the part of speech); not lyric sequences of analogies but schematic, parabolic narrative:

> The cannibal God
> shutters his lids of night   on the day's gluttony
> the partially   devoured humanity
> warms its unblessed beds   with bare prostrations
> (LLB 113)

Here is Loy's version of late Victorian London, with its alien devouring deity presiding over the sordid nighttime couplings ("bare prostrations") in the "unblessed beds" of the dreary mass metropolis. If this passage brings to mind Eliot's "Preludes" ("One thinks of all the hands / That are raising dingy shades / In a thousand furnished rooms"), Loy's "unblessed beds" are purposely left unspecified, their occupants never quite materializing as actual human beings.

In this respect, Loy is much closer to Wyndham Lewis than to Eliot or Pound, Williams or Stevens, or, for that matter, to Moore, to whom critics from Pound on down have linked her, evidently because of gender. The departicularization of "Exodus," as of "English Rose" in the next section, and of "Ova" (Mina Loy herself), "Esau Penfold" (Stephen Haweis), and "Colossus" (Arthur Cravan), is symptomatic of Loy's larger metaphysical perspective. Whereas Marinetti (and the Imagists as well) put his faith in objects, lining up catalogs of concrete nouns (*torpedo-boat-battleship-machine gun*) and onomatopoeic sounds ("zang-tumb-tuum," "ta-ta-ta-ta") for their immediate presentational value, Loy is a satirist, a diagnostician who is willing to regard her very own parents as nasty stereotypes, representative of a late Victorian imperialist England in which the outsider, especially an Eastern European Jewish outsider ("Exodus") could only gain a foothold by marrying an "English Rose," no matter how great the mismatch.

Indeed, in her portrait of her father Sigmund Löwy, Loy seems to accept all the anti-Semitic stereotypes of her time and place. Exodus's mother has "hair long as the Talmud" and "tamarind eyes" (LLB 111); his father stuffs him "with biblical Hebrew and the seeds of science exhorting him / to vindicate / his forefathers' ambitions" (LLB 111–12). In the passage I have cited above, "the senile juvenile / calculating prodigies of Jehovah" (senile because even as children they must push and shove and make their way) learn to "scrape / the gold gold golden muck" from the "hoofs" of the Occident [read "gentile"] ox." Arriving in London, Exodus is soon the "highest paid tailor's / cutter in the City," masters "business English," "stock exchange quotations / and conundrums of finance / to which unlettered immigrants are instantly initiate" (LLB 115). His gift to his daughter, we learn later, is none other than "The Jewish brain!" (LLB 132). But the stereotype is not only of the shrewd, money-grubbing Jewish immigrant. Loy endows her father with the reputed "Jewish" artistic bent (a Sunday painter, "Painting feeling his pulse . . . Under his ivory hands / his sunflowers sunwards / glow" [LLB 118]), as well as with the powerful sex drive of dark "Eastern" males: "He / loaded with Mosaic / passions that amass / like money" (LLB 124), and again, "Exodus / Oriental / mad to melt / with something softer than himself" (LLB 126).

Inevitably, the union with his opposite, the cold, virginal "English Rose," is bound to prove disastrous. Loy's portrait of her mother in part 2 of "Anglo-Mongrels" contains some of her most devastating satire, satire in which, again, the language itself is as "mongrelized" as are the principals of her narrative. Here is the opening:

> Early English everlasting
>   quadrate Rose
>   paradox-Imperial
> trimmed with some travestied flesh
> tinted with bloodless duties   dewed
> with Lipton's teas
> and grimed with crack-packed

herd-housing
petalling
the prim gilt
penetralia
of a luster-scioned
core-crown

Rose of arrested impulses
self-pruned
of the primordial attributes
a tepid heart   inhibiting
with tactful terrorism
the Blossom Populous
to mystic incest with its ancestry
establishing
by the divine right of self-assertion
the post-conceptional
virginity of Nature.

                              (LLB 121)

Here Loy has produced a brilliant parody of *Le Roman de la Rose,* her Skeltonic rhymes inverting the value of virginity in Machaut's medieval romance so as to make it an absurd value, a cash commodity whereby the British empire plies its trade. The opening "litany" might be interestingly compared to Eliot's slightly later (1930) quite serious litany in "Ash Wednesday" ("Rose of Memory / Rose of forgetfulness / . . . The single Rose / Is now the Garden"). Loy's alliterating opening, "Early English everlasting" also echoes parodically Gerard Manley Hopkins's "Earnest, earthless, equal, attuneable" (from "Spelt from Sybil's Leaves"), while the reference to the four-petaled rose ("quadrate") refers to the Rose of fin-de-siècle occultists, most notably Yeats's "Far-off, most secret, and inviolate Rose."

But what is entirely Loy's own poetic signature is that her rose images, far from producing an imagist or symbolist landscape, jostle with conceptual nouns, puns, and aggressive rhymes, in a curious "mongrelization" of linguistic registers. The poet's rose is "paradox-Imperial" in that her vaunted purity and modesty can "work" on male suitors only because this "Blossom Populous" can bank on its "mystic incest with its ancestry," its "divine right of self-assertion." Rose's very "flesh" is "travestied" by its class origin, "tinted with bloodless duties," and "dewed / with Lipton's teas."

Here not only do the suffixes match, but "dewed . . . teas" nicely puns on the "duties" this "pouting / pearl beyond price" has been trained to perform. And a further pun relates those "teas" to the "tease" which "She / simpering in her / ideological pink" (LLB 124) turns out to be. For what are those "petals" but the "prim gilt" ("guilt") or fake "luster" covering the "penetralia" to Rose's "core-crown"—"crown" by virtue of the "divine right of self-assertion," the assertion of her illustrious imperial pedigree. Even the lady at Exodus's boardinghouse dinner table, after all, excuses what are evidently her bad table manners by saying, "Our Dear Queen picks chicken bones / in her fingers" (LLB 115). Why, then, should Exodus not pick a few chicken bones of his own? Trained as he is to "scrape / the gold gold golden / muck" from the hoofs of the "Occident ox" (LLB 112), why not a little "prim gilt" from the "luster-scioned / crown"?

The narrative of Exodus's meeting with and courtship of "Alice the gentile" is high comedy:

> While she
> expecting the presented knee
> of chivalry
> repels
> the sub-umbilical mystery
> of his husbandry
> hysterically
>
> His passionate anticipation
> of warming in his arms
> his rose   to a maturer coloration
> which was all of aspiration
> the grating upon civilization
> of his sensitive organism
> had left him
>
> splinters upon an adamsite
> opposition
> of nerves like stalactites
>
> This dying chastity
> had rendered up no soul
> yet they pursued their conjugal
> dilemmas   as is usual
> with people

```
who know          not what they do
but know          that what they do
is not illegal
```

(LLB 126–27)

In the first stanza above, the six "leash" rhymes—"she" / "knee" / "chivalry" / "mystery" / "husbandry" / "hysterically"—concisely and bitingly define the misalliance of Exodus and his Rose. To be brought up to expect the chivalry of the "presented knee," only to be exposed to that "subumbilical mystery" of his "husbandry" (the phrase combines euphemism and pun to describe, from Rose's perspective, the act that can't be named) culminates in that free-floating adverb that destroys, in more ways than one, the decorum of the preceding noun sequence. "Hysterically" is what we're left with. The same effect is rendered in the next stanza by the rhyming of suffixes of abstract nouns—"anticipation" / "coloration" / "aspiration" / "civilization"—where the last word "civilization" doesn't belong semantically in the catalog of mental states that precede it, the irony being that this "civilization" consists precisely of such foolish forms of flirtation.

Rose's resistance to Exodus's "passionate anticipation" is defined in terms of minerals: "adamsite" (a greenish-black mica) and "nerves like stalactites." Again, the two geological terms rhyme. "No soul," it seems, in this "conjugal" union. But—and now Loy switches to ordinary diction to make a fine point—these Victorians were "people / who know not what they do / but know that what they do / is not illegal." The indictment of marriage as an institution could hardly be more scornful.

The logopoeia of these early sections of "Anglo-Mongrels" is extremely intricate. Punning will often depend on foreign words or on breaking up words into their morphemes. "Deep in the névrose night," for example, enables Loy to embed her "rose" in the French word for "neurotic." The "disciplining" of "the inofficial / 'flesh and devil' / to the ap parent impecca bility / of the English," plays on "parent" and sinning (i.e., "non peccavi"). And perhaps most wittily, Loy uses personification and circumlocution to create burlesque scenes of virginal defensiveness:

```
For of this Rose
wherever it blows
it is certain
that an impenetrable pink curtain
hangs between it and itself
and in metaphysical vagrance
```

it passes beyond the ken
of men unless
possessed
of exorbitant incomes
And Then—
merely indicates its presence
by an exotic fragrance

(LLB 128)

The image of the hymenal "impenetrable pink curtain" hanging "between it and itself . . . in metaphysical vagrance" is wonderfully absurd, especially since the reference is embedded in the nursery rhymes "Rose" / "blows," "certain" / "curtain," "unless" / "possess," and especially the crescendo of "ken" / "men" / "And Then—." The only "presence" here, as the final pararhyme suggests, is not of a living body but only a teasing fragrance. Withholding is all.

In the course of the poem, Loy pulls out all the generic stops—allegory, mock epic, biography, realist narrative—so as to foreground the ironies inherent in her tale. But it is the tone of the poem, the distance between its aloof narrator and her cartoonish characters, that makes Loy's work distinctive. For who, after all, talks about her parents this way? Who would characterize her own birth as the extraction from her mother's loins of "A clotty bulk of bifurcate fat" (LLB 130), or describe her baby self as "feed[ing] / its mongrel heart on Berger's food / for infants" (LLB 132)? Is the poet too cruel to the memory of her parents? Too intolerant and unforgiving? Just plain nasty?

In the later sections of "Anglo-Mongrels," the poet details Ova's coming to consciousness, her gradual separation from "the heavy upholstered / stuffing" of the "netherbodies" of both mother and nurse (LLB 139), whose presence can no longer stifle the child's curiosity about words, for example "iarrhea," which the two-year-old toddler overhears and transforms into a kind of magic wand. Yet neither her precocious love of language nor her later forging of her own version of Christianity[15] can quite break the family tie:

Suburban children
of middle-class Britain
ejected from the home
are still connected
with the inseverable

navel-cord of the motherland

and

need never feel alone

(LLB 154)

This extract from "Ova among the Neighbors" lacks the punning, sound play, and high-spiritedness of the earlier satire: indeed, Loy consistently seems less comfortable talking about herself than about her cold and hypocritical mother, her ineffectual father, and the series of nursemaids and governesses who try to control her childhood activities. In the course of the narrative, the emphasis remains squarely on the indictment of the imperial England of the poet's childhood, with its "bland taboo / from the nursery to the cemetery" (LLB 156) and its "twilight turbulence / of routine in coma" (LLB 157).

But—and I want now to come back to Virginia Kouidis's representation of the American Mina Loy—the poet does not, at least not in this poem, turn to French models;[16] she does not adopt natural speech rhythms (as do Eliot and Pound), and by no means is hers the Cubist aesthetic one associates with Gertrude Stein. Cubism, after all, implies multiplicity of perspectives, the blurring of figure-ground relationships, and the indeterminacy of reference, the outlines of a wine glass doubling as the stick figure of a man, guitar strings as letters of the alphabet or body parts, and so on. And further: unlike the Marinetti who invented *parole in libertà,* or the Dadaists of the Cabaret Voltaire, or the Eliot of the *Waste Land* and Pound of the *Cantos,* Loy was not a collagist. She does not paste together disparate verbal fragments, letting their spatial juxtapositions create a complex network of meanings.[17] Rather, hers is a temporal mode, a satiric narrative, however broken and self-interrupting, in which structures of voice and address take precedence over the "constatation of fact," as Pound called it, of the image.

Where, then, does this logopoeic mode come from? Perhaps the first place to look is at the Yellow Nineties of Loy's London childhood: the England of Oscar Wilde and Aubrey Beardsley, of art nouveau and her one-time art teacher Augustus John. Like the calla lily lamps she invented in the late twenties, her verbal compositions are highly stylized, intentionally artificial, extravagantly mannered. As she herself put it in an unpublished homage to Dante Gabriel Rossetti, "Tipped off as it were by the poet I preferred, I at last began to function" (LLB 315).[18]

At the same time, she infuses the language of the fin de siècle with solecisms, neologisms, foreign phrases (characterizations of Cravan, for example, seem to demand French as in Loy's designation of him as *"un brute mystique"* or *"le dieu qui se conserve et le fou qui s'evade"* [LLB 318–19]), Jewish inflections, and realistic references to bodily functions that would not have been tolerated by the Rhymers' Club or the *Savoy*. Indeed, her curious polyglossia reflects her own "Anglo-mongrel" ancestry as well as the expatriation of her adult life.

"Anglo-Mongrels and the Rose," written in Paris after the traumatic loss of Cravan—a loss from which, by her own account, Loy never recovered[19]—thus represents a rupture with a lyrical tradition that parallels Gertrude Stein's break with conventional narrative some ten years earlier. Like Stein (or, for that matter, like Loy's American expatriate friend Djuna Barnes), Loy maintains an ironic distance from her materials. The "Buda Pest" of the Löwys was not, after all, a place she really knew but largely a mythic space she herself had invented. And, compared to the "Unreal city" of Eliot's *Waste Land,* published the year she began "Anglo-Mongrels," her own London locales remain curiously abstract and schematic. The "isolate consciousness / projected from back of time and space" that Loy explores in her narrative poem is not given to fantasies of shoring fragments against its ruins. Rather, as Pound and Rexroth recognized, the poet's sardonic wit and bitter acerbity find their outlet in the play of language itself, the logopoeia that finds satisfaction in discovering the paragrams and puns latent in any given vocabulary.

If this logopoeic poetry has finally come into its own, it may well be because our own "American" English has become so thoroughly mongrelized. Interestingly, Loy herself predicted this turn of events. "It was inevitable," she remarked in one of her rare critical essays, "that the renaissance of poetry should proceed out of America, where latterly a thousand languages have been born, and each one, for purposes of communication at least, English—English enriched and variegated with the grammatical structure and voice-inflection of many races. . . . Out of the welter of this unclassifiable speech, while professors of Harvard and Oxford labored to preserve 'God's English,' the muse of modern literature arose, and her tongue had been loosened in the melting pot."[20]

This was written in 1925, the same year "Anglo-Mongrels" was published. At the end of the century, as "English" in the United States becomes increasingly other, no longer the language of the mother country but an amalgam of "névrose" locutions and syntactic structures taken from African, Latin American, and Asian as well as European cultures, Loy's poetic language no longer appears all that eccentric.[21] Such neologisms as "increate altitudes" (LLB 169) or "the more formulate education" (LLB 152) no longer seem, as they did even to favorable critics like Rexroth, "lapses of skill" (see KR 69), and the campy artifice of her Exodus/Colossus narrative can now be understood as deploying verbal displacement and syntactic dislocation for essential satirical ends.

Roger Conover recounts an anecdote that is apropos in this regard:

> [Loy] wrote under an elaborate system of anagrammatically and nu-merologically derived pseudonyms. Was she impersonating herself or did she have a double? . . . Was it her pseudomania, perhaps, which ac-counts for a rumor that was circulating around Paris in the Twenties — that Mina Loy was in fact not a real person at all, but a forged persona, a hoax-of-critics. Upon hearing this, the story goes, Mina Loy turned up at Natalie Barney's salon in order to convince guests of her existence:
>
> I assure you I am indeed a live being. But it is necessary to stay very unknown. . . . To maintain my incognito the hazard I chose was— poet. (LLB xvii–xviii)

It is a nice parable of the grim advantages of what we might call negative identity. Mina Loy's "pseudonymity" may well have been the signature that gave her the "American" freedom to invent a verbal world of her own. "I began," she recalls, "to 'furnish' England with a small pattern, an in-cipient rhythm, a wisp of folklore" (LLB 315). And again, in "Ladies in an Aviary," "It is so sweet this sugar, the sugar of fictitious values" (LLB 316).

9. Poetry in Time of War

The Duncan-Levertov Controversy

In 1952 Denise Levertov, then living in New York, received a poem-letter titled "For a Muse Meant" signed only "R. D." and bearing a San Francisco postmark. The poem begins:

> in
>
> > spired/the aspirate
> > the aspirant almost
>
> > without breath

and refers, some lines later, to "A great effort, straining, breaking up / all the melodic line (the lyr- / ick strain?)," and to the brewing of "another cup" of "flavor stinking coffee . . . in that Marianne Moore— / E. P.— Williams—H. D.—Stein— / Zukofsky—Stevens—Perse— / surrealist— dada—staind / pot."[1] Levertov mistook these elliptical passages as a slur on her writing and wrote its author a note to say that if "R. D." was indeed the Robert Duncan who had written *Heavenly City, Earthly City*, a book she had recently read with great admiration, she was truly sorry he disliked her own work so much. To which Duncan responded with a bemused "on the contrary" letter, its envelope bearing the words "It is as it was in admiration."[2]

So began the intense and voluminous correspondence between the two poets. For the first decade or so of their conversation (the two finally met in 1955), Duncan was Levertov's ardent admirer; indeed, his letters are almost deferential. Praising "the non-dream daylight facts of the imagination" in "The Departure," he exclaims, "How nervous my tensions seem to me compared!" (12 February 1957). And his blurb for *Overland to the Islands* (1957) goes like this:

> Denise Levertov in these poems brings me again and again to the most intense thing, to that crossing of the inner and the outer reality where we have our wholeness of feeling in the universe. . . . She has no superior in [the] clarification of a scene—moving traffic, mexican girls after First Communion kicking a baseball, or the arrival of sharks off shore at sundown. . . . In the dance of word and phrase to express feeling, in the interior music of vowels, in subtlety of changing tempo within the form, in the whole supple control of freedom, she excels. (Included in letter of 1 October 1957)

Notice that it is Levertov's phenomenology, her tracking of perceptual realities that Duncan admires. "In range," he writes in an introduction to her San Francisco reading (19 January 1958), "her poetry moves between this impending reality—what we call the objective world . . . and another world, equally objective, of the imagination that springs into life and voice from the ground of common things." [3]

But by 1968 something had changed. That something was of course the Vietnam War and the two poets' increasingly conflicting views of the relation of poetry to politics. Interestingly, the rift that now occurred and that came to a head in an angry exchange of long letters in the fall and winter of 1971–72 is much less an ideological difference than it is a question of how poetry positions itself vis-à-vis politics. Both poets were outraged by U. S. policy toward Vietnam, both deplored the bombing of Hanoi, the duplicity of the Johnson and later the Nixon administrations, and so on. Both read their poetry at antiwar rallies. But by 1968, Levertov was on the barricades, writing and reading from the antiwar poems she was to publish in *Relearning the Alphabet* (1970) and *To Stay Alive* (1971). Duncan's own "antiwar" poems published in *Bending the Bow* (I am thinking of "The Multiversity," "Up Rising," and "The Soldiers," all of them part of *Passages*), are, by contrast, more properly understood, Ian W. Reid points out, as "war poems, studies in struggle." "While the Vietnam conflict is of course substantially present there," writes Reid, "a ganglion of pain, it becomes simply the most salient manifestation in our day of an abiding social and spiritual reality which brings to poetry a mythic dimension." [4] "War, as Duncan had put it in the early fifties in *A Book of Resemblances*, is like love and poetry in that it expresses "the deepest forces and cleavings . . . of man's hidden nature." [5]

Consequently, Duncan had little use for what we might call Levertov's agitprop. "It's hard to write [to you] now," he tells Denise and her husband Mitchell Goodman in June of 1968, "because you both stand now so definitely at the front of—not the still small inner voice of conscience that cautions us in our convictions but the *other* conscience that drives us to give our lives over to our convictions, the righteous Conscience—what Freudians call the Super Ego, that does not caution but sweeps outside all reservations." Such submission to the super ego is a "tyranny of the will," and Duncan declares:

> No, I very much do not subscribe to the Old Testament idea of a covenant or a commitment as a morality. The righteousness, the revival of the Judaic-Puritanic convenanter's Salvation Army against the evil of war in RESIST [a radical anti-war group] repels me. The "Thou shalt not . . ." written in stone or written in the heart. . . . and the "Thou shalt not kill" . . . is the very evil of a resolution of free immediate individual experience of choice.

As for the Eugene Debs demand, then very much cited, that "so long as any man is in prison, I am not free," Duncan objects, "I am but the more aware that this is the very imprisoning message itself."

The poet, in Duncan's view, cannot become anyone's mouthpiece, not even the mouthpiece of a righteous cause. Freedom is of the essence, the freedom to represent the human universe as the poet imaginatively reconstructs it. Indeed poetry's function, as Duncan was to put it in his long, closely argued letter of 19 October 1971, "is not to oppose evil, but to imagine it: what if Shakespeare had opposed Iago, or Dostoyevsky opposed Raskolnikov—the vital thing is that they *created* Iago and Raskolnikov [so that] we begin to see betrayal and murder and theft in a new light." And he adds, "It is a disease of our generation that we offer symptoms and diagnoses of what we are in the place of imaginations and creations of what we are."

In our current Foucauldian climate with its adherence to the various models of cultural construction, these comments may seem hopelessly retro, outmoded romantic notions of personal freedom, individual agency, and the uniqueness of the poetic self. Levertov herself has attributed Duncan's reservations about *poetry engagé* to his anarchist upbringing, which, she believes, led him to mistrust group action. "His political awareness," she remarks, "formed in the '40s and early '50s, remained static. . . . He did not experience the comradeship, the recognition of apparent strangers as brothers and sisters" from which she herself drew sustenance in the difficult Vietnam years (SM 111–12).

But Duncan's romanticism is more complicated than such comments would lead one to believe. Poetry, he suggests again and again, is always already political in that it presents us with the motives and results of the political process. Great political poetry, moreover, is apocalyptic in the Blakean sense, visionary in presenting the events in question as part of larger and more universal paradigms. From this perspective, the use of poetry to support a particular revolutionary cause is, for Duncan, "one of the great falsehoods." "The question," he writes in response to Levertov's "Revolution or Death" poem ("Staying Alive, Part 1"), "is the poetry and not the revolution—the book clearly isn't 'revolutionary' in the sense of the poem—and the theme may be *anguish*. I feel that revolution, politics, making history is one of the great falsehoods—is Orc in his burning madness" (4 October 1971).

Let us look at this reaction more closely. "Staying Alive, Part 1 (October '68–May '69)," begins with the lines:

> Revolution or death. Revolution or death.
> Wheels would sing it
> > but railroads are obsolete,
> we are among the clouds, gliding, the roar
> a toneless constant.
> > *Which side are you on?*
> Revolution, of course, Death is Mayor Daley.[6]

In the October 4 letter, Duncan cites this passage and responds:

Do we believe in unilateral peace? Then surely it is *we* who must create it where we are. But the revolution, like Nixon, believes in inflicting peace on their own terms. I do not ask for a program of peace; but I do protest the war waged under the banner of Peace, no matter who wages it. It is false to the word. Men at war against the State are one thing—and that can at least be true to itself—even if it is not successful; but men at war against war are hypocrites if they argue that there can be no peaceful ways in a time of war. THERE HAS BEEN NO TIME IN

HUMAN HISTORY THAT WAS NOT A TIME OF WAR. And any peaceful ways and deeds of peace have had to be created in the face of the need for war—for war against oppression, for war against injustice, etc.

It's the Altars in the Street I am for, the acts of care in making and attendance. In the midst of apocalypse, that present most vividly the test of Art. Revolutions have all been profoundly opposed to the artist, for revolutions have had their power only by the rule that power not be defined. And as workers in words, it *is* our business to keep alive in the language definitions as well as forces, to create crises in meaning, yes—but this is to create meanings in which we are the more aware of the crisis involved, of what is at issue. In posing "revolution or death" you seem to feel that evolution—which as far as we know is the way in which life actually meets its test and creates its self—does not come into the picture. As if, i.e., Man got to "overthrow" reptiles. (4 October 1971)

And in a subsequent letter, Duncan expands on this distinction: "Let's take that word *Revolution,* which I reminded you referred to the figure of time and space, the universe and man's loss as a wheel turning. The wheel of torture. The card in the Tarot shows the wheel turning *to the right* with Anubis "the underdog" rising. . . . And the idea of revolution belongs to the old Ptolemaic universe picture with its revolving concentric spheres" (8 November 1971).

What is striking about this commentary on "Revolution or Death" is a quality not usually associated with Duncan (perhaps because in his essays he writes more formally, more self-consciously and manneredly)—namely a hard-headed and clear-eyed common sense. From Marinetti to Breton, after all, the avant-garde of the early century had claimed to be producing a new "revolutionary" art—a revolutionary art that, as theorists from Peter Bürger on down have been telling us for decades, never had any real impact at the political level. But to go so far as to declare that revolution is the enemy of art because revolution must, to succeed, betray the poet's *language,* that revolution belongs to the old Ptolemaic universe and should be supplanted by evolution—this is to give avant-garde theory a curious spin.

To begin with, Duncan discriminates between the use of community as poetic *subject* (Levertov's mode in *To Stay Alive*) and a communal vision. "It is not," he explains, "that, as writers, we should not be immodest, but that we must go into the depths of immodesty; not that we should not be narcissistic, but that we should go into the depths of Narcissus. The *impulse* that informs (and makes *necessary* the artist's craft), the hidden and

life-creative and destructive ID-entity underlying and overriding the con-
veniences of personal identity is what makes the difference between mere
craft . . . and significant craft; is why many a good craftsman is even an
enemy of Art" (19 October 1971). What this means in practice is, in the
words of Duncan's own title, *ground work*—the grounding of abstraction
and morality in the particulars that might give them life. "I am certain,"
says Duncan, "'language charged with meaning to the utmost possible
degree' [Pound's phrase] is our responsibility if we be language workers"
(8 November 1971).

The 19 October letter, which goes on for some fourteen long and
crowded handwritten pages, spells out the responsibility of the poet as
"language worker." Here Duncan's "Exhibit A" is Levertov's "Tenebrae,"
which I cite in full:

> Heavy, heavy, heavy, hand and heart.
> We are at war,
> bitterly, bitterly, at war.
>
> And the buying and selling
> buzzes at our heads, a swarm
> of busy flies, a kind of innocence.
>
> Gowns of gold sequins are fitted,
> sharp-glinting. What harsh rustlings
> of silver moiré there are,
> to remind me of shrapnel splinters.
>
> And weddings are held in full solemnity
> not of desire but of etiquette,
> the nuptial pomp of starched lace;
> a grim innocence.
>
> And picnic parties return from the beaches
> burning with stored sun in the dusk;
> children promised a TV show when they get home
> fall asleep in the backs of a million station wagons,
> sand in their hair, the sound of waves
> quietly persistent at their ears.
> They are not listening.
>
> Their parents at night
> dream and forget their dreams.

They wake in the dark
and make plans. Their sequin plans
glitter into tomorrow.
They buy, they sell.
They fill freezers with food.
Neon signs flash their intentions
into the years ahead.

And at their ears the sound
of the war. They are
not listening, not listening.

(TSA 17–18)

"The opening voice of the poem," Duncan comments, "proposes a *tremendum* in which all the empty-headed and heartless meaningless campaigns of Viet Nam even may be seen as 'war,' and speak for a being at war that is significant at the level of the individual soul life." The critique here is Poundian—the demand for *le mot juste,* for an accuracy which the lines do not fulfill. "War" presented in the abstract is no more than a counter, "We are at war," is like a flash card to which we must respond with predictable horror. The poem leaves the reader no freedom to interpret.

But it is the reference to the "gowns of gold sequins" and their wearers that makes Duncan especially angry:

> In "Tenebrae" it is moralizing that sets in, to deny any ground the heaviness and the bitterness might have verity in. And we get in its place the displaced bigotry in which women are concerned about their gowns of gold, sequins . . . [and] TV watchers are accused of "not listening."
>
> If we were to read this protest of "*they* are not listening" with the possibility that the message of the poem does have content as a dream has content—then we would read that following the opening lines, it is the *poem* itself that is not listening, that has turned to the vanity that all moralizing is in order to evade the imminent content of the announced theme. . . . I think the poems like . . . "Tenebrae" . . . are not to be read properly in relation to Viet Nam . . . but in relation to the deep underlying consciousness of woman as a victim in War with the Man. . . .
>
> It is as if women would give their assurance that although they are filled with rage, they will be good helpmates in the politics of the revolution. (19 October 1971)

Here Duncan's psychologizing (Levertov, he suggests, is subconsciously acting out the beliefs of her radical husband Mitch Goodman, one of the Chicago Seven, so as to please him) may well be overdetermined: the "sincerity" of her antiwar crusade is, in any case, less important than its poetic execution. In her (not surprisingly) angry response in an equally long letter, typed in snatches for a week between 25 October and 2 November 1971, Levertov protests that it would have been hypocritical to identify with those who were "not listening" to the sounds of war, that these sequined-gowned women, whose weddings are reported in the newspaper next to the war news, blindly go on with their lives no matter what catastrophe might be threatening. To excoriate these "consumers," she explains, is by no means a case of "moralizing" but rather a form of "keening," a lament or dirge. As for Duncan's "misapprehensions" that her Vietnam poems "are really about the sex war," she responds, "Bullshit!" and insists that she has never been a member of what was then called a women's lib group.

But whatever the motive behind Levertov's protest poetry (and we can hardly expect her to agree with Duncan's harsh assessment of it), her explanation that the society news ("gowns in gold sequins") is next to the war news in the daily paper does nothing to dispel the larger charge that it is the poem that is "not listening." "While you tell us that 'they' are not listening," he writes in his next letter, "not hearing the war, I am listening and hearing more than you consider it legitimate to hear" (11 November). What Duncan means here, I think—and this is an important critique, not only of "Tenebrae" but of social protest poems in general—is that a genuinely "listening" poem would not present those who "fill their freezers with food" or the kids who watch television and go to beach picnics as an aggregate to be dismissed condescendingly by an "I" who knows better, who presents herself as sensitive and "above" the mere routines of ordinary people. It is this us-versus-them attitude, here and in neighboring poems like "Life at War," that prompts Duncan to speak of the poem's "displaced bigotry," its empty moralizing. Even those who wear gowns of gold sequins or silver moiré, after all, deserve to have their lives *imagined* rather than merely dismissed as vain and futile. And so, when Levertov explains in her letter that "the families are the innocent/ignorant millions of families who do keep the kids quiet with the promise of TV or candy bars or hot dogs," she is, from Duncan's perspective, refusing to engage her subject. The "insight and devotion to the world around us" that Duncan had found so moving and exciting in the earlier poetry, he holds, has now given way to facility.

"The poet's role," in Duncan's view, "is not to oppose evil, but to imagine it." Such imagining depends on "the idea of the multiphasic character of *language* and of the poem as a vehicle of the multiplicity of phases," which, says Duncan, "is more and more central to my thought." Indeed, "The most important rimes are the resonances in which we sound these phases in their variety of depths [in Charles Olson's *Maximus* this appears as taking soundings of the ocean bottom, and knowing the patterns of the fishing rods] — the resonances that depend upon our acknowledgement in our work of what we know of the range of meanings in the language . . . the sexual content so active everywhere in human discourse, the existential propositions of syntax" (19 October 1971). Without such soundings, political poetry is left, says Duncan, with the "Polonius pieties of those who do not want to question their unmixed good will," their commitment to what Levertov calls "a solidarity of hope and struggle with the revolutionary young" (author's preface, TSA viii).

Duncan's emphasis on the poet's need to master "the range of meanings in the language" (e.g., Olson's expertise in recognizing the patterns of fishing rods) might suggest that his is a formalist, indeed a New Critical poetics. But as a theorist, Duncan is closer to Plato or Sidney than he is to Cleanth Brooks or even Roman Jakobson. For he is making the case, later to be made by, say, Steve McCaffery or Susan Howe, that poetic form is itself what Wittgenstein called a form of life and hence a form of knowledge. One cannot, Duncan's letters to Levertov imply throughout, present the horrors of a particular battle or bombing, a government edict or military law, without contextualizing it. To talk of War in the abstract is meaningless. There is no War (as in "We are at war, / bitterly, bitterly at war"), but there are always wars — wars that become the subject of the most varied and contradictory discourses. "You remember," Duncan tells Levertov, "that you are committed to 'opposition to the whole system of insane greed, of racism and imperialism' [see TSA viii] — a political stance: but we are the more aware that it comes to forestall any imagination of what that system is, any creation of such a system of greed, racism and imperialism. These, Denny, are empty and vain slogans" (19 October 1971). Empty, no doubt, because the abstract nouns in question can point to any number of conditions and situations, because there is no map on which to locate them. How about, for example, another event of 1968 — one never mentioned in *To Stay Alive* — namely the Soviet invasion of Czechoslovakia, with its attendant purges, arrests, and killings, designed to squelch the liberation movement known as the Prague Spring? What "system of imperialism" was involved here?

At the microlevel, poetic knowledge involves the interrogation of words, images, or metaphors. One of the most interesting debates in the Duncan-Levertov correspondence has to do with the meaning of specific terms, for instance *spider web* and *coprophilia*. In "Life at War," Levertov laments the callousness of modern man:

> the knowledge that humankind,
>
> delicate Man, whose flesh
> responds to a caress, whose eyes
> are flowers that perceive the stars,
>
> whose music excels the music of birds,
> whose laughter matches the laughter of dogs,
> whose understanding manifests designs
> fairer than the spider's most intricate web,
> still turns without surprise, with mere regret
> to the scheduled breaking open of breasts whose milk
> runs out over the entrails of still-alive babies.
>
> (TSA 13–14)

"There is of course," Duncan comments drily, "an immediate sinister extension of meaning here—for where designs are fair as a spider's web, they remind us of the cruel machinations of Louis XIV who in the poetry of his subjects' speech became 'the spider king.'" And he adds, "Us flies have a grim sense of the fairness of spider webs. And as poets we be spiders who must keep alive the imagination of the flies' relation to the web."

This commentary on the spider image may sound like mere nitpicking, and Levertov responds with irritation, explaining that she had in mind "designs having the beauty of the spider's web but not having the purpose that flaws that beauty and makes it sort of creepy" (25 October–2 November 1971). To which Duncan responds in turn:

> . . . which reading of a spider's web is *careless*, the one that remembers what an actual spider's web is and is designed for and so sees the word "fairer than" charged with more than one level of meaning? or that one that argues against any further thought about spider webs past the visual delight? . . . Images in poems like images in dreams are not inci-

dental or mere devices of speech, chance references, but go deep into our experience. And who in this world has not watched with fascination the activities murderous and cannibalistic of a spider in its web? What child does not know the spider's invitation to the fly?

I'm sure it is perfectly possible to exclaim how lovely! upon seeing a spider-web dew, bejewelled in the sun or moonlight. And I care not if it seem creepy. What is demanded by poetry is that we see (as [Henry] Adams sees his beloved Gothic) the web in its full truth and loveliness.

This is, I think, a very important statement about metaphor. If the nature of "man's understanding" is to be represented by means of an image, Duncan implies, then that image better be an applicable one. If we have to suppress one of the crucial meanings of a given word or phrase in order to make the implied comparison convincing, then surely language is not doing its work.

Duncan lodges a similar objection to the passage in "Staying Alive, Part I," in which the poet longs for a meaningful death, a death

that's not the obscene sellout, the coprophiliac spasm
that smears the White House walls with its desensitized thumbs.

(TSA 30)

"Where and why," asks Duncan with mock naïveté, "this image of a baby smearing the walls with shit? . . . Since I know of no story of Johnson's being a coprophiliac, I can only imagine that your projection alone supplies this as an image of evil" (19 October 1971). Levertov answers with exasperation that Duncan is purposely quibbling, knowing full well as he does that her metaphor is designed to excoriate Johnson and Nixon, whose lies "smear shit all over the White House walls." The coprophiliac image, she insists, has nothing to do with babies, who would just as soon play with applesauce or mud as with shit. As for the reference to "thumbs," Levertov explains that she liked the ugly sound of this monosyllable, and that she wanted to remind her reader of the clumsy and gross gesture of Little Jack Horner (25 October–2 November 1971).

But of course if we "know damn well" that shit is used metaphorically and that the "White House connection" is obviously one to lies and evil deeds, isn't this tantamount to admitting that the metaphor is a well-worn cliché? What, in other words, does it tell us about the Johnson or Nixon White House that we don't already know? And what *is* the relation of the president to Little Jack Horner, an innocent if there ever was one?

Levertov evidently assumes that Duncan didn't understand what she meant, but of course he knows only too well. On 11 November, he replies:

> My complaint about the passage about the coprophiliac spasm that smears the White House walls with its desensitized thumbs *is* that unless there is some actuality to the President or someone smearing the White House walls with shit then there can be nothing but projection. The idea of coprophilia as having to do with desensitized thumbs and with murderous phantasies (and hence with war) does have to do with Freudian ideas of a phase—thinking the unthinkable."

Quite possibly, Duncan is also reading Levertov against the Blake of "London" ("I wander thro' each charter'd street"), where the city's perceived "marks of evil, marks of woe" include the "hapless soldier's sigh" that "Runs in blood down Palace walls." It is possible to unpack this famous symbolic image as meaning that the anguish of the young man who is forced to be a soldier is a ceaseless reproach to the government that has conscripted him. But one needn't have a particular view of the French Revolution, the reactionary government of George III, or the ministry of William Pitt to be moved by Blake's image; indeed, his apocalyptic vision ("In every cry of every man, / In every Infant's cry of fear, / In every voice in every ban, / The mind-forg'd manacles I hear") transcends the petty finger-pointing of Levertov's slurs on Johnson and Nixon.[7] Petty, because the violent image does not go beyond the cliché that the president is an evil man who spreads shit wherever he goes. If this is indeed the case, surely it demands more thorough treatment. Was it Johnson who started the war? Or is he carrying out the Pentagon's wishes? Or trying to fulfill the mandate of his assassinated predecessor? And if the latter is the case, would it make sense to say that Kennedy's tomb at Arlington Cemetery is also "smeared" by "coprophiliac spasm"? If not, why not?

These are the issues raised by Duncan's doggedly literal interrogation of Levertov's war poems. Her outrage, he implies, does not have what Eliot called an objective correlative. And whereas Levertov's earlier poetry beautifully "caught" the nuances of persons, places, and things observed, *To Stay Alive* seems to suffer from hubris. Where it should present, it merely preaches with righteous indignation. "Criticism," says Duncan, must "make clear some crisis in reading. . . . Criticism enlarges our sense of how language works" (19 October 1971). Thus his attack on the war poetry is never petty or personal, never directed against Denise herself but against what Duncan takes to be a wrong turn in what was heretofore an impor-

tant poetic oeuvre. And he tries to convince her how much more successful the Olga poems, which form the first section of *To Stay Alive,* are.

It is hardly surprising, however, that the pressure of this extensive and
insistent commentary was too much for Levertov. Having patiently written a dozen typed pages of self-defense in the 25 October–2 November
letter, a letter to which Duncan responded on 8 November with yet again
the same criticism, she wrote him in December a cool letter of farewell,
telling him she could never really be his friend again, that their close bond
had been irrevocably destroyed by his "coercive" behavior. Duncan took
this hard. On 25 January 1972, he responded apologetically: "My contention with you [was a] contention with my own *anima.* . . . For much of
what I suspect you of, or accuse you of, I suspect as some womanish possibility in myself." In subsequent short letters, he talks about his partner
Jess, about his garden, about his own weaknesses. But to no avail. Levertov was not the forgiving type and, although she later wrote on her early
friendship with Duncan for *Scales of the Marvelous* and occasionally commented on his work in a blurb or book promotion, she kept her distance
right up to the time of his death in 1988.

But from our perspective a quarter century after the Vietnam War, the
question is not whether Duncan was too cruel to Levertov, whether his
authoritative pronunciamentos may or may not have been sexist, or even
whether he was unfair to specific passages in her poems. Rather, the interest the correspondence raises is in the larger issue of the poetry/politics
debate—a debate very much with us today in the guise of the so-called
Culture Wars. Is what seems like a one-dimensional and simplistic lyric
outburst against injustice or racism to be praised because its author is a
member of a minority group and hence not to be subjected to the literary norms of the dominant race and class? Is every poem about AIDS
ipso facto moving and worthy? Is there a taboo against offering any sort
of critique of Amy Tan's *Joy Luck Club* or bell hooks's vituperative essays
attacking the black middle class? Or, for that matter, is there an unstated
taboo against one language poet actually criticizing the work of another?

Whether or not we agree with its premises, Duncan's stringent, learned,
and brilliant critique suggests otherwise. It suggests that precisely those
who know each other well should be willing to argue about their work;
that if all we say is "Yeah, great" and let it go at that, as increasingly poets
and critics are doing at readings and in journals, there can be no meaningful poetic discourse at all. Duncan's pointed and passionate criticism may
have lost him Levertov's friendship, but it won him, I would posit here, a

place among the major poetic theorists as well as major poets of his time. The "coprophiliac" Johnson administration lasted only four years, Chicago's Mayor Daley, long dead, has been replaced by many more sinister politicians (not to mention his son, Chicago's current mayor, and from all accounts a perfectly decent one). But poetry continues in its task, which is, in Duncan's words, "to reveal what is *back of* the political slogans and persuasions." "The questions," as he puts it in response to the "Revolution or Death" option, "are not ideological but have to do with where I feel you do not get to the truth of your ideology." It is an interesting and important distinction.

—You will start with the third chapter, Arkadii said, and the first sentence must be attributed to Emmanuel Kant as follows: everything happens so often, that speaking of it makes no sense.

—*Oxota*, Book 3, chapter 89 [1]

10. How Russian Is It

Lyn Hejinian's *Oxota*

Arkadii, in the above passage, is Arkadii Dragomoschenko, the remarkable Russian poet Lyn Hejinian has been translating for the past decade or so, a poet she first met in 1983 when she accompanied her husband Larry Ochs and other members of the Rova Saxophone Quartet on a tour to Moscow and Leningrad. Few poetic journeys of our time have proved to be more fruitful. Dragomoschenko and Hejinian have collaborated on a film script, a theater piece, poems, and translations of each others' work; they also organized, in 1989, an international conference on avant-garde writers, the first such conference since the Russian Revolution. The four American poets who attended—Michael Davidson, Ron Silliman, Barrett Watten, and Hejinian herself—wrote a collaborative account of their trip called *Leningrad* (Mercury House, 1991), in which their four alternating voices run together, the individual poets "distinguished only by the icons used as a visual key to identify them: a formal element of the text as poem." The result makes for a fascinating collage travel narrative, tracking as it does the rapid unraveling of the Soviet Union, as seen from a set of related but quite different positions. [2]

Hejinian's own narrative in *Leningrad* sets the stage for *Oxota*, subtitled *A Short Russian Novel*, a 3,780-line poem, written in the fourteen-line stanza of Pushkin's *Evgeny Onegin* and divided, like *Onegin*, into eight books. *Oxota* is not only one of the most ambitious long poems of the nineties; it is, I think, one of the very best—eloquent testimony that despite all the gloomy journalistic predictions about the death of poetry, and especially narrative poetry, in the information age, there are still important stories to be told. In *My Life* (first version, 1980; second, 1987), Hejinian submitted her own "story" to a new kind of simultaneous vision, her girlhood experience intersecting that of "everygirl's" in a series of deliciously comic and moving permutations. In *Oxota* (the title means "the hunt"),[3] the story broadens out to include a host of Russian and American characters, but its mysteries—what it doesn't tell us—make even greater demands on the reader. As Hejinian, following her Russian formalist mentors Viktor Shklovsky and Jurij Tinjanov, puts it, "The very idea of reference is spatial: over here is word, over there is thing at which the word is shooting amiable love-arrows," and thus "the struggle between language and that which it claims to depict or express" is what determines the very shape narrative takes. "Language discovers what one might know, which in turn is always less than what language might say."[4]

But how, we might ask, do we reconcile the poetics of the language movement with the demands of narrative? If language games—paranomasia, paragram, epigraphy—and syntactic dislocations abound, if the reader can't even tell "what's going on," how can *Oxota* claim to be a novel? And how can Hejinian's ruminations on what she calls in *Leningrad* "juxtaposition, happenstance, double vision, vistas, and a flow of observations and expectations kept in suspense" bear comparison, parodic or otherwise, to the great Russian epic poem *Evgeny Onegin?*

As it happens, I brought along my copy of *Oxota* to India (my first visit), where much time was spent waiting in local airports, sitting in countless crowded lounges or waiting for takeoff on small planes that were invariably delayed and often simply canceled. Even in these distracting circumstances, I found, to my own surprise, that I couldn't put *Oxota* down—and not because I couldn't wait to see what happened next, for it is never clear, in this poem of dislocations, irruptions, and veiled allusions, what is actually happening. Rather, I read avidly because Hejinian's "short Russian novel" actively engages us in the poet's own "hunt" for meaning, for greater understanding of daily life in the Soviet Union, as that life is perceived by the uninitiated but not quite innocent American visitor. What game, for example, is the sinister colonel playing? Why are "they" hunting for Gavronsky and what crime, if any, did he commit? Is "Lyn" falling in love with Arkadii or is theirs primarily a literary friendship? How does Arkadii's wife Zina view the situation? Are specific events described "real" or experienced in dreams? What is it that "Lyn" learns about herself? And, on a more pedestrian level, does the terrible freeze ever let up? Are certain images signs of spring or just momentary changes in the weather? Each fourteen-line stanza seems to promise disclosure of these and other "realities," but the disclosure never quite comes, even though we notice a gradual transformation in phenomenology: something, we know, is changing, being digested, increasingly understood; some of the initial strangeness of the Russian world is gradually diminishing even if it never quite disappears.

What, asks John Bayley in his introduction to Charles Johnston's translation of *Evgeny Onegin* (Penguin Classics), did Pushkin mean by calling his poem "a free novel"? "Apparently a work of art which did not conform to the rules of a single genre, but which, as he put it in the stanza that opened the poem by way of a preface, offered 'a collection of parti-coloured chapters half-funny, half-sad, ideal and folk-simple' (*prostonarodny*)." And Bayley cites Shklovsky, who said that Pushkin's real subject was not the story of his lovers, Eugene and Tatyana, "but a game with this story." Like the Byron of *Don Juan,* Pushkin's "I" is the poem's central character, providing ironic commentary, judging his characters' behavior, and digressing on larger social and political themes. At the same time, the poem's playfulness is kept in check by the fixity of its stanza form: fourteen lines of octosyllabic verse, rhyming *ababccddeffegg.*

The appeal this particular equilibrium evidently held for Hejinian is spelled out most fully in chapters 192 and 193 of *Oxota.* The latter begins:

> *Evgeny Onegin* is a novel of manners (Belinsky called it encyclopedic), a
> family saga, an autobiography, an aimless plot with the symmetry of
> time, an impression of philosophy, and *Dead Souls* is an epic, hope-
> ful of resurrection
> The epic, said Mikhail Kheraskov, will remember important, memo-
> rable, famous events occurring in this world to cause important
> change, or it will sing of events occurring in a certain state to glorify
> life, or occasion peace, or finally to provoke a transition to a differ-
> ent condition

Here is the paradox Hejinian embodies in *Oxota. Dead Souls* is written in prose but its domain is that of epic; *Onegin* is in verse, but it is more properly understood as a novel of manners or autobiography. One needn't choose one or the other ("Equally marvelous, as Gogol said, are the lenses that contemplate a star and those that study a bug"), but Hejinian's personal predilection is for the freedom of the Pushkin model: "Every fact could break through deterministic constraints," and moreover "Everyone has to eat and many eat potatoes, but some of those also eat pineapples."

How, then, to adapt such an outwardly formal model? "Once in Moscow," the poet recalls in chapter 149, "I was asked to recite and the man was antagonized," evidently by the absence of meter and rhyme in her poems. But "Even 'it' is irregular," she responds, referring both to *Evgeny Onegin* and to the word "it," with its myriad uses.[5] "There are irregularities for all that's permitted / Or I see it backward / Or it has its choice of contemporary resemblance." What such "contemporary resemblance" might look like is suggested in chapter 192, which opens as follows:

> But to return to the theme of the novel and poetry
> That is, one theme
> The time comes when each individual poem reveals not only its own internal connections but also spreads them out externally, anticipating the integrity each poem requires in order to explain obscure points, arbitrary elements, etc., which, if they were kept within the limits of the given text, would seem otherwise to be mere examples of the freedom of expression

If we read *Oxota* as a self-enclosed text, its "obscure points" and "arbitrary elements" will look like "mere examples of the freedom of expression." But if we pay attention, the poem "reveals not only its own internal connections but also spreads them out externally." For Pushkin's "irregularities" of storytelling, his countless digressions, observations, interruptions, Hejinian substitutes the "irregularity" of "free verse," but only within the limits of the temporal and spatial frames provided by the original: the fourteen-line stanza, the eight-book structure, the shift from Petersburg (Hejinian's Leningrad) to the pastoral setting of Tatyana's country house, and so on.

The resulting design resembles, as Hejinian herself notes, those picture books where little figures are buried inside the outlines of larger images, their detection presenting a challenging "quandary for children":

> Things in the picture are hidden but once found one can never not see them though to someone's who's never looked they're still out of sight, lost in the lines
>
> (chap. 209)

This is precisely what happens to the reader of *Oxota*. "Things . . . hidden," for example, the frequent references to Pushkin—his house, his tomb, his lovers and habits of writing—and the equally frequent allusions to the story motifs of *Onegin* —Tatyana's sexually charged dream of meeting a bear in the snow, the insomnia she and Eugene alternately experience, the rivalry between Eugene and Lensky, and so on—make *Oxota* a kind of roman à clef, though not in the usual sense of the word.

Consider the title *Oxota* (*The Hunt*). The first overt explanation of its meaning comes near the end of the "novel" in chapter 259:

> It's characteristic of a Russian novelist to reveal some lack of
>   confidence in the relationship between words and their things
> A chair but not sure what sits and what will match it
> Noon freezing on the spot we don't remember
> Each action hangs, inconsequentially, over objects
> How many alternatives there must be
> How many patient comparisons await fulfilling
> Unextracted paradoxes, breathless empty ice streets, anticipated
>   catastrophes with
>   no one approaching, love not provided with intrigue
> It was Zina who called it *oxota*
> The hunt

Here Hejinian refers obliquely to Roman Jakobson's famous distinction between the metaphoric and metonymic poles of language, the former (or figure of similarity) said to belong to poetry, the latter (or figure of contiguity) more properly to realistic prose fiction. Postmodern poetry has challenged and undermined this opposition; the metonymic mode Jakobson associated with Tolstoy's and Chekhov's fiction has become prominent in lyric as well. Then, too, theorists from Lacan and Genette on down have been at pains to show that Jakobson's sharp dichotomy between the two will not stand up to scrutiny. Metaphors can work metonymically and vice versa; figures of similarity and contiguity are always intertwined.

Hejinian, in any case, adapts the Jakobson model to her own purposes. In a 1988 lecture to the Kootenay School of Poetics at Vancouver, she described her desire for a phenomenological "description" that would avoid both "after-the-fact realism, with its emphasis on the world described (the objects of description)" and the "organizing subjectivity (that of the perceiver-describer)." Description, she suggests, should be "a method of invention and of composition . . . with a marked tendency toward effecting isolation and displacement, that is, toward objectifying all that's described and making it strange." And she adds:

If one posits descriptive language and, in a broader sense, poetic language as a language of inquiry, with analogies to the scientific methods of the explorers, then I anticipate that the principal trope will be the metonym, what Roman Jakobson calls "association by contiguity." . . . Metonymy moves attention from thing to thing; its principle is combination rather than selection. Compared to metaphor, which depends on code, metonym preserves context, foregrounds interrelationship. And again in comparison to metaphor which is based on similarity, and in which meanings are conserved and transferred from one thing to something said to be like it, the metonymic world is unstable. . . . Comparing apples to oranges is metonymic.[6]

Here Hejinian stresses the instability rather than the supposed realism of the metonymic world. "How many patient comparisons await fulfilling," we read in chapter 259, "Unextracted paradoxes . . . anticipated catastrophes with no one approaching." And in chapter 258, "The hunter knows the resource / The hunter resorts / She doesn't think and then decide / She follows word to word in words' design." Whereas Pushkin's Tatyana is "hunted by love's anguish" (bk. 3, 20), Hejinian's "describer-perceiver" hunts among words and sentences for clues and connections. "A woman is hunting for sleep," we read in chapter 153, "but she is sleeping to hunt." Book 5, from which these lines are taken, was published separately as *The Hunt*,[7] and it abounds in images of pursuit and pursuers, a "hunt syntax" as it is called in chapter 248.

In "The Formative Properties of Words" (chap. 135), Hejinian gives us some idea of what such a "hunt syntax" involves:

I cannot imagine a glass prose
But I was losing interest in the phenomenology of my dreams
Daylight was thicker than it seemed—with augmentation, odor, air
Where are words changed?

If the language of transparency (a "glass prose") is inadequate, "reality" does make its demands on the poet: "Daylight was thicker than it seemed —with augmentation, odor, air." And later in the stanza:

It's the principle of connection not that of causality which saves us
    from a bad infinity
The word *hunt* is not the shadow of an accident

The postmodern narrative poem, these lines imply, cannot adopt the language of transcendence ("a bad infinity"), nor can its incidents and events unfold according to the laws of "causality." Rather, the "principle of connection," of metonymic structuring that animates *Oxota,* is designed to produce what Hejinian calls an "intervalic" or "unstable" form, in keeping with the poem's destabilization of identity.

From *Writing Is an Aid to Memory* (1978) and the first version of *My Life* to her recent long metaphysical poem "The Person," Hejinian has refused all notions of the self as "some core reality at the heart of our sense of being," the still dominant myth of the "artist's 'own voice,' issuing from an inner, fundamental, sincere, essential irreducible, consistent self, an identity which is unique and separable from all other human identities." In Russian, she points out, "the closest representation of my notion of the self occurs in (but only in) the reflexible pronoun *sebya* (oneself, myself), which never appears in the nominative case and is most frequently seen in form of the suffix *sya* at the end of reflexive verbs. This suggests that when speaking Russian a self is felt but has no proper name, or that the self occurs only in or as a context but is insufficiently stable to occur independently as a noun." [8]

This explanation of Russian reflexive verb forms is somewhat fanciful: from Pushkin to Pasternak, after all, Russian poetry has displayed a very strong sense of personal identity, even if there is no single word that defines selfhood. Just the same, this particular peculiarity of Russian grammar helps Hejinian articulate her own view that "the person . . . is a mobile (or mobilized) reference point; or to put it another way, subjectivity is not an entity but a dynamic." "Certainly," Hejinian concedes, "I have an experience of being in position, at a time and place, and of being conscious of this, but this position is temporary, and beyond that, I have no experience of being except in position." And again, "[The] sense of contingency is ultimately intrinsic to my experience of the self, as a relationship rather than an existence" (PJ 167).

What this means in practice is that ideas, sensations, overheard remarks, and so on, are *seen* from a particular perspective but these perspectives never wholly cohere into anything like a fixed identity or self. We come to know the way Hejinian's language works—her stylistic choices are highly particularized—but we learn little about the poet's past or present circumstances, and it would be difficult to say that she has such-and-such attributes and character traits, or to comment on her "nature." Psychology, in this scheme of things, means not self-revelation but, in Wallace Stevens's words, "description without place," the anchor being the buried but ever present analogy to *Evgeny Onegin.* Here is chapter 1:

This time we are both
The old thaw is inert, everything set again in snow
At insomnia, at apathy
We must learn to endure thé insecurity as we read
The felt need for a love intrigue
There is no person—he or she was appeased and withdrawn
There is relationship but it lacks simplicity
People are very aggressive and every week more so
The Soviet colonel appearing in such of our stories
He is sentimental and duckfooted
He is held fast, he is in his principles
But here is a small piece of the truth—I am glad to greet you
There, just with a few simple words it is possible to say the truth
It is so because often men and women have their sense of honor

In good epic tradition, the poem opens in medias res with "This time," the implication being that "this time" (arriving again in the Soviet Union?) will be measured against another time which was somehow different. But "This time we are both" immediately displays Hejinian's deceptive flatness: the language seems totally ordinary, and yet it throws out any number of plot lines. Perhaps it means that "we are both here," but then who are "we"? And what is it we both are? Both poets, one American, one Russian, or one woman and one man? Both guests of the Soviet government? Both ready for a relationship? Or, if "both" is construed, not as the predicate nominative but as the modifier of the predicative adjective(s), we might read it as "both tired and hungry, both frightened and elated," and so on.

Something, in any case, is about to happen "this time." The "thaw" of line 2 may well refer to the brief political respite of the Khrushchev years as well as the actual weather conditions; soon "everything [is] set again in snow." And just as Pushkin's dedicatory stanza describes his poem as the product "of carefree hours, of fun, / of sleeplessness, faint inspirations," Hejinian refers to "insomnia" and "apathy," warning her reader even as she warns herself that "We must learn to endure the insecurity as we read / The felt need for a love intrigue / There is no person—he or she was appeased and withdrawn." The "need for a love intrigue" refers, of course, to the Onegin-Tatyana romance which is Pushkin's "subject"; in our own fractured world, such "love intrigue" seems to have given way to the diminished romance of "relationship," and even then a relationship that "lacks simplicity." Indeed, all sorts of sexual and familial relationships, all more or less complicated, will be presented for our inspection, and part of the fun of reading *Oxota* will be to figure out who is drawn to whom, for how long, and what the sexual and/or political dynamics are.

In the meantime, the stage is set for the unfolding of events: "People are very aggressive and every week more so," where the reference to "week" is a play on the standard complaint that "Things get worse every day!" The "duckfooted" colonel, who will appear and reappear throughout the narrative, an embodiment of "principles" and "sentimental" old truths, is introduced and then, like a stock character in a cheap thriller, mysteriously disappears again. And now the stanza ends on a turn of phrase that is brilliantly deployed throughout *Oxota*, especially in the early chapters, where the poet records how it feels to be a linguistic alien in a country one wants so badly understand. "Here is a small piece of the truth—I am glad to greet you" is the poet's rendition of the way "polite" Russian hosts greet their American guests, the excessive formality of phrasing being a function of unfamiliarity rather than good manners.

Many of us have had the experience of meeting foreigners who seem extremely, if not excessively, polite until we realize they are speaking a careful English based on the classroom model or grammar book. Translated into colloquial English, line 12 carries something like the locution, "Believe me, I am really happy to meet you." But in bringing "the truth" into speech twice, and in concluding that "It is so because often men and women have their sense of honor," we are immediately *in* a language world—and, in Wittgensteinian terms, the limits of my language are the limits of my world—that is largely alien to the American visitor. Accordingly, for the "we" who are "both," assimilation will depend not on finding out what the words mean but how they are used, how to read the signs. And, as Hejinian wittily implies throughout, this is no easy matter. When someone says to us "There, just with a few simple words it is possible to say the truth," we surmise the presence of a sensibility that may not be there at all.

But then words like "there" are always suspect in Hejinian's scheme of things, origin and location, whether of speech or event, being all but impossible to define. As in Ingeborg Bachmann's poetic novel *Malina,* individual phrases and sentences (whether thoughts or portions of dialogue) are often not assigned to a particular subject: a phrase like "People are very aggressive and every week more so," for instance, sounds like a snatch of conversation overheard while waiting in line at the butcher shop. But it may also refer to something quoted from the newspaper or, for that matter, it may record Lyn's own appraisal of her surroundings. Even the stilted

Russian constructions of the English language cannot always be attributed to X or Y; often, they may be Hejinian's own, as she tries to make herself understood to those who have schoolbook English. They may even be approximations of Russian syntax, as laboriously translated into English by the poet. The pattern is further complicated by the gaps between statements and/or lines, one perception thus failing to lead, as Charles Olson would have it, immediately (or even remotely) to a further perception.

Yet Hejinian's disjunctiveness does not go together with an imagistic or filmlike verbal surface, or even with the free association of stream of consciousness. Language does not represent "thought"; on the contrary, linguistic artifice is emphasized by the embedding of images in a network of abstractions, as in "everything set again in snow," or by the positioning of abstractions in unlikely grammatical constructions, as in the locution "At insomnia, at apathy," on the model of "at school" or "at home." The resulting poem-novel is, as Hejinian puts it in chapter 2, "something neither invented nor constructed but moving through that time as I experienced it unable to take part personally in the hunting." It is as if the text avoids the requisite distance between subject and object and lets "events" unfold so that the reader feels as if she has come in on a conversation whose participants cannot be located. There is nothing obscure about what's being said or thought, but we don't know who is doing the thinking or talking. *Oxota* is thus a novel in which we have any number of actions and events but can't quite tell who the actors are. We only know that there are many and that their lives sharply intersect Lyn's own.

Book I might be called, in oblique homage to Gertrude Stein's *Tender Buttons* (about which Hejinian has written so interestingly in "Two Stein Talks"),[9] "Rooms." The first preoccupation of the American guest is to become accustomed to her immediate surroundings. In chapter 3:

Something hangs in the drawing room and it's green
A painted herring hung where it's harder to recognize
I slept there in a corner on the sofa called America
In a bed near the Vyborg by a crowbar with magpie-dog duo singing a
    ballad without the neighbor's shaking out his blanket
I dreamed I was walking somewhere in the Crimea with my mother
    when we met two soldiers and their man in handcuffs
He was a criminal of passion
The riddle depending on delayed recognition of a thing like a herring-
    Armenian

A maiden name
A visa
I answered the top man at the consulate and said the word was marital
Rubble—so you see that our people must squat in their ditch and
    speak of beauty
The enemy freezes to its trees
The old women who survived had to have been witches, said Misha
Bitches, said Arkadii Trofimovich—the crime of passion is our Soviet
    kindness

"Metonymy moves attention from thing to thing." The first few lines chart the poet's "night thoughts" as she tries to acclimate herself to her new sleeping quarters in Arkadii's drawing room, where she occupies "the sofa called America," so-called, no doubt, because it's where visiting Americans are put up. As she tries to make out the "something" hanging on the wall, which looks like a "painted herring," two comic riddles come to mind: the popular Jewish joke about the green herring,[10] and the more personal "riddle depending on delayed recognition of a thing like a herring-Armenian"—a comic reference to the attempt, evidently by the Russian immigration officials, to pronounce the name "Hejinian," which, further and confusingly, is assumed by them to be "a maiden name." "I answered the top man at the consulate and said the word was marital." A name can be marital ("Hejinian" is the name of the poet's first husband) but an undesignated word can't, the phrasing pointing up the disparity between the two kinds of words. Then, too, "marital," followed as it is by the word "Rubble," becomes, by the merest reversal of its fourth and fifth letters, "martial," the word making perfect sense in the context of the language of war and imprisonment that dominates the stanza.

Such linguistic play is at the heart of what Hejinian calls "description as a method of invention and of composition." The conventional auto-biographical travel narrative, whether in verse or prose, would talk *about* alienation and the difficulty of communication. *Oxota,* by contrast, allows the language itself to generate the ideas. Thus, when Hejinian refers to the dream of "walking somewhere in the Crimea with my mother when we met two soldiers and their man in handcuffs," and concludes, "He was a criminal of passion," the reader is initially confused. People everywhere commit "crimes of passion" but what does it mean to *be* a "criminal of passion"? The mystery is partially cleared up when Arkadii refers, in the stanza's final line, to the Soviet practice of putting people in camps on trumped up charges of sexual offense:

> The old women who survived had to have been witches, said Misha
> Bitches, said Arkadii Trofimovich — the crime of passion is our Soviet
>   kindness

It is the phrase "crime of passion" that haunts the narrator, reappearing in her dream as a visual image of a "man in handcuffs," who is identified, as if for life, as a "criminal of passion." The simple nominal shift from deed to doer serves to define the Soviet system more tellingly than might a didactic account of the camps. The word, for Hejinian thus plays a constructive rather than a representational role; it is itself the creator of the images we claim to "see."

What is it that we "see" in the course of the poem? The events depicted in *Oxota* are characterized by their dailiness: people shop, cook dinner, talk endlessly about their feelings and (since these are poets) about art and literature, make love, suffer from occasional insomnia, complain about the weather, try to inure themselves to daily economic and political upheavals, and so on. But if "everything happens so often, that speaking of it makes no sense" (chap. 89), the poet must find ways of representing those happenings so that their actual feel, their texture is reexperienced. Take Hejinian's strategy of opening a "chapter" (stanza) with an aphorism or wise generalization:

Neither art nor life is opposite (chap. 39)
All tender winds are foreseen tunes (chap. 45)
Truth is not precision but evidence (chap. 71)
Passion is the alienation that love provides (chap. 75)
Metaphor hides the paranoia of writing (chap. 103)
Divination by clouds must be renounced under a colorless sky (chap. 135)

Does this last statement mean that if the sky were blue, "Divination by clouds" should be practiced? Does the relation of "truth" to "evidence" rather than "precision" mean that the truth mustn't be exact? These dada versions of proverbial wisdom prefigure the narrator's overwhelming sense of difference, confronted by the Other which is Russia. "Dreams don't understand, they're what's being understood," begins chapter 21, evidently playing on an earlier discussion of the power of dreams to interpret ("understand" in Russian-English speak) reality. The stanza continues:

A commentator in the kitchen on television gives the official
   explanation that the reason there's no food in the stores is that
   people are eating too much
But the television is only a three-inch square
Rice with horseradish and bread
We had bought some daffodils and had taped the petals erect
Following Zina I had felt slightly exposed, but as a child does out
   of bed
She had previously enraged a group of the enormous courtyard crows
A face they heard. . . .

Here the comparison of apples and oranges Hejinian made in her lecture "Strangeness" is apposite. The authority of the television is undercut by the absurd premise that its three-inch screen is too small to convey truth, much smaller, at any rate, than the reality that there is nothing for dinner but "rice with horseradish and bread." And if there is not enough food there might as well, again by the logic of the absurd, be flowers, in this case daffodils, whose wilted petals need to be taped erect. The anger that should be directed at the economy that produces chronic food shortages is now vented on "a group of the enormous courtyard crows"; the "face they heard" is Zina's, her mouth evidently open in a scream. As for the "I" who witnesses these events, she recalls feeling "slightly exposed" (on the aggressive hunt for food in the markets), "but as a child does out of bed," which is to say a naughty child which has sneaked out of its room when it's supposed to be asleep. "Slightly exposed" perhaps also, in that Zina may suspect the malaise she feels in these hospitable but still wholly alien surroundings.

Throughout this chapter, indeed throughout *Oxota,* catachresis (e.g., "A face they heard") emphasizes the difficulties of perception, even as incorrect usage ("She had previously *enraged* a group of . . . crows") calls attention to the constructedness of this poetic discourse. Even repetition serves to point up difference: the spread at Misha's party (chap. 21, lines 12–14), for example, is as meatless as the dinner at Zina's, but this time "potatoes with mushrooms, two different cabbage salads . . . bread" are enhanced by wine and vodka, so that the conversation proceeds enjoyably enough "in stages of anecdote," despite the "poor dog with pecked eyes" and, again, the crows.

The crows, like so many of the "characters" in *Oxota,* reappear frequently—in this case, as emblems of a loving but slightly squalid and even oppressive domesticity. In chapter 58, for example, the poet has evidently been taken ill and is being nursed by Zina and her son Ostap, while Arkadii attends a poetry meeting in a neighboring town. "Some possibilities take place on a plate," the stanza begins, the "possibilities" probably referring to something Lyn ate that has made her sick. Such food poisoning is "A process whose pace doesn't coincide with comprehension's pace." One can be told over and over again not to eat X or Y ("I remember the instructions") but when the plate of food actually appears, one forgets: "To see is such deferred." Someone, in any case (Ostap? Zina? Or maybe Lyn herself?) declares, "I am to interrupt myself tonight at exactly 8 and propose a toast to our colleagues who at this moment are reading verses in Tambov." And the toast is followed by the line "Both largeness and lozenge to collide." Now the scene shifts to the crows:

> The crows voices in winter light like copper pliers
> The reading an open word shutter
> Only slats, and they faded into winter. . . .

Here constriction is the order of the day. To the feverish patient sucking on lozenges, the crows' voices "light" (i.e., "alight" but "light" can also be an adjective), grating on the ear "like copper pliers," but the poetry reading itself appears to her as "an open word shutter," a closure of something that should remain free. Meanwhile, she is confined in the apartment, the "slats," now of the window shutters, "fad[ing] into winter" as night comes on. In this landscape, Hejinian's crows, rather like Wallace Stevens's blackbirds, "mark the edge of one of many circles." Later, when the spring thaws come (chap. 64), the crows give way to the "mumbling as of wasps or sheep," and "I said that a fly had appeared in the operating room / It sat like a crystal of black salt on the bed."

Book 1 (chaps. 1–70) circles around these images and themes, the changes that take place, both seasonal and personal, being so gradual as to be almost imperceptible. Book 2 (chaps. 71–80) has a different rhythm. For one thing, each of its ten poems has a title: in sequence, "Truth," "Nature," "Innocence," "Conspiracy," "Passion," "Design," "Suffering," "Betrayal," "Death," and "Redemption." All of these conceptul abstractions relate to the romance of Onegin and Tatyana, the initial passion the "innocent" girl living in the country conceives for him, Lensky's death in the duel, Onegin's betrayal, Tatyana's suffering, and then, in the stunning reversal, Onegin's own suffering, which looks ahead to death and perhaps redemption. Not only, then, does Pushkin provide Hejinian with a frame for this section; book 2 also contains many references to him, to his house (now a museum), his tomb, his admirers, his mistresses, and to imaginary scenes in which Pushkin may be lying "naked in his room on the rug writing in solitude or visiting with friends."

But it is not just a matter of chapter titles or Pushkin references. The mood of Book 2 is quite different from that of Book 1. The parties, conversations, meals, and poetry debates give way to solitude in nature although the setting is not made clear. The weather has changed ("The frost falls from a tree"; "gray birches"), and although there are still occasional snowfalls, the air is warmer. The sequence opens with the line "Truth is not precision but evidence"; the body, it seems has its own truth ("Body and truth at the thought / Crazy who says no longer") and the poet, formerly so upbeat, so busily engaged in exploring her new territory, now appears (when she appears at all, for her identity is increasingly fractured), troubled and somehow guilty: "I was feeling an inferior weariness, an inability to acknowledge anything." At the middle of the sequence (chap. 75) is the elliptical poem called "Passion":

Passion is the alienation that love provides
Drifting winter tinted where we lifted, plowed
Jealousy is a flake of a different passion
It was hungry to be plunging in disruption
The wobble and mattering the sensing muscles which combine
People are not joined in passion but divulged
They diverge—but that sight was unseen
But all is muffled in banalities, I said
It is not passion to nod in
It is passion for no one to listen
One with closed eyes and the other one's opened
The snowfall offered all the colors of apple
There was passion in its thud and exhilaration
Patience itself pushes over—given a body for what

The language of this curious love poem is chaste in comparison to the earlier exuberant stanzas; sound repetition (the assonance, for example, of "Drifting winter tinted where we lifted") and the repetition of the word "passion" (it occurs five times in the space of fourteen lines) chiming with other nouns ending with the "-ion" suffix ("alienation," "disruption," "exhilaration"), give the poem a formal air. At the same time, the sexual allusions ("Drifting," "lifted," "plowed," "plunging," "The wobble and

mattering of the sensing muscles which combine") have a slightly histri-
onic tone—like bowdlerized Meredith or slightly souped-up Rossetti—so
that one is not surprised to read "But all this is muffled in banalities, I
said." Banalities like "The snowfall offered all the colors of apple," with its
allusion to forbidden fruit.

We never know much more about the poem's "love intrigue" than this.
The focus is not on the lovers as individuals but again on the feel or texture of "love." In *Oxota,* it seems to lead to frustration: "Suffering" (chap.
77) begins:

> A stench left from cooking fish lay frenzied, fell inert
> Or a yellow rose frustrated in the Summer Garden

And "Death" (chap. 79) ends on a note of regret: "Why not have waited."
Only in the final chapter "Redemption," does the mood shift once more:
a certain serenity now colors the atmosphere:

> We were laughing at the Russian novel
> We will say, the slower you go the farther you'll get and plain water is
>   glad to get a crow
> We will be redeemed, we will be rescued
> We will believe everything we say

The image of the "crow," associated with the family scenes of book 1,
marks a return to what is usually called "reason," a return at least to the
desire for something different: "We will be redeemed, we will be rescued."
And by the time we open Book 3 and read the pseudoepic and punning
lines, "Leningrad lies in the haze of its sides / It lies as a heroine" (chap.
81), we are back in a more public space, where the "I" functions as visiting
poet and foreign observer.

"You will start with the third chapter, Arkadii said." In this opening
stanza of the third book, Hejinian gives us what is perhaps the poem's
clearest statement of poetics. After the opening gesture toward Leningrad,
we read:

> Now it is both
> How not—the not is sometimes impossible to reach
> It was
> But then is the work of art not an act but an object of memory
> Then from a great disturbance
> The most delicate message accumulates

But you must know why you write a novel, said Vodonoy
It's not to displace anything
It has context and metronome
By insisting on a comprehension of every word I am free to signify
    place though not to represent it.
So I must oppose the opposition of poetry to prose
Just as we can only momentarily oppose control to
    discontinuity, sex to organization, disorientation to domestic time
    and space, and glasnost (information) to the hunt

In the short compass of a single stanza, Hejinian traces her own response to romanticism and its offshoot, the New Criticism. One's first poetic model, she posits, is the Faustian lyric of yearning, whose "not is sometimes impossible to reach," a model that easily gives way to the doctrine of the poem as formal artifact ("not an act but an object of memory"), together with the New Critical doctrine (made famous by I. A. Richards) of poetic tension and resolution: "Then from a great disturbance / The most delicate message accumulates." Perhaps Hejinian calls her poem a "novel" so as to avoid the heavy weight of lyric tradition. "It's not to displace anything," for of course her text isn't like a novel either: "It has context and metronome," a network of interrelated images and realistic settings together with a strong verse line that, if not guided by the metronome, is not innocent of rhythm and metrical tradition either: "Leningrad lies in the haze of its sides," for that matter, is a ten-syllable line having only four strong stresses, in the tradition of Eliot's *Waste Land* or *Four Quartets*.

But it is the long twelfth line that is especially revealing:

By insisting on a comprehension of every word I am free to signify
    place though not to represent it

Once writing is no longer regarded as the vehicle that conveys an already present speech, every word, indeed every morpheme can be seen to carry meaning, to enter relationships with its neighbors. There are, in this scheme of things, no "fillers" or function words, and syntax is at least as important as the invention of striking images. And here the distinction between "signify[ing] place" and "represent[ing] it" becomes clear. The rejection of *representation* does not, as many readers have assumed, entail the loss of *reference*. A Hejinian stanza, that is to say, does not present us with a coherent picture of something external to it, a photograph *of* or picture *of.* But reference, whether to persons (Zina, Olga, Natasha, Vodonoy, Alexei, Arkadii, Gavronsky) or places (cities, rivers, streets, houses), is essential to the poem, the necessary peg upon which speculation can be hung.

A frequent objection of mainstream poetry criticism is that, without some measure of representation—the mirror held to nature, to social custom and the "march of events"—the poetic text becomes meaningless. But it is reference, not representation, that we cannot do without: words, after all, must point to something, even if that something is only a small part of their structures of meaning. By the same argument, the conventional opposition of poetry to prose, an opposition still central to curricula, literary journals, and critical discourse, must itself be opposed. For the long poems consonant with our times, Hejinian suggests, cannot be pigeonholed; the four- or five-line strophes of *Oxota,* for example, are always approaching the condition of prose, without ever quite becoming coherent sentences. To illustrate the perils of dichotomizing, Hejinian concludes the stanza by comparing that division to a series of others, by no means obviously analogous:

poetry	prose
control	discontinuity
sex	organization
disorientation	domestic time and space
glasnost (information)	the hunt

This opposition would make much more sense if we could switch the items in the second pair: "discontinuity" would seem to go with poetry and sex, and certainly with "disorientation," whereas "control" belongs to "organization" and the order of prose. "Domestic time and space" goes here too because, for the woman poet, this is the space of "organization," where one takes care of others rather than oneself. As for the title noun, "the hunt," the reference is to the relentless power structure that pursues its recalcitrant victims, that forces the person to obey certain laws. If the information provided by the new *glasnost* seems to provide the necessary opening, such free inquiry may not be able to resist "the hunt"—*Oxota.*

At first the initiation into the Soviet order, an order softened by *glasnost* and sweetened by the presence of close friends and colleagues, provides amusement and pleasure; somewhat later, sexual love and perhaps jealousy come into the picture to complicate matters. But after the recognition in Book 3 (chap. 89) that "names are relationships with a remarkable economy while descriptions are profligate," a certain distancing occurs. "Rested by winter" (chap. 108), the "describer-perceiver" can enjoy the coming of spring with equanimity:

> And so in a truly magical manner it has come about in
> > apparently one continuous morning that I have become the
> possessor of
> > multitudes of wide open windows and of sunlight tumbling
> into other minute
> > fissures of an almost invisible brightness
>
> > > > > > (chap. 109)

"Sex will begin again" (chap. 111), but it is now viewed with more detachment, with a greater sense of the absurd: "sex is all feature and has no destiny / an enormous toe, a dusty skin, breast hair. . . . At such an age the features fatten." When Lyn and Zina dawdle in the morning over their "Cuban grapefruit," they are "very relaxed with sophistication" (chap. 121). More comfortable with the "person" she is becoming, Lyn is learning about the Russian avant-garde that is so central to *Oxota:*

> Lyosha, I said, please
> Explain to me, the two avant garde traditions after Mandelstam
> > and Pasternak
> With no indolence, he said
>
> > > > > (chap. 133)

Here is one of those phrases that deliciously mimic Russian speech trying to approximate English idiom. "With no indolence" means more or less "I'd be happy to." And Lyosha's explanation is rendered with similar humor:

> But, for example—can one say that a huge sun is a damp whole
> > in English
> It would be very difficult, I said
> For instance, I could not have said so before 1985
> Unbirth and birth
> No, prebirth
> Nonbirth
> Petersburg
> I agree

Here Lyosha is making a case for the extravagant imagery of Dada and Surrealism, suppressed during the long years of Socialist Realism. But the irony is that the American poet says "It would be very difficult" to use such imagery in English as well, and the reference to 1985 refers not only to *glasnost* but, quite possibly, as the stichomythia of the next lines suggests, to the situation of poetry in the United States, it being unclear which of the two is speaking.

Despite the principle of indeterminacy that operates here and throughout, *Oxota* is nothing if not formally finished. Book 8 recycles the ten stanza titles of Book 2 ("Truth," "Nature," "Innocence," etc.), but the content is quite different. "Truth" (Book 2) begins with the line "Truth is not precision but evidence," "Truth" (Book 8) with the line, "Truth is not a likeness—not of depicted sense." "Redemption" (Book 2) concludes with the lines, "We will be redeemed, we will be rescued / We will believe everything we say," whereas "Redemption" (Book 8) is more resigned:

> After something into somewhere—they await each other
> Each is how bewildered and not only to the setting
> Instigated, half out of spiral, split
> Why halt
> We will not lead what we mean
> Each time in obverse as perceived
> Spring doesn't follow winter but it shadows it reversed
> Now
> Morning, morning—nothing less
> It's real to the season—the most passing
> Just being there
> And we will continue to acquire existence
> And to confuse it
> We are both

The last line brings us full circle to the opening of the poem, "This time we are both." "After something into somewhere"—and much has happened—"they await each other." The "love intrigue" seems about to take place, but, for the moment, "Just being there" is enough. Hejinian's coda slyly alludes to *Onegin*'s concluding stanzas. In book 8, chapter 49, Pushkin's narrator declares:

> Whatever in this rough confection
> you sought—tumultuous recollection,

a rest from toil and all its aches,
or just grammatical mistakes,
a vivid brush, a witty rattle—
God grant that from this little book
For heart's delight, or fun, you took
for dreams, or journalistic battle,
God grant you took at least a grain.

This becomes, in Hejinian's counterstatement,

Say a name and someone appears, someone without the same name
Then it's quiet
We cross some distance in the pale pulverizations of the rosy marsh
Mist on dusts of orange light, partial preparations
We will find what we want
Describer's hunter, narrator's hunt
Half-visible, emerging, merged. . . .

Pushkin's "rough confection" reappears in Hejinian's "pale pulverizations," but whereas the Russian poet prays that "God grant you took at least a grain" from "this little book," Hejinian's narrator has fewer illusions: "We will find," she shrugs, "what we want." And that, I take it, is precisely the way *Oxota* works. Many readers, accustomed to the "glass prose" of more user-friendly poems, will find its contrived corridors impassable. Others like myself will enter the "Half-visible, emerging, merged" labyrinth which is *Oxota* and find that the absence of designated exits is itself a special pleasure.

11. What Really Happened

Roland Barthes's Winter Garden/Christian Boltanski's Archives of the Dead

I begin with two photographs, both evidently family snapshots of a young mother and her little boy in a country setting (figures 1 and 2). Neither is what we would call a "good" (i.e., well-composed) picture, although the one on the left is more "expressive," the anxious little boy clinging somewhat fearfully to his mother, while the impassive woman and child on the right look straight ahead at the camera.

And then a second pair of photographs, this time class pictures (figures 3 and 4). On the left, an end-of-the-year group photo of a smiling high school class with their nonsmiling male teacher in the center of the first row; on the right, a more adult (postgraduate?) class, with their teacher (front row, third from the left) distinguished by his white hair, smiling ever so slightly in keeping with the apparently collegial spirit of the attractive young group.

Both sets may be used to illustrate many of the points Roland Barthes makes about photography in his last book, *Camera Lucida* (*La Chambre claire* of 1980). First, these pictures are entirely "ordinary"—the sort of photographs we all have in our albums. Their appeal, therefore, can only be to someone personally involved with their subjects, someone for whom they reveal the that-has-been (*ça a été*) which is, for Barthes, the essence or *noeme* of photography. "The photographic referent," we read in chapter 32, "[is] not the *optionally* real thing to which an image or a sign

Figure 1. Anonymous, *La Demande d'amour* (1923).

refers but the *necessarily* real thing which has been placed before the lens, without which there would be no photograph. . . . In Photography I can never deny that *the thing has been there.*"[1] And again, "The photograph is literally an emanation of the referent" (CL 80). In this sense, "every photograph is a certificate of presence" (CL 87).

But "presence," in this instance, goes hand in hand with absence, with death. "What the Photograph reproduces to infinity has occurred only once: the Photograph mechanically repeats what could never be repeated existentially" (CL 4). As soon as the click of the shutter has occurred, that which was photographed no longer exists; subject is transformed into object, "and even," Barthes suggests, "into a museum object" (CL 13). When we look at a photograph of ourselves or of others, we are really looking at the return of the dead. "Death is the *eidos* of the Photograph" (CL 15).

Two of these pictures are illustrations from Barthes's autobiographical reflections, *Roland Barthes by Roland Barthes*.[2] I have paired them with two similar photographs from the work of the artist Christian Boltanski. Boltanski shares Barthes's predilection for the ordinary photograph, the photograph of everyday life. Like Barthes, he dislikes "art photography," photography that approaches the condition of painting. For him, too, the interesting photograph is one that provides the viewer with the testimony that the thing seen *has been,* that *it is thus.* In Barthes's words, "the Photograph is never anything but an antiphon of 'Look,' 'See,' 'Here it is'; it points a finger at certain *vis-à-vis,* and cannot escape this pure deictic language" (CL 5). But in Boltanski's work, as we shall see, this pointing at "what has occurred only once," what Barthes calls the "pure deictic language" of photography (CL 4), takes on an edge unanticipated in the phenomenology of *Camera Lucida.*

Consider the mother-and-child snapshots shown here. Both identify an apparent referent, the outdoor scene that the camera reproduces. But in what sense are the photographs "certificates of presence"? The photo on the left (figure 1) portrays Roland Barthes, aged five or six, held by his mother, who stands at some distance from a house (her house?) in an unspecified countryside. The mother's clothes and hairstyle place the photograph somewhere in the 1920s; the long-legged boy in knee socks, shorts, and sweater seems rather big to be held on his mother's arm like

Figure 2. Christian Boltanski, from *Album de photos de la famille D., 1939–64.*

Figure 3. Christian Boltanski, from *Classe terminale du Lycée Chases en 1931*.

Figure 4. "L'espace du séminaire . . . [de l'Ecole des Hautes Etudes]."
Photograph by Daniel Boudinet (1974).

a baby. The caption Barthes gives on the facing page (RB 7) accounts for this awkwardness: it reads, "The demand for love" (*La demande d'amour*).

The photograph on the right (figure 2) is part of a work by Boltanski (also of the early 1970s) called *Album de photos de la famille D., 1939–64*, which depicts a "family" (are they a family?) Boltanski didn't know at all. He had borrowed several photo albums from his friend Michel Durand-Dessert (hence the *D*), reshot some 150 snapshots from these albums and tried to establish their chronology as well as the identities of their subjects, using what he called an ethnological approach: for example, "the older man who appeared only at festive occasions, must be an uncle who did not live in the vicinity," as Lynn Gumpert writes in the catalog *Lessons of Darkness*.[3] But the sequence he constructed (see figure 5) turned out to be incorrect: "I realized," the artist remarked, "that these images were only witnesses to a collective ritual. They didn't teach us anything about the Family D. . . . but only sent us back to our own past."[4] And, since the snapshots in the sequence date from the French Occupation and its immediate aftermath, the viewer begins to wonder what really went on in this bourgeois provincial family. Were these men on the battlefield? Were they Nazi collaborators or Resistance fighters? Did these women have to harbor the enemy? And so on. What, in short, is it that *has been* in the snapshot of the young woman and small boy, resting in a shady meadow?

Figure 5. Christian Boltanski, "24 photographies extraites de *l'Album de photos de la famille D., 1939–64*" (1971).

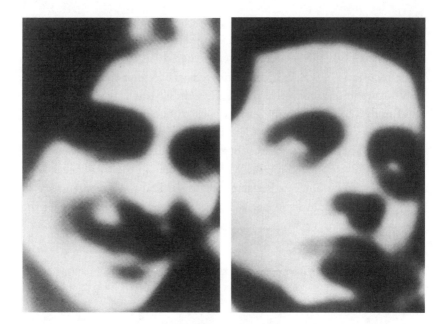

Figure 6. Christian Boltanski, from *Le Lycée Chases* (1987).

Similar questions are raised by the second Boltanski photograph. Again, the two class pictures make an interesting pair. On the bottom (figure 4), we have one of the entries Barthes made under the letter "S" in *Roland Barthes by Roland Barthes:* a photograph of *le séminaire,* taken some time in the 1970s. The very ordinariness of the class picture, Barthes suggests, becomes the occasion for the viewer's most private fantasies. This is the pleasure of the *ça a été.* The caption reads: "The space of the seminar is phalansteric, i.e., in a sense, fictive, novelistic. It is only the space of the circulation of subtle desires, mobile desires; it is, within the artifice of a sociality whose consistency is miraculously extenuated, according to a phrase of Nietzsche's: 'the tangle of amorous relations' " (RB 171). The "real," "referential" photograph thus becomes an occasion for pleasurable erotic fantasy.

In contrast, the other class photograph (figure 3) is a picture Boltanski came across by chance. It portrays the 1931 graduating class of the Chases Gymnasium, a Jewish high school in Vienna, which was shut down shortly after this end-of-the-year group photograph was taken: here the "death" the camera invokes for the photograph's subjects echoes with the imminent but unseen possibility of their real death in the camps. For his 1986 installation *Le Lycée Chases,* Boltanski rephotographed the individual smiling faces in this "ordinary" class photograph, enlarging and obscuring them until they lost any sense of individuality and began to look like skeletal X-rays, or even death masks (figure 6). Yet this version is no more "real" than the other, Boltanski never having learned what actually happened to the members of the class of 1931. When *Le Lycée Chases* was shown in New York in 1987, one of the students in the photograph, now a man in his late sixties, came forward and identified himself to Boltanski. But, ironically, this "real" Chases graduate, who had emigrated to the United States in the early 1930s, knew nothing of the fate of the other students.[5]

"Every photograph," says Barthes, "is somehow co-natural with its referent" (CL 76). But what is the referent of the Chases graduation picture? What "evidential force" does it possess, and for whom? To answer this question, we might begin with Barthes famed Winter Garden photograph. Barthes wrote in *Camera Lucida* that the *punctum* of this photograph (the prick, sting, or sudden wound that makes a particular photograph epiphanic for a particular viewer) was for him so powerful, so overwhelming, so redolent with his own anticipation of death, that he simply could not reproduce it:

> (I cannot reproduce the Winter Garden Photograph. It exists only for me. For you, it would be nothing but an indifferent picture, one of the thousand manifestations of the "ordinary"; it cannot in any way constitute the visible object of a science; it cannot establish an objectivity, in the positive sense of the term; at most it would interest your *studium:* period, clothes, photogeny; but in it, for you, no wound.) (CL 73)

The Winter Garden photograph thus becomes the absent (and hence, more potent) referent of this paean to presence, a paean that, at this crucial point, turns from the image and takes the form of an elegiac *ekphrasis.*

"One November evening, shortly after my mother's death," Barthes recalls, "I was going through some photographs. I had no hope of 'finding' her. I expected nothing from these 'photographs of a being before which one recalls less of that being than by merely thinking of him or her'" (CL 63). And Barthes puts in parentheses following the quote, the name of the writer who is the tutelary spirit behind his own lyric meditation — Proust. Like the Proust of *Les Intermittances du coeur,* Barthes's narrator has learned from the repeated disillusionments of life to expect nothing. The mood is autumnal, sepulchral, and the image of the dead mother cannot be recovered — at least not by voluntary memory. Different photographs capture different aspects of her person but not the "truth of the face I had loved": "I was struggling among images partially true and therefore totally false" (CL 66).

As in Proust, the miraculous privileged moment, the prick of the *punctum,* comes when least expected. The Winter Garden photograph—an old, faded, album snapshot with "blunted" corners—allows Barthes to "see" his mother, not as he actually saw her in life (Barthes calls such "normal" attention to the object of one's contemplation the *studium*), but as the child he had never known, a five-year-old girl standing with her seven-year-old brother "at the end of a little wooden bridge in a glassed-in conservatory" (CL 67). We learn that brother and sister are united "by the discord of their parents, who were soon to divorce" (CL 69). But in Barthes's myth, this little girl is somehow self-born. "In this little girl's image I saw the kindness which had formed her being immediately and forever, without her having inherited it from anyone; how could this kindness have proceeded from the imperfect parents who had loved her so badly—in short, from a family?" (CL 69). In an imaginative reversal, the mother-as-child in the Winter Garden photograph now becomes his own child: "I who had not procreated, I had, in her very illness, engendered my mother" (CL 72). The tomblike glass conservatory thus becomes the site of birth.

"The unknown photographer of Chennevières-sur-Marne," Barthes remarks, "had been the mediator of a truth"—indeed, of *the* truth; his inconsequential little snapshot "achieved for me, utopically, *the impossible science of the unique being*" (CL 71). Impossible, because the uniqueness of that being is, after all, only in the eye of the beholder. Like Proust's Marcel, the narrator of these reflections seems driven by guilt of his own "deviation" (sexual or otherwise) from the bourgeois norms of his childhood world, a course which he believes to have caused his mother great pain. Like Marcel, he invents with this picture a mother who was a perfect being, her goodness and purity deriving from no one (for family is the enemy in this scheme of things). Gentleness is all: "during the whole of our life together," writes Barthes in a Proustian locution, "she never made a single 'observation'" (CL 69). Thus perfected, the mother must of course be dead; the very snapshot that brings her to life testifies as well to the irreversibility of her passage. The intense, violent, momentary pleasure (*jouissance*) that accompanies his reception of the photograph's "unique being" is individual and "magical," for, unlike all other representations, the photograph is an image without a code (CL 88), the eruption of the "real" into the signifying chain, a "*satori* in which words fail" (CL 109).

As an elegy for his mother, as well as a kind of epitaph for himself, *Camera Lucida* is intensely moving. But what about Barthes's insistence on the "realism" of the photograph, his conviction that it bears witness to what-has-occurred-only-once? "From a phenomenological viewpoint," says Barthes, "in the Photograph, the power of authentication exceeds the power of representation" (CL 89). Authentication of what and for whom? Here Boltanski's photographic representations of everyday life raise some hard questions. Indeed, the distance between Barthes's generation and Boltanski's—a distance all the more remarkable in that Boltanski's important photo installations *La Famille D., Le Club Mickey,* and *Détective* date from the very years when Barthes was composing *Roland Barthes by Roland Barthes, The Lover's Discourse,* and *Camera Lucida* —can be measured by Boltanski's revisionist treatment of the phenomenology of authentication articulated in Barthes's late discussions of photography.

Roland Barthes was born in the first year of World War I (26 October 1915); Christian Boltanski in the last year of World War II, specifically, on the day of the liberation of Paris (6 September 1944)—hence his middle name Liberté. Barthes's Catholic father was killed in October 1916 in a naval battle in the North Sea; the fatherless child was brought up in Bayonne by his mother and maternal grandmother in an atmosphere he has described as one of genteel poverty and narrow Protestant bourgeois rectitude. Boltanski's father, a prominent doctor, was born a Jew but converted to Catholicism; his mother, a writer, was Catholic, and young Christian was educated by Jesuits. To avoid deportation in 1940, the Boltanskis faked a divorce and pretended the doctor had fled, abandoning his family, whereas in reality he was hidden in the basement of the family home in the center of Paris for the duration of the Occupation. The death of Barthes's father may thus be contrasted to the simulated "death" of Dr. Boltanski at the time of his son's birth. Indeed, this sort of simulation, not yet a central issue in World War I when battle lines were drawn on national rather than ideological grounds, became important in the years of the Resistance, when simulation and appropriation became common means of survival. For example, in his fictionalized autobiography *W; or, The Memory of Childhood,* Georges Perec (a writer Boltanski greatly admires and has cited frequently) recalls that his widowed mother, who was to die at Auschwitz, got him out of Paris and into the Free Zone by putting him on a Red Cross convoy for the wounded bound for Grenoble. "I was not wounded. But I had to be evacuated. So we had to pretend I was wounded. That was why my arm was in a sling." But ironically this tale of simulation turns out to be itself a simulation. In the very next paragraph, Perec admits that, according to his aunt, his arm was not in a sling; rather "It was as a 'son of a father deceased,' a 'war orphan,' that I was being evacuated by the Red Cross, entirely within regulations." [6] Perec's double simulation suggests that when events are sufficiently intolerable, their very memory can only be a fiction.

Under such circumstances, "authentication" becomes a contested term. How does one document what-has-occurred-only-once when "events" are themselves often simulations? And to what extent has the experience of *studium* versus *punctum* become a collective experience, rather than the fiercely personal one it was for Barthes? In a 1984 interview held in conjunction with the Boltanski exhibition at the Centre Pompidou in Paris, Delphine Renard asked the artist how and why he had chosen photography as his medium. "At first," he replied, "what especially interested me was the property granted to photography of furnishing the evidence of the real [*la preuve du réel*]: a scene that has been photographed is experienced as being true. . . . If someone exhibits the photograph of an old lady and the viewer tells himself, today, she must be dead, he experiences an emotion which is not only of an aesthetic order." [7]

Here Boltanski seems to accept the Barthesian premise that the "photographic referent" is "not the *optionally* real thing to which an image or a sign refers but the *necessarily* real thing which has been placed before the lens, without which there would be no photograph. . . . In Photography I can never deny that *the thing has been there*." But for Boltanski, this "reasonable" definition is not without its problems:

> In my first little book, *Tout ce qui reste de mon enfance* of 1969, there is a photograph that supplies the apparent proof that I went on vacation to the seashore with my parents, but it is an unidentifiable photograph of a child and a group of adults on the beach. One can also see the photograph of the bed I slept in when I was five years old; naturally, the caption orients the spectator, but the documents are purposely false. . . . In most of my photographic pieces, I have utilized this property of the proof one accords to photography to expose it or to try to show that *photography lies, that it doesn't speak the truth but rather the cultural code.* (BOL 75, emphasis added)

Such cultural coding, Boltanski argues, characterizes even the most innocent snapshot (say, the Winter Garden photograph). The amateur photograph of the late nineteenth century, for example, was based on a preexisting image that was culturally defined—an image derived from the painting of the period. And even today, the amateur photographer "shows nothing but images of happiness, lovely children running around on green meadows: he reconstitutes an image he already knows" (BOL 76). Tourists in Venice, for example, who think they are taking "authentic" photographs of this or that place, recognize the "reality" only through the lens of a set of clichés they have unconsciously absorbed; indeed they want these pictures to resemble those they already know. So Boltanski makes an experiment. Together with Annette Messager, he produces a piece called *Le Voyage de noces à Venise* (1975), composed of photographs taken elsewhere (BOL 76). And another book, *Dix portraits photographiques de Christian Boltanski, 1946–1964* (1972), supposedly depicts the young Boltanski at different ages, but in fact all the photographs were taken the same day (figure 7). "This little book," says the artist, "was designed to show that Christian Boltanski had only a collective reality . . . [that of] a child in a given society" (BOL 79). In a related book, *Ce dont ils se souviennent,* we see what looks like an updated version (figure 8) of a Proustian scene in which the narrator and Gilberte play together in the Champs Elysée; here, ostensibly, are young Christian's friends playing on seesaws in the park.

This simple little photograph is enormously tricky. There are actually three seesaws, as evident from the three horizontal shadows stretching across the ground in the bottom of the frame.[8] The two little girls next to one another on parallel seesaws on the left look normal enough, but what is happening at the other end? The slightly crouching boy in the center (his legs straddling a third seesaw) seems to be staring at what looks like an extra leg, its knee bent on the board opposite—a leg that suggests a body on the rack rather than a child at play. The impression is created by the photograph's odd lighting: the figure on the far right, who is evidently holding down one seesaw in balance, blocks the second figure (feet dangling) and the head and torso of the third. Moreover, the ropelike thin line of the third seesaw extends from that bent leg on the right to the head of the little girl at its opposite pole, creating the illusion that she is chained to it. Thus the little playground scene takes on an aura of isolation and imprisonment. Is it winter (the white area could be snow) or a scorchingly sunny summer? The more one looks at this "ordinary" photograph (actually, Boltanski tells us, a found photograph taken from the album of a young woman), the less clear the "emanation of the referent" becomes.

But Boltanski's is by no means a simple reversal of the Barthesian *noeme.* For the paradox is that, again like Perec, there is nothing he finds

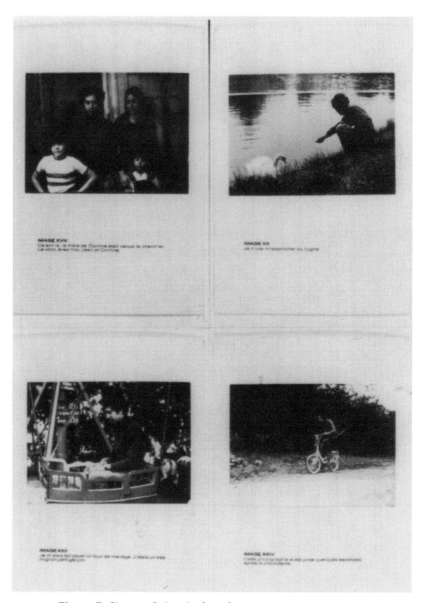

Figure 7. Christian Boltanski, from *Dix portraits photographiques de Christian Boltanski, 1946–1964.*

as meaningful as the ordinary object, the trivial detail. Photography, for him, is a form of ethnography, and he has often spoken of his early fascination with the displays in the Musée de l'Homme, not so much the displays of imposing African sculpture but of the everyday objects—Eskimo fishhooks, Indian arrows from the Amazon valley, and so on:

I saw large metal boxes in which there were little objects, fragile and without signification. In the corner of the case there was often a small faded photograph representing a "savage" in the middle of handling these little objects. Each case presented a world that has disappeared: the savage of the photograph was no doubt dead, the objects had become useless, and, anyway, no one knew how to use them any more. The Musée de l'Homme appeared to me as a great morgue. Numerous artists have here discovered the human sciences (linguistics, sociology, archeology); here there is still the "weight of time" which imposes itself on artists. . . Given that we have all shared the same cultural references, I think we will all finish in the same museum." (BOL 71)

Does this mean that art discourse can be no more than a cultural index, that the individual artwork no longer counts? On the contrary. For whereas Barthes locates *"the impossible science of the unique being"* in a given spectator's particular reading of a photograph in itself perfectly "ordinary," Boltanski enlarges the artist's role: it is the artist who creates those images (and captions) that are "imprecise enough to be as communal as possible"—images each viewer can interpret differently, as when a picture from, say, an elementary school history book every child has used is repro-

Figure 8. Christian Boltanski, *Ce dont ils se souviennent,* #86.

Figure 9. Christian Boltanski, from *Inventaire des objets ayant appartenu à un jeune homme d'Oxford* (1973).

duced, bearing a caption (see BOL 79) like *Ce jour-là, le professeur entra avec le directeur* ("That day, the teacher entered with the principal").

Thus one of Boltanski's favorite genres is the inventory. If many of his "albums" use "fake" photos to tell what are supposedly "true" stories, the *Inventar* series works the other way around. Here, for example, is the *Inventaire des objets ayant appartenus à un jeune homme d'Oxford* of 1973 (figure 9). Boltanski had read of the untimely death of an Oxford student and wrote to his landlord asking if all his personal effects, "significant" or otherwise, could be sent to him. Photographed against a neutral background, these objects take on equal value: the pope's photograph, a folded shirt, a suit jacket on a hanger, a set of pamphlets, a toothbrush. The question the inventory poses is whether we can "know" someone through his or her things. If the clothes make the man, as the adage has it, can we recreate the absent man from these individual items? Or does the subject fragment into a series of metonymic images that might relate to anyone? Is there, in other words, such a thing as identity? And, if so, how does it express itself?

Here again Barthes offers an interesting *point de repère.* One of the sections in *Roland Barthes by Roland Barthes* is called "*Un souvenir d'enfance*— A memory of childhood," and goes like this:

> When I was a child, we lived in a neighborhood called Marrac; this neighborhood was full of houses being built, and the children played in the building sites; huge holes had been dug in the loamy soil for the foundations of the houses, and one day when we had been playing in one of these, all the children climbed out except me—I couldn't make it. From the brink up above, they teased me: lost! alone! spied on! excluded! (to be excluded is not to be outside, it is to be *alone in the hole,* imprisoned under the open sky; *precluded*); then I saw my mother running up; she pulled me out of there and took me far away from the children—against them. (RB 121-22)

Beyond the obvious psychosexual symbolism of this passage lies Barthes's assumption that the *souvenir d'enfance* has meaning, that memory can invoke the past, can revive the fear, panic, and sense of release the boy felt when his mother rescued him, that these memories are intelligible within the spectrum of adult emotions. The little filmic narrative relates past and present to create the sense of identity that is Barthes's.

Memory plays no such role in Boltanski's work. "I have very few memories of childhood," Boltanski tells Delphine Renard, "and I think I undertook this seeming autobiography precisely to blot out my memory and to protect myself. I have invented so many false memories, which were collective memories, that my true childhood has disappeared" (BOL 79). Again Perec's *W; or, The Memory of Childhood* comes to mind: "I have no childhood memories. Up to my twelfth year or thereabouts, my story comes to barely a couple of lines" (W 6). For writers and artists born in the France of World War II, and especially for Jewish artists like Perec and Boltanski,

Figure 10. Christian Boltanski, from *Les Archives Détective* (1987).

the Proustian or Barthesian *souvenir d'enfance* seems to have become a kind of empty signifier, a site of assumed identities and invented sensations.

Take the installation *Détective* (a first version was mounted in 1972, a more extensive one in 1987), which consists of 400 black-and-white photographs, 110 metal boxes with magazine articles and 21 clamp-on desk lamps (detail, see figure 10). "These photographs," we read in the headnote, "originally appeared in the magazine *Détective*. A weekly specializing in news items, it presents an indiscriminate blend of assassins and victims, the unintentional heroes of forgotten dramas."[9] The immediate occasion, Boltanski explains, was the 1987 trial in Lyons of the Nazi war criminal Klaus Barbie. "Barbie has the face of a Nobel Peace Prize Winner," Boltanski remarked. "It would be easier if a terrible person had a terrible face." And in an interview for *Parkett* called "The White and the Black," Boltanski explains that his ideas of original sin and grace stem from his Christian upbringing even as his longing for a lost Jerusalem is part of Jewish mythology. "My work is caught between two cultures as I am."[10]

The mystery of *Détective* is that the criminals and the victims are not identified. Inevitably one tries to rise to the challenge by distinguishing them: the bald man whose head and cheeks have been cropped (top row, third from the left) is surely a killer, isn't he? Or—wait a minute—couldn't he be an innocuous person, the local butcher or pharmacist, perhaps, who has been murdered? Or is he a mental patient? And what about the little boy with blond curls (second row, third from right), surely he is an innocent victim? Or is it the baby picture of someone who turned out to be an ax murderer? The pictures don't *reveal* anything. Each and every photograph can be read both ways, and there are all sorts of metonymic linkages: compare the woman (is that a woman?) with glasses (bottom row, second from right) to the man in the top row I refer to above. The cropping, lighting, and pose are similar. One wears glasses, the other one doesn't. One is probably female, the other definitely male. Throughout the sequence, each person looks a bit like someone else. Just so, the se-

Figure 11. Christian Boltanski, from *Portraits des élèves du C.E.S. de Lentillères [Dijon] en 1973* (1973).

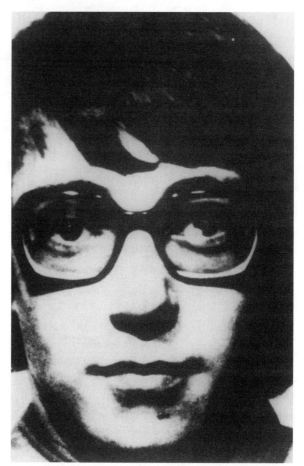

Figure 12. Christian Boltanski, from *Monument:
Les Enfants de Dijon* (1986).

quence implies, the middle-class Nazis and Jews of prewar Berlin, for
example, were quite indistinguishable.

What sort of evidence, then, does the photograph supply? I have
already mentioned the students of *Le Lycée Chases,* whose faces Boltanski isolated and enlarged until they resembled death masks. But the same
phenomenon can be found much closer to home: in 1973, in the foyer of a
junior high school in Dijon, Boltanski installed the portrait photographs
of each of the students attending the school who were then between the
ages of ten and thirteen (see figure 11). Thirteen years later he mounted an
installation using the same photographs, which had been supplied by the
children's parents, and called it *Monument.* As Günter Betken explains in
his catalog description of the installation, Boltanski "tightened the format,

closing in on the subject, so that the clothing, hairstyle and background disappeared, and only the faces, standardized by their identical presentation remained" (COL 155). Typically Boltanski enhanced the black and white contrast and added glasses—a logical enough development for a woman now in her mid-twenties (see figure 12). As in the case of *Le Lycée Chases,* the artist merely brings out what is already there.

The figurative "death" of the Dijon schoolgirl, reborn a plain woman in glasses, prefigures death itself, which is for Boltanski, as for Barthes, the very essence of photography. In 1991, he produced a piece called *Les Suisses morts* (detail, figure 13) that can be read as an interesting public counterpart to Barthes's very private Winter Garden. The "subjects" are some three thousand dead Swiss citizens as depicted in obituary announcements published in the Swiss regional newspaper *Le Nouvelliste du Valais.*

Figure 13. Christian Boltanski, from *Les Suisses morts* (1991).

Why Swiss? "Because," Boltanski explains, "Switzerland is neutral. There is nothing more neutral than a dead Swiss. Before, I did pieces with dead Jews but 'dead' and 'Jew' go too well together. It is too obvious. There is nothing more normal than the Swiss. There is no reason for them to die, so they are more terrifying in a way. They are us" (PAR 36). The "normalcy" of the three thousand Swiss is further heightened by the conventions of the obituary photograph: "The thing about pictures of dead people is that they are always alive, all tanned, muscular, and smiling. The photo replaces the memory. When someone dies, after a while you can't visualize them anymore, you only remember them through their pictures" (PAR 36).

But remember what, exactly? One looks in vain at these obituary photos of men and women, some old, some younger, and even a child or two, for clues about the meaning of their lives. Is theirs anything other than a national identity? At moments the viewer persuades herself that it is, that these white Aryan Europeans look stolid and bourgeois—the representatives of a country that has never known war, genocide, famine, natural disaster. But what about their private lives? Was the pretty woman in the second row far left happily married? Was the man to her right a successful businessman? And what were all these people doing when they weren't smiling at the camera?

"Why," asks Georgia Marsh, in the *Parkett* interview, "this delectation of the dead?" And Boltanski answers:

> I don't really know myself. We are all so complicated, and then we die. We are a subject one day, with our vanities, our loves, our worries, and then one day, abruptly, we become nothing but an object, an absolutely disgusting pile of shit. We pass very quickly from one stage to the next. It's very bizarre. It will happen to all of us, and fairly soon too. Suddenly we become an object you can handle like a stone, but a stone that was someone. There is no doubt something sexual about it. (PAR 36)

This linkage of sexuality and death takes us back to Barthes's elegy for his mother-turned-child in *Camera Lucida*. "What is always fascinating," says Boltanski, "is that every being is interchangeable, and at the same time each one has had a very different life with different desires" (PAR 37). For Barthes, still writing in the late modernist tradition, the reception of the photograph is a kind of rescue operation: the *punctum* of the Winter Garden photograph is achieved when its viewer (Barthes) is able to turn the object back into a subject, a sentient and sexual being.

For Boltanski, such unique presence is no longer possible. The referent, to paraphrase Barthes, adheres all right, but that referent is *they* not *she,* and the shock of recognition comes when the viewer recognizes the *interchangeability* of human beings—an interchangeability paradoxically born out of difference, each of us having different desires, agonies, aspirations. Personal tragedy—the loss of an adored mother—gives way to a scene of collective mourning, individuality mattering less than positionality (the *à côté de*) in the larger space of inscription. The image of the Winter Garden (a specific, clearly defined area within a larger structure) gives way to the amorphous, dimly lit space of *Détective* and Boltanski's later "altar pieces." Thus may what-has-occurred-only-once recur again and again, thus the phantom uniqueness of the endlessly reproducible photograph.

It is wonderful how a handwriting which is illegible can be read, oh yes it can.

—Gertrude Stein

Consider the page not as a space but as a death occuring in the gap between "writing" and "wanting to say"

—Steve McCaffery[1]

12. "Inner Tension / In Attention"
Steve McCaffery's Book Art

"The materiality of language," Steve McCaffery has suggested in a 1978 essay on the poet bill bissett, "is that aspect which remains resistant to an absolute subsumption into the ideality of meaning. . . . To see the letter not as a phoneme but as ink, and to further insist on that materiality, inevitably contests the status of language as a bearer of uncontaminated meaning(s)" (NI 105). Consider the following scenario, provided by Michael Coffey as an illustration of McCaffery's argument:

> You drive into a parking garage. After taking a ticket, you see a red arrow pointing to the right. Or:
>
> You drive into a parking garage. After taking a ticket, you read a sign that says, "Parking to the Right." Or:
>
> You drive into a parking garage. After taking a ticket, an attendant nods over his shoulder and says "There are spaces to the right."[2]

Coffey comments: "Each of these directional episodes 'means' the same thing: proceed to the right to park your car. In that all three messages convey the same meaning, the material differences in the composition are devalued, made irrelevant. Despite three entirely different modes of presentation (graphic; lexical/phonetic; oral/gestural), the idea from each converges at the same terminus and all else falls away" (OL 32–33).

Steve McCaffery's writing project has, from the first, foregrounded the "all else," what Georges Bataille has defined as the "excesses of energy" inherent in the economy of distribution and circulation (NI 201). In literary terms, "excess" is equivalent to the *paragram,* which McCaffery defines, following Julia Kristeva and Leon S. Roudiez, as a text whose "organization of words (and their denotations), grammar, and syntax is challenged by the infinite possibilities provided by letters or phonemes combining to form networks of signification not accessible through conventional reading habits." The paragram "is that aspect of language which *escapes* all discourse" (NI 63–64). An analogy to the paragram or what he calls the "cipheral text" (NI 19) would be the biotopological form known as the Klein worm—"a form which differs from conventional geometric forms in its characteristic absence of both inner and outer surfaces. . . . Any part of the form can touch, contact, communicate with, flow with any other part" (NI 20). The Klein worm provides the model for a form "without 'walls' with milieu and constellation replacing syntax. The letter—in its major and minor registrations—not the word forms the basic unit of organization" (NI 21).

If this defense of the paragrammatic, of what McCaffery calls "a first order experience of graphemes" (NI 19), is reminiscent of the manifestos of concrete poetry prominent in the fifties and sixties, the difference between a "postconcrete" poet like McCaffery and his mentors—the *Noigandres* group in Brazil, Ian Hamilton Finlay in England—is that McCaffery's unit has always been the page rather than the individual concrete poem, and, beyond the page, the book. In a fanciful Cratylian study, McCaffery (writing together with bpNichol) points out that the word *book* is etymologically connected with the name of the beech tree (Old English *bok, boce,* Old Norse *bok*) as well as the Gothic *boka* (letter of the alphabet), whose plural form *bokos* means writing or document. Book as beech leaf (an organic object), book as document: the double meaning, McCaffery and Nichol suggest, denies the book the passive role we generally assign to it. Similarly, *page* comes from the Latin *pagina,* whose stem *pag-* is also that of *pangere,* to fasten, fix in, fix together. A page, the authors conclude, is not just a blank sheet, waiting for "meaningful" print to be affixed to it, but a kind of trellis, upon which words and letters are fastened visually as well as semantically.[3] Thus the "book of the writer" becomes the "book of the written" (KNK 56).

Artist's Book may not seem like quite the right term for the resultant productions. Illustrations, for example the reproductions of old engravings underlying the text of *In England Now That Spring* and the anatomical drawings in *Panopticon,* are sparse, and the innovative typography, used in the early works like *Ow's Waif,* gives way, in the recent *Black Debt,* to a long, continuous block of large type with justified left and right margins. Compared to, say, John Baldessari's or Martha Rosler's artists' books, McCaffery's look amateurish and a shade drab. One would not expect to see them in art galleries or at "book art" exhibitions.

But as Johanna Drucker has shown in her recent *Century of Artists' Books,* the only distinguishing feature of "artists' books," a genre that has come into its own only in the twentieth century, is that "they call attention to the specific character of a book's identity while they embody the expressive complexity of the book as a communicative form."[4] Drucker places McCaffery's work in the chapter "Books as Verbal Exploration," and more specifically under "Typewriter Works." Her emphasis on the book qua book, with its tension between the apparent conventionality of the codex form and the "inexhaustible possibilities" of its composition, echoes an earlier discussion of artists' books by Richard Kostelanetz. "[An] essential distinction," he writes, "separates imaginative books from conventional books. In the latter, syntactically familiar sentences are set in rectangular blocks of uniform type (resembling soldiers in a parade), and these are then "designed" into pages that look like each other (and like pages we have previously seen). An imaginative book, by definition, attempts to realize something else with syntax, with format, with pages, with covers, with size, with shapes, with sequence, with structure, with binding—with any or all of these elements."[5] In this sense, McCaffery's are certainly exemplars of book art, pages functioning as "trellises" upon which lettrist and verbal experiments are hung, the whole giving a very different impression from the individual page on the one hand and the conventional illustrated book on the other.

McCaffery's first book experiment or, more accurately, page experiment was called *Carnival, The First Panel: 1967–70* and published by the Coach House Press in Toronto in 1973. The work was made by placing masks on each of sixteen standard 8½-by-11-inch pages, arranged in groups of four to make a square (or, strictly speaking, rectangle) measuring 44 by 36 inches. The sixteen pages were then perforated and arranged in sequential book form, accompanied by the instructions, "In order to destroy this book please tear each page carefully along the perforation. The panel is assembled by laying out pages in a square of four." The readerly dilemma thus created was that in order to take in the whole panel, the book has to be destroyed.

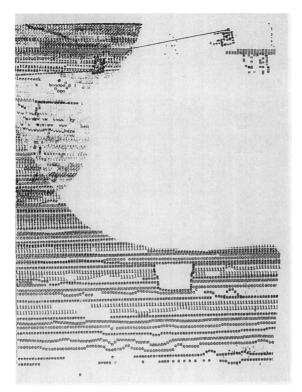

Figure 1. Steve McCaffery, *Carnival, The First Panel: 1967–70.*

As for the mask technique itself, McCaffery has explained his procedures as follows:

> *Carnival* was essentially a cartographic project; a repudiation of lin-
> earity in writing and the search for an alternative syntax in "mapping".
> . . . The panels grew directly through the agency of the typewriter and
> through the agency of marginal link-ups. . . . As a mask bled off a page
> I would devise another shape that picked up the bleed of the text at the
> margin. . . . the mask came about as a way to create a painterly shape
> by censoring the flow of typewritten line. It was a method of arriv-
> ing at a collage effect without resort to the actual adhesion of different
> fragments to a support surface. . . . It's important to remember that
> the mask excludes and deletes much of the written text. What results
> are deliberately induced fragments, parts of inscription whose termina-
> tions and commencements are not determined by a writing subject or
> a logical intention but by a material, random intervention. (OL 72–73)

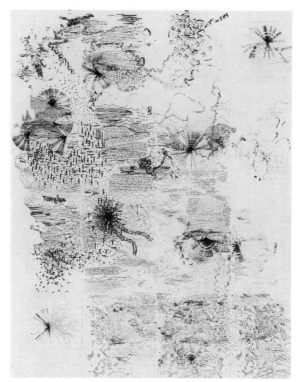

Figure 2. Steve McCaffery, *Carnival, The Second Panel: 1971–75.*

Since the writing in this "multi-panel language environment" was a "spontaneous emission into the space set up by the mask for writing," there are large areas of "non-semantic type, zones of repeated letters and lettristic clusters that attempt a sort of abstract expressionism through the typewriter" (OL 72; see figure 1). Such coherent words and phrases as do appear in the panels were later repudiated by McCaffery as "incredible naive . . . I built the text around certain biblical allusions. Adam as the power of nomination; Babel as the source of polyglossia and so on. All of this I would now scrap" (OL 72).

Carnival, The Second Panel: 1971–75 (published 1977) takes what Mc-Caffery calls "a structure of strategic counter-communication" even further. Whereas the first panel was entirely typewriter generated, the second "places the typed mode in agonistic relation with other forms of scription: xerography, xerography within xerography . . . electrostasis, rubber-stamp, tissue texts, hand-lettering and stencil." [6] The effect (figure 2) is a distancing of language so as to foreground its "neglected qualities of immanence and non-reference," language as a "seen thing," as McCaffery puts it in the introduction (C2). But although the sixteen-panel overview, as depicted here, allows for little comprehension of individual words or phrases, the individual panel-pages make various "reading paths" available. Thus the spokes of the wheel on the tenth page (figure 3) are rubber-stamped "CHANGE OF ADDRESS" signs, underneath which we find a complicated set of tissue texts and xerographies, the fragmented words referring to a text by Charpentier "on how the gothic cathedral is built up palimpsesti-cally," to "geomantic syntax often depicted as snakes." And indeed those "snakes" do appear as part of the graphic page design (see figure 2).

Carnival represents the first stage of McCafferian language experimen-tation, the stage when the "death of the referent" as well as the fabled "death of the subject" were taken to be de rigueur.[7] As the poet's book art evolved, the drive toward nonreferentiality began to give way to the rec-ognition that the referent never wholly "dies," even if the "trace structure" and "scriptive play" (Derrida's terms) of poetic language complicate its determination (NI 148–49). The same holds true for the speaking subject. "The most enduring accusation against early Concrete [poetry]," McCaf-fery was to note in the Yale symposium, was "its failure to engage the

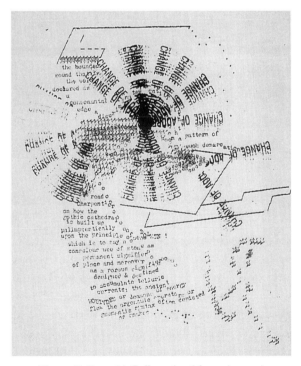

Figure 3. Steve McCaffery, detail from the tenth (unnumbered) sheet of *Carnival, The Second Panel: 1971–75.*

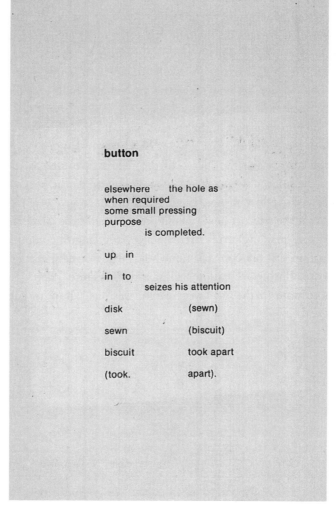

button

elsewhere   the hole as
when required
some small pressing
purpose
        is completed.

up   in

in   to
      seizes his attention

disk   (sewn)

sewn   (biscuit)

biscuit   took apart

(took.   apart).

Figure 4. Steve McCaffery, Dr. Sadhu's Muffins: A Book of Written Readings.

social base of language as an interactive heteroglossia," the "divorce from social utterance which instantly de-politicizes the work" (EVC 373).

A first step toward this reengagement with social utterance is found in the book works of the mid-seventies, *Dr. Sadhu's Muffins* and *Ow's Waif,* where the writing is based entirely on "supply texts chosen at random from whatever happened to be on or near my desk when I was working" (DSM). These "supply texts" — the Concise Oxford Dictionary, the works of Shakespeare, the *I Ching,* various newspapers, magazines, and abandoned drafts of earlier poems — were subjected to "numerous chance and random techniques to assist me in word selection and partial syntactic structuring to a degree such as would keep me excluded from the content part of the compositions." The reader will recognize this as a technique similar to Jackson Mac Low's chance-generated poems and especially to John Cage's "writings through" texts from the Bible to *Finnegans Wake*.

How does this "writing through" work in *Dr. Sadhu's Muffins?* In the "Note on the Method of Composition," from which I have been quoting, McCaffery explains:

> as a poet i took responsibility for the page but not necessarily for everything that found its way onto the page. what i did was set up the sufficient conditions for an open field to form into which a word could find its own way settling in its own syntactic space. . . . having no responsibility whatsoever for the lexical material found that i could concentrate exclusively on the invention of form—on the realignment of discrete semantic units into either open or closed fields of independent energy and image.

But if *Carnival* subordinated the semantic to visual effects, *Dr. Sadhu's Muffins* works the other way around. It looks, to begin with, like a perfectly normal book of poems. True, the endpapers feature witty collage drawings with letters from "Steve" to "Tim" about matters of production concerning the very book we're reading (see figure 4), and each poetic sequence has a separate title page, facing a page of abstract black and white graphics. But the texts themselves are printed conventionally enough. Take the section called "Anamorphoses," which the note describes as "attempts to 'describe out of definition,' to transform a comprehension into a perception, the known thing into the thing seen, by having a text generate itself out of the dictionary definition of its title." [8] The eighteenth anamorphosis is called "button," immediately recalling Gertrude Stein's *Tender Buttons,* which provides McCaffery with the epigraph to the sequence, "Act so that there is no use in a centre." But "button" is centered on its numbered page like any little Imagist lyric:

Here the nonparallel columns—"disk" is matched to "(sewn)", "sewn" to "(biscuit)" and so on—recall dada rather than Imagist lyrics, but the poem, however dependent it may be on its "supply texts," is fairly straightforward, referring as it does to a "required" "hole," to "some small pressing," to a movement that goes "up in / in to," and then to "sewn" and "took apart," counterposed to the "disk"/"biscuit" rhyme. Stein's own *Tender Buttons* is, to use McCaffery's own vocabulary, more radically paragrammatic.

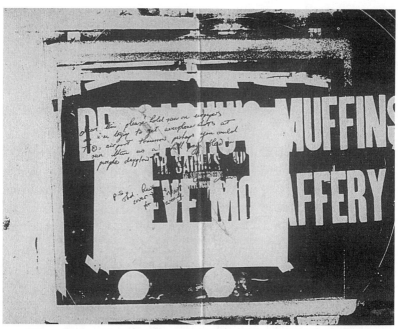

Figure 5. Steve McCaffery, *Dr. Sadhu's Muffins: A Book of Written Readings.*

Much more effective is the title prose poem, which uses a "core structure of 13 phrases selected at random from the *Toronto Globe and Mail* and repeated and permuted according to a predetermined chance programme." Among these phrases, most of them marvelously vapid, are "the virtues of middle age were the ones that marked the Fifties," "That was a terrible day I could eat nothing. I felt faint," and "the foundations for the new world are being laid right now." Dr. Sadhu makes his appearance in the sentence, "Let me put the matter allegorically, friends of Dr. Sadhu Singh Dhami are invited to attend a lecture entitled 'Between Two Worlds'" (DSM 12). As for the muffins, these have nothing to do with Dr. Sadhu, except in McCaffery's scheme of things; their actual entrance cue comes on the opening page in the phrase, "dropping him a scented note or a flower or a bran muffin baked with her own little hands." Dr. Sadhu makes only three appearances in the poem that bears his name, but the "dropping . . . muffin" phrase appears six times, always in different contexts, and then begins to permutate, "dropping him a scented note" splitting off from the rest of the phrase and undergoing reshuffling, so that we read:

> sick. tired. i am sick of the amount
> great trouble. the foundations for this new

    indeed. guilty. i'll try to be another
    muffin. baked. scented note or flower
    fact for. the unseen cook

and the poem ends with the lines:

    the cold scented with her own little hands
    a bran muffin baked with her

where the syntactic displacement of "own little hands" creates an entirely different meaning: the unnamed she is now baking in the oven along with the bran muffin. And if that can happen, why not attribute muffins to the evening's lecturer on the topic "Between Two Worlds," the eminent Dr. Sadhu Singh Dhami?

The parodic word play of these found texts looks ahead to the profoundly satiric *Black Debt* of 1989. As book art, however, *Dr. Sadhu's Muffins* is less interesting than another book of this period, *Ow's Waif,* which is a comically abbreviated version of Longfellow's [as in Henry Wadsworth] *The Waif.* Again, the poet's stated aim is to create "a near to total separation of form from content, the entire 'borrowing' of content as a prepared word-supply (a 'supply-text') and a creative concentration on the invention of the poems' forms as verbal fields free of presupposed or prerequisite rule structures of grammar and syntax." The supply text functions "as the total available language system for the poem"; this time these texts include Newton's *Optics* (1705 ed.), an Evelyn Waugh biography of Edmund Campion, Susanna Moodie's *Roughing It in the Bush,* a trigonometry textbook, Jacques Maritain's *Creative Intuition in Art and Poetry,* Edgar Allen Poe's *Poetic Principle,* and John Cage's *A Year from Monday.* There is also a set of poems called "Ten Portraits," whose supply text is a transcribed interview with some New York prostitutes. As in *Dr. Sadhu's Muffins,* word choice, frequency, recurrence, and so on are produced by systematic chance operations, although there are instances of "careful conscious choice." The "operating analogy," in any case, is "cubism: the process of fragmentation and reconstitution of a known thing in a fresh form." Or, we might say, using McCaffery's own designation, anamorphosis.

Unlike *Carnival* and *Dr. Sadhu's Muffins, Ow's Waif* is something of a collaboration: the design and instant lettering collages were made for the Coach House Press by Robert MacDonald. The miniature (6-by-4-inch) book is beautifully produced and all of a piece, typographical design in primary colors being integrated with the printed texts. The title page

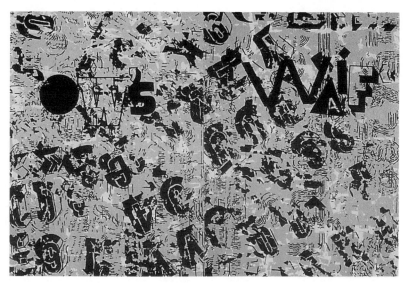

Figure 6. Steve McCaffery, *Ow's Waif and Other Poems.*

foregrounds red letters and numbers, some in bold type, some transparent, against a busy yellow background: the title itself is rendered in
black or outlined letters, the first and second **W**s having opposite designs
(figure 6). The **O** is rendered as a black circular disk, a black sun or an
apple with a stemlike shape (the dot of an **i**? an apostrophe?), even as the
first **W** is transparent and the **A** of "Waif" is an "empty" letter silhouetted against a black triangle. The black/white, full/empty contrast is then
reversed in the book's centerfold (figure 7): now it is the **O** that is merely
outlined (and almost invisible) and the two giant-size bold **W**s, letters that
here dwarf everything else, are identical. The typefaces of "Waif," furthermore, produce paragrams in the form of "a" and "if." "What if?" the
second page seems to ask. And the long dash, followed by what looks like
a colon, leaves the question open. What if what? Given the background
pictographs—letters, numbers, houses, dollar signs, telephone shapes—
the possibilities for narrative are intriguingly open.

The visual representation of the words, in any case, reenforces the
paragrammatic play of the title: "Ow's" seems to be Cockney dialect for
"How's," in which case the phrase, spoken aloud, sounds like "How's the
wife?" "Ow's" also suggests "Owl's," and since owls are solitary nocturnal
creatures the sense of "waifhood" is made more prominent. And when
we turn to the individual "poems," we note that the layout of the titles
(taken from the supply texts) is often striking, calling attention to its own

meanings, which are often intensified by, or in competition with, the individual texts.

Take the double page spread for "E. A. Poe The Poetic Principle" (figure 8). Here POE anticipates the first two syllables of POETIC, but, at the same time, the title can be read as **Ea**'s THE POE PRINCIPLE, even as THE POET, printed in lighter dotted letters, is subordinated. And this is of course what Poe's famous essay does: it applies the "Poe Principle" to all "Poetry" and equates the two:

> With inspired limit,
> inculcation, not demands thy dispensable
> but her we need
>
> language
> > We word as poetical
> > perceive between inculcation.

Poe's "Poetic Principle" is, of course, a famous instance of "poetical . . . inculcation." And McCaffery buries other puns and double entendres in his title designs: The textbook title *Elementary Trigonometry* contains, inside a "so-called 'perfect' figure," the three-dimensional circle or **O**, a second letter, **N**. That letter becomes, in turn, the first letter of NOM (NAME), but **M**

Figure 7. Steve McCaffery, *Ow's Waif and Other Poems,* unnumbered double page near the center of the book.

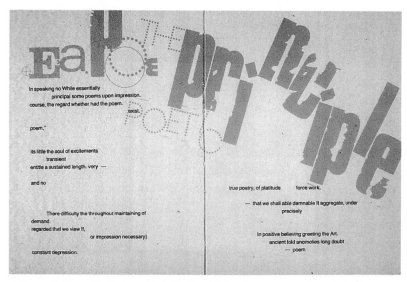

Figure 8. Steve McCaffery, *Ow's Waif and Other Poems*, unnumbered double page featuring "E. A. Poe, *The Poetic Principle*."

also goes with **E** to spell ME. **Try** is placed above the letter line by itself, a reminder that even elementary trigonometry takes a good deal of TRY[ing]:

> a ladder is placed with its foot at a distance
>
> > Find Sin
> find navigation
> > > Find the height of window
> > *all circles*
>
> hence
> > write down all ratios.

Here is the "first order system of graphemes," the "trace structure" or "cipheral play" McCaffery wants to produce. The titles are paragrammatic, the found texts themselves often providing clues as to how the titles should be read. Indeed, what the poet has done is to infuse even as dry a supply text as *Elementary Trigonometry* with, if not his own personality, at least his own signature. One of McCaffery's recurrent themes, for instance, is the human inability to draw proper conclusions, to make correct syllogisms and analogies. So the "writing through" the elementary trigonometry book produces passages like the following:

                    man runs each minute
                    traverses yards two places

                                subtends centre hence
                    flywheel

                                        clock is 20 minutes
                    hence navigation   *all circles*

    Dr. Sadhu's Muffins and *Ow's Waif* represent the "writing through" or "supply text" stage of McCaffery's book art, but by the later seventies, the poet was moving on to other experiments. *Knowledge Never Knew* (figure 9), published in 1983 although composed some years earlier, turns to a different language game: the recharging of a time-honored genre, the aphorism, coupled with a rethinking of Pound's famous definition of the epic as a "poem including history." In *Open Letter,* McCaffery recalls the genesis of the book:

> *Knowledge Never Knew* was written as a reaction to those awful collections of aphorisms such as Chazal's *Sens Plastique* (great title/terrible book) and Dahlberg's *Reasons of the Heart* (terrible title/terrible book). . . . The aphorism is a defiant and extremely presumptious form. It's intellectually cheeky. Its force derives not just from the classical brevity of its appearance (that would link it to the epigram) but also from the successful excision of the discursive elements that make it possible. It is thus an ideal model of parricide. (OL 76)

Whereas the "language of the critical essay is normally contextual and integrative, and of a cumulative, linked, propositional nature," the aphorism, inherently "brief" and "non-integrative," "calls attention to its own scenic disposition" (OL 77).

    The aphorisms are placed at the bottom of each page; at the top (with a large expanse of white space between), McCaffery has placed a series of dates, times of day, and pointless historical facts ostensibly relating to those dates, thus playing the "audacity" of the aphorism against the "banality" of historical "fact." The dialogic format of double bands is designed to make the reader ponder the very nature of facticity, both upper and lower bands providing what at first looks like "information." To put it another way: when "knowledge" is tested by placing it in the unexpected context of the aphorism, it moves from "knew" to "new."

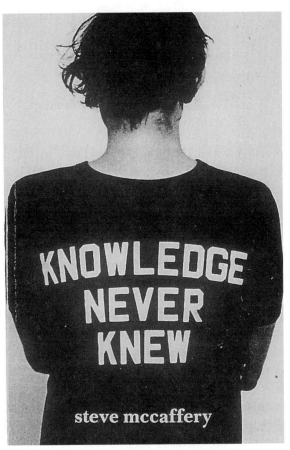

Figure 9. Steve McCaffery, *Knowledge Never Knew*,
front cover.

The calendar (upper band) runs from 1 January to 19 April, but the year designated shifts randomly from century to century, and the historical tag often doesn't go with the time frame. On page 12, for example, we read:

january 7 1259
Rev. Thomas Malmsbury leaps into a pool of burning gasoline

and on the facing page:

january 8 1943
Knowledge declared to be a venal sin by the fourteen monks of Wearmouth

Here the "encounters with history" are themselves absurd. But further, these "facts" are "penetrated" (McCaffery's own word) by the aphorisms in the bottom band. Here are the full pages 12 and 13: On the "january 7

Figure 10. Steve McCaffery, *Knowledge Never Knew*, page 12.

january 8 1943

Knowledge declared to be a venal sin by the fourteen monks of Wearmouth

a motion?
e motion!

13

Figure 11. Steve McCaffery, *Knowledge Never Knew,* page 13.

1259" page, "to write is to reach a surface through the holes named things" obliquely refers to the Rev. Thomas Malmsbury's leap into the burning gasoline pool. The writer reaches a "surface" denied the priest. And on the "january 8 1943" page, the declaration that knowledge is a venal sin can be understood, via the aphorism, as "a motion" that deals with "e motion."

Or again, a pointless piece of information like that on page 15:

january 10, 1344
Wichlaf, Bishop of Kingston, celebrates Easter at Croyland

may take on a new edge when juxtaposed to an aphorism like:

the dream of the written is always to be somewhere else

—the irony here being that to write about "somewhere else," in this case Wichlaf's Easter mass at Croyland, doesn't necessarily put the writing somewhere else at all.

A similar sleight of hand occurs on the "january 18, 1392" page, where "*Hippocentaur found preserved in honey*" is juxtaposed to the phrase:

once upon a time
twice inside a space

The medieval tale, not inappropriately designated by "once upon a time," actually recounts what is "twice inside a space," the first being the time of preservation and the second the time when the Hippocentaur was found.

To avoid predictability, the steady recurrence of the A + B pattern, McCaffery introduces pages that have no upper "history" band at all. Page 31, for example, provides only the date, "january 31" (with no year), the aphorism reading:

grammar is skeletal
words are glandular

followed on the next page by "february 1 211 b.c.," and again no "history" entry, the bottom band reading:

the essence of the sign is to be a margin emerging

Here the pages enact what the words say: the "glandular" words are given full force by subordinating the "skeletal" grammar and placing a line of type at the bottom of a nearly blank page so that the "sign" can indeed "be a margin emerging." The final entry in the book is for "5.42 A.M.," no date or fact being given. What does the dawn hour signify? The aphorism reads:

> never read
> never write
> always continue to learn

The pun on "never wrong, never right" and the emphasis in the third line on continuity, on the projection forward in the direction of the empty page beyond, provides a nice form of anticlosure.

Knowledge Never Knew thus constitutes an important statement of aesthetic, an artist's commonplace book where the briefest aphorisms force us to think through the question of how writing works. When, for example, the entry "March 18 1923 / *Frank Sinatra baptized*" is "penetrated" by the lines

> to be rooted in anything
> one must be rotated in something

the reader has an image of the infant Sinatra "rotated" in the baptismal font, the relation of "rootedness" to rotation thus making perfect sense. Nothing, the poet seems to be saying, is as irrelevant as you think it is. Watch those words you merely "read"! Or, as the "march 20" entry would have it,

> to ground yourself in words always lean against your reading
> and balance on the weight of what you don't know

Such "balancing" acts have characterized McCaffery's more recent books, *Evoba, Panopticon,* and *The Black Debt.* Since I have written of the latter two elsewhere,[9] I want to conclude here with a discussion of *Evoba: The Investigation Meditations 1976–78,* published in 1987. *Evoba* is "above" spelled backward, and the book's "Meditations" are on Wittgenstein's *Philosophical Investigations,* which are quoted extensively. *Evoba* thus follows up the implications of *Knowledge Never Knew,* which is written under the sign of the *Tractatus Logico-Philosophicus.* Whereas *Knowledge* plays on the individual Wittgenstein proposition, *Evoba* takes up the more expansive language games of the *Investigations.*

Let us begin with the source of the title *Evoba,* Wittgenstein's proposition 160:

Suppose that a man who is under the influence of a certain drug is presented with a series of characters (which need not belong to any existing alphabet). He utters words corresponding to the number of characters, as if they were letters, and does so with all the outward signs, and with the sensations, of reading. . . . In such a case some people would be inclined to say the man was *reading* those marks. Others, that he was not.—Suppose he has in this way read (or interpreted) a set of five marks as A B O V E—and now we show him the same marks in the reverse order and he reads E V O B A; and in further texts he always retains the same interpretation of the marks: here we should certainly be inclined to say he was making up an alphabet for himself *ad hoc* and then reading accordingly.[10]

In opting for the "reverse order," McCaffery announces his aim to call our normal language habits into question, to produce an oppositional text. The frontispiece plays on Wittgenstein's proposition 309 ("What is your aim in philosophy?—To show the fly the way out of the fly-bottle," PI 103e), declaring:

> If the aim of philosophy is, as
> Wittgenstein claims, to show the fly the
> way out of the fly-bottle, then the aim of
> poetry is to convince the bottle that
> there is no fly.

Poetry, in McCaffery's witty spin on Wittgenstein's theorem, has no inside or outside, no "fly" that can be removed from the bottle. There is only the bottle itself, the material object to be reconstructed textually. "The limits of my language," as Wittgenstein put it, "are the limits of my world."

The first step is to get rid of the Augustinian notion, called into question on the opening page of the *Philosophical Investigations,* that *verba rerum nomina sunt,* that "the individual words in language name objects" (PI 2e). The passage from Augustine's *Confessions* (1.8) cited by Wittgenstein is rendered by McCaffery as a page from a comic book (figure 12). The first band, for example, plays on the caption *"Cum ipsi (majories homines apellabant secundum each vocem corpus ad aliquid movebant, videbam* (When they [my elders] named some object, and accordingly moved toward something, I saw this)" by taking the "mov[ing] toward something" quite literally as the cliché image of a passionate lovers' kiss.

The opening comic strip is further juxtaposed to the photograph, which appears on the cover as well as on the recto and verso of front and back endpapers (see figure 13) of two men in hats, looking at books evidently taken from a floor-to-ceiling bookcase, which is surrounded by rubble—a library, as it were, in the process of demolition or, at the very least, transit.

Figure 12. Steve McCaffery, *Evoba. The Investigation Meditations 1976–78*, page 13.

Figure 13. Steve McCaffery, *Evoba,* cover and endpaper photograph.

Here, McCaffery seems to be saying, is what philosophical meditations look like. And throughout the text there are cartoon drawings, rebuses, witty diagrams like the "line"/"nile" crossing on page 23 (figure 14) that are an integral part of the poetic composition. Indeed, layout is everywhere a part of the meaning. On facing pages (24–25), for example, we have the opening sentence of proposition 162 (PI 65e):

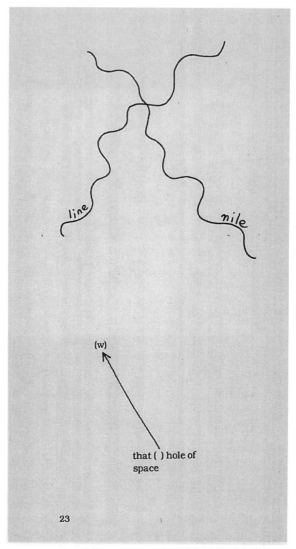

Figure 14. Steve McCaffery, *Evoba*, page 23.

You are reading when you *derive*
the reproduction from the original

Wittgenstein now goes on to demonstrate that this definition could apply
to someone who has been taught the Cyrillic alphabet and, not knowing
what words are being spelled out, tries to pronounce every letter, one by
one. Strictly speaking, such a person is *reading*. But McCaffery's poetic

```
          red colour
blue   red definition   sky
       red judgement


                       a private syntax &
                       a common language


'has'


                       'something'


       once you know what
       you know, once
       it was a whole use
       he had

               to the right
               of a meaning out of sequence


memory:
        in time
        in page
        in process

                       a dictionary (inwardly)
                       a table


then her lips
her eyes
        the pain of a wheel

or what each thing would like to say
```

25

Figure 15. Steve McCaffery, *Evoba*, page 25.

version (the fly-bottle without the fly) carries the proposition much further: "Red" is by definition a "colour," but what do we know about it when we have so designated it? Can a "judgement" be "red"? Yes, in the sense that it is "read." Poetry draws on a "common language" but it is inevitably a "private syntax," McCaffery's own poem juxtaposing verbs without subjects, pronouns without antecedents, and the image of "her lips" and "her eyes," juxtaposed to "the pain of a wheel" that can refer to any number of narratives, especially when that pain is juxtaposed to "or what each thing would like to say," where the "or" follows no "either." Indeed, McCaffery's meditation on memory and time, a dictionary and a table, lips and eyes, red and blue, once and then, private syntax and common language, never makes clear what it is that "each thing would like to say."

Evoba culminates in a series of pages that brings McCaffery's intense scrutiny of language to a remarkable verbal/visual resolution. On page 98, a child's drawing of a cloud is suspended in space over a diagonal block **E** that looks rather like a doormat or grate. On the facing page (99), McCaffery reproduces the conclusion of Wittgenstein's proposition 426: "In the actual use of expressions we make detours, we go by sideroads. We see the straight highway before us, but of course we cannot use it, because it is permanently closed." The book we have been reading has, in fact, enacted this very insight and so, we read at bottom right, "The book exploded in his hand. Slowly, at first." As the book gets ready to disappear, the poet turns his attention to Wittgenstein's meditation on the meaning of "pain" and "feeling," especially Wittgenstein's (proposition 284): "And so, too, a corpse seems to us quite inaccessible to pain." What, then, is it to be alive? The last page of the book looks like this (figure 16):

Take the I (the individual self) out of ALIVE and what do you have? AL VE, perhaps the truncated SALVE of SALVE REGINA, with its reminder of the Mass. Or perhaps an anagram on VALE (AVE ATQUE VALE—"Hail and Farewell"). Then again, the I is only a lower-case "i," so maybe its removal, along with those little raindrop circles falling from the AL VE cloud, doesn't damage ALIVE all that much. It would be pretty to think so except that near the bottom of the page on the right, we have the single word *dead*. Language, as Wittgenstein argues and as McCaffery knows full well, has its own power. Take the "i" out of ALIVE, and you have *dead*. Read sequentially, this is what the page "says." But read spatially—and in McCaffery's books we must always read spatially—what dominates is the oval containing AL VE, dropping its "i." Poetry, the text tells us, needn't focus on

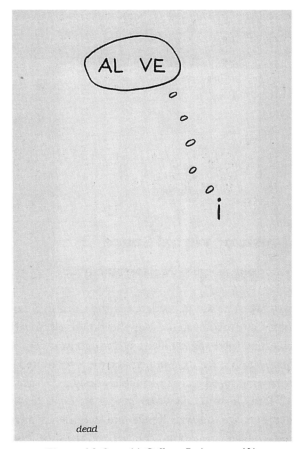

Figure 16. Steve McCaffery, *Evoba*, page 101.

individual sensibility. When the "i" drops out, emphasis shifts from the author to the reader. As the first page of *Evoba* would have it:

> *The water in this space*
> *disappears*

> a reader enters.

Thus it is that *Evoba* challenges the notion of the book as "machine," designed "to accommodate printed linguistic information in a linear form" (RG 60). "The emphasis on the visual element in writing," as McCaffery and nichol put it, "[has] a *poetic* emergence." The page, in this scheme of things, is no longer "an obstacle to be overcome" (RG 61) but "a profoundly active space" (RG 65). And so "a reader enters."

Syntax, like

government, can only be obeyed.   It is

therefore of no use except when you

have something particular to command

such as: Go buy me a bunch of carrots.

—John Cage, *M* 1

13. The Music of Verbal Space

John Cage's "What You Say . . ."

As early as 1939, when he was in residence at the Cornish School of Music in Seattle, John Cage investigated the application of electrical technology to music. His first (perhaps *the* first) electroacoustic composition was *Imaginary Landscape No. 1,* a six-minute radio piece for muted piano, cymbal, and two variable-speed record turntables, designed to accompany the production of Jean Cocteau's play *Marriage at the Eiffel Tower.* The piece was performed by Cage, his wife Xenia, and two friends in two separate studios, mixed in the control room, and beamed the short distance to the theater.[2] *Imaginary Landscape No. 1* looks ahead to any number of Cage compositions involving radio, magnetic tape, and computer technologies. And yet the irony is that, having produced so many complex intermedia works using the most varied acoustic materials, by 1970 or so, Cage started to write a series of "mesostics," performance works that made use of only a single instrument—the human voice—and a single medium—language.

"My first mesostic," Cage writes in the foreword to *M* (1), "was written as prose to celebrate one of Edwin Denby's birthdays. The following ones, each letter of the name being on its own line, were written as poetry. *A given letter capitalized does not occur between it and the preceding capitalized letter.* I thought I was writing acrostics, but Norman O. Brown pointed out that they could properly be called 'mesostics' (row not down the edge but down the middle)."

Here is the Edwin Denby mesostic of 1970 called "Present":

rEmembering a Day i visited you—seems noW
as I write that the weather theN was warm—i
recall nothing we saiD, nothing wE did; eveN so
(perhaps Because of that) that visit staYs.

This first attempt, as Cage suggests, was clearly not quite satisfactory. The four-line text, with its justified left and right margins, doesn't have much visual interest, the capital letters merely appearing in a linear sequence. More important, the Denby mesostic doesn't have much aural or musical complexity, its prose format being that of normal writing of the sort we all do when we write a note to a friend on an occasion like a birthday. True, the mesostic rule (Cage was later to call this a 50 percent mesostic since the given letter capitalized can occur between it and the *following* capitalized letter, whereas a 100 percent mesostic doesn't allow for occurence of the letter either preceding or following its appearance) is observed, but hearing this particular text read, one would not especially notice the structuration of language by the EDWIN DENBY string, although—a harbinger of things to come—the Y-word, "staYs," rhymes with the D-word, "Day."

The difficulty at this stage was that Cage was still using normal syntax. In another early mesostic, entitled "On the windshield of a new Fiat for James K[losty] (who had not made up his mind where to go) and Carolyn Brown," we read:

asK
Little
autO
Where it wantS
To take
You.
(*M* 94)

Unlike the Denby mesostic, this one is "written as poetry," in that each capital letter gets a line to itself (and as a 100 percent mesostic, its wing words are of necessity very short), but again, the poem's syntax and sound are almost those of ordinary conversation. Thus, although the Klosty mesostic is visually more of a "poem" than is the Edwin Denby one, the poetic problem has not yet been resolved.

Cage was quite aware of this quandary. When, in the early seventies, the French philosopher Daniel Charles posed the question, "Aren't your lectures, for example, musical works in the manner of the different chapters of Walden?" Cage replied, "They are when sounds are words. But I must say that I have not yet carried language to the point to which I have taken musical sounds. . . . I hope to make something other than language from it." And he adds, "It is that aspect, the *impossibility of language,* that interests me at present." Again, in a later exchange, when Charles remarks, "You propose to musicate language; you want language to be heard as music," Cage responds, "I hope to let words exist, as I have tried to let sounds exist" (FB 113, 151).[3]

Making language as interesting as music, Cage was to learn, depended on the dismantling of "normal" syntax. Much as he loved Joyce, Cage felt that even *Finnegans Wake* was conventional in this respect:

> Reading *Finnegans Wake* I notice that though Joyce's subjects, verbs, and objects are unconventional, their relationships are the ordinary ones. With the exception of the Ten Thunderclaps and rumblings here and there, *Finnegans Wake* employs syntax. Syntax gives it a rigidity from which classical Chinese and Japanese were free. A poem by Basho, for instance, floats in space. . . . Only the imagination of the reader limits the number of the poem's possible meanings. (*M* 2)

In the former case, the words themselves are made strange, Joyce being, of course, a master of word formation, punning, metaphor, and allusion, but the syntax is left intact; "Joyce," Cage remarks elsewhere, "seemed to me to have kept the old structures ('sintalks') in which he put the new words he had made" (EW 133). The alternative (Basho's) is to use "ordinary" language but to explode the syntax, a process Cage regularly referred to as the "demilitarization of the language." "Speaking without syntax," he explains in a note on "Sixty-Two Mesostics Re Merce Cunningham," "we notice that cadence, Dublinese or ministerial, takes over. (Looking out the rear-window.) Therefore we tried whispering. Encouraged we began to chant. . . . To raise language's temperature we not only remove syntax: we give each letter undivided attention setting it in unique face and size; *to read* becomes the verb *to sing*" (JCW 97). But he admits in the foreword to *M* that "My work in this field is tardy. It follows the poetry of Jackson Mac Low and Clark Coolidge, my analogous work in the field of music, and my first experiments, texts for *Song Books*. . . . Concrete and sound poets have also worked in this field for many years, though many, it seems to me, have substituted graphic or musical structures for syntactical ones" (*M* 2).

Cage is quite right to refer to his "work in this field" as "tardy." As early as 1960, Jackson Mac Low had written a sequence called *Stanzas for Iris*

Lezak based on chance operations. "Call Me Ishmael," for example, takes the first three words of *Moby Dick* as its acrostric string, and finds the words that begin with the thirteen consecutive letters C-A-L–L-M-E-I-S-H-M-A-E-L in the novel's first few pages, as determined partly by *I Ching* chance operations.[4] The text has five three-line stanzas, with the pattern 4-2-7 words per line respectively:

> Circulation. And long long
> Mind every
> Interest Some how mind and every long
>
> Coffin about little little
> Money especially
> I shore, having money about especially little
>
> Cato a little little
> Me extreme
> I sail have me an extreme little
>
> Cherish and left, left,
> Myself extremest
> It see hypos myself and extremest left,
>
> City a land. Land.
> Mouth; east,
> Is spleen, hand, mouth; an east, land.[5]

When Cage began to write mesostics, he adopted Mac Low's acrostic procedures, but with an important difference. Whereas in the example above, Mac Low lets chance operations generate the entire text, Cage, as we shall see, uses these operations to generate the word pool to be used and the rules to be followed, but he then fills in lines with "wing words," generated, as he repeatedly put it, "according to taste."[6] The result is an idiom markedly different from Mac Low's, especially in its vocal quality, Cage preferring softer, blending sounds to the harshly stressed monosyllabic nouns, separated by strong caesuras, that we find in "Call Me Ishmael." A similar difference may be observed between Cage and such concrete poets as the Brazilian *Noigandres* group (Augusto de Campos, Haroldo de Campos, and Decio Pignatari), with whom he shared many aesthetic principles and who have assiduously translated and disseminated his writings. In concrete poetry—say Augusto de Campos's *Luxo* or Pignatari's *Beba coca cola* —the visual image predominates, the actualization of performance not giving the listener the full effect of the figure the poem makes, a figure depending on complex patterns of typography, spacing, color contrasts, and so on. In Cage, by contrast, it is the aural that dominates. Indeed, however visually striking Cage's verbal scores may be, with the mesostic column creating an interesting pattern and the punctuation marks of the original often strewn around the page (as in *Roaratorio*), poetic density depends primarily on sound, as actualized in performance. Cage was, after all, a composer even when the materials he worked with were linguistic rather than musical.

The influences Cage cites in *M* could thus take him only so far. A decade of experimentation followed. While the earliest mesostics, like the "25 Mesostics Re and not Re Mark Tobey" (*M* 186–94) were written in Cage's own words (the first "MARK" mesostic reads "it was iMpossible / to do Anything: / the dooR / was locKed"), and while what we might call the middle ones were "writings through" such great literary texts as *Finnegans Wake* or Ezra Pound's *Cantos*,[7] in his last years, Cage turned increasingly to making mesostics out of texts not in themselves consciously "poetic." In Tokyo in 1986, for example, Cage performed a mesostic piece called "Sculpture Musicale," which used as its source text for the mesostic string only that title and the following words of Marcel Duchamp: "sons durant et partant de differents points et formant une sculpture sonore qui dure." A second Tokyo piece submitted to "writing through" Cage's own "Lecture on Nothing," even as his "Rhythm, etc." (1988) takes a passage from *A Year from Monday* ("There's virtually nothing to say about rhythm") and uses the four sentences of this passage as the mesostic string.

Discussions of Cagean mesostic have usually ignored this evolution from mesostic strings based on single proper names, repeated throughout (as in the case of the name "JAMES JOYCE" in the *Roaratorio*), to strings derived from larger statements or paragraphs, whose individual words are part of the standard lexicon. The turning point from the "proper name" string to what we might call the "sentence" string may well have come with the writing, in the early eighties, of the performance piece "James Joyce, Marcel Duchamp, Erik Satie: An Alphabet." In this complex work, the hypothetical "conversation" between the three artists is presented, partly by means of found text, artfully collaged from their writings, partly by Cage's own discourse, structured by the proper names of the three artists, repeated as mesostic strings according to chance operations. In "A Conversation about Radio in Twelve Parts" with Richard Kostelanetz conducted a few years later, Cage expressed dissatisfaction with "Alphabet" because its "scenes [are] in a very simple way differentiated from one another. They don't overlap so that it's as simple as a work by Stravinsky, but within each part there's a great disparateness with the next part; so that the act of listening is very uncomfortable." "All those scenes," he explained, "have beginnings and endings. It's a multiplicity of beginnings and endings. That's what annoys me. I don't mind it as something to read; but as something to hear." [8]

What Cage means, I think, is that proper-name mesostics, derived not from a "writing through" but from sentences made up for the occasion, have a tendency to form independent strophes of four to six lines, strophes divided by a sharp pause and hence not sufficiently "interpenetrating" phonemically. For example:

> from his Jumping
> the older one is Erik SAtie
> he never stops sMiling
> and thE younger one
> iS joyce, thirty-nine
>
> he Jumps
> with his back tO the audience
> for all we know he maY be quietly weeping
> or silently laughing or both you just Can't
> tEll [9]

Here the syntactically straightforward narrative perhaps too easily yields the requisite mesostic letters: J-A-M-E-S and J-O-Y-C-E; if, say, an O were needed as the final mesostic letter, Cage could substitute "knOw" for "tEll" without it making much difference. Then, too, the stanza break follows the normal syntactic break: "the younger one is Joyce, thirty-nine. // He jumps. . . ," thus producing the "differentiat[ion] from one another" Cage criticizes.

The solution was to use a seemingly inconsequential prose text as the source, not only for his own "writing through" but for the mesostic string as well. There would be, in other words, a rule to follow, but that rule would be so hidden that "beginnings and endings" would not call attention to themselves. Moreover, the discourse of ordinary prose—a passage from an interview, a newspaper paragraph, a statement from a lecture— could now be decomposed and recharged so as to uncover the mysteries of language. "You see," Cage told Niksa Gligo in an interview, "language controls our thinking; and if we change our language, it is conceivable that our thinking would change" (K 149). For this purpose, "empty words" are more useful than "full" ones. "Full words," Cage explains to Richard Kostelanetz, "are words that are nouns *or* verbs *or* adjectives *or* adverbs," whereas "empty words" (what we call function words or deictics) are "connective[s] or pronoun[s] — word[s] that refer to something else" (K 141).

As an example of such an "empty word" mesostic, I have chosen a short piece called "What you say . . ." from 1986, an "autoku" on an informal statement on aesthetics made by Jasper Johns in an 1979 interview with Christian Geelhaar.[10] This is the first of two companion texts by Cage based on Johns's commentary on his own work, the second being "Art Is Either a Complaint Or Do Something Else," which is taken from a series of statements cited by Mark Rosenthal in his *Jasper Johns: Work Since 1974* (Philadelphia Museum of Art, 1988). Cage discusses this mesostic piece with Joan Retallack in the first of the interviews in *Musicage* called "Words." As Cage explains the piece:

> it's all from words of Jasper Johns, but they're used with chance operations in such a way that they make different connections than they did when he said them. On the other hand, they seem to reinforce what he was saying . . . almost in his way. And why that should surprise me I don't know because all of the words are his. (*laughs*) But they make different connections.[11]

Consider the "different connections" in "What You Say . . . ," which draws on a statement Johns makes at the very end of the Geelhaar interview:

> What you say about my tendency to add things is correct. But, how
> does one make a painting? How does one deal with the space? Does
> one have something and then proceed to add another thing or does
> one have something; move into it; occupy it; divide it; make the
> best one can of it? I think I do different things at different
> times and perhaps at the same time. It interests me that a part can
> function as a whole or that a whole can be thrown into a situation
> in which it is only a part. It interests me that what one takes to
> be a whole subject can suddenly be miniaturized, or something, and
> then be inserted into another world, as it were.

Notice that Cage's reproduction of Johns's response is already a kind of writing through, the sentences being arranged as line lengths and centered so as to give the whole an accordion-like visual shape. At the Los Angeles performance I attended (at UCLA, 4 September 1987, in conjunction with the opening of the exhibition of the Samuel Beckett-Jasper Johns collaboration *Fizzles*), "What you say . . ." was preceded by the reading of three short mesostics on the name JASPER JOHNS, one of them having appeared in *Empty Words* (1979) under the title "Song":

> not Just
>   gArdener
> morelS
>   coPrini,
>   morEls,
>   copRini.
>
>   not Just hunter:
> cutting dOwn
>   ailantHus,
>   cuttiNg down
> ailanthuS.
>
>   (EW 10)

Notice that this mesostic belongs to Cage's earlier "concrete poetry" phase, the lines built primarily on catalogs of nouns, and the game being that each of two words (or phrases) per stanza can supply the poet with the necessary capital letters (e.g., the "S" and "E" of "morels"). These are primarily eye devices. By the time Cage wrote "What you say. . .," his aim was to "musicate" the language, letting it do the sorts of things he had hitherto done with musical sounds. Indeed, at the UCLA performance, the piece was performed by a dozen or so readers, according to the following program notes:

> For any number of readers able to read in one breath any of the 124 "stanzas" (a "stanza" is a line or lines preceded and followed by a space).

> Each reader, equipped with a chronometer, and without intentionally changing the pitch or loudness of the voice quietly reads any 4 "stanzas" at any 4 times in each minute of the agreed-upon performance time.

> The readers are seated or stand around the audience or both within and outside it [12].

Whether performed chorally or by Cage himself (and I have heard it done both ways), the "frame" is now no longer the decision on how many times to repeat a given proper name like JAMES JOYCE but the "agreed-upon performance time." Cage's initial experiments with magnetic tape in the late forties and early fifties, Margaret Leng Tan has pointed out, "emphasized the fact that duration (time length) is synonymous with tape length (space) and it is the application of this principle which forms the basis for the space-time proportional notation used in the *Music of Changes* and the *Two Pastorales* of 1951."[13] The same principle, Cage came to see, could be applied to language texts. In the case of "What you say . . . ," duration would seem to be determined by the need to provide one line for each of the 512 letters in Johns's paragraph. But in fact "What you say . . ." is much longer than 512 "lines" because of the spacing (silence) Cage introduces between word groups, with extra rests replacing the missing letters—missing because "For several letters there were no words: the v of have (twice); the v of move; the j of subject; and the z of miniaturized. Spaces between lines take the place of the missing letters" (F 53).

The selection of words from the source pool, Cage explains in his note to "What you say . . ." (F 53), is based on MESOLIST, "a program by Jim Rosenberg, extended for this particular piece by a second program made by Andrew Culver, which extended the number of characters in a search string . . . to any length; this extended MESOLIST was used to list the available words that were then subjected to IC (a program by Andrew Culver simulating the coin oracle of the *I Ching*)." Although I have not seen this program, it seems clear that even though the MESOLIST-derived "chance operations" do govern the sequencing of the words that contain the requisite letters for the mesostic string, the variable length of the search string made it possible for Cage to create precisely the semantic and phonemic juxtapositions that suited him. In this particular case, he had to begin with a line containing the *W* of the first word "What," followed by the *h*, the *a*, and so on, and the first *W*-word designated by MESOLIST is the last word of Johns's statement—"were." But although chance operations dictated the selection of "were" as the first capitalized word to be used in "What you say . . . ," it was Cage's own choice to place, in the opening line, the whole phrase, "as it Were." Indeed, as we shall see, in this instance as elsewhere, Cage's poetic composition is nothing if not *designed*. As he put it in the foreword to *Silence:* "As I see it, poetry is not prose simply because poetry is in one way or another formalized. It is not poetry by reason of its content or ambiguity but by reason of its allowing musical elements (time, sound) to be introduced into the world of words" (S x).

The world of words, in this case, consists of seven "ordinary" sentences (three of them questions), containing 127 words, 99 of them monosyl-lables. This is already an unusual linguistic situation, but what is even odder is that there are only seven words in the entire passage that have more than two syllables.[14] And further: the majority of monosyllables and disyllables are deictics or function words: "it" appears seven times, "thing" six times, "one" five times, "something" three times, "how," "what," and "whole" twice each. In this context, the word that stands out is the five-syllable "miniaturized" in the next to last line.[15]

The sentence structure is as elementary as is the word pool. "How does one" with the variant "does one" appears four times; "it interests me that" twice, and simple parallel structure occurs in "move into it; occupy it; divide it; make the best one can of it." Johns's statement, at least as lineated here, thus has a naive or childlike sound structure, especially since the artist hesitates or withdraws statements, as in "I think I do different things at different times and perhaps at the same time," or when he de-clares that "a whole subject can suddenly be miniaturized, or something." Finally, the paragraph concludes with the qualifier, "as it were."

Why would Cage, who has previously written through the incredibly rich word pool of *Finnegans Wake* or the hieratic rhythms of Pound's *Can-tos*, select such an ordinary flat discourse to "write through"? After all, Johns's statement is just an unrehearsed response to a question from an interviewer. This is of course Cage's point. "There is no such thing as an empty space or an empty time. There is always something to see, some-thing to hear" (S 8). Even in his off-the-cuff remarks about his art making, Johns, so Cage posits, is saying something significant, is posing basic ques-tions about painting. And, moreover, Johns's own vocal patterns, with which Cage was of course deeply familiar, produce a sound curve to which Cage's own sound curve is designed to respond. Indeed, the composer-poet's role, in this scheme of things, is to bring Johns's "something," his particular signature—the visual made verbal and vocal—out into the open by "demilitarizing" the syntax so as to controvert the chosen state-ment's linearity and permit its components to realign themselves. Let me try to elaborate.

"What you say . . ." opens with the final "as it Were" of Johns's para-graph and comes full circle to "wEre" on its last page. Here is the begin-ning:

as it Were

anotHer world

A whole or
The best one can of it

suddenlY
sOmething

move

miniatUrized

Perhaps the first thing to notice here is the elaborate sound structure, a structure especially notable in Cage's own reading of the text in which each line, spoken slowly, is followed by a silence the length of a short syllable.[16] The first three lines are linked by stress pattern (two stresses per line), anaphora of short *a*s and internal rhyme ("Were"/"world"/"or"). In line 4, the sound shifts to short vowels, embedded in *t*s and *th*s; the lightly stressed monosyllabic line "The best one can of it" being related to the first three by the repetition of "it," the internal rhyme of "an" (in "another") and "can," and of "-tHer" and "The" (*t*s and *th*s, incidentally, constitute 52 or roughly one tenth of the poem's phonemes). Lines 5 and 6—"suddenlY / sOmething"—are again related by stress pattern and alliteration, and "move," with its open vowel followed by a voiced spirant, opens the way for the alliterating *m* of the passage's longest (and perhaps least musical) word, "miniatUrized," a word that appears again and again, furnishing the different letters of the "What you say . . ." string.

But there is also a curious clinamen in this passage. Line 7, "move" is not part of the mesostic string at all, "WHAT YOU" being complete without it. The source text reads: "does one have to do something; move into it." Cage might have put "move" on line 6 along with the semicolon, or he might have left the word out completely since the search string can be, as Cage points out, of any length. Yet "move," physically moved over to the right here, has an important effect. The domain of art, the text suggests, is "as it Were / anotHer world / A whole or / The best one can of it." This other world is "suddenlY / sOmething," and it is, in Cage's elliptical construction, "move"—which is to say, moving, on the move, in movement, in a move toward, the "miniaturization" of "subject" which is art.

But of course the text itself we are reading (or hearing) is precisely this miniaturization, this creation of "suddenlY / sOmething." Lift the ordinary out of the zone of saying, Cage seems to say ("The best one can of it") and "it" will become "something." Just as Johns would paint ordinary numbers (0 to 9; see figure 1) or the letters of the alphabet (A to Z), or a clothes hanger or beer can, so Cage will take words as uninteresting as "as," "it," "or," "of," and "a," place those words in particular spatial configurations, white space (silence) being at least as prominent as the written and spoken language itself, and create a minimalist *ars poetica*.

That Cage's work continues to go unrecognized as poetry by those who produce books like the *Norton Anthology of Poetry*—as well as those who read and review them—has to do with our general inability to dissociate "poetry" from the twin norms of self-expression and figuration. "What you say . . . ," it is argued by Cage's detractors (and they are legion), is, after all, no more than a reproduction of someone else's text: the "I" is not Cage's and, in any case, there is no psychological revelation of a personal sort. Moreover, in the passage we have just read there isn't a single metaphor (except for that dead metaphor "world") or arresting visual image. Indeed, Cage's diction, so this line of reasoning goes, is merely trivial, isn't it?

This is to ignore the crucial role played by the context in which words occur, by their temporal and spatial arrangement, and especially by their sound. Take, for example, the common phrase "make the best one can of it" in Johns's paragraph. Eliminate the initial "make" and the phrase becomes the strange "The best one can of it," made even stranger by its insertion in the text between "A whole or" and "suddenlY." Yet the realignment produces a new meaning: "a whole or / the best" may now be read as adjectives modifying "world," and "the best one can" may be construed as a noun phrase. Certainly a "can" is a kind of whole. Aural performance, in any case, activates any number of meanings, especially since the spacing (the visual equivalence of silence) ensures very slow reading, whether one or more persons are reading simultaneously. "SuddenlY / sOmething / move / miniatUrized"—one word per line, a rest between lines: the audience is forced to listen carefully, to pay attention to the sound of each unit.

The strategy of "What you say . . ."—and this is where the mesostic mode, with its dependence on a fixed word pool, can work so effectively—is to recharge individual words by consistently shifting their context and hence their use. Take the word "whole," used three times in Johns's statement: "It interests me that a part can function as a **whole** or that a **whole** can be thrown into a situation in which it is only a part. It interests me that what one takes to be a **whole** subject can suddenly be miniaturized" (my emphasis). In Cage, this "normal" syntax gives way to astonishing variations. "Whole" appears twenty-eight times, each of its letters appearing in the mesostic string of the text. Along the way it yields such stanzas as:

oF it

a whole sUbject
aNd then
a whole Can be
whaT you say about
It

Occupy it

a whole caN
hAve
different timeS and
tAkes
can be throWn
and perHaps at the same time

Or
how does one deaL with
diffErent times and

(F 62)

Here the mesostic string is "FUNCTION AS A WHOLE." But the poem itself questions this "function"; the "whole sUbject" is in apposition to a mere "it"; "a whole Can be" "whaT you say about / It," "a whole caN / hAve / different timeS and / takes," it can be "throWn / and perHaps at the same time." On the next page "wHole" furnishes Cage with the *H* mesostic letter and thus becomes a "hole."

Now let us look again at the source text which reads "What one takes to be a whole subject can suddenly be miniaturized." Cage's own text enacts precisely this statement: what we "take to be a whole" dissolves into a number of possibilities. Not only can this "whole" be "miniaturized" but it "caN / hAve / different timeS and / tAkes"; there is no essential truth behind the word: "a whole Can be / whaT you say about it." A neat illustration, as it were, of Wittgenstein's proposition that "the meaning of a word is its use in the language."

Again, consider the couplings and uncouplings given to the word "tendency," which appears only once in Johns's statement, in the opening sentence: "What you say about my tendency to add things is correct":

hoW
about my tenDency

thrOwn into a
thEn
and then be inSerted
my tendency tO
move iNto it

What tendency, we wonder, is this? ThrOwn into a / thEn? "My tendency tO / move iNto it"? It sounds risky. Two pages later, we read:

How does one
It
my teNdency to
have somethinG
deAl

where "deal" may be either noun or verb, either indicative or imperative, the "tendency to / have somethinG" therefore being quite mysterious. Further down on the same page, the plot thickens:

i Think
a situatiOn in which
you sAy about
one Deal with
tenDency
As it were

Let's make a deal and take care of the situation in which the tendency in question arises, as it were. Two pages later, we find the stanza:

moVe
It
make
i Do
movE
whIch
Tendency
My
situAtion in which
i thinK
onE
can funcTion as

The instructions are to "moVe it" (reenforced by the verb "make," another one of what we might call outriders in the text, "make" not being part of the mesostic chain, which here is "[DI]VIDE IT MAKE T[HE BEST OF IT]"), to which the response is "i Do movE," and now "tendency" is explicitly linked to "situation," a "situAtion in which / i thinK / one can funcTion as." Function as what? Johns's "tendency to add things" now takes on a darker cast, his tendency producing a situation in which the artist only thinks he can function. When "tendency" reappears some time later in the performance, it is "thAt / teNdency to / oF it," where the "tendency" can be interpreted in a variety of ways. Or again, it becomes a "whoLe / tendencY to / whAt one / occuPy." The last three pages of "What you say . . ." accelerate the repetition, "tendency" appearing six more times:

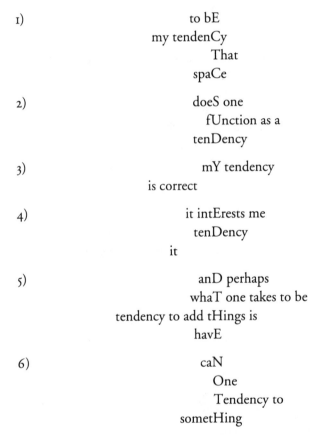

1)
           to bE
      my tendenCy
              That
        spaCe

2)
           doeS one
              fUnction as a
           tenDency

3)
                mY tendency
       is correct

4)
               it intErests me
           tenDency
       it

5)
           anD perhaps
        whaT one takes to be
    tendency to add tHings is
          havE

6)
           caN
         One
          Tendency to
     sometHing

This is Cage at his most Steinian, charging language by means of permutation, words like "tendency" taking on a different aura with every repetition. What makes these pieces so remarkable is that they are, to use Joyce's term, "verbivocovisual." Visual, to take it backward, in that the spacing and mesostic chain produces its own meanings, so that "tenDency," with that "ten" separating out, is not the same as "tendenCy," and the construction of larger units will depend on word placement and spacing. "Verbi," in that Cage is always constructing new meanings, in this case giving new connotations to a "tendency" Johns mentions only casually. But it is the "voco" ("musical") element which perhaps dominates here. For given the nature of the "writing-through" process, there are only so many words at the composer's disposal, and these words—"what," "world," "perhaps," "another," "something," "interest," "function"—appear again and again, becoming familiar counters. "Miniaturized," for example, has nine lives, supplying the mesostic string with necessary letters (aurally phonemes) at frequent intervals, even as its z, as Cage notes, cannot be used.

As such, Cage's sound structure has a decisive semantic import. Unlike most actual art discourse, the mesostic "written-through" lecture or essay cannot just continue, cannot move from point to point, from thesis statement to exemplification or analogy, in a logical way. Rather, the discourse must "say something" about aesthetic, using no more than its baseline of 127 words, whose rule-governed permutations take us from "as it Were" to "a wholE can / peRhaps / wEre."

That it does "say something" is, of course, the work's great feat. "What You Say . . . ," what Cage's work "says" takes us back to the famous (perhaps too famous) theorem of "Experimental Music" that the "purposeless play" of art means "waking up to the very life we're living, which is so excellent once one gets one's mind and one's desires out of its way" (S 12). Purposeless play is not a matter of making "just any experiment." It does not mean that anything goes, that anyone can be an artist, that any random conjunction of words or sounds or visual images becomes art. What it does mean, as a reading of "What you say . . ." teaches us, is that the ordinary (in this case, Jasper Johns's not terribly edifying comment about his painting habits) can provide all that the artist needs to make "something else." Indeed, the challenge is to take the ordinary—words like "it" and "one" and "function" and "situation"—and "miniaturize" it into "something."

And that is of course what Johns himself does in his paintings (Figure 1). When he remarks, "Does one have something and then proceed to add another thing **or** does one have something; move into it; occupy it; divide

Figure 1. Jasper Johns, *Figure 5* (1955). Encaustic and collage on canvas. 44.5×55.6 cm. Collection of the artist. Copyright © Jasper Johns/Licensed by VAGA, New York, NY.

it; make the best one can of it?" we should note the allusion to his own famous warning to "Avoid a polar situation." For of course there is no meaningful opposition between "add[ing] another thing" or "hav[ing] something [and] mov[ing] into it"; the either-or proposition is falsely posed. Johns is playing similar games when he says, "I think I do different things at different times and perhaps at the same time." At one level, the tautology is absurd. But as we learn from Cage's "What you say . . . ," such tautologies are integral to the process whereby we learn that there *is* no essential truth about art making, no way of saying for sure what art is or what the artist does.

"I think," Cage remarked a few months before his death, "a very impressive quality [of Johns's painting] is the absence of space. Something has been done almost everywhere. So it leads very much to the complexity of life" (*Musicage* 106). The verbal equivalent of this "absence of space" can be seen in a passage like the following:

<pre>
                    Or does one
            function As
        another WorlD

                Do
                Time
        and tHen proceed to
            dIvide it

                oNe
        a paintinG
                            (F 54)
</pre>

In the source-text interview, Johns speculates on the ways "a whole subject" might "be inserted into another world." Cage shows how such insertion is performed by presenting himself as "one" who can actually "function **As** / another WorlD." And just as Johns's painting is characterized by an "absence of space" (which is to say, unused space), so Cage's performance poem is characterized by an absence of time, in that each word, each morpheme, each phoneme must do double duty: look, for example, at the way *d*s, *o,* and *n*s are modulated in the "miniaturizing" sequence "Or—does—one—function—another—world—do—proceed—to—divide—one—painting."

When Cage began to experiment with mesostics, he worried that he had not yet hit upon a way of "carry[ing] language to the point to which I have taken musical sounds." The solution, it seems, was to learn to "Do / Time / and tHen proceed to / dIvide it." But even this stanza, taken out of context, may seem too assertive, too dogmatic to suit those like Cage and Johns who want to avoid polar situations. And so the poem makes a tentative circle back to the "as it Were" of the opening:

<pre>
        a wholE can
            peRhaps
            wEre
</pre>

where the last two lines introduce internal rhyme—"peR" / "wEre"—only to qualify repetition by the intrusion of that little particle "haps," which repeats the "p" sound but combines it with a prominent spirant so as to produce dissonance. "A wholE can / peRhaps / wEre": the difference, as Gertrude Stein would put it, is spreading.

The twentieth-century artist is not necessarily someone who draws well,
but someone who thinks well.
—Bill Viola, "The Porcupine and the Car"

I don't like the label "video artist." I consider myself to be an artist. I
happen to use video because I live in the last part of the twentieth century.
—Bill Viola, Statements for *Summer 1985* [1]

14. The Morphology of the Amorphous
Bill Viola's Videoscapes

Video art has now been around for over thirty years, but, in the world
of literary and cultural studies, one would barely know it. Television as
medium and television culture have, of course, been endlessly dissected:
from Raymond Williams's *Television, Technology and Cultural Form* (1974)
and Louis Althusser's study of "Ideological State Apparatuses" (1971) to
Baudrillard's "Requiem for the Media" (1981) and, more recently, to such
essay collections as Constance Penley and Andrew Ross's *Technoculture*
(1991) and Gretchen Bender and Timothy Druckrey's *Culture on the Brink:
Ideologies of Technology* (1994). A whole library of studies has grown up
that unmasks television discourses, power mechanisms and markets, ideological control, and especially, in recent years, media representations of
race, gender, class, and ethnicity.[2] Video, it seems from this flood of media
critique, is that which is seen on broadcast television—period.

Even in the art world, where video pieces are, of course, exhibited,
discussed, and studied, video art has been accused of "technocratic ideal-
ism"; "an uneasy relationship," in Benjamin Buchloch's words, "with the
institutions of reception and distribution of the high-art avant-garde—the
museum and the gallery—and an even uneasier one with the customers
of the distribution system, the private collectors." "Many of the potentially most progressive features of the medium," says Buchloch, "have by
now turned out to be a trap for the artists who find themselves caught

between the vigorous reaffirmation of traditional values and techniques in the worlds of high-art . . . and an attitude of increasing certainty that culture, consumption, and ideology are congruent." Only when the video maker recognizes this complicity and engages in direct political critique, as in Dan Graham's *Rock My Religion* or Martha Rosler's *A Simple Case for Torture,* does video art become useful and interesting.[3]

This argument is itself undercut by a naive utopianism. For surely the number of viewers who take in an agitprop video like Rosler's *Simple Case for Torture* or Dara Birnbaum's *Damnation of Faust* (both 1983) is by no means greater than those who look at videos by Nam June Paik or John Baldessari; in either case, the audience is hardly the audience that watches *Wheel of Fortune* or *Beverly Hills Cop* or even *Masterpiece Theatre.* Indeed, no artist today would make the undue claim that video art has the power to subvert, much less overturn, the vast circuitry of mass television. No technical tool—whether paint brush, pencil, chisel, or lithographic stone—is in itself the means to a revolutionary art. Walter Benjamin, we recall, insisted that film was inherently a more subversive form than dada or surrealist painting, because painting, however "provocative" its images and daring its "word salad," was "in no position to present an object for simultaneous collective experience."[4] But within a decade of Benjamin's death, the films distributed for "simultaneous collective experience" had become at least as commercial and commodified as the art forms they had replaced, a prime exemplar, for that matter, of what the Frankfurt school scornfully dubbed the consciousness industry.

What tends to be ignored in all these discussions about the "revolutionary" potential (or lack thereof) of this or that new medium is that, once a given medium is in place—as was the case with photography in the mid-nineteenth century, film in the early twentieth, and today, the various digital technologies—the most interesting artists will naturally gravitate toward it, exploring its potential and displacing attention, at least for a time, from the more conventional media. Then, too, the return, say, to painting, once a medium like video is in place, will obviously produce a different kind of painting, just as postfilm theater has adapted certain filmic qualities in its staging, scenic design, and spatial relationships.

How, we might begin by asking, does video art relate to its most immediate relatives, television and film? In one of the first (and still best) considerations of the distinctive features of video, David Antin discusses the use of *time* in broadcast television:

For television, time has an absolute existence independent of any imagery that may or may not be transmitted over its well-defended airwaves and cables. It is television's only solid, a tangible commodity that is precisely divisible into further and further subdivisible homogeneous units, the smallest quantum of which is measured by the smallest segment that could be purchased by a potential advertiser, which is itself defined by the minimum particle required to isolate a salable product from among a variable number of equivalent alternatives. The smallest salable piece turns out to be the ten-second spot, and all television is assembled from it.[5]

And Antin goes on to show, with great wit and finesse, how the medium is driven by the extreme segmentation of transmission time mainly through the intense development of multiple sponsorship. "What is called news on television," for example, "is a chain of successive, distinct, and structurally unrelated narrations called stories. These average from thirty seconds to two minutes in length, are usually presented in successions of three or four in a row, and are bracketed between packets of commercials from one to two minutes long" (DA 158). As minute segments proliferate, the distinction between commercials and programs breaks down, in that "every genre of program appears also as a commercial: Dramas, comedies, documentaries, science talks, lists, all show up in thirty- and sixty-second forms" (DA 159). The resulting linear succession of logically independent units of nearly equal duration is the basic syntax of television, as we all know it. And although Antin wrote his essay before the advent of cable, it is amazing how little difference it has made in the time sequence of television as he describes it.

To turn from television to artist's videotapes is thus, as Antin notes, a strange experience. Viewers not accustomed to such videos tend to find them long and boring, even when their running time is actually shorter than that of the standard commercial. The perception of length has everything to do with the way "normal" television presents its ten- or thirty-second "message," so that absence of fixed "content" becomes peculiarly disconcerting, and a startling form of defamiliarization occurs. In forcing the viewer to "see" and "hear" what may be "normal" television images at a different speed and rate of transformation, avant-garde video may well constitute, as the curator David Ross has observed, "the only meaningful critique of television's form and practice."[6]

If time in video art is thus significantly different from television time (and I will exemplify this in a moment), it also deviates significantly from film time. In a 1981 catalog essay called "The Porcupine and the Car," Bill Viola explains it this way:

> Looking at the technical development of both video and film, we immediately notice a profound difference: as film has evolved basically out of photography (a film is a succession of discrete photographs), video has emerged from audio technology. A video camera is closer to a microphone in operation than it is to a film camera; video images are recorded on magnetic tape in a tape recorder. Thus we find that video is closer in relationship to sound, or music [and I would interject here, to a verbal art like poetry] than it is to the visual media of film and photography. . . .
>
> One of the most fascinating aspects of video's technical evolution, and the one that makes it most different from film, is that the video image existed for many years before a way was developed to record it. . . . Taping or recording is not an integral part of the system. Film is not film unless it is filming (recording). Video, however, is "videoing" all the time, continually in motion, putting out 30 frames, or images, a second. . . . *Video's roots in the live, not recorded, is the underlying characteristic of the medium.* Somehow, in a way no one has really been able to explain, time becomes more precious when dealing with video. . . . When one makes a videotape, one is interfering with an ongoing process, the scanning of the camera. . . . In film . . . the basic illusion is of movement, produced by the succession of still images flashing on the screen. In video, stillness is the basic illusion: a still image does not exist because the video signal is in constant motion scanning across the screen. (PC 62–63, my emphasis)

Perhaps the easiest way to understand the distinction Viola is trying to make is to think of film in its original definition as a *motion picture,* the succession of still images composed so as to produce the illusion of motion, whereas the video camera as *scanner* operates the other way around. As a cousin to the microphone, the video camera, as many artists have testified,[7] becomes a kind of prosthesis, an extension of the body that exists to record what is out there. And since, given the nature of the video signal, supplying "realistic" renditions of specific events is no longer a problem, the real challenge for the video artist is to use electronic editing (available since the mid-seventies) to *leave out.* Whereas film is an art of *composition,* of framing, arrangement, structuring, so as to create a particular set of images, video is, Viola suggests, an information art. Given the current glut of books, magazines, newspapers, radio and television programs, records, videotapes, films, and so on in our culture, he points out, "the major task of today is not information production but information management" or retrieval. . . . In this light, the main problem for artists using video these days lies in deciding what *not* to record. Making a videotape, therefore, might not be so much the creation or building up of some thing, but more like the cutting or carving away of everything else until only a specific thing remains" (PC 60). The most interesting connections, in this regard, become those between "areas of low, or ambiguous, information, so-called 'gaps' in recognition" that involve the participation of the viewer. "The process of learning itself," as Viola puts it, "demands that initially one must be confronted with something one does not understand" (PC 67). And he cites René Magritte's well-known comment: "People who look for symbolic meanings fail to grasp the inherent poetry and mystery of the image. No doubt they sense this mystery, but they wish to get rid of it. They are afraid. By asking 'what does this mean?' they express a wish that everything be understandable. But if one does not reject the mystery, one has quite a different response. One asks other things." [8]

Let us see how this works in a specific Viola video. In 1986, the artist released an eighty-nine-minute videotape called *I Do Not Know What It Is I Am Like,* the title taken from the *Rig Veda.* It has five "chapters": "Il Corpo Scuro" (The dark body), "The Language of the Birds," "The Night of Sense," "Stunned by the Drum," and "The Living Flame," all of them related by a concern for the relationship of human to animal consciousness within a natural world of great extremes with respect to climate and topography. The video was two years in the making: during part of that time, Viola was artist-in-residence at the San Diego Zoo.[9] Some of the images were gathered in places as far apart as Wind Cave National Park and Jewel Cave National Monument in South Dakota (where Viola spent several weeks scanning the movements of a freely roaming herd of buffalo and studying cave formations), a glacial lake near Banff in the Canadian Rockies, and the Mahadevi Hindu Temple on the island of Fiji, where Viola attended a week-long firewalking ritual.

But in this parodic nature documentary (a brilliant deconstruction of documentaries like PBS's *Nova* as well as of television travelogues), the exotica are never far removed from the scanning of the artist's own study in Long Beach, California—a rather ordinary room with a large desk, on

Figures 1–5. Outtakes from *I Do Not Know What It Is I Am Like.*

which sits a fluorescent swivel lamp. We first see the artist in chapter 2, reflected in the pupil of the owl, whose watchful presence (see figure 1) is one of the highpoints of *I Do Not Know.* In chapter 3, we see Viola sitting at his desk for minutes at a time, reading and taking notes as he studies the footage of the preceding bird sequence on a tiny monitor (see figure 2). A coffee mug, a pencil, a rock, a little gold jewelry casket, an egg—these are situated on the desk or the neighboring table. Occasionally a cat meows and a dog barks somewhere out of sight. This quiet sequence is followed by the artist's solitary late-night dinner, a slow motion scene that begins as a kind of Dutch still life and gradually becomes a Swiftian cartoon in its huge close-ups of the artist's knife and fork dissecting an ordinary fish—a fish that in turn defamiliarizes those in the blow-ups we have seen in slow motion in the prior chapter, the artist himself reflected in the giant pupils of their huge eyes. In the eating sequence, an ominous silence is punctuated by loud intermittent cutting, crackling, and swallowing sounds that suggest large-scale dismemberment.

In a diary entry of 1980, Viola writes: "I want to look so close at things that their intensity burns through your retina and onto the surface of

your mind. The video camera is well suited to looking closely at things, elevating the commonplace to higher levels of awareness. I want each image to be the first image, to shine with the intensity of its own first-born being" (RKW 78). And he cites, as he frequently does, Rilke's lines, "When a question is posed ceremoniously, / the universe responds."

But the "closeness of things" is based on sound as much as it is on light. "We usually think of the camera," says Viola, "as an 'eye' and the microphone as an 'ear,' but all the senses exist simultanenously in our bodies, interwoven into one system that includes sensory data, neural processing, memory, imagination, and all the mental events of the moment. This all adds up to create the larger phenomenon we call experience" (RKW 151–52). In *I Do Not Know What It Is I Am Like,* reflection plays a central role: the artist sees his reflection in the chrome of the kitchen faucet, in the eyes of fish, buffalo, and birds, in a glass of water on his desk that turns out to have a miniature tree in it—everywhere there are black pupils that give the artist his self-image even as the sounds of water and wind, intermittent barking and chirping create a disquieting counterpoint to the visual. In Viola's work, sound and image are never fully in sync.

One especially arresting sequence, about halfway through the video,

follows the tracking of a snail, emerging very slowly, first one antenna and then the other, from the little gold jewelry box (it looks like a miniature version of Cleopatra's golden barge) on the polished wooden table (see figure 3). Again, the allusion is to still life, this time surrealist rather than seventeenth-century, but the still life comes to life in a frightening way—all the more frightening because what happens is quite normal. As the snail moves out of the field of vision, the camera focuses on an egg we have seen sitting on the artist's table in an earlier shot of his study. Only now that perfect white egg—an elegant shape like an Arp or Brancusi sculpture, a shape that fills up two thirds of the screen and is seen against a totally plain background, has a crack in it (figure 4).

The individual segments in the egg sequence are in real time but the tape is edited so that some phases of the hatching process are omitted. The slow but sure cracking of the egg is, to my mind, an image as fearful as it is astonishing. One wants—at least I want—the egg to look perfect and pristine again, one wants that irritating scar to disappear. And at first the crack is so small that closure seems possible. For a moment, in a painterly blow-up, we seem to be looking at a white-on-white abstract composition with broken texture—an Antoni Tàpies perhaps. But when the egg begins to rock, when the silence (throughout the sequence only a very faint hum is heard) is broken by an almost imperceptible infant's cry, when movement (of what we don't yet know) appears inside the shell, and when the wet and yellow feathers are glimpsed inside it, we know it's all over. The bits of egg-shell litter the previously clean table, the yellowish membrane behind the shell flutters, and now the crack cuts the egg in two. We hear the faint monotonous chirping of the chick and it emerges from its shell, as grotesque a creature as one can imagine (figure 5). The camera slowly scans its face and eye, and then its claws with their long hideous humanoid nails, wiggling and reaching up into the air, even as the shell becomes barely visible behind it. And now the camera finally cuts away, resting its eye on another white shape, this time the coffee mug—a manufactured object, whose whiteness and shiny smooth surface provide a stark contrast to the egg.

The egg-and-chicken sequence is, of course, designed to be seen and heard as part of the larger composition, but even in itself it has striking features. First, its normalcy—what is it but a chicken hatched from its egg?—in a curiously abnormal setting of a table top. Second, its perfectly obvious struggle-of-birth symbolism, rather like that in William Carlos Williams's *Spring and All:* "Rooted we grip down / and begin to awaken." Third, its also obvious eroticism: the dilating opening, the breaking of the membrane, the not quite visible moving organ within. And the contrast,

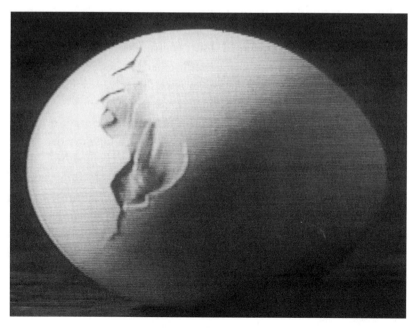

in this connection, between the smooth exterior and the mysterious interior, a kind of heart of darkness, audible before it is visible.

But such connections are only a first step in assessing Viola's composition. In alternately speeding up the birth cycle (all steps in the cycle are not photographed) and slowing it down (shifting to real time in the case of each shot), the artist asks the viewer/listener to consider what "birth" means. No adorable chickens here as in television advertising, no paeans to the "incredible, edible egg." And no tribute to the "beauty" of labor as in a still shot in *The Family of Man* or in one of those elegant television documentaries about "birth." Who wants to be born, one wonders, more important, who wants to give birth when this is what it's like? And yet the tape bears no signs of artistic manipulation: It really *is* the thing itself, as witnessed by the video camera and rewitnessed by us. The artist has not composed his picture as would a filmmaker; he has not added shadows or enhanced the resolution. His focus is less on image as such than on *time*— the time it takes for the shell to crack, for the first chirp to be heard, for the egg to shake, for the membrane to burst. The whole segment lasts only five minutes, shorter than the 8:25 local news broadcast, but it seems to take an eternity, as our eyes take in what they normally—and purposely—

miss. Here slow-down is as important as speed-up. For seconds, almost a minute, at a time, nothing changes, so that the sudden breaking of the shell is as dramatic as sudden movement after stasis is in a Noh drama.

A videotape like Viola's *I Do Not Know* also foregrounds what we might call a fractal sense of reality. Viola does not literally use fractal geometry in his work, but his aesthetic makes much of the "fractals" or irregular fragments perceived in nature when we refine our ways of measuring and describing what we see. "Clouds," as Benoit Mandelbrot remarks in his introduction to *The Fractal Geometry of Nature*, "are not spheres, mountains are not cones, coastlines are not circles, and bark is not smooth, nor does lightning travel in a straight line. . . . Nature exhibits not simply a higher degree but an altogether different level of complexity. . . . The existence of these patterns challenges us to study those forms that Euclid leaves aside as being 'formless,' to investigate the morphology of the 'amorphous.' "[10] Thus the length of a curve—say, the length of the coastline of Britain, to take Mandelbrot's famous example, will vary according to what principle of measurement we apply to it. Far from being the total of individual segments of coastline, length varies according to the scale of units to be included: the greater the detail, which is to say, the smaller the measurable subbays and subpeninsulas, the greater the difficulty in assigning anything like a "true length" to the coastline's curve (BM 25–26).

Much of Viola's reductionism, his slow, patient analysis of a buffalo's eye or the branches of a tree, has to do with this new form of fractal measure. Look at a standard travel poster featuring a glacial lake and the blue oval, surrounded by snowy mountains, and it will not seem all that remarkable. But now take the same lake and focus on an inch of rippling lake water, and all sorts of things become apparent. Again, the dialectic here is with television on the one hand, film on the other. In a given film, the minute particle of lake water would function as a telling detail: it might, for example, refer us to the body drowned on this spot, and the camera would soon get on with it, relating this detail to the larger narrative structure. In commercial television, the detail (say, water bubbles), would function as a signifier: once recognized (look, it's Glacier Lake!) it would be replaced by, say, the bottle of Evian, which represents its real value, or by the Chateau Lake Louise, which represents its real use as a vacation setting. But in video, as Viola sees it, the aim is to slow down the viewer's attention and witness what has always already been there but never quite seen. In the words of Viola's favorite poet William Blake, "If the doors of perception were cleansed, every thing would appear to man as it is, infinite."[11]

Viola is much given to citing Blake, Rilke, and other poets[12] and to referring to his own work as "poetic." From the early *Songs of Innocence* (1978), a visual counterpart to Blake's poems, to the recent *Déserts* (1994), based on the sound landscape of Edgar Varèse's music, Viola has expressed the desire to give his video piece "a form of visual poetry" (RKW 263). And *Slowly Turning Narrative*—a two-channel video installation that juxtaposes a large screen with a mirrored surface on one side to a normal projection screen on the other—uses as voice-over a set of anaphoric lineated phrases, recited slowly and deliberately by Viola. In the course of this monologue, the opening phrase, "the one who goes," undergoes dozens of permutations: "the one who discovers / the one who does / the one who fights / the one who fears" or again, as "the one who spits / the one who pisses / the one who blinks / the one who hears / the one who touches" (RKW 228–31). Text and image are closely related.

What makes such an installation "poetic"? Is "poetic" just another epithet for "imaginative" or "moving" or "intense"? Or does Viola's video have some more meaningful relation to "poetry"? My own take on this difficult question is that the attraction poetry has had for Viola is that it provides video with a turn away from the merely visual. "Traditionally in television," he remarks, "fidelity has been to vision, to the visual image and not to reality, and rarely to the retinal image in the eyeball. . . . The human visual image is binocular, it includes overlapping areas, double images, indistinct edges, and only a very small part of the center, called the fovea, shows focus in rich detail. Of course, human software, the mind, integrates this with information from the other senses. . . . The camera only sees three faces of a cube, for example, yet our hands can tell us that the other three simultaneously exist" (RKW 221).

The *poetic* thus translates roughly as the *other,* the *visionary*—the missing piece in the puzzle, the fourth dimension that "normal" television can never convey. It is a surprisingly romantic notion, as is Viola's repeated insistence that, finally, video art must use the latest technology—hardware and software—to enhance the "development and understanding of the self." "This," Viola insists, "is where the really hard work is. The level of use of the tools is a direct reflection of the level of the user. Chopsticks can either be a simple eating utensil or a deadly weapon, depending on who uses them" (RKW 71).

Such claims for video as the medium of self-discovery, its potential for transcendence and "poetic" vision, may well strike us as excessive. But perhaps Viola's drive to videate poetry and poeticize video, to transfer, for example, Blake's *Songs of Innocence* to the video screen, not by reproducing the poet's words, much less by talking *about* the poetry, but by inventing a visual and sonic analogue that can serve as intertext,[13] is best understood as a form of pragmatism. In a piece called "Between How and Why" (1993), Viola observes:

> The new technologies of image-making are by necessity bringing us back to fundamental questions, whether we want to face them or not. The development of schemes for the creation of images with computers is an investigation into the structure and fabric of the world we observe and participate in. . . . Faced with the content of the direct images and sounds of life in one's daily practice as an artist, questions of form, visual appearance, and the "how" of image-making drop away. You realize that the real work for this time is not abstract, theoretical, and speculative—it is urgent, moral, and practical." (RKW 257)

Urgent, moral, and practical: even as cultural critique continues to insist that "high" art is dead, that, at the very least, there is no domain of art distinct from commodification and popular culture, artists like Viola are rediscovering the function of art as a form of practical knowledge—in Plato's words in the *Ion, techne kai episteme*.[14] At the end of the twentieth century, as Viola puts it, "the artist is not necessarily someone who draws well, but someone who thinks well."

Notes

Essay I: "Postmodernism / Fin de Siècle"

1. David Antin, "Modernism and Postmodernism: Approaching the Present in American Poetry," *boundary 2: an international journal of postmodern literature* 1, no. 1 (fall 1972): 98–133, see 98–99, 109–12. Subsequently cited in the text as DA. This essay, as well as Charles Altieri's "From Symbolist Thought to Immanence" (see n. 2) have recently been reprinted in Paul Bové, ed., *Early Postmodernism: Foundational Essays* (Durham, NC: Duke University Press, 1995), the title of Bové's volume nicely confirming my own configuration here. Antin enlarges on the argument of the *boundary 2* essay, especially with relation to modernism, in an important piece called "Some Questions about Modernism," *Occident* (spring 1974): 7–38.

2. Charles Altieri, "From Symbolist Thought to Immanence: The Ground of Postmodern American Poetics," *boundary 2* 1, no. 3 (spring 1973): 605–41.

3. See Altieri, *Enlarging the Temple: New Directions in American Poetry* (Lewisburg, PA: Bucknell University Press, 1979); James E. B. Breslin, *From Modern to Contemporary: American Poetry, 1945–65* (Chicago: University of Chicago Press, 1984); Marjorie Perloff, *The Poetics of Indeterminacy: Rimbaud to Cage* (Chicago: University of Chicago Press, 1981).

4. Ihab Hassan, "POSTmodernISM: A Paracritical Bibliography," *New Literary History* 3, no. 1 (fall 1971); rpt. in *Paracriticisms: Seven Speculations of the Times* (Urbana: University of Illinois Press, 1975), and *The Postmodern Turn: Essays in Postmodern Theory and Culture* (Columbus: Ohio State University Press, 1987), 25–45. All subsequent references are to this collection, cited as IHPT. Hassan lists seven rather than nine categories because three (elitism, irony, abstraction) are subsumed under "Dehumanization." For purposes of clarity, I have thought it best to break this unit up, since the subsections get as much attention as the other sections. A related essay by Hassan, "The New Gnosticism: Speculations on an Aspect of the Postmodern Mind," appears in *boundary 2* 1, no. 3 (spring 1973): 547–69.

5. Jean-François Lyotard, *The Postmodern Condition: A Report on Knowledge,* trans. from the French by Geoff Bennington and Brian Massumi (Minneapolis: University of Minnesota Press, 1984), xxiv–xxv, 3–8, and esp. 31–37. Subsequently cited in the text as PC. Interestingly, the blurb for the Minnesota edition was written by Ihab Hassan.

6. Fredric Jameson, *Postmodernism; or, The Cultural Logic of Late Capitalism* (Durham, NC: Duke University Press, 1991), 2. Subsequently cited as FJ.

7. See Andreas Huyssen, *After the Great Divide: Modernism, Mass Culture: Postmodernism* (Bloomington and Indianapolis: Indiana University Press, 1986);

Rosalind Krauss, intro. to special issue "High/Low," *October* 56 (spring 1991): 3–4. But cf. Stephen Connor, *Postmodern Culture: An Introduction to Theories of the Contemporary* (Oxford: Basil Blackwell, 1989). Connor puts his finger on the difficulty of making definitive statements about postmodernism, which is supposedly so undefined and open. Referring to Foucault's account in *The Order of Things* of Borges's Chinese encyclopedia as a "structure of radical incommensurability" or "heterotopia," Connor comments: "The obvious problem . . . which Foucault does not here confront, is that, once such a heterotopia has been named, and, more especially, once it has been cited and re-cited, it is no longer this conceptual monstrosity which it once was, for its incommensurability has been in some sense bound, controlled and predictively interpreted, given a centre and illustrative function." In this sense, postmodern theory regularly "names and correspondingly closes off the very world of cultural difference and plurality which it allegedly brings to visibility. What is striking is precisely the degree of consensus in postmodernist discourse that there is no longer any possibility of consensus, the authoritative announcements of the disappearance of final authority, and the promotion and recirculation of a total and comprehensive narrative of a cultural condition in which totality is no longer thinkable" (9–10).

8. For the printed version of the performance piece, in which the voice-over becomes a caption, see Laurie Anderson, *United States* (New York: Harper & Row, 1984), part 1, unpaginated. Craig Owens's reference is to the earlier version in *Americans on the Move,* in which the wording is slightly different. See Owens, "The Discourse of Others: Feminists and Postmodernism" in *The Anti-Aesthetic: Essays on Postmodern Culture,* ed. Hal Foster (Port Townsend, WA: Bay Press, 1983), 60; subsequently cited in the text as AA.

9. Herman Rapaport, " 'Can You Say Hello?': Laurie Anderson's *United States,*" *Theatre Journal* 38, no. 3 (October 1986): 340.

10. When Owens does briefly mention Luce Irigaray, Hélène Cixous, and Monique Wittig, he refers to their work as "the writing of women influenced by Lacanian psychoanalysis" (AA 63).

11. Brenda K. Marshall, *Teaching the Postmodern: Fiction and Theory* (New York and London: Routledge, 1992). Subsequently cited as BM.

12. In the five years since this essay first appeared, this has increasingly been the tenor of discussion. See, e.g., John McGowan, *Postmodernism and Its Critics* (Ithaca: Cornell University Press, 1991) and Christopher Norris, *The Truth about Postmodernism* (Oxford, 1993). A recent essay for *Critical Inquiry* by Charles Altieri, once the proponent of a postmodern theory, begins with the sentence, "I think postmodernism is now dead as a theoretical concept and, more important, as a way of developing cultural frameworks influencing how we shape theoretical concepts." See "What Is Living and What Is Dead in American Postmodernism: Establishing the Contemporaneity of Some American Poetry," *Critical Inquiry* 22 (summer 1996): 764. As Altieri's title suggests, he is not averse to salvaging certain

aspects of the postmodern paradigm: it is, as he suggests in his appendix (788–89), the increasingly political definitions of postmodernism that must go.

13. David Harvey, "Looking Back on Postmodernism," *Architectural Digest* (1990): 12. Harvey is here rethinking some of the notions in his *The Condition of Postmodernity* (Oxford: Blackwell, 1989).

14. Charles Bernstein, *A Poetics* (Cambridge: Harvard University Press, 1992), 4. Subsequently cited in the text as CB.

15. Henry Louis Gates Jr., "Goodbye, Columbus? Notes on the Culture of Criticism," *American Literary History* 3, no. 4 (winter 1991): 716.

16. Benjamin Alire Sáenz, *Calendar of Dust* (Seattle: Broken Moon Press, 1991), 45–46.

17. Alfred Arteaga, *Cantos* (Berkeley: Chusma House, 1991), 28–31.

18. Steve McCaffery, *Theory of Sediment* (Vancouver: Talon Books, 1991), 38–39. A related poetic text, *The Black Debt,* is discussed in my *Radical Artifice: Writing Poetry in the Age of Media* (Chicago: University of Chicago Press, 1992), chap. 4 passim. See also essay 14 below.

19. Johanna Drucker, *Narratology* (New York: Druckwerk, 1994), unpaginated last page.

Essay 2: "Tolerance and Taboo"

1. "How many kilometers it took to make us feel we were finally on the threshold of exoticism!" Michel Leiris, *L'Afrique fantôme* (1934; Paris: Editions Gallimard, 1981), 226; my translation. Subsequently cited in the text as AF.

2. Marianna Torgovnick, *Gone Primitive: Savage Intellects, Modern Lives* (Chicago: University of Chicago Press, 1990), 21. Subsequently cited in the text as GP. In the *New York Times Book Review,* 24 June 1990, Arthur C. Danto pronounced *Gone Primitive* "powerful" and "provocative," "a superb book." In *Modern Philology* 89 (February 1992), Sander Gilman similarly declares, "Marianna Torgovnick has now provided us all (academic and nonacademic specialists) with a brilliant, exciting, and innovative reading of our 'modern' . . . fascination with the image of the primitive" (437). And he concludes by remarking, "I put down this book feeling that cultural studies in this country had come a lot further than I had imagined" (439). And in "Otherness Is in the Details," *The Nation* (5 November 1990): 530–36, Micaela di Leonardo, who does comment on some of the book's "key lacunas," calls Torgovnick's goal "laudable," her critique of humanism "valuable," and "her interpretations of the shifting meanings and wildly enhanced monetary value of primitive art . . . particularly acute" (533).

3. James Clifford, *The Predicament of Culture: Twentieth-Century Ethnography, Literature, and Art* (Cambridge: Harvard University Press, 1988), 42. Subsequently cited as JCP.

4. See, for example, GP 17–18. Torgovnick also cites Edward Said and Christopher Miller as ignoring the gender issue. In keeping with her own assessment, Torgovnick's book has been marketed as a "corrective" to Clifford's. In her book blurb, for example, Catharine R. Stimpson calls *Gone Primitive* "an extraordinary account of the ways in which race, gender, and a terrible romance with 'the primitive' have structured Western culture."

5. Leiris is now coming into his own in the United States. See the special number *On Leiris, Yale French Studies* 81 (1992), which contains an excerpt of Lydia Davis's new translation of *Fourbis* and essays by Marc Blanchard, Edouard Glissant, Francis Marmande, Jean-Christophe Bailly, Jean-Luc Nancy, Denis Hollier, Leah D. Lewitt, Michèle Richman, and J. B. Pontalis, as well as extracts from earlier essays by Emmanuel Levinas and Maurice Blanchot. This issue is subsequently cited in the text as YFS. For a good recent overview, see Richard Sieburth, "The Librettist of Self," *Times Literary Supplement*, 5 March 1993, 3–4.

6. I have seen all these except the Livre de Poche, for which I owe the relevant information to Philippe Lejeune's important *Lire Leiris* (Paris: Editions Klincksieck, 1975), 109–10. Lejeune points out that the Livre de Poche blow-up projects the idea of violence exercised on oneself (Lucrece) onto the figure of Judith, whereas the Folio card-game image, "ne produit pas pour autant l'effet érotique du nu de Cranach."

7. Michel Leiris, *Manhood*, trans. Richard Howard (San Francisco: North Point, 1984), 94–95. Subsequently cited as MLM. Leiris, *L'Age d'homme* (Paris: Gallimard, 1939), 142–43. Subsequently cited as LD.

8. GP 111. For a good treatment of the complexity of Leiris's representation, see Michèle Richman, "Leiris's *L'Age d'homme*: Politics and the Sacred in Everyday Ethnography," YFS 91–110. Richman writes, "In [Leiris's] favorite mythological pantheon, Judith and Lucretia transform their horrific situations into parables of strength, offering dramas in which the victim/executioner relationship is played out with unexpected heroism" (95). But "the particular mixture of sacred terror and pity [Judith and Lucretia] evoke is tinged with a sense of remorse due to [the narrator's] own cowardice as well as cruelty, which in turn promote the 'crainte superstitieuse d'un châtiment' " (99).

9. Paul Gilroy warns of this ahistoricism (vis-à-vis the treatment of Black Britain) in "Cultural Studies and Ethnic Absolutism," in *Cultural Studies*, ed. Lawrence Grossberg, Cary Nelson, and Paula Treichler (New York and London: Routledge, 1992), 187–98.

10. Cf. Leiris's "Civilization," one of the short pieces written for *Documents* (1929), collected in *Brisées* (1966), trans. Lydia Davis (San Francisco: North Point, 1989):

However little taste one might have for proposing metaphors as explanations, civilization may be compared without too much inexactness to the thin greenish layer—the living magma and the odd detritus—that forms on the surface of calm water and sometimes solidifies into a crust, until an eddy comes to break it up. All our moral practices and our polite customs, that radiantly colored cloak that hides the coarseness of our dangerous instincts, all those lovely forms of culture we are so proud of—since it is thanks to them that we can call ourselves "civilized"—are ready to disappear at the slightest turbulence, to shatter at the slightest impact (like the thin mirror on a fingernail whose polish cracks or roughens) allowing our horrifying *primitiveness* to appear in the interstices, revealed by the fissures just as hell might be revealed by earthquakes. (19)

11. Even this assumption is unfounded, since the circumcision practices described at length in the passage Torgovnick cites are those of men, not women.

12. See James Clifford, Headnote to section on "Phantom Africa," *Sulfur* 15 (1986), "Special Section: New Translations of the Work of Michel Leiris," ed. James Clifford: 42. This journal issue is subsequently cited as S. For the original, see AF, 350: "Amertume. Ressentiment contre l'ethnographie, qui fait prendre cette position si inhumaine d'observateur, dans des circonstances ou il faudrait s'abandonner."

Excerpts from Leiris's *La Possession et ses aspects théâtraux chez les Éthiopiens de Gondar* (1958), which deals specifically with the Zâr cult, may be found in S 113–17.

13. John Guillory, *Cultural Capital: The Problem of Literary Canon Formation* (Chicago: University of Chicago Press, 1993), 22.

14. Velimir Khlebnikov, "My Own" (1919), cited in Rainer Crone and David Moos, *Kazimir Malevich: The Climax of Disclosure* (Chicago: University of Chicago Press, 1991), 137.

15. Cited by Charlotte Douglas, intro. to *Collected Works of Velimir Khlebnikov*, vol. 1, *Letters and Theoretical Writings,* trans. Paul Schmidt, ed. Charlotte Douglas (Cambridge: Harvard University Press, 1987), 8.

16. Michel Leiris, "Glossary: My Glosses' Ossuary" (1925), in *Brisées,* 3–4.

17. Lyn Hejinian, *Oxota: A Short Russian Novel* (Great Barrington, MA: The Figures, 1991), 235. For discussion of Hejinian's long poem, see essay 10 below.

Essay 3: " 'Barbed-Wire Entanglements' "

1. *Poetry* 37 (January 1931): 231.

2. *Poetry* 37 (March 1931): 332–33.

3. Letters to Louis Zukofsky, 5 July 1928 and 18 July 1928, in *The Selected Letters of William Carlos Williams,* ed. John C. Thirlwall (New York: New Directions, 1957; rpt. 1984), 101. Subsequently cited in the text as WCWL.

4. "Memory of V. I. Ulianov" is the first poem in the sequence "29 Poems," first published in *All: The Collected Short Poems, 1923–1964;* see Louis Zukofsky, *Complete Short Poetry* (Baltimore: Johns Hopkins University Press, 1991), 21–22. This edition is subsequently cited in the text as CPLZ.

5. Ezra Pound, letter to Louis Zukofsky, 24 October [1930], in *Pound/Zukofsky: Selected Letters of Ezra Pound and Louis Zukofsky,* ed. Barry Ahearn (New York: New Directions, 1987), 45, 47, 49. Subsequently cited in the text as PZ.

6. Ezra Pound, "A Retrospect," *Literary Essays of Ezra Pound,* ed. T. S. Eliot (London: Faber & Faber, 1954), 5.

7. Richard Johns (born Richard Johnson in 1904) was the son of a well-known Boston attorney named Benjamin N. Johnson, who had studied with William James at Harvard. The young Johns attended Classical High School in Lynn, Massachusetts, but dropped out before graduating and did not go on to college; rather, he traveled with his father to Greece, haunted the Boston bookshops and read voraciously, wrote poems and short stories, and between 1927 and 1929 studied comparative poetry and literary theory at Columbia. Having no regular job, Johns decided in the late twenties to start a literary magazine. For this background and for an excellent scholarly study of the *Pagany* archive, with selections from the magazine itself, see *A Return to PAGANY: The History, Correspondence, and Selections from a Little Magazine, 1929–1932,* ed. Stephen Halpert with Richard Johns (Boston: Beacon Press, 1969). This book is subsequently cited in the text as ARP.

8. This role is usually thought to have been played by Williams: see Stephen Halpert in ARP, passim. But Peter Quartermain, who has read the unpublished (and currently inaccessible) correspondence between Richard Johns and Louis Zukofsky, has suggested to me in conversation that the poetry selections may well reflect the choices of Zukofsky rather than Williams. This would explain why Zukofsky is never listed under "Contributors' Notes" in *Pagany* and why Johns published so many of the Objectivists at a time when they were little known.

9. Richard Johns, "Announcement," *Pagany* 1, no. 1 (January–March 1930): 1. Subsequently cited in the text as P, followed by volume, issue, and page number. For Johns's early reading of admiration of Williams, see the correspondence between the two in ARP 3–5 and Halpert's commentary beginning on 6.

10. Mary Butts's first husband was the English poet, critic, printer and publisher John Rodker, who befriended Pound in Paris and worked with him on various projects; the surrealist poet Georges Hugnet, of whose friendship with Stein more below, had written appreciative essays on Virgil Thomson; Atget, virtually unknown at the time of his death except by the surrealist cenacle and other fellow artists, was rescued from oblivion by the photographer Berenice Abbott, who saved his negatives, printed them, and brought them to the United States for exhibition and sale when she returned to her native country from Paris in 1929.

Johns's chief contact with Rodker, Thomson, Hugnet et al. was Sherry Mangan, Harvard graduate, classicist, and cosmopolitan writer-critic, whom Johns had befriended in Boston; see ARP 17–20. On 28 August 1929, Mangan wrote Johns from Paris that he would round up some of the foreign and expatriate talent. "Djuna [Barnes]," he remarked, "is getting very snooty, but may be approachable" (see ARP 18). As it turned out, Barnes, in contrast to Stein, never published in *Pagany*.

11. Fredric Jameson, *Postmodernism; or, The Cultural Logic of Late Capitalism* (Durham, NC: Duke University Press, 1991), 17.

12. Mary Butts, "Brightness Falls," *From Altar to Chimney-Piece: Selected Stories of Mary Butts,* preface by John Ashbery (Kingston, NY: McPherson, 1992), 203. Subsequently cited in the text as MB.

13. P1, 1:39. Johns published Stein on the warm recommendation of Williams, who insisted that his own essay on Stein (see below) be published in the first issue. In response to this issue, Stein wrote Johns (ARP 129–30), "I like you and Pagany, so there we are. Later I will send you a little thing when it gets done, a play in which only contemporaries appear, it will amuse you, and Virgil may later do music for it, anyway, we are all active and pleasant."

14. See Williams, *Selected Essays* (New York: New Directions, 1954), 113–20, and 162–66. In the latter essay, Williams writes, "Stein has gone systematically to work smashing every connotation that words have ever had, in order to get them back clean" (163).

15. Stein met Georges Hugnet, a young surrealist poet, through Virgil Thomson in 1927. He admired her work, translated some of her portraits and selections from *The Making of Americans,* and together they translated *Composition as Explanation.* She then offered to reciprocate by translating into English his suite of poems called *Enfances.* But translation was not Stein's game, and, as she proceeded, her version became increasingly "free," Hugnet's thirty stanzas being rendered by prose paragraphs as well as brief sentences and his erotic imagery being almost entirely elided. Hugnet nevertheless planned to publish the two versions in book form, again side by side, but Stein objected to what she saw as her subsidiary position in the venture and broke off all further contact with Hugnet, as her new title *Before the Flowers of Friendship Faded Friendship Faded* suggests. See Richard Bridgman, *Gertrude Stein in Pieces* (New York: Oxford University Press, 1970), 201–2; *A Gertrude Stein Companion,* ed. Bruce Kellner (New York: Greenwood Press, 1988), 24, 207; James R. Mellow, *Charmed Circle: Gertrude Stein and Company* (New York: Avon, 1975), 408–12; Renée Riese Hubert, "Gertrude Stein and the Making of Frenchmen," *SubStance* 59 (1989): 71–92.

In *The Autobiography of Alice B. Toklas* (in *Selected Writings of Gertrude Stein,* ed. Carl Van Vechten [New York: Vintage, 1972], 218) "Alice" recalls "In the meantime, Georges Hugnet wrote a poem called 'Enfance.' Gertrude Stein offered to translate it for him, but instead wrote a poem about it. This at first pleased Georges Hugnet too much and then did not please him at all. Gertrude Stein then called the poem 'Before the Flowers of Friendship Faded Friendship Faded.'"

16. Stephen Halpert reproduces Stein's telegram (22 December 1930) to Johns, which reads: "TITLE MY POEM IS POEM PRITTEN ON PFANCES OF GEORGES HUGNET IMPERATIVE" (see ARP 216).

17. Marianne DeKoven, *A Different Language: Gertrude Stein's Experimental Writing* (Madison: University of Wisconsin Press, 1983), 105–6.

18. Peter Quartermain, " 'The Tattle of Tongueplay': Mina Loy's *Love Songs*," forthcoming in *Mina Loy: Essays on the Poetry* (Orono, ME: National Poetry Foundation, 1997).

19. The allusion is to Eliot's "The Hollow Men," part 5: "Between the idea / And the reality / Between the motion / And the Act / Falls the Shadow. . . . Between the desire / and the spasm / Between the potency / And the existence / Between the essence / And the descent / Falls the Shadow / *For Thine is the Kingdom.*" See T. S. Eliot, *The Complete Poems and Plays, 1909–1950* (New York: Harcourt, Brace, and World, 1962), 58–59.

20. James E. Devlin, *Erskine Caldwell* (Boston: Twayne Publishers, 1984), 139.

21. Johns was introduced to Caldwell's work by Charles Henri Ford, who was then editing *Blues: A Magazine of New Rhythms,* a journal which went through nine issues in 1929–30 and shared many of *Pagany's* predilections, including a taste for Williams, Rexroth, and the objectivist poets. Caldwell was a willing contributor because he was, at this moment, involved in a censorship suit over his first novel, *The Bastard; Hound and Horn* had turned down "Hours before Eternity," evidently for fear of obscenity charges, so that this and the earlier "Strawberry Season" (printed in the first issue) fell into Johns's lap; see ARP 25–31, 219–21.

22. Kenneth Burke, "Caldwell: Maker of Grotesques," *New Republic* 82 (1935): 232–35; rpt. in *The Philosophy of Literary Form: Studies in Symbolic Action,* 3d ed. (Berkeley: University of California Press, 1973), 350–60, 350–51. Subsequently cited in the text as KB.

23. See *In Love, in Sorrow: The Complete Correspondence of Charles Olson and Edward Dahlberg,* ed. Paul Christensen (New York: Paragon House, 1990). Dahlberg is not mentioned in Cary Nelson's *Repression and Recovery: Modern American Poetry and the Politics of Cultural Memory, 1910–45* (Madison: University of Wisconsin Press, 1989). Subsequently cited in the text as CNRR.

24. See CPLZ 23–24, 27, 36.

25. Burton Hatlen, "Zukofsky, Wittgenstein, and the Poetics of Absence," *Sagetrieb* 1, no. 1 (winter 1982): 66, 76. I am greatly indebted to this important discussion, which first suggested to me that thirties poetics was "different," not just in degree but in kind, from its modernist forebear.

26. See, e.g., Joseph M. Conte, *Unending Design: The Forms of Postmodern Poetry* (Ithaca: Cornell University Press, 1991), 142–54. "Virtually all the poems of *All* are songs," says Conte (151).

27. For the details, which are interesting in that Johns's case is not at all un-

typical of young men who saw their trust funds and inheritances shrink to almost nothing as a result of the Depression, see ARP 423–24, 445–46, 476–80.

28. CNRR 114. Cf. Nelson's preface and introduction to *Edwin Rolfe: Collected Poems,* ed. Cary Nelson and Jefferson Hendricks (Urbana: University of Illinois Press, 1993). Nelson calls Rolfe "one of the more inventive political poets of the Great Depression . . . the writer Americans who fought in the Spanish Civil War regard as their poet laureate" (13).

29. For another good example of Rolfe's poetic (at least before he wrote his Spanish Civil War poems, which use somewhat more concrete vocabulary), see "Eventualities" in P3, 1:45–46:

> when I shall   laughing   find the giddy
> spring receiving me   aware of lunacy
> in the bestowal raptly hung upon a threat
>
> When both of us   quite dead
> declare the cleaving done for both of us
> quite dead
>   when laughter loses resonance
> and grates upon the raucous wheel still
> turning   swiftly
>
>   then no more the blending
> will demand our fealty
>   no more the sugar
> in the cup be stirred against its chemistry
> no more the listless villified
>   no more defied
> the murdering of many moments built of sun
> (though shades be drawn from dawn to darkening)
> no more the thou cupped close. . . .

Here the spacing is evidently designed to look "modernist" but the well-worn Poetic Diction—"giddy / spring," "bestowal raptly hung," "cleaving," "fealty," "the listless villified"—belies this modernism at every turn.

30. *Partisan Review* 1, no. 1:32; the poem is reprinted in *Edwin Rolfe: Collected Poems,* ed. Nelson and Hendricks, 89–91.

31. Henri Meschonnic, *Théorie du Rythme* (Paris: Editions Verdier, 1982); Anthony Easthope, *Poetry as Discourse* (London: Methuen, 1983).

1. Richard Wilbur, "Love Calls Us to the Things of This World," *Things of This World* (New York: Harcourt, Brace, and World, 1956), 5–6.

2. According to Jed Rasula's very useful table of anthology appearances between 1945 and 1990, Wilbur is Number One, his inclusion in seventy anthologies surpassing even the sixty-seven of Robert Lowell. See Rasula, *The American Poetry Wax Museum: Reality Effects, 1940–1990* (Urbana, IL: National Council of Teachers of English, 1996), 509. This text, subsequently cited as WM, is indispensable for anyone studying the poetics of the period.

3. Richard Wilbur, in *Poets in Progress* (1966); rpt. in Richard Ellmann and Robert O'Clair, *Modern Poems: A Norton Introduction,* 2d ed. (New York and London: W. W. Norton, 1973), 575, n. 6.

4. See *The Contemporary Poet as Artist and Critic: Eight Symposia,* ed. Anthony Ostroff (Boston and Toronto: Little, Brown, 1964), 2–21. Subsequently cited in the text as AO.

5. Peter Stitt et al., "The Art of Poetry: Richard Wilbur," *Paris Review* 72 (Winter 1977); rpt. in *Conversations with Richard Wilbur,* ed. William Butts (Jackson: University Press of Mississippi, 1990), 200. Subsequently cited as Butts.

6. Carl Sandburg, preface, *The Family of Man: The Greatest Photographic Exhibition of All Time—503 Pictures from 68 Countries—Created by Edward Steichen for the Museum of Modern Art* (New York: Museum of Modern Art, 1955), unpaginated.

7. "The war was over," Frank later recalled, "and I wanted to get out of Switzerland. I didn't want to build my future there. The country was too closed, too small for me." Soon after his arrival in 1947, he wrote his parents, "this country is really a free country. A person can do what he wants. Nobody asks to see your identification papers." See Martin Gasser, "Zurich to New York: 'Robert Frank, Swiss, unobtrusive, nice. . . ,'" in *Robert Frank: Moving Out,* ed. Sarah Greenough and Philip Brookman (Washington, DC: National Gallery of Art, 1994), 46–47. Subsequently cited in the text as RF. Frank himself also had a few pictures in the *Family of Man* show.

8. Jack Kerouac, introduction, *The Americans* (New York: Grove Press, 1959; rpt. New York, Zurich, and Berlin: SCALO Publishers in association with the National Gallery of Art, Washington, 1994), 6. Subsequently cited as RFA.

9. John Brumfield, "'The Americans' and the Americans," *Afterimage* 8, no. 1–2 (summer 1980): 10.

10. The phrase comes from "Memories of West Street and Lepke," Robert Lowell, *Life Studies* and *For the Union Dead* (New York: Farrar, Straus, & Giroux, 1959, 1964), 85. A neighboring poem "Man and Wife" opens with the line "Tamed by *Miltown,* we lie on mother's bed" (87), referring to the first of the commonly used tranquilizers.

11. Mistrust of "Tricky Dick" is a central theme of political articles in 1956. See, e.g., Selig S. Harrison, "The Old Guard's Young Pretender," *New Republic*, 30 August; "Did Ike Really Want Nixon?" *Colliers*, 26 October.

12. The equivalent today would be about four thousand dollars a month.

13. For this story, see Allen Ginsberg, *Journals Mid-Fifties 1954–1958*, ed. Gordon Ball (New York: HarperCollins, 1995), 3–7; James E. B. Breslin, *From Modern to Contemporary: American Poetry 1945–1965* (Chicago: University of Chicago Press, 1984), 94–95. Subsequently cited in the text as JEB.

14. In the case of foreign high culture, as this list reminds us, "writer" almost invariably equaled "male writer," Simone de Beauvoir's *Mandarins* being a major exception. At the same time—and this puts an interesting spin on the culture industry—the U.S. novel (as well as a fair amount of the poetry, from Leonie Adams, Elizabeth Bishop, and Louise Bogan, to Babette Deutsch, Carolyn Kizer, Elizabeth Spencer, and Ruth Stone) was largely the domain of women. Katharine Anne Porter's *Ship of Fools*, serialized in the *Atlantic* in 1956, was one of the major literary events of a year that also boasted the publication of Mary McCarthy's *A Charmed Life* and Caroline Gordon's *The Malfactors*. An important story by Flannery O'Connor, "Greenleaf," appeared in the summer issue of the *Kenyon Review*. And, although I haven't done a count, reviewers in the mainstream journals and little magazines were more likely to be women in 1956 than in 1996: Bishop, Miles, and Kizer reviewed frequently for the *New Republic*, McCarthy, Vivienne Koch, Mary O. Hivnor, and Margaret Avison for the *Kenyon Review*, Dorothy Van Ghent and Marie Boroff for the *Yale Review*, and so on. Given the large number of women among fiction readers, women were allowed—indeed encouraged—to write fiction, but they were almost never editors or publishers, and, with such exceptions as Hannah Arendt and Suzanne Langer, not eligible to be major "thinkers."

15. As Wilbur put it, "I have no case whatever against controlled free verse. Yet I think it is absurd to feel that free verse—which has only been with us in America for a little over a hundred years—has definitely 'replaced' measure and rhyme and other traditional instruments." See "Craft Interview with Richard Wilbur" (1972), in *The Craft of Poetry: Interviews from the "New York Quarterly,"* ed. William Packard (New York: Doubleday, 1974), 183–84.

16. Brumfield, "'The Americans,'" *Afterimage*, 7.

17. Allen Ginsberg, "Robert Frank to 1985—A Man," in Anne Wilkes Tucker and Philip Brookman, *Robert Frank: New York to Nova Scotia*, exhibition catalog (Museum of Fine Arts, Houston; Boston: Little, Brown, 1986), 74.

18. O'Hara dated most of his manuscripts carefully. According to Donald Allen's notes for *The Collected Poems of Frank O'Hara* (1971; Berkeley: University of California Press, 1995), the poems on pages 239–64 all date from 1956. Among these we find such key poems as "To John Wieners," "In Memory of My Feelings," "Digression on *Number 1, 1948*," and "Why I Am Not a Painter," as well

as "A Step Away from Them," which is discussed below. The *Collected Poems* is subsequently cited as FOH.

19. Allen Ginsberg, "Howl," *Collected Poems 1947–1980* (New York: Harper & Row, 1984), 126. Subsequently cited in the text as AGCP. "Howl" first appeared in *Howl and Other Poems,* The Pocket Poet Series Number 4 (San Francisco: City Lights, 1956).

20. AGCP 146. "America" first appeared in *Howl and Other Poems,* 31–34.

21. Warren Tallman, "Mad Song: Allen Ginsberg's San Francisco Poems," *Open Letter,* 3d ser. (winter 1976–77); rpt. in *On the Poetry of Allen Ginsberg,* ed. Lewis Hyde (Ann Arbor: University of Michigan Press, 1984), 384.

22. Ginsberg avoided the draft because of his nearsightedness, a common fifties exemption.

23. The phrase is Warren Tallman's; see "Mad Song," 384.

24. See William Carlos Williams, "Asphodel, That Greeny Flower," *The Collected Poems of William Carlos Williams,* vol. 2, *1939–62,* ed. Christopher Mac-Gowan (New York: New Directions, 1988), 321–25.

25. FOH 257–58. The poem is dated 16 August 1956 and was first published in *Evergreen Review* 1, no. 3 (1957).

26. I have commented on the specific stylistic traits in this and related poems in *Frank O'Hara: Poet among Painters* (New York: George Braziller, 1977), 124–39. Subsequently cited as MPFO.

27. For a discussion of O'Hara's "Personism: A Manifesto," see MPFO 1–30, 135–39; cf. Charles Altieri, "Varieties of Immanentist Expression," *Enlarging the Temple: New Directions in American Poetry during the 1960s* (Lewisburg, Pa.: Bucknell University Press, 1979), 108–22. As late as 1970, Richard Wilbur dismissed O'Hara, Ashbery, and Kenneth Koch as not of "sufficient consequence to deserve such a magnificent title as the New York School." "The limitation of this school," he added, "is the limitation which the dada tradition has—the inclination to silliness." See Willard Pate and Panel/1970, "An Interview with Richard Wilbur," in BUTTS 68–69.

28. See, e.g., William Atwood, "Fear Underlies the Conflict," *Look,* 3 April 1956, 27.

29. *Some Trees,* published in an edition of 817 copies, was, strictly speaking, Ashbery's second book. His first, *Turandot and Other Poems,* was a paper-covered pamphlet published by the Tibor de Nagy Gallery in 1950 in an edition of 300 copies. For bibliographical information, see David K. Kermani, *John Ashbery: A Comprehensive Bibliography* (New York and London: Garland, 1976). In an unpublished interview of 1974, Ashbery gave Kermani an account of how W. H. Auden happened to award the Yale Younger Poets Prize to *Some Trees,* although, so Ashbery believes, he really didn't like it very much (see Kermani, 6). It was Auden who referred to the book's style as "surrealistic."

30. Cited by Brad Gooch in his *City Poet: The Life and Times of Frank O'Hara* (New York: Alfred A. Knopf, 1993), 190.

31. John Ashbery, *Selected Poems* (New York: Viking, 1983), 3. Subsequently cited as JA.

32. The two are Herbert Morris's "Twenty-Eight" and Theodore Holmes's "The Life of the Estate," the latter containing such passages as "The house sits up on the hill; and has that satisfied look / Of a head taking credit for the comfort the body enjoys in bed." See *Kenyon Review* 18, no. 2 (spring 1956): 270–75. "Two Scenes" is on 272–73.

33. Michael Davidson, letter to the author, 29 July 1996. I am indebted to Davidson for much helpful advice and useful debate throughout this paper.

Essay 5: "Lucent and Inescapable Rhythms"

1. Stephen Fredman, *Poet's Prose: The Crisis in American Verse* (Cambridge: Cambridge University Press, 1983), 1. Subsequently cited as SFPP. A second expanded edition of this book was published by Cambridge in 1990, after this essay was written.

2. Unpublished letter to the members of the Stanford University English Department, Stanford, California, March 1984.

3. Charles O. Hartman, *Free Verse: An Essay on Prosody* (Princeton: Princeton University Press, 1980), 11. Subsequently cited in the text as COH.

4. Richard Lanham, *Analyzing Prose* (New York: Charles Scribner's Sons, 1983), 79.

5. "Historiquement, poétiquement, linguistiquement, il y a des différences de degré, non de nature, entre *les proses et les vers.*" See Henri Meschonnic, *Critique du rythme: Anthropologie historique du langage* (Paris: Editions Verdier, 1982), 458, and see chap. 9, "Prose, Poésie," 393–518 passim. The book is subsequently cited as HM. Translations are my own.

6. Anthony Easthope, *Poetry as Discourse* (London: Methuen, 1983), 24. Subsequently cited as AE.

7. J. W. von Goethe, *Briefe,* Hamburger Ausgabe, ed. Karl Robert Mandelkow, 4 vols. (Hamburg: Christian Wegner, 1962–67), 1:314–15. Translations here and of the poetry are mine. Of the countless Goethe biographies, the English-speaking reader may find especially interesting the classic *Life of Goethe* by George Henry Lewis, 3d. ed. (London: Smith, Edler, 1875).

8. Goethe, *Werke,* 6 vols. (Wiesbaden: Insel, 1949–52), 1:59. Note that this is the second of two short lyrics by the same title. The earlier one (1776) has the opening line, "Der du von dem Himmel bist." In Insel's more recent edition for the Deutscher Klassiker Verlag, "Wandrers Nachtlied" is retitled "Ein Gleiches" and reads as follows:

Über allen Gipfeln
Ist Ruh'
In allen Wipfeln
Spürest Du
Kaum einen Hauch;
Die Vögelein schweigen im Walde.
Warte nur! Balde
Ruhest du auch.

Since the minor orthographic changes (an apostrophe after "Ruh" in line 2 to indicate the elision of the "e" of "Ruhe" and the substitution of an exclamation point for a comma in line 5) don't affect the poem's metrical form, I have preferred to use the earlier, more familiar version.

9. Arthur Rimbaud, *Oeuvres,* ed. Susanne Bernard (Paris: Garnier, 1966), liv–lxii. This edition is subsequently cited as SBAR.

10. Friedrich Engels, *The Condition of the Working Class in England,* cited in Edward J. Ahearn, *Rimbaud: Visions and Habitations* (Berkeley: University of California Press, 1983), 239. Subsequently cited as RV.

11. SBAR 273. The translation used is Edward J. Ahearn's; see RV 322 as well as the interesting commentary on 323.

12. See Marjorie Perloff: *The Poetics of Indeterminacy: Rimbaud to Cage* (Princeton: Princeton University Press, 1981; Evanston, IL: Northwestern University Press, 1983), chap. 2 passim. Subsequently cited as MPPI.

13. See LeRoy Breunig, "Why France?" in *The Prose Poem in France: Theory and Practice,* ed. Mary Ann Caws and Hermine Riffaterre (New York: Columbia University Press, 1983), 7–11. Subsequently cited as PPF.

14. The so-called "Lettres du Voyant" are (1) a letter to Georges Izambard, 13 May 1871; and (2) a letter to Paul Démeny, 15 May 1871. They appear with facing English translations in Arthur Rimbaud, *Complete Works,* ed. Wallace Fowlie (Chicago: University of Chicago Press, 1966), 302–11.

15. Albert Sonnenfeld, "L'Adieu suprème and Ultimate Composure: The Boundaries of the Prose Poem," PPF 200–201.

16. Michel Beaujour, "Short Epiphanies: Two Contextual Approaches to the French Prose Poem," PPF 55–56.

17. The essay was submitted to *Poetry* in 1913, but Harriet Monroe returned it as incomprehensible. The text is cited in Mike Weaver, *William Carlos Williams: The American Background* (Cambridge: Cambridge University Press, 1971), 82–83.

18. See Hugh Kenner, *The Pound Era* (Berkeley: University of California Press, 1971), 58. Subsequently cited as HK.

19. *The Collected Poems of William Carlos Williams,* vol. 1, *1909–39,* ed. A. Walton Litz and Christopher MacGowan (New York: New Directions, 1986), 85–86.

20. Allen Ginsberg, "Williams in a World of Objects," in *William Carlos Wil-*

liams: Man and Poet, ed. Carroll F. Terrell (Orono, ME: National Poetry Foundation, 1983), 36.

21. Williams, "Author's Introduction to *The Wedge*" (1944), in *Selected Essays of William Carlos Williams* (New York: Random House, 1954), 256. Subsequently cited as WCWE.

22. Martin Heidegger, *Poetry, Language, Thought,* trans. Albert Hofstadter (New York: Harper & Row, 1971), 216.

23. See, on this point, AE 13–18. Easthope provides here a convenient summary of Derridean-Lacanian theory as it might be applied to the question of lyric form.

24. *Still* was first published in 1974, in a limited edition of 160 copies with original etchings by Stanley William Hayter (Milan: M'Arte Edizioni, 1974). It was translated into French as *Immobile* and published in Paris by Les Editions de Minuit in 1976. The English version is included in *Fizzles* (New York: Grove Press, 1976), where it appears as #7, 47–51. All references in my text are to this edition. For the publishing history, see Carlton Lake, *No Symbols Where None Intended: A Catalogue of Books, Manuscripts and Other Material Relating to Samuel Beckett in the Collections of the Humanities Research Center* (Austin, TX: Humanities Research Center, 1984), 160–62.

25. Enoch Brater, "Still/Beckett: The Essential and the Incidental," *Journal of Modern Literature, Samuel Beckett Special Number,* ed. Enoch Brater, 6 (February 1977): 8.

26. On the concept of "copresence" in Williams's work, see J. Hillis Miller, *Poets of Reality: Six Twentieth Century Writers* (1965; rpt. New York: Atheneum, 1969), 285–359, esp. 287–92.

27. John Ashbery, *Three Poems* (New York: Viking Press, 1972), 38; John Ashbery, *As We Know* (New York: Viking Press, 1979), 74.

28. Charles Bernstein, *Islets/Irritations* (New York: Jordan Davies, 1983), 47.

29. See Deirdre Bair, *Samuel Beckett: A Biography* (New York: Harcourt Brace Jovanovich, 1978), 606–7.

30. Wallace Stevens, "The Snow Man," *The Palm at the End of the Mind: Selected Poems and a Play,* ed. Holly Stevens (New York: Alfred A. Knopf, 1984), 54. Subsequently cited as WS.

31. "A Mythology Reflects its Region," WS 398.

Essay 6: "After Free Verse"

1. See the entry "Vers Libre" by Clive Scott, *The New Princeton Encyclopedia of Poetry and Poetics,* ed. Alex Preminger and T. V. F. Brogan (Princeton: Princeton University Press, 1993), 1344–45. This book is subsequently cited in the text as EPP.

2. Ezra Pound, "A Few Don'ts," *Poetry* 1, no. 6 (March 1913); rpt. in "A Retro-

spect," *Literary Essays of Ezra Pound,* ed. T. S. Eliot (London: Faber & Faber, 1954), 3. Subsequently cited as LEEP. See also the entries on free verse by Donald Wesling and Eniko Bollobás and on imagism by Stanley F. Coffman in EPP.

3. T. S. Eliot, "The Music of Poetry" (1942), *On Poetry and Poets* (New York: Farrar, Straus, 1957), 31.

4. Eliot, "Reflections on 'Vers Libre'" (1917), *To Criticize the Critic and Other Writings* (New York: Farrar, Straus, 1965), 183–89. The citations are from 189, 185, 187 respectively, but the whole essay should be read carefully.

5. Annie Finch, *The Ghost of Meter: Culture and Prosody in American Free Verse* (Ann Arbor: University of Michigan Press, 1993), 139. For Wright, Finch maintains, "the connotations of iambic pentameter remain positive" (134); for Lorde, "both iambic pentameter and dactylic rhythms carry abundant stores of wordless energy" (135).

6. Derek Attridge, *Poetic Rhythm: An Introduction* (Cambridge: Cambridge University Press, 1995), 172. Subsequently cited as DA.

7. Timothy Steele, *Missing Measures: Modern Poetry and the Revolt against Meter* (Fayetteville: University of Arkansas Press, 1990), 10.

8. Helen Vendler, *London Review of Books* (4 July 1996): 6.

9. Charles O. Hartman, *Free Verse: An Essay on Prosody* (Princeton: Princeton University Press, 1980), 24–25. Subsequently cited in the text as COH. I discuss this definition of free verse in relation to "prose" in essay 5.

10. In *Rational Geomancy: The Kids of the Book-Machine: The Collected Research Reports of the Toronto Research Group, 1973–1982* (Vancouver: Talon Books, 1982), Steve McCaffery and bpNichol have this entry on "Verse & Prose":

> *verse*—from the Indo-European root "wert": to turn, from this root derives the medieval Latin "versus" literally to turn a furrow, in subsequent usage the furrow became the written line by analogy. . . .
>
> *prose*—deriving from the same Indo-European root—is a contraction of the Latin "proversus" contracted thru "prorsus" to "prosus": literally the term forward, as adjectivally in "prosa oratio"—a speech going straight ahead without turns. (106) Subsequently cited in the text as RGEO.

11. Northrop Frye, *The Well-Tempered Critic* (Bloomington: Indiana University Press, 1963), 21. Cf. Frye, "Verse and Prose," EPP 885.

12. Robert Pinsky, "Commentary," in "Symposium on the Line," ed. Rory Holscher and Robert Schultz, *Epoch 29* (winter 1980): 212. The symposium is subsequently cited as EPOCH.

13. Derek Attridge, e.g., defines *rhythm* as "the continuous motion that pushes spoken language forward in more or less regular waves, as the musculature of the speech organs tightens and relaxes, as energy pulsates through the words we speak and hear, as the brain marshals multiple stimuli into ordered patterns" (DA 1).

14. A classic account of this position is Eleonor Berry's "Visual Form in Free

Verse," *Visible Language* 23, no. 1 (winter 1989): 89–111. I have discussed the visual form of Williams's and Oppen's lyric in *The Dance of the Intellect* (1985; rpt. Evanston, IL: Northwestern University Press, 1996), chaps. 4 and 5. For statements by poets who stress the visual component, see e.g., Margaret Atwood, EPOCH 172: "The line, then, is a visual indication of an aural unit and serves to mark the cadence of the poem." Cf. Allen Ginsberg, EPOCH 189, George MacBeth 203, Josephine Miles 207. In their introduction to their collection *The Line in Poetry* (Urbana: University of Illinois Press, 1988), Robert Frank and Henry Sayre state that "the line—its status as a 'unit of measure,' what determines its length, the effects which can be achieved at its 'turn'—has come to be the focus of . . . concern" (ix). But the portfolio called "L=A=N=G=U=A=G=E Lines," edited by Bruce Andrews and Charles Bernstein, that concludes *The Line in Poetry* (see 177–216) actually calls this statement into question, as does my essay 5 here, "Lucent and Inescapable Rhythms: Metrical Choice and Historical Formation." I shall come back to the Language essays below. The Frank-Sayre collection is subsequently cited as LIP.

15. See COH, chaps. 7 and 8 passim; Donald Wesling, "Sprung Rhythm and the Figure of Grammar," *The New Poetries: Poetic Form Since Coleridge and Wordsworth* (Lewisburg, PA: Bucknell University Press, 1985), 113–44; Jonathan Holden, "The Free Verse Line," LIP 1–12. "The most fundamental rhythmical unit in verse," writes Holden, "is *not* the line but the syntactical unit" (LIP 6).

16. Henri Meschonnic, *Critique du rythme: Anthropologie historique du langage* (Paris: Verdier, 1982), 21. All translations are mine. Subsequently cited as HMC.

17. HMC 593, 595, my emphasis. A similar argument is made by Anthony Easthope in *Poetry as Discourse* (London: Methuen, 1983). For Easthope, all verse forms—from the feudal medieval ballad to the courtly sonnet to the transparency of the "ordered" eighteenth-century heroic couplet—are ideologically charged: blank verse, for instance, has to serve as *the* bourgeois subjective verse form for the romantic period, a form that gives way to free verse when the transcendental ego is replaced by the dispersal of the subject and the dominance of signifier over signified. Easthope's analysis is overly schematic and he seems to accept the common wisdom that free verse is the end point of prosody. But his basic premise— that verse forms are not just arbitrary or "neutrally available" to everyone at any time—is important.

18. See, on this point, Jonathan Culler, *Structuralist Poetics: Structuralism, Linguistics, and the Study of Literature* (Ithaca: Cornell University Press, 1975), 161–64. Culler borrows from Gerard Genette the example of a lineated version of "banal journalistic prose" ("Yesterday / on the A 7 / an automobile / travelling at sixty miles per hour / crashed into a plane tree. / Its four occupants were / killed") to show that lineation transforms reader expectation and interpretation.

19. Consider, e.g., the airline menu on "easy SABRE" that gives commands like "Return to the first line." Or again, consider the following protest poem by Wilma

Elizabeth McDaniel, the so-called Gravy Poet of the San Joaquin Valley, cited in an article by Peter H. King in the *Los Angeles Times* (11 August 1996, A1): "You can put your trust in gravy / the way it stretches out / the sausage / the way it stretches out / the dreams." Earlier in the century, such versifying would have demanded meter and rhyme; now even polemic jingles are as likely as not to be in free verse.

20. I discuss Williams as a representative free-verse poet in essay 5. Pound's "visualized" page, especially in those Cantos that make frequent use of Chinese and other ideograms, has been a key source for concrete and post-concrete poetry and contemporary experiments with visual poetics.

21. *Naked Poetry: Recent American Poetry in Open Forms,* ed. Stephen Berg and Robert Mezey (New York and Indianapolis: Bobbs Merrill, 1969) is subsequently cited in the text as NAK. *Out of Everywhere: Linguistically Innovative Poetry by Women in North America and the U.K.,* ed. Maggie O'Sullivan (London: Reality Street Studios, 1996), which has an afterword by Wendy Mulford, is subsequently cited in the text as OOE.

22. Charles Olson, "Projective Verse," *Selected Writings,* ed. Robert Creeley (New York: New Directions, 1966), 18–19. Subsequently cited as COSW. Donald Allen, who reprints "Projective Verse" in his *The New American Poetry* (New York: Grove Press, 1960), obviously has Olson's rejection of "closed verse" in mind when he writes that the poets in his anthology "have shown one common characteristic: a total rejection of all those qualities typical of academic verse" (xi), the most obvious of those "qualities" being, of course, metrical form.

23. COSW 16. Here and elsewhere, Olson attributes this aphorism to Robert Creeley, and the attribution has stuck, although Creeley never gave a systematic account of the proposition.

24. The editors do claim that they had wanted to include LeRoi Jones and Michael Harper but were constrained "because of cost and space" (xii). As for the U.S. focus, "We decided to keep it American because we knew nothing much new has happened in English poetry since Lawrence laid down his pen and died" (xii). It is true that English and American poetics were probably furthest apart in the fifties and sixties when "The Movement" dominated in Britain. But note that it never even occurs to the editors to include Canadian poets or poets of other English-speaking countries; their chauvinism is characteristic of the U.S.-centered imperialist ethos of the sixties.

25. The notation used here is the standard one adopted by George Trager and Henry Lee Smith Jr. in *An Outline of English Structure* (Washington, DC: American Council of Learned Societies, 1957). Trager and Smith identify four degrees of stress in English: primary (/), secondary (∧) as in a compound noun like "bláckbîrd," tertiary (\), as in the first syllable of "èlevátor"; and weak or unstressed ( ), as in the second syllable of "elevator." A double bar (‖) is used to indicate a caesura, and I use a right arrow (→) to indicate that the line is runover.

26. In this regard, it differs from its free-verse precursors: in Williams's lyric, as we have seen in essay 5, line break was brilliantly used for visual effect.

27. The count of syllables per line here is: Levertov: 2–8, Merwin: 9–13, Snyder: 4–10, Lowell: 3–10. Ginsberg's strophes are visually even more unified because of the dropped indented lines.

28. Andrews and Bernstein, "L=A=N=G=U=A=G=E Lines," LIP 177–216.

29. See Susan Howe, "Making the Ghost Walk about Again and Again," *A Bibliography of the King's Book or Eikon Basilike* (Providence, RI: Paradigm Press, 1989), unpaginated. This preface is reproduced in Susan Howe, *The Nonconformist's Manual* (New York: New Directions, 1993), 47–50. The poetic sequence itself follows (51–82) but the page design is not quite that of the original, largely because of page size.

30. In *Poetic Rhythm* (171), Derek Attridge describes an extract from Howe's *Pythagorean Silence,* part 3, as follows:

> Susan Howe's poetry illustrates the potential that free verse possesses to fragment and dislocate the normal sequentiality of language, beyond even the techniques deployed by Pound and Williams. This extract . . . uses the disposition of words on the page in combination with disruptions of syntax to suggest bursts of utterance interspersed with silences. The morsels of language demand maximal attention. . . . [These lines] indicate something of the resonating power phrases can have when the connectivity provided by syntax, phrasing, rhythm, and visual linearity is partly—though only partly—broken.

It is interesting that although Attridge puts his finger on exactly what makes Howe's verse quite unlike the earlier model, he still categorizes it as "free verse," as if there could be no other name for Howe's obviously very "different" page layout.

31. They are in order of appearance (but not chronology or nationality) Susan Howe, Joan Retallack, Tina Darragh, Paula Claire, Diane Ward, Carla Harryman, Lyn Hejinian, Maggie O'Sullivan, Meilanie Neilson, Denise Riley, Rae Armantrout, Catriona Strang, Nicole Brossard, Wendy Mulford, Rosmarie Waldrop, Deanna Ferguson, Hannah Weiner, Carlyle Reedy, Geraldine Monk, Karen Mac Cormack, Kathleen Fraser, Lisa Robertson, Marjorie Welish, Barbara Guest, Grace Lake, Caroline Bergvall, Fiona Templeton, Fanny Howe, Bernadette Mayer, Leslie Scalapino.

32. Ezra Pound, "Papyrus," *Personae: The Shorter Poems; A Revised Edition,* ed. Lea Baechler and A. Walton Litz (New York: New Directions, 1990), 115.

33. Steve McCaffery, "Diminished Reference and the Model Reader," *North of Intention: Critical Writings, 1973–1986* (New York: Roof Books, 1986), 21. McCaffery's discussion of the Klein worm (20–21) as emblem of a poetry "without walls," in which "milieu and constellation replace syntax," is also very helpful.

Essay 7: "What We Don't Talk about When We Talk about Poetry"

1. The choice of books to be reviewed, here as elsewhere, is of course the assigning editor's. But we should bear in mind that, in the case of omnibus reviews, the reviewer normally reserves the right to omit specific items (and could in any case decline the commission). In what follows, then, I attribute responsibility to Maxwell rather than to the *TLS* editor.

2. *New York Times Book Review,* 15 January 1995, 15.

3. See Dana Gioia, *Can Poetry Matter?* (New York: Graywolf Press, 1992). Gioia claims that, until 1960 or so, poetry had a wide circulation—it appeared in newspapers and popular magazines, along with political journalism, humor, fiction and reviews—and it was widely reviewed and discussed in the leading papers. But the quality of that "it" is open to question, as I argue here.

4. The Brown introduction (unpaginated) is reprinted as the headnote to each of the seventy-two Arno reprint volumes, followed by Alfred Kazin's "A Sense of History."

5. See Pierre Bourdieu, "The Field of Cultural Production; or, The Economic World Reversed" (1983), trans. Richard Nice, *The Field of Cultural Production: Essays on Art and Literature,* ed. Randal Johnson (New York: Columbia University Press, 1993), 51, and cf. fig. 2 on 49.

6. Jimmy Carter, "Sport," *Always a Reckoning* (New York: Random House, 1995), 23.

7. T. J. G. Harris, "In the Labyrinth," *PN Review* 80 (July/August 1991): 71.

8. Eavan Boland, "Identities and Disguises" (review of Michael Longley, *Poems 1963–1983* and E. A. Markham, *Living in Disguise*), *PN Review* 55 (1987): 95.

9. For an excellent sociological account of how and why poetry still occupies this privileged position, in name if not in fact, see Pierre Bourdieu, *The Field of Cultural Production: Essays on Art and Literature,* ed. Randal Johnson (New York: Columbia University Press, 1993), chap. 6, "Principles for a Sociology of Cultural Works," 176–91.

10. An earlier version of this discussion of *Exact Change* may be found in *Sulfur* 37 (fall 1995): 236–50, and I compare the *Yearbook* to various anthologies of postmodern poetries in "Whose New American Poetry? Anthologizing in the Nineties," *Diacritics* 26, nos. 3–4 (1997): 119–22.

11. The compact disc is disappointing, there being no explanation of the eclectic mix of poets represented, many of whom (e.g., Alice Notley, Kenward Elmslie) are not in the book at all; some readings, such as Jack Spicer's "Imaginary Elegies" (1957) and John Ashbery's "They Dream Only of America" (1962), stem from earlier decades. One could argue that the aim here, as in the book, is to produce telling juxtapositions, but in practice the sequence from Michael Palmer to Ted Berrigan creates more confusion than insight.

12. Ming-Qian Ma, a Chinese doctoral candidate at Stanford who has published essays on Carl Rakosi, George Oppen, Susan Howe, and Lyn Hejinian, and who is working on further translations of the Original poets with Jeff Twitchell, tells me that in the Mandarin Chinese, the poems in question are much more nonsyntactic and disjunctive than in these translations.

13. One should bear in mind that in the United States, almost 50 percent of the appropriate population attends university and that university campuses also draw in a larger public that shares the concerns of particular departments, attends lectures and readings, and so on. But this public, though surprisingly large, is by no means equivalent to, say, the general *TLS* or *NYTBR* readership.

14. To date, in the United States, *A Poetics* has been reviewed in the following mix of scholarly journals and "little magazines": *Agni Review, American Literature, College Literature Common Knowledge, Comparative Literature Studies, Contemporary Literature, Harvard Review, Modernism/Modernity, Sulfur, Virginia Quarterly Review, West Coast Line, World Literature Today*.

Essay 8: "English as a 'Second' Language"

1. Ezra Pound, "A List of Books," *Little Review,* March 1918; rpt. in Ezra Pound, *Selected Prose 1909–1965,* ed. William Cookson (New York: New Directions, 1973), 424–25.

2. The Haweises' first child, Oda, was born in 1904 in Paris but died on her first birthday. My biographical sketch is largely based on Carolyn Burke, *Becoming Modern: The Life of Mina Loy* (New York: Farrar, Straus Giroux, 1996). See also Roger Conover's introduction and timetable, in Mina Loy, *The Last Lunar Baedeker,* ed. Roger L. Conover with a note by Jonathan Williams (Highlands, NC: Jargon Society, 1982), xv–lxxix. This book is subsequently cited in the text as LLB. Conover's more recent edition of Loy's poems, *The Last Lunar Baedeker: Poems of Mina Loy* (New York: Farrar, Straus Giroux, 1996), provides corrected versions of many of Loy's poems and excellent notes, but since it doesn't include "Anglo-Mongrels and the Rose," and since many textual questions are left unresolved, I rely here on the earlier edition. For a discussion of Burke's biography and Conover's *Lost Lunar Baedeker,* see my "The Mina Loy Mysteries: Legend and Language," *American Book Review* 18, no. 1 (1996): 16–17, 26.

3. In LLB, Roger Conover lists Loy's father as Lowy, the Anglicized spelling of the German Löwy. The umlaut is important, for Löwy derives, of course, from Löwe (lion), Löwenthal (lion valley) and so on.

4. In the *Egoist* 5 (1918): 70, T. S. Apteryx [Eliot's pseudonym] called Loy's "The Effectual Marriage" (a thinly veiled account of her relationship with Papini) "extremely good." And years later, Ezra Pound recalled "Effectual Marriage" as

one of the poems of the last thirty years which by virtue of its "individual character" remained in his memory. See Pound, *Profile: An Anthology Collected in 1931* (Milan: John Scheiwiller, 1932), 13.

5. Virginia M. Kouidis, *Mina Loy: American Modernist Poet* (Baton Rouge: Louisiana State University Press, 1980); subsequently cited in the text as VK. The American label is all but ubiquitous: see, e.g., Jane Augustine, "Mina Loy: A Feminist Modernist Americanizes the Language of Futurism," *Mid-Hudson Language Studies* 12, no. 1 (1989): 89–101; Carolyn Burke, "The New Poetry and the New Woman: Mina Loy," in *Coming to Light: American Women Poets in the Twentieth Century,* ed. Diane Wood Middlebrook and Marilyn Yalom (Ann Arbor: University of Michigan Press, 1985): 37–57; Linda A. Kinnahan, *Poetics of the Feminine: Authority and Literary Tradition in William Carlos Williams, Mina Loy, Denise Levertov, and Kathleen Fraser* (Cambridge and New York: Cambridge University Press, 1994).

6. T. S. Eliot, "The Music of Poetry" (1942), *On Poetry and Poets* (New York: Noonday Press, 1961), 23; Ezra Pound, "A Retrospect," *Literary Essays of Ezra Pound,* ed. with an introduction by T. S. Eliot (New York: New Directions, 1954), 5.

7. Alfred Kreymborg, *Our Singing Strength: An Outline of American Poetry (1620–1930)* (New York: Coward-McCann, 1929), 488–89.

8. Ezra Pound, "How to Read" (1928), in *Literary Essays of Ezra Pound,* ed. T. S. Eliot (London: Faber & Faber, 1954), 25.

9. Kenneth Rexroth, "Les Lauriers Sont Coupés," *Circle* 1, no. 4 (1944): 69–70. Subsequently cited as KR.

10. LLB 112–13. Conover normalizes Loy's dramatic spacing and omits her dashes, hyphens, and other special punctuation devices. In my citations, I reproduce the spacing of the original: for the passage cited here, see *Little Review* 9 (spring 1923): 11–12.

11. William Carlos Williams, *Spring and All,* in *Imaginations,* ed. Webster Schott (New York: New Directions, 1970), 109.

12. See T. V. F. Brogan, "Skeltonic," in *The New Princeton Encyclopedia of Poetry and Poetics,* ed. Alex Preminger and T. V. F. Brogan (Princeton: Princeton University Press, 1993), 1154–55. An example from Skelton's "To Mistress Margaret Hussey" goes like this:

> Merry Margaret,
>   As midsummer flower,
> Gentle as falcon
> Or hawk of the tower
> With solace and gladness,
> Much mirth and no madness,
> All good and no badness;

So joyously,
So maidenly,
So womanly . . .

13. See VK 49–59; Carolyn Burke, "The New Poetry and the New Woman: Mina Loy," 39–43; Rachel Blau DuPlessis, " 'Seismic Orgasm': Sexual Intercourse, Gender Narratives and Lyric Ideology in Mina Loy," in *Studies in Historical Change,* ed. Ralph Cohen (Charlottesville: University Press of Virginia, 1992), 264–91; and esp. Elizabeth Arnold, "Mina Loy and the Futurists," *Sagetrieb* 8, nos. 1–2 (1989): 83–117.

14. F. T. Marinetti, "Technical Manifesto of Futurist Literature" (1912), in *Let's Murder the Moonshine: Selected Writings,* trans. R. W. Flint (Los Angeles: Sun & Moon, 1991), 92–97.

15. For a discussion of Loy's brand of Christianity and Freudianism, see Keith Tuma, "Anglo-Mongrels and the Rose," *Sagetrieb* 11, nos. 1–2 (1992): 207–28.

16. Virginia Kouidis suggests Jules Laforgue as a model (see VK 91–94), but Laforgue is much more lyrical than Loy, and, despite his ironic registers, much more concerned with self-expression.

17. See, on this point, chap. 2 of my *Futurist Moment: Avant-Garde, Avant-Guerre and the Language of Rupture* (Chicago: University of Chicago Press, 1986), and my essay "Collage," in the *Encyclopedia of Aesthetics,* ed. Michael Kelly (New York: Columbia University Press, 1996), forthcoming.

18. The first person to have noted Loy's debt to Rossetti and fin-de-siècle English poets is Marisa Januzzi: see her "Mongrel Rose: The 'Unerring Esperanto' of Loy's Poetry," forthcoming in *Mina Loy, Essays on the Poetry* (Orono, ME: National Poetry Foundation, 1997). "The Rossettis," writes Januzzi (n. 20), "seem to have influenced Loy's early ideas of subject matter and style. In her notes on Dante Gabriel Rossetti, however, Loy could not resist teasing his work on both grounds. [For example,] she assails his famous 'stunning subjects': that influential 'rubber corps' of his 'wide-eyed women stricken with fried hair.' "

19. In the final issue of the *Little Review* (1929), Margaret Anderson and Jane Heap gave their authors a questionnaire to fill out. One question was "What has been the happiest moment of your life? The unhappiest? (if you care to tell)." Mina Loy responded: "Every moment I spent with Arthur Cravan. The rest of the time." See LLB 305–6; cf. Loy's apotheosis of her lover in "Arthur Cravan Is Alive!" LLB 317–22.

20. Mina Loy, "Modern Poetry," *Charm* 3, no. 3 (April 1925): 17. I owe the discovery of this essay to Marisa Januzzi, whose Columbia University dissertation, *Reconstru[ing] Scar[s]: Mina Loy and the Matter of Modernist Poetics,* provides the most thorough critical analysis of Loy's poetry to date.

21. Not everyone, of course, assents to this view. In her review of Burke's biography and the Conover *Last Lunar Baedeker,* Helen Vendler remarks critically, "it

is not clear to me that Loy was innately a lyric poet," as if to say that, in this case, she cannot be a very good poet, and, indeed, Vendler concludes that "what is disappointing is that [Loy] was unable to go beyond poems that were, for the most part, brittle, jittery, digressive, and unmusical." See Vendler, "The Truth Teller," *New York Review of Books,* 19 September 1996, 60.

Essay 9: "Poetry in Time of War"

1. See Robert Duncan, *Selected Poems,* ed. Robert J. Bertholf (New York: New Directions, 1993), 35–37. Subsequently cited in the text as RDSP.

2. Denise Levertov, "Some Duncan Letters—A Memoir and a Critical Tribute," *Scales of the Marvelous,* ed. Robert J. Bertholf and Ian W. Reid (New York: New Directions, 1979), 86–87, 90–91. The collection is subsequently cited as SM. The 1953 letter is in the Robert Duncan Archive at Stanford University. Copyright © The Literary Estate of Robert Duncan. All subsequent references to the Duncan-Levertov correspondence are to the Stanford archive. I wish to thank William McPheron, the curator of English and American Literature, Stanford University Libraries, Stanford University, for his help on this project. I also want to thank Robert J. Bertholf, the executor of the Duncan estate, for granting me permission to cite extracts from the Duncan letters.

3. Robert Duncan, "Introductory Notes: Denise Levertov," in *A Selected Prose,* ed. Robert J. Bertholf (New York: New Directions, 1995), 161.

4. Ian W. Reid, "The Plural Text: "Passages," SM 169.

5. Robert Duncan, *A Book of Resemblances: Poems 1950–53* (New Haven, CT: Henry Wenning, 1966), vii.

6. Denise Levertov, *To Stay Alive* (New York: New Directions, 1971), 29. Subsequently cited in the text as TSA.

7. It is only fair to say here that Duncan is sometimes guilty of the same fault. "Up Rising," for example, begins with the lines, "Now Johnson would go up to join the great simulacra of men, / Hitler and Stalin, to work his fame / with planes roaring out from Guam over Asia." And later in the poem there is reference to "this black bile of old evils arisen anew, / takes over the vanity of Johnson." See *Bending the Bow* (New York: New Directions, 1968), 81–82. Perhaps Duncan is recognizing his own earlier weakness in his critique of Levertov.

Essay 10: "How Russian Is It"

1. Lyn Hejinian, *Oxota: A Short Russian Novel* (Great Barrington, MA: The Figures, 1992). All subsequent references to this text are to this edition.

2. See my review of *Leningrad* in *Sulfur* 29 (fall 1991): 216–21.

3. "The title, *Oxota*," Hejinian explains, "is a transliteration of a Russian word which could be translated as *the hunt* or *hunting*. It comes from a friend's characterization of herself as "oxotnitsa," the huntress (one of Artemis's epithets); she was referring to the work of providing for daily life in conditions of worsening shortages of food and basic goods and to the spirit in which people have to hunt for them." See Hejinian, "On *Oxota*: A Short Russian Novel," headnote to extract from the poem in "Focus on the Long Poem," special issue, *Pequod* 31 (1990): 67.

4. "The Rejection of Closure," in "Women & Language," special issue, *Poetics Journal* 4 (May 1984): 138–39.

5. In a letter to me (23 September 1992), Hejinian remarks how drawn she is to "the all-purpose, fluid, ambiguous, forever serviceable It. . . . I find this pronoun and its usage fascinating, because of its flexibility:

It's raining tonight. What is?
It's a question of being accurate. What is?
It's okay to be confused in a foreign country. What is it?"

6. Lyn Hejinian, "Strangeness," *Poetics Journal* 8 (June 1989): 32, 38–39.

7. Lyn Hejinian, *The Hunt* (Tenerife, Canary Islands: Zasterle Press, 1991). Manuel Brito, the editor of Zasterle, regularly publishes experimental poetry from the United States.

8. Lyn Hejinian, "The Person and Description," symposium on "The Poetics of Everyday Life," in "The Person," special issue, *Poetics Journal* 9 (1991): 166–67. Subsequently cited as PJ.

9. See Lyn Hejinian, "Two Stein Talks: (1) Language and Realism, (2) Grammar and Landscape," *Temblor* 3 (1986): 137.

10. The joke goes like this:

A: What's green, hangs on the wall, and whistles?
B. A herring.

A. But a herring isn't green.
B. You can paint it green.

A. But a herring doesn't hang on the wall.
B. You can nail it to the wall.

A. But a herring doesn't whistle.
B. So it doesn't whistle.

Essay 11: "What Really Happened"

1. Roland Barthes, *Camera Lucida: Reflections on Photography*, trans. Richard Howard (New York: Farrar Straus, 1981), 76; originally published as *La Chambre*

claire (Paris: Editions du Seuil, 1980). The English text is subsequently cited in the text as CL.

2. *Roland Barthes by Roland Barthes,* trans. Richard Howard (New York: Farrar, Straus and Giroux, 1977); originally published as *Roland Barthes par Roland Barthes* (Paris: Seuil, 1975). The English text is subsequently cited as RB.

3. Lynn Gumpert, "The Life and Death of Christian Boltanski," in *Christian Boltanski: Lessons of Darkness,* ed. Lynn Gumpert and Mary Jane Jacob (Chicago: Museum of Contemporary Art, 1988), 59. This catalog is subsequently cited in the text as LD.

4. Christian Boltanski, interview with Suzanne Pagé in *Christian Boltanski— Compositions,* exhibition catalog (Paris: A.R.C./Musée d'art moderne de la Ville de Paris, 1981), 7; cited in Lynn Gumpert's translation, LD 59.

5. See *Christian Boltanski, Catalogue, Books, Printed Matter, Ephemera 1966– 91,* ed. Jennifer Flay, with commentaries by Günter Metken (Cologne: Walther König, 1992), 155. This catalog is subsequently cited as COL.

6. Georges Perec, *W; or, The Memory of Childhood,* trans. David Bellos (Boston: David Godine, 1988), 54–55, originally published as *W ou le souvenir d'enfance* (Paris: Editions Denoel, 1975); subsequently cited as W. See also David Bellos, *Georges Perec: A Life in Words* (Boston: David Godine, 1993), 55–59.

7. Delphine Renard, "Entretien avec Christian Boltanski," in *Boltanski* (Paris: Centre Georges Pompidou, 1984), 75. This catalog is subsequently cited in the text as BOL. All translations are my own.

8. In the first version of this essay (*Artes* 2 [1995]: 110–25) I read this photograph as containing two rather than three seesaws (see 118). The presence of the third (the thin ropelike one at the furthest distance) was pointed out by Gerard Malanga in a letter to the editor in *Artes* 3 (1996): 146. Malanga discovered (and his interpretation is quite convincing) that the shadows demonstrate the existence of a third seesaw. I am very grateful for his correction, which actually corroborates my reading of the sinister potential of the lighting in this complex image.

9. See LD 14. The entire run of photographs is reproduced in this catalog: see 15–48.

10. Georgia Marsh, "The White and the Black: An Interview with Christian Boltanski, *Parkett* 22 (1989): 37. This issue of *Parkett* is subsequently cited as PAR.

Essay 12: "'Inner Tension / In Attention'"

1. Steve McCaffery, *Knowledge Never Knew* (Montreal: Vehicule Press, 1983), 24. Subsequently cited in the text as KNK. McCaffery's books and broadsides cited in this essay are listed chronologically, preceded by the acronyms I have used to designate them and followed by bibliographical information. Derived from bp nichol, "The Annotated, Anecdoted, Beginnings of a Critical Checklist of the

Published Works of Steve McCaffery," *Open Letter,* 6 series, no. 9 (fall 1987): 67–92; this special Steve McCaffery issue is subsequently cited as OL.

C *Carnival, the first panel: 1967–70* (Toronto: Coach House Press, 1973), 18 sheets, offset, perforated.

DSM *Dr. Sadhu's Muffins: a book of written readings* (Erin, Ontario: Press Porépic, 1974), 142 pp., offset, printed endpapers.

OW *Ow's Waif and other poems* (Toronto: Coach House Press, 1975), 160 pp., offset, hardbound, printed endpapers.

C2 *Carnival, the second panel: 1971–75* (Toronto: Coach House Press, 1977), 22 sheets, offset, perforated.

IEN *In England Now That Spring,* with bpNichol (Toronto: Aya Press, 1979), 128 pp., offset.

PAN *Panopticon* (Toronto: Blew Ointment Press, 1984), 160 pp., offset, perfect bound.

NI *North of Intention: Critical Writings 1973–1986* (New York/Toronto: Roof Books/Nightwood Editions, 1986), 239 pp., offset, perfect bound.

EV *Evoba: The Investigation Meditations 1976–78* (Toronto: Coach House Press, 1987), 101 pp., offset, perfect bound.

BD *The Black Debt* (London, Ontario: Nightwood Editions, 1989), 202 pp., offset, perfect bound.

RG *Rational Geomancy: The Kids of the Book-Machine: The Collected Research Reports of the Toronto Research Group, 1973–1982,* by Steve McCaffery and bpNichol; ed. Steve McCaffery (Vancouver: Talon Books, 1992), 320 pp. offset, perfect bound.

2. Michael Coffey, "Grammatology and Economy," OL 32.

3. See the *Oxford English Dictionary* (OED) and Steve McCaffery and bpNichol, "Manifesto as Interlude," *Open Letter,* 2d series, no. 9 (fall 1974): 78–79, rpt. in RG 105–10. And for a good critical overview of the TRG (Toronto Research Group), formed by McCaffery and Nichol and their various manifestos on questions of language and etymology, see Caroline Barnard, *The New Poetics in Canada and Quebec: From Concretism to Post-Modernism* (Toronto: University of Toronto Press, 1989), 56–67.

4. Johanna Drucker, *The Century of Artists' Books* (New York: Granary Press, 1996), 359–60. McCaffery's *Carnival* is discussed on 239–40.

5. Richard Kostelanetz, "Book Art," in *Artist's Books: A Critical Anthology and Sourcebook,* ed. Joan Lyons (New York: Visual Studies Workshop, 1985), 29. This work is subsequently cited in the text as AB.

6. Introduction to C2, pages unnumbered. In *Open Letter,* McCaffery further explains that "Panel Two, thanks to the xerox disintegration sections, stages entropy . . . I've long felt that a large part of the history of writing has been the sociological impact of its materiality upon its agents and users" (OL 73).

7. In the 1995 "Yale Symphosymposium on Contemporary Poetics and Concretism: A World View from the 1990s," in *Experimental—Visual—Concrete: Avant-Garde Poetry Since the 1960s,* ed. K. David Jackson, Eric Vos, and Johanna Drucker (Amsterdam and Atlanta, GA: Rodopi, 1996), McCaffery observes: "I believe that aspect of contemporary poetics that might be termed the critique of voice is a central and persistent presence within concretism. It is important to distinguish vocality from voice. The latter, like the Freudian phallus, is to be understood less as a physical organ than an ideologically saturated signified fundamentally complicit with the logocentric tradition. A further dimension is the abrogation of linearity. The latter we have come to understand not merely as a spatial arrangement but as a way of thinking" (372). The book is subsequently cited as EVC.

8. *Anamorphosis,* according to OED, means 1. "A distorted projection or drawing of anything, so made that when viewed from a particular point, or by reflection from a suitable mirror, it appears regular and properly proportioned; a deformation," and 2. "*Bot.* Such a degeneration or change in the habit of a plant from different conditions of growth as gives it the appearance of a different species or genius; abnormal transformation."

9. Marjorie Perloff, " 'Voice Whisht through Thither Flood': Steve McCaffery's *Panopticon* and *North of Intention,*" *Poetic License: Essays in Modernist and Postmodernist Lyric* (Evanston, IL: Northwestern University Press, 1990), 285–96; and on *The Black Debt,* Marjorie Perloff, "Signs Are Taken for Wonders: The Billboard Field as Poetic Space," *Radical Artifice: Writing Poetry in the Age of Media* (Chicago: University of Chicago Press, 1991), 105–11.

10. Ludwig Wittgenstein, *Philosophical Investigations,* 3d ed., trans. G. E. M. Anscombe (New York: Macmillan, 1968), 64e. Subsequently cited in the text as PI. For a larger discussion of the way Wittgenstein's writing enters the domain of poetry, see my *Wittgenstein's Ladder: Poetic Language and the Strangeness of the Ordinary* (Chicago: University of Chicago Press, 1996).

Essay 13: "The Music of Verbal Space"

1. John Cage, *M: Writings '67–72,* 215. The following texts by Cage are cited in this essay:

"Art Is Either a Complaint Or Do Something Else." *Aerial* 6/7 (Washington: Edge Books, 1991), 1–35. Rpt. in *Musicage,* 3–42.

"Diary: How to Improve the World (You Will Only Make Matters Worse) Continued 1971–72," *M* 195–217.

Empty Words, Writings '73–78 (Middletown, CT: Wesleyan University Press, 1979). Cited as EW.

For the Birds: John Cage in Conversation with Daniel Charles (Boston and London, Marion Boyars, 1981). Cited as FB.

"James Joyce, Marcel Duchamp, Erik Satie: An Alphabet," *X: Writings '79–82.* (Middletown, CT: Wesleyan University Press, 1983), 53–101. Cited as *X*.

John Cage, Writer: Previously Uncollected Pieces. Selected and edited by Richard Kostelanetz (New York: Limelight Editions, 1993). Cited as JCW.

M: Writings '67–72. (Middletown, CT: Wesleyan University Press, 1973). Cited as *M*.

Musicage: John Cage in Conversation with Joan Retallack (Hanover, NH: Wesleyan University Press/University Press of New England, 1996). Cited as *Musicage*.

Roaratorio: An Irish Circus on Finnegans Wake, ed. Klaus Schöning (Munich: Atheneum, 1985). Cited as *R*.

Silence: Lectures and Writings (Middletown, CT: Wesleyan University Press, 1961). Cited as *S*.

"Time (Three Autokus)" (1986), in *John Cage II,* ed. Heinz-Klaus Metzger and Rainer Riehn, special issue of *Musik-Konzepte* 2 (Munich 1990): 264–304. "What you say . . ." appears on 267–77. Cited as HKM.

"Tokyo Lecture and Three Mesostics" (1986), in *John Cage, Writer* 177–82.

"What You Say . . . ," *Formations* 4, no. 1 (spring–summer 1987): 52–67. Cited in the text as F. Reprinted in "Time," see above.

2. In *The Roaring Silence: John Cage: A Life* (New York: Arcade Publishing, 1992), David Revill notes that "It was also in the *Imaginary Landscape* that Cage first employed his system of rhythmic structure. The simple figures that constitute the piece fit into a scheme of four sections consisting of three times five measures which are separated by interludes which increase in length additively from one to three measures; the piece ends with a four-measure coda" (65–66).

3. The English version, *For the Birds: John Cage in Conversation with Daniel Charles,* was published by Marion Boyars (Boston and London) in 1981. The actual interviews were begun in 1968 but were submitted by Charles to Cage for revision and commentary and not published until 1976 under the title *Pour les oiseaux.*

4. The *I Ching or Book of Changes* has, of course, been a source book for many poets and artists. Cage's own use of the *I Ching* began in 1950, when Christian

Wolff gave him the new Bollingen (Princeton) two-volume edition of the English translation by Cary F. Baynes of Richard Wilhelm's German translation with the introduction by C. G. Jung. The magic square of sixty-four hexagrams, Cage explains in "Tokyo Lecture," transferred to the computer, "works musically to tell me for instance how many sound events take place in what length of time, at what points in time, on which instruments, having what loudnesses, etc. And in my writing it lets me continue, in a variety of ways, my search for a means which comes from ideas but is not about them but nevertheless produces them free of my intentions" (178–79). Mac Low has used similar techniques, first by throwing coins and dice, later with the computer, to determine factors of sixty-four; that govern individual lineation and stanzaic structure. But Mac Low's acrostics are more ad hoc than Cage's: he has tended to devise the methodology as he goes along.

5. Jackson Mac Low, "Call Me Ishmael," in *Representative Works: 1938–1985* (New York: Roof Books, 1986), 89.

6. See, e.g., R 173.

7. Cage was not satisfied with his "writing through" of Pound's *Cantos.* "Now that I've done so [i.e., "written through" them]," he remarks in an interview, "I must say that I don't regard them as highly as I do the *Wake.* The reason is that there are about four or five ideas that keep reappearing in the *Cantos,* so that in the end the form resembles something done with stencils, where the color doesn't really change. There's not that kind of complexity, or attention to detail, as there is in Joyce"; see Richard Kostelanetz, *Conversing with Cage* (New York: Limelight Editions, 1988), 152; subsequently cited as K.

No doubt, Cage also objected to Pound's studious elimination of the very words Cage himself liked best—prepositions, conjunctions, articles, pronouns—and that Pound's parataxis of nouns and noun phrases made any "writing through" extremely difficult. Much more suitable for his purposes was Allen Ginsberg's "Howl"; I have written of Cage's brilliant deconstruction of that poem in "A Lion in Our Living Room: Reading Allen Ginsberg in the Eighties," *Poetic License: Essays in Modernist and Postmodernist Lyric* (Evanston, IL: Northwestern University Press, 1990), 219–22.

8. See Richard Kostelanetz and John Cage, "A Conversation about Radio in Twelve Parts," in *John Cage at Seventy-Five,* ed. Richard Fleming and William Duckworth (Lewisburg, PA: Bucknell University Press, 1989), 293–94. Subsequently cited as RF.

9. On the piece as a whole, see my "'A Duchamp unto Myself': Writing through Marcel," in *John Cage: Composed in America,* ed. Marjorie Perloff and Charles Junkerman (Chicago: University of Chicago Press, 1994), 100–124.

10. See Christian Geelhaar, "Interview with Jasper Johns," in *Jasper Johns: Working Proofs,* exhibition catalog, ed. Christian Geelhaar, (Basel: Kunstmuseum, 1979); rpt. in Jasper Johns, *Writings, Sketchbook Notes, Interviews* (New York: Mu-

seum of Modern Art, 1996), 188–97. The citation of "What you say . . ." is from 197. In his introduction to "Time (Three Autokus)," Cage explains, "An autoku uses its entire source as the string down the center of the mesostic, providing, at the same time, all the wing words" (HKM 266). The "autoku" is, in other words, a self-referential (auto) mesostic.

11. *Musicage* 54. This interview was originally published in *Aerial* in 1991 (see n. 1). Unlike "What You Say . . . ," "Art Is Either a Complaint or Do Something Else" is based on separate statements made by Johns, appearing in different contexts.

12. These program notes were not included in the printed version in *Formations*, evidently because there is no way the instructions could be followed during a silent reading of the text. What status, then, does the printed text have? It is, we might say, a score that must be activated, an incomplete verbal-visual construct that needs to be "audited."

13. Margaret Jeng Tan, "'Taking a Nap I Pound the Rice': Eastern Influences on John Cage,'" in RF 51.

14. I am not counting "different" or "interests" because in standard American speech (and certainly in Jasper Johns's southern idiolect) both words are pronounced as having only two syllables: "dif-rent," "in-trests." The seven words are "another" (used twice), "tendency," "occupy," "suddenly," "inserted," "situation," and "miniaturized."

15. Again, syllable count is not the same in the oral performance as in the written. When spoken, "miniaturized" usually has four syllables: "min-ya-tyuw-riyzd."

16. Cage's reading of this and related mesostics is, in many ways, inimitable, his soft, neutral California speech rhythms giving the pattern of sounds and silences of the lineated text an edge not quite duplicatable when anyone else (myself included) reads the "score."

Essay 14: "The Morphology of the Amorphous"

1. "The Porcupine and the Car," *Image Forum* (Tokyo) 2, no. 3 (January 1981): 46–55, and *Summer 1985,* group exhibition catalog, ed. Julia Brown (Los Angeles: Museum of Contemporary Art, 1985), both rpt. in Bill Viola, *Reasons for Knocking at an Empty House: Writings 1993–94* (Cambridge: MIT Press, in conjunction with Anthony d'Offay Gallery, London, 1995), 59–72 and 149–52 respectively; the citations are from 64 and 152. The collection is subsequently cited in the text as RKW. "The Porcupine and the Car" is subsequently cited as PC.

2. See, e.g., Raymond Williams, *Television, Technology and Cultural Form* (1974; rpt. Middletown, CT: Wesleyan University Press, 1992); Louis Althusser, "Ideology and Ideological State Apparatuses (Notes towards an Investigation)," *Lenin and Philosophy,* trans. Ben Brewster (New York: Monthly Review Press,

1971); Jean Baudrillard, "Requiem for the Media," *For a Critique of the Political Economy of the Sign,* trans. Charles Levin (St. Louis: Telos Press, 1981); Peter d'Agostino, ed., *Transmission: Theory and Practice for a New Television Aesthetics* (New York: Tanam Press, 1985); Tania Modelski, *Studies in Entertainment: Critical Approaches to Mass Culture* (Bloomington: Indiana University Press, 1986); Todd Gitlin, ed., *Watching Television: A Pantheon Guide to Popular Culture* (New York: Pantheon, 1986); Andrew Ross, ed., *Universal Abandon? The Politics of Postmodernism* (Minneapolis: University of Minnesota Press, 1988); Constance Penley and Andrew Ross, *Technoculture* (Minneapolis: University of Minnesota Press, 1991); Gretchen Bender and Timothy Druckrey, *Culture on the Brink: Ideologies of Technology* (Seattle: Bay Press, 1994). In the case of foreign works, the dates are those of translation, since this is when they began to have an influence on media studies in the United States.

3. Benjamin H. D. Buchloch, "From Gadget Video to Agit Video: Some Notes on Four Recent Video Works," in *Video: The Reflexive Medium,* ed. Sara Hornbacher, *Art Journal 45* (fall 1985): 217, 224–25.

4. Walter Benjamin, "The Work of Art in an Age of Mechanical Reproduction" (1936), *Illuminations, Essays and Reflections,* ed. Hannah Arendt, trans. Harry Zohn (New York: Schocken Books, 1968), 234–35, 247–48.

5. David Antin, "Video: The Distinctive Features of the Medium" (1975), in *Video Culture: A Critical Investigation,* ed. John G. Hanhardt (Rochester, NY: Visual Studies Workshop Press, distributed by Gibbs M. Smith, Inc., Layton, UT: 1986), 156. Subsequently cited as DA; the Hanhardt collection is subsequently cited as JGH. This is the best of the general collections of video culture, including early "historical" pieces by Bertolt Brecht, Hans Magnus Enzensberger, and Walter Benjamin's "Work of Art in the Age of Mechanical Reproduction" as well as important pieces by David Ross, Rosalind Krauss, and Stanley Cavell.

6. See David Ross, "Truth or Consequences: American Television and Video Art" (1984), JGH 169. Ross follows Antin in suggesting that all talk of "improving" television represents a misunderstanding of the way the medium works. One might add that the frequently heard complaints of elder statesmen like Walter Cronkite and David Brinkley that newscasting has "deteriorated" since their day are beside the point, television velocity, fueled by the increasing competition for viewer attention, creating its own demands.

7. See, e.g., Robbert Flick, in conversation with me, December 1996.

8. PC 67. For Magritte's statement, see Suzy Gablick, *Magritte* (Boston: New York Graphic Society, 1976), 11.

9. The video credits list Daphne, emu, Wahuhi, horned owl, Shaman, horned owl, and Barney, barn owl, all residents of the San Diego Zoo, and Nita, elephant in the San Diego Wild Animal Park.

10. Benoit B. Mandelbrot, *The Fractal Geometry of Nature* (New York: W. H. Freeman, 1983), 1. Subsequently cited as BM.

11. See William Blake, "The Marriage of Heaven and Hell," in William Blake, *Jerusalem, Selected Poems and Prose,* ed. Hazard Adams (New York: Holt, Rinehart and Winston, 1970), 131. Cited by Viola in "The Porcupine and the Car," RKW 60. Viola doesn't quote it quite accurately: he adds a "then" before "every thing," runs the words together, and puts a dash before "infinite" rather than a comma. For other references to Blake, see RKW 168. References to Blake aphorisms occur regularly in Viola's essays and interviews: see RKW 168, 200, 219, 240, 273, 283.

12. For example, the Persian Sufi poet of the thirteenth century, Jalladin Rumi, Saint John of the Cross, the anonymous *Cloud of Unknowing,* and so forth.

13. See Bill Viola, *Songs of Innocence.* Color, mono sound, 9:34 minutes, in *Four Songs,* produced on videotape in association with WNET/Thirteen Television Laboratory, New York, 1976.

14. The phrase *techne kai episteme* refers to two kinds of knowledge: technical (hence "techne" is often translated as "technique" or "art") and conceptual.

Illustration Sources

Essay 1

Figure 1. Laurie Anderson, "Say Hello," from the book *United States* by Laurie Anderson, originally published by Harper & Row. Copyright © 1984 by Laurie Anderson. Reprinted with permission of the author.

Figure 2. Laurie Anderson, "Say Hello," from the book *United States* by Laurie Anderson, originally published by Harper & Row. Copyright © 1984 by Laurie Anderson. Reprinted with permission of the author.

Figure 3. Brenda K. Marshall, *Teaching the Postmodern: Fiction and Theory* (New York: Routledge, 1992), 1. Copyright © 1991. Reproduced by permission of Routledge, Inc.

Figure 4. Vincent van Gogh, *A Pair of Boots* (1887). Oil on canvas. 33 x 41 cm. The Baltimore Museum of Art: The Cone Collection, formed by Dr. Claribel Cone and Miss Etta Cone of Baltimore, Maryland, BMA 1950.302.

Figure 5. Andy Warhol, *Diamond Dust Shoes* (1980). Copyright ©1988 by the Andy Warhol Foundation for the Visual Arts/ARS, New York.

Figure 6. Johanna Drucker, from *Narratology* (Druckwerk, 1994), unpaginated. Reprinted by permission of the author.

Essay 3

Figure 1. Eugène Atget, *Avenue des Gobelins* (1927). Gelatin-silver print. Courtesy of Weyhe Gallery. From *Pagany* 2 (January–March 1931).

Figure 2. Eugène Atget, untitled [Window with Stuffed Animals] (1927–30). Collection of Berenice Abbott. From *Pagany* 2 (January–March 1931).

Figure 3. Eugène Atget, untitled [Puppet-Theater Curtain] (1927–30). Courtesy of Weyhe Gallery. From *Pagany* 2 (January–March 1931).

Figure 4. Eugène Atget, untitled [Palais des singes] (1927–30). Gelatin-silver print. Courtesy of Weyhe Gallery. From *Pagany* 2 (January–March 1931).

Figure 5. Berenice Abbott, untitled [Manhattan Skyline near 42nd Street] (1930–31). Gelatin-silver print. From *Pagany* 2 (spring 1931).

Figure 6. Berenice Abbott, untitled [The Old Union Square Cigar Store] (1930–31). Gelatin-silver print. From *Pagany* 2 (spring 1931).

Figure 7. Berenice Abbott, untitled [Barbershop] (1930–31). Gelatin-silver print. From *Pagany* 2 (spring 1931).

Figure 8. Berenice Abbott, untitled [Manhattan Skyline from Downtown] (1930–31). Gelatin-silver print. From *Pagany* 2 (spring 1931).

Essay 4

Figure 1. *The Family of Man: The Greatest Photographic Exhibition of All Time—503 Pictures from 68 Countries—Created by Edward Steichen for the Museum of Modern Art* (New York: Museum of Modern Art, 1955), unpaginated. Photo by Gottard Schuh. Copyright © 1988 by the Artists Rights Society (ARS), New York/Pro Litteris, Zurich.

Figure 2. *The Family of Man.* Photo by Laurence LeGuay.

Figure 3. *The Family of Man.* Photo by George Rodger.

Figure 4. *The Family of Man.* Photo by Elliot Erwitt.

Figure 5. Robert Frank, *Parade—Hoboken, New Jersey,* in *The Americans* (New York: Grove Press, 1959; rpt. New York, Zurich, and Berlin: SCALO Publishers in association with the National Gallery of Art, Washington, 1994), 11. Copyright © Robert Frank. Reprinted courtesy of PaceWildensteinMacGill, New York.

Figure 6. Robert Frank, *Ranch Market—Hollywood,* in *The Americans,* 37. Copyright © Robert Frank. Reprinted courtesy of PaceWildenstein-MacGill, New York.

Figure 7. Robert Frank, *Trolley—New Orleans,* in *The Americans,* 45. Copyright © Robert Frank. Reprinted courtesy of PaceWildensteinMac-Gill, New York.

Essay 5

Figure 1. Stanley William Hayter, etching, from *Still*, by Samuel Beckett (Milan: M'Arte Edizioni, 1974). Reproduced by permission of Harry Ransom Humanities Research Center, The University of Texas at Austin.

Essay 6

Figure 1. Susan Howe, from *A Bibliography of the King's Book, or Eikon Basilike* (Providence, R.I.: Paradigm Press, 1992), in *Out of Everywhere: Linguistically Innovative Poetry by Women in North America and the UK*, ed. Maggie O'Sullivan (London: Reality Street Studios, 1996), 11.

Figure 2. Rosmarie Waldrop, from *Lawn of Excluded Middle* (New York: Tender Buttons, 1993), in *Out of Everywhere*, 125. Reprinted by permission of the author.

Figure 3. Karen Mac Cormack, "Multi-Mentional," from *Marine Snow* (Toronto: ECW Press, 1995), in *Out of Everywhere*, 162. Reprinted by permission of the author.

Figure 4. Maggie O'Sullivan, "A Lesson from the Cockerel," from *Unofficial Word* (Newcastle upon Tyne: Galloping Dog Press, 1988), in *Out of Everywhere*, 74. Reprinted by permission of the author.

Figure 5. Joan Retallack, from "Afterrimages," in *Afterrimages* (Hanover, NH: Wesleyan University Press, 1995), in *Out of Everywhere*, 23. Copyright © 1995 by Joan Retellack, Wesleyan University Press, by permission of University Press of New England.

Essay 11

Figure 1. "Le Demande d'amour," anonymous photograph (1923), *Roland Barthes par Roland Barthes* (Paris: Seuil, 1975), 7 ["The Demand for Love," in *Roland Barthes by Roland Barthes*, trans. Richard Howard (New York: Farrar, Straus and Giroux, 1977), unpaginated photo section preceding text]. Courtesy of Editions du Seuil.

Figure 2. Christian Boltanski, from *Album de photos de la famille D., 1939–1964*. Artist's book, album of 150 black-and-white photographs (self-published, 1971). Courtesy of Marian Goodman Gallery, New York.

Figure 3. From *Classe terminale du Lycée Chases en 1931.* Artist's book of 38 black-and-white photographs (Saint-Etienne: Maison de la culture et de la communication de Saint-Etienne, 1987). Courtesy of Marian Goodman Gallery, New York.

Figure 4. "L'espace du séminaire . . . [de l'Ecole des Hautes-Etudes]." Photograph by Daniel Boudinet (1974), in *Roland Barthes par Roland Barthes,* 173 ["The Space of the Seminar . . . ," in *Roland Barthes by Roland Barthes,* 171]. Copyright © Ministère de la Culture-France.

Figure 5. Christian Boltanski, "24 photographies extraites de *l'Album de la famille D., 1939–64*" (1971). Courtesy of Marian Goodman Gallery, New York.

Figure 6. Christian Boltanski, from *Le Lycée Chases* (1987). Courtesy of Marian Goodman Gallery, New York.

Figure 7. Christian Boltanski, from *Dix photographiques de Christian Boltanski, 1946–1964.* Artist's book (Paris: Editions Multiplicata, 1972). Courtesy of Marian Goodman Gallery, New York.

Figure 8. Christian Boltanski, *Ce sont ils se souviennent,* #86. Artist's book (self-published, 1972). Courtesy of Marian Goodman Gallery, New York.

Figure 9. Christian Boltanski, from *Inventaire des objets ayant appartenu à un jeune homme d'Oxford,* 1973.

Figure 10. Christian Boltanski, from *Les Archives-Détective* (1987). Installation: 400 photographs, 110 metal boxes with magazine articles, and 21 clamp-on desk lamps. Photographs 18 x 24 cm. Collection of the Ydessa Art Foundation, Toronto.

Figure 11. Christian Boltanski, from *Portraits des élèves du C.E.S. de Lentillères [Dijon] en 1973* (1973). Courtesy of Marian Goodman Gallery, New York.

Figure 12. Christian Boltanski, from *Monument: les Enfants de Dijon* (1986). Courtesy of Marian Goodman Gallery, New York.

Figure 13. Christian Boltanski, from *Les Suisses morts* (1991). Courtesy of Marian Goodman Gallery, New York.

Essay 12

Figure 1. Steve McCaffery, *Carnival, The First Panel: 1967–70* (Toronto: Coach House Press, 1973). 18 sheets, offset, perforated. A sheet dated 1970.

Figure 2. Steve McCaffery, *Carnival, The Second Panel: 1971–75* (Toronto: Coach House Press, 1977). 22 sheets, offset, perforated. Postcard rendering of the whole, 1977.

Figure 3. Steve McCaffery, *Carnival, The Second Panel,* detail from the tenth (unnumbered) sheet.

Figure 4. Steve McCaffery, *Dr. Sadhu's Muffins: A Book of Written Readings* (Erin: Press Porcepic, 1974). Offset, page 43.

Figure 5. Steve McCaffery, *Dr. Sadhu's Muffins,* double-page frontispiece.

Figure 6. Steve McCaffery, *Ow's Waif and Other Poems* (Toronto: Coach House Press, 1975). Offset, hardbound. Double title page.

Figure 7. Steve McCaffery, *Ow's Waif,* unnumbered double page near book's center.

Figure 8. Steve McCaffery, *Ow's Waif,* unnumbered double page featuring "E. A. Poe, *The Poetic Principle.*"

Figure 9. Steve McCaffery, *Knowledge Never Knew* (Montreal: Vehicule Press, 1983). Front cover.

Figure 10. Steve McCaffery, *Knowledge Never Knew,* 12.

Figure 11. Steve McCaffery, *Knowledge Never Knew,* 13.

Figure 12. Steve McCaffery, *Evoba: The Investigation Meditations 1976–78* (Toronto: Coach House Press, 1987), 13.

Figure 13. Steve McCaffery, *Evoba,* cover and endpaper photograph.

Figure 14. Steve McCaffery, *Evoba,* 23.

Figure 15. Steve McCaffery, *Evoba,* 25.

Figure 16. Steve McCaffery, *Evoba,* 101.

Essay 13

Figure 1. Jasper Johns, *Figure 5* (1955). Encaustic and collage on canvas. 44.5 x 55.6 cm. Collection of the artist. Copyright ©Jasper Johns/Licensed by VAGA, New York, NY.

Essay 14

Figures 1–5. Outtakes from *I Do Not Know What It Is I Am Like.* Video-tape. Color, stereo sound, 80 minutes. Record on ¾″ and ½″ VHS tape, mastered on 1″ tape. Production assistant Kira Perov. Produced in association with the American Film Institute, Los Angeles; the Contemporary Art Television (CAT) Fund, a project of the WGBH New Television Workshop, the Institute of Contemporary Art, Boston; and ZDF, Mainz, West Germany.

Poetry Sources

John Ashbery, "As We Know" from *As We Know* by John Ashbery (New York: Viking, 1979). Copyright © 1979 by John Ashbery. Reprinted by permission of Georges Borchardt, Inc. "As We Know" from *As We Know: Poems* by John Ashbery (Manchester: Carcanet New Press, 1981). Reprinted by permission of Carcanet Press Limited.

Excerpt from *Three Poems* by John Ashbery (Hopewell, N.J.: Ecco Press, 1997). Copyright © 1970, 1971, 1972 by John Ashbery. Reprinted by permission of Georges Borchardt, Inc. Also included in *The Mooring of Starting Out* (Manchester: Carcanet Press, 1997). Reprinted by permission of Carcanet Press Limited.

"Two Scenes." Published in the *Kenyon Review* o.s. 18, no. 2 (spring 1956). Copyright © *The Kenyon Review.*

Samuel Beckett, "Still." Published in *Fizzles* 7 (1976): 47–51. Reprinted by permission of Grove Press.

Charles Bernstein, "The Klupzy Girl." Published in *Islets/Irritations.* Reprinted by permission of the Segue Foundation.

John Cage, "Present," "On the Windshield of a new Fiat for James K. (who had not made up his mind where to go) and Carolyn Brown." Published in *M: Writings '67–'72,* pp. 89, 94, 215. Copyright © 1973 by John Cage and Wesleyan University Press. Reprinted by permission of the University Press of New England.

"Song." Published in *Empty Words: Writings '73–'78,* p. 10. Copyright © 1979 by John Cage and Wesleyan University Press. Reprinted by permission of the University Press of New England.

"James Joyce." Published in *Roaratorio: An Irish Circus on Finnegan's Wake* (Munich: Athenaeum, 1985). Courtesy of the John Cage Trust.

"What You Say . . ." Published in *Time (Three Autokus)* (1986) in *John Cage II: Musik-Konzepte* II, ed. Heinz-Klaus Metzger and Rainer Riehn (1990). Courtesy of the John Cage Trust.

Jimmy Carter, "Sport," from *Always a Reckoning.* Copyright © Random House, Inc. Reprinted by permission of Random House, Inc.

Allen Ginsberg, "America." Published in *Collected Poems 1947–1980* by Allen Ginsberg. Copyright © 1956, 1959 by Allen Ginsberg. Copyright renewed. Reprinted by permission of HarperCollins Publishers, Inc.

Lyn Hejinian, *Oxota: A Short Russian Novel* (Great Barrington, MA: The Figures, 1991). Reprinted by permission of The Figures.

Denise Levertov, "Tenebrae," "Staying Alive." Published in *Poems 1968–1972* by Denise Levertov. Copyright © 1968, 1970 by Denise Levertov. Reprinted by permission of New Directions Publishing Corporation.

Index

Abbott, Berenice, 55, 65, 72–78, 328n10
Adam, Paul, 141
Adams, J. Donald, 177
Adams, Leonie, 333n14
Ahearn, Barry, 328n5
Ahearn, Edward J., 336nn10, 11
Akhmatova, Anna, 114
Aldington, Richard, 52
Allen, Donald, 333n18; *The New American Poetry*, 4, 340n22
Althusser, Louis, 15, 24, 309, 353n2
Altieri, Charles, 5, 323nn1, 3, 324–25n12, 334n27
Anderson, Laurie, 33; *United States*, 11–15, 324n8
Anderson, Margaret, 345n19
Anderson, Sherwood, 64
Andrews, Bruce, 157, 166, 339n14
Anouilh, Jean, 95
Antin, David, 4–8, 10, 13, 18, 32, 116, 310–11, 323n1, 354n5
Apollinaire, Guillaume, 18, 105, 128
Aragon, Louis, 184–85
Arendt, Hannah, 333n14, 353n4
Arensberg, Walter, 193
Armantrout, Rae, 159, 341n31
Arnold, Elizabeth, 345n13
Arp, Hans, 316
Arteaga, Alfred: "The Small Sea of Europe," 25–28, 32
Ashbery, John, 8, 101, 119, 180, 184, 334n27, 342n11; "As We Know," 138; *Some Trees*, 110, 116, 334n29; *Three Poems*, 137–38; "Two Scenes," 110–15
Atget, Eugène, 55, 65, 72–74, 328n10
Attridge, Derek, 142–44, 341n30
Atwood, Margaret, 339n14
Atwood, William, 98–99, 334n28
Auden, W. H., 180, 334n29

Augustine, St.: *Confessions*, 283
Augustine, Jane, 344n5
Avison, Margaret, 333n14

Bachmann, Ingeborg, 114, 183, 230
Baechler, Lea, 341n32
Bailly, Jean-Christophe, 326n5
Bakhtin, Mikhail, 117
Balanchine, George, 109
Baldessari, John, 266, 310
Ball, Hugo, 185
Barnard, Caroline, 349n3
Barnes, Djuna, 206, 329n10
Barney, Natalie, 207
Barthes, Roland, 8, 14, 15, 181, 243–63; *Camera Lucida* (*La Chambre Claire*), 243–61; *Roland Barthes by Roland Barthes*, 245, 248, 257
Bataille, Georges, 18, 265
Baudelaire, Charles, 7, 59, 124, 125, 126
Baudrillard, Jean, 8, 14, 309, 354n2
Bayley, John, 224
Baynes, Cary F., 352n4
Beardsley, Aubrey, 205
Beatty, Paul, 185
Beaujour, Michel, 127–28
Beauvoir, Simone de, 333n14
Beckett, Samuel, 8, 17, 118, 133, 138–39, 297; *Fizzles*, 337n24; *Still*, 133–40
Bellos, David, 348n6
Bender, Gretchen, 309, 354n2
Benjamin, Walter, 310, 354n5
Bennington, Geoff, 323n5
Bentham, Jeremy, 116
Bentley, Phyllis, 176
Berg, Stephen, 146–54
Bergvall, Caroline, 159, 341n31; "Of Boundaries and Emblems," 166–67
Bernstein, Charles, 21–22, 157, 166,

Caws, Mary Ann, 36, 336n13
Celan, Paul, 114
Celine, Louis Ferdinand, 18, 44
Cendrars, Blaise, 18, 105, 128
Chambers, Whittaker, 51
Champion, Martha, 51
Charles, Daniel, 291–92, 351nn1, 3
Chaucer, Geoffrey, 165
Chekhov, Anton, 226
Cixous, Hélène, 181, 324n10
Claire, Paula, 159, 341n31
Clifford, James, 35, 36, 46–48, 327n12
Coan, C. Arthur, 177
Cocteau, Jean, 59, 290
Coetzee, J. M., 15, 17
Coffey, Michael, 264
Cohen, Jean-Louis, 168–69
Cohen, Ralph, 345n13
Cohn, Ruby, 133
Cole, Norma, 24
Colomina, Beatriz, 168
Commager, Henry Steele, 95, 113
Connor, Stephen, 324n7
Conover, Roger, 207, 343n2, 344n10, 345n21
Conrad, Joseph, 40, 48, 175
Conte Joseph M., 330n26
Coolidge, Clark, 166, 171, 185, 292
Cranach, Lucas, *Lucrece and Judith*, 36–38, 44–45
Crane, Hart, 70
Crapsey, Adelaide, 195
Cravan, Arthur, 193, 199, 205–6, 345n19
Creeley, Robert, 5, 147, 154, 165, 184; "Anger," 154–56, 157, 340nn22, 23
Crone, Rainer, 327n14
Cronkite, Walter, 354n6
Culler, Jonathan, 339n18
Culver, Andrew, 298
cummings, e. e., 52
Cun, Yi, 186

Cunningham, Merce, 5, 292
Curtis, James, 3
Curtis, Mina, 95

d'Agostino, Peter, 354n2
Dahlberg, Edward, 54, 73, 330n23, "Graphophone Nickelodeon Days," 67–69
Danto, Arthur, 172, 325n2
Dao, Bei, 187
Darragh, Tina, 159, 341n31
Davidson, Arthur, 79
Davidson, Michael, 113–14, 222, 335n33
Davis, Lydia, 326n6, 326–27n10
de Campos, Augusto, 293
de Campos, Haroldo, 293
de Chirico, 184
DeKoven, Marianne, 57
deLauretis, Teresa, 15
Deleuze, Gilles, 8
de Man, Paul, 3, 7, 181
Demuth, Charles, 65, 73
Denby, Edwin, 109, 290–91
Dent, Tory, 185
Derrida, Jacques, 8, 10, 12, 13, 14, 15, 17, 24, 188, 269
Deutsch, Babette, 333n14
Devlin, James E., 65, 66
Dickinson, Emily, 171, 177–78, 181
Diderot, Denis, 96
Di Leonardo, Micaela, 325n2
Dobyns, Stephen, 172–73
Donne, John, 85, 86
Donoghue, Denis, 180
D[oolittle], H[ilda], 74, 181, 208
Dos Passos, John, 7, 54, 73, 76
Douglas, Charlotte, 327n15
Dowson, Ernest, 79
Dragomoschenko, Arkadii, 222
Dreiser, Theodore, 175
Drucker, Johanna, 24, 157, 266, 350n7; *Narratology*, 30–32

"Life at War," 217–18; "Staying Alive," 211, 218; "Tenebrae," 213–15

Lévi-Strauss, Claude, 14

Levin, Charles, 354n2

Levinas, Emmanuel, 326n5

Levine, Philip, 147

Levine, Sherrie, 14–15

Lewis, Mary Owens, 177

Lewis, Sinclair, 176

Lewis, Wyndham, 199

Lewitt, Leah D., 326n5

Libby, Anthony, 172–73

Litz, A. Walton, 336n19, 341n32

Liu, Hong, 186

Longfellow, Henry Wadsworth, 81, 273

Longley, Michael, 182, 342n8

Lorde, Audre, 142, 338n5

Love, Adelaide, 177–78

Lowell, Robert, 4–5, 93, 133, 147, 180, 332nn2, 10; "The Mouth of the Hudson," 149–52, 341n27;

Loy, Mina, 54, 63, 65, 75, 79, 82, 193–207; "Anglo-Mongrels and the Rose," 194–207; "Lady Laura in Bohemia," 61–63, 69

Lumpkin, Grace, 81

Lyons, Joan, 349n5

Lyotard, Jean-François, 8, 9, 10, 15, 17, 181

Ma, Ming-Qian, 343n12

McAlmon, Robert, 51, 195

MacBeth, George, 339n14

McCaffery, Steve, 24, 159, 166, 172, 186, 216, 264–89, 341n33; *Carnival*, 266–69; *Dr. Sadhu's Muffins*, 269–73; *Evoba*, 282–89; *Knowledge Never Knew*, 277–82; *Open Letter*, 348–49n1; *Ow's Waif*, 269–77; *Rational Geomancy*, 338n10; "Staged Dia-

logue with Failed Transit Actiant Opposition," 28–29, 32

McCarthy, Mary, 333n14

Mac Cormack, Karen, 341n31; "Multi-Mentional," 159–60, 162–63, 164

McDaniel, Wilma Elizabeth, 339–40n19

MacGowan, Christopher, 334n24, 336n19

McGowan, John, 324n12

McGowran, Alec, 135

Mac Low, Jackson, 96, 271, 352n4; *Stanzas for Iris Lezak*, 292–93

McLuhan, Marshall, 3, 6–7

McPheron, William, 346n2

Malanga, Gerard, 348n8

Malevich, Kasimir, 48

Malinowski, Bronislaw, 40, 48

Mallarmé, Stephane, 8

Mandelbrot, Benoit, 319

Mangan, Sherry, 328–29n10

Mann, Thomas, 7, 175

Marcuse, Herbert, 8

Marin, John, 125

Marinetti, F. T., 175, 179, 193, 198–200, 205, 212

Maritain, Jacques, 273

Marivaux, Pierre, 95

Markham, E. A., 342n8

Marmande, Francis, 326n5

Marsh, Georgia, 262

Marshall, Brenda K., 15–17

Marx, Karl, 8

Masina, Giulietta, 109

Massumi, 323n5

Masters, Edgar Lee, 51

Maxwell, Glyn, 168–72, 178–79, 185, 188, 342n1

Mayakovsky, Vladimir, 105, 114, 118, 128, 145

Mayer, Bernadette, 341n31